CONGRESS

at the Crossroads

by GEORGE B. GALLOWAY

THOMAS Y. CROWELL COMPANY

NEW YORK

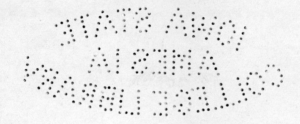

To

Senator Robert M. La Follette, Jr.

and

Representative Mike Monroney

Preface

THE CONGRESS OF the United States is the central citadel of American democracy. The framers of the federal constitution defined its structure and powers in the first article of that immortal charter; and the architects of the national legislature later erected its marble halls on the commanding heights of Capitol Hill—acts reflecting the primacy of our parliament in the minds of the founding fathers. One hundred years afterwards, when Woodrow Wilson penned his remarkable study, "congressional government" was still the dominant feature of the American system, despite intervening swings of the political pendulum.

But after 1910–1911, when the overthrow of Speaker Cannon dispersed leadership in the House of Representatives, the nation witnessed the gradual decline of Congress in the federal scheme and the growing centralization of power in the executive branch. Recurring national crises, induced by two world wars and a Great Depression, called forth strong popular-leader presidents, accelerating the trend toward presidential government and threatening to convert Congress into a mere ceremonial appendix to bureaucracy. While the onward sweep of science and technology and the mammoth wartime mobilization of our human and industrial resources were raising the nation to new pinnacles of power in world affairs, Congress still was working with the tools and techniques inherited from the wig and snuff-box era. And when, after the Second World War, the Administration sought to streamline its sprawling agencies, many legislators seemed content to carry on with their antiquated stagecoach equipment.

Alarmed, meanwhile, by the growing imbalance between the legislative and executive branches of the national government, and warned as well by the fate of parliaments in the totalitarian countries of Europe, the protagonists of efficient representative government began to consider ways and means of strengthening Congress. Firm in the democratic faith that legislative assemblies are the first defense of civil liberties, they launched an inquiry on the eve of Pearl Harbor into the causes of congressional decline and possible remedies. They soon found sympathizers among several of the younger and progressive members of Congress such as Representatives Dirksen, Gore, Kefauver, Monroney, Outland, and Voorhis and Senators La Follette, Maloney, and Pepper—all under 50 years of age—who had long been disturbed by the trend of events at both ends of Pennsylvania Avenue. Meanwhile, civic and professional groups such as the National League of Women Voters, the American Political Science Association, and the National Planning Association also became actively interested and put their influential weight behind the movement. Leading newspapers and magazines supported these efforts editorially. Gradually the movement spread within and outside Congress until, by 1945, it was evident that the American people were embarked, not on a short-run crusade, but upon a real campaign to modernize their national legislature.

Recognizing alike its own serious deficiencies and the rising popular demand for positive reform, Congress created during the winter of 1944-1945 a joint committee to study its internal organization and operation. The recent report of that committee, ably led by Senator Robert M. La Follette, Jr. and Representative Mike Monroney, furnishes a fitting occasion for a fresh and full examination of the role of Congress in the American scheme of government. In the following chapters I shall undertake to analyze the evolution of the essential functions of Congress since 1789, to describe how Congress works under modern conditions, to diagnose its defects, and to prescribe a comprehensive program for its reconstruction as an effective instrument of representative government adequate to meet its responsibilities in the postwar world.

ACKNOWLEDGMENTS

MANY PEOPLE HAVE helped me in many ways in the preparation of this book. For professional advice and counsel I am indebted to the members of the Committee on Congress of the American Political Science Association. Since its appointment early in 1941 this committee has been the chief catalytic agent of congressional reform and its ideas can be traced throughout the fabric of this work. Special acknowledgment is due Arthur N. Holcombe, Robert D. Leigh, and Benjamin B. Wallace for many constructive suggestions, and to Roland Young for the opportunity to read his unpublished *Study Outline on Congress.*

Many other political scientists have also contributed to this book through their writings and testimony, as the footnotes indicate. I am especially grateful to Ernest S. Griffith, director of the Legislative Reference Service in the Library of Congress, for the stimulating suggestions in his pioneer prewar study: *The Impasse of Democracy;* for his survey of the history of congressional reorganization which appears as Chapter 5 in this book; and for his careful reading and comment upon this entire work in manuscript form. I am also greatly indebted to Herman Finer of Harvard University for his vivid analysis of question-time in the House of Commons, which he made at the invitation of the Joint Committee on the Organization of Congress, and upon which I have drawn in Chapter 7; to Belle Zeller of Brooklyn College for her helpful memorandum on the federal regulation of lobbies, which she prepared at a similar invitation and which I have used in Chapter 9; and to William Anderson of the University of Minnesota for his thoughtful paper on legislative-executive relations in the national government, a partial summary of which appears at the end of Chapter 4.

I want also to express sincere appreciation to the many members of both houses of Congress and both political parties who, in conversation, conference and testimony have contributed so much during the past five years to my understanding of the legislative process. Their names are too numerous to list here, but I am especially indebted to Senator Robert M. La Follette, Jr., and to Representative Mike Monroney who made it possible for me to obtain an inside view of Congress in action. Without their aid and cooperation this book could not have been written. I am also deeply grateful to Senator Elbert D. Thomas and Senator Wallace H. White, Jr., and to Congressmen Everett M. Dirksen and Estes Kefauver for much wise advice and counsel.

Among the veteran officers and employees of Congress are several who generously contributed to my political education out of their long experience on Capitol Hill. I extend my sincere thanks for their many favors and helpful assistance to Charles L. Watkins and Lewis Deschler, parliamentarians of the Senate and the House of Representatives; to Carl A. Loeffler and Felton M. Johnston, secretaries to the Minority and the Majority of the Senate; to George H. E. Smith, research assistant to the Senate minority leader, for much helpful advice and counsel and invaluable aid and cooperation; to Oco Thompson and J. C. Shanks, Senate and House financial clerks; to John C. Pugh and Marcellus Sheild, present and former clerks of the House Committee on Appropriations; to William A. Duvall, assistant clerk of the House Appropriations Committee; to James D. Preston, Senate clerk, for the opportunity to examine his collection of historic papers relating to Congress and the press; and to Agnes Strauss Wolf, staff member of the Truman-Mead Committee.

I am also indebted to Hadley Cantril of the Office of Public Opinion Research at Princeton University for permission to make use of unpublished material on Congress and public opinion in Chapter 9; to Lawrence K. Frank for his stimulating thoughts on the psycho-cultural approach to social planning; to Raymond R. Zimmerman, administrative assistant to the President, for data on civilian nominations; to W. Darlington Denit, expert in administrative management, for the reorganization chart (Chart III in the Appendix); and to the Legislative Reference Service and the financial clerks of the House and Senate for valued research assistance on various aspects of the congressional committee system and legislative expenditures.

My special thanks are finally reserved for my wife, Eilene-Marie Galloway, for her constant encouragement and counsel; to Jean Sulzberger and Kathleen Lucas, interns of the National Institute of Public Affairs, for much appreciated research assistance on many important aspects of congressional organization and operation; and last but not least to Mary-Louise Walpole for her competent and indispensable secretarial services.

CONTENTS

1.

The Functions of Congress

WHEN THE DIRECTOR of the Budget appeared before
the Joint Committee on the Organization of Congress in May, 1945, he
challenged the twelve Senators and Congressmen who composed it to
consider at the outset what the role of Congress should be in the government of the United States. "This is a different sort of world,"
he said, "from that which existed when the Constitutional Convention devised the framework of our government. Yet we still lack
a penetrating and practical restatement of the role of representative
assemblies in the light of the changed problems with which they
deal and the altered conditions under which they operate . . . Your
own talents and the keenest minds you can command could very well
be devoted to rethinking the functions of the Congress under present
conditions. A sound reformulation of the role of the representative
body is basic to all the work of your committee." Only on such a basis,
he added, could the effectiveness of its organization and operation and
proposals for change be appraised.

Let us accept this forthright challenge and begin our inquiry by
considering what functions were assigned to Congress by the framers
of the federal constitution and how they have evolved and been
modified during the intervening 160 years.

ORIGINAL DESIGN

Before the Revolution all the higher functions of government were
exercised in the American colonies by the British Crown and Parliament through the royal governors and courts and their agents. After
striking for independence the Revolutionists adopted articles of confederation which set up a Congress composed of delegates elected by
the state legislatures. In effect this Congress was little more than a

council of ambassadors from sovereign states, for the local legislatures were supreme under the articles. Congress, to be sure, could declare war and appropriate money, but it was dependent upon the states for troops and funds. It could make treaties, but it was powerless to enforce them. Nor could it lay and collect taxes or control banking and currency or regulate foreign and domestic commerce. Under the articles of confederation, in short, Congress was a weak and incompetent creature of sovereign states which retained control over the essential functions of government.

Called to Philadelphia in 1787 merely to amend the articles, the delegates to that historic convention discarded them entirely and, after long debate and much travail, drafted a new constitution deemed "adequate to the exigencies of government and the preservation of the nation." To this great document we must look for the original and authentic ideas of the framers concerning the powers and functions of Congress and its place in the governmental scheme of things.

At the very outset, immediately after the preamble, in the first section of the first article the constitution-makers vested "all legislative powers herein granted . . . in a Congress of the United States, which shall consist of a Senate and House of Representatives." Clearly, Congress was originally designed to exercise the *legislative function* of lawmaking.

Then, after providing for the election and qualifications of members of the House and Senate and their officers, the framers gave the House "the sole power of impeachment" and the Senate "the sole power to try all impeachments" (Sections 2 and 3) of civil officers accused of high crimes and misdemeanors. Thus, Congress was also assigned a *judicial function,* in the performance of which the Senate in its rules long described the House, when acting in an impeachment, as the "grand inquest of the nation" and referred to itself as a "high court of impeachment." Each house was also made the judge of the elections, returns and qualifications of its members (Section 5)—a further judicial function.

Each house was also authorized to determine the rules of its proceedings, to compel the attendance of absent members, and to punish its members for disorderly behavior (Section 5), from which is derived part of what may be called the *housekeeping function* of Congress.

The specific powers of Congress in the realm of public policy are enumerated in Section 8 of Article I of the federal constitution. This section empowers Congress to act in eighteen particular fields. Here we find the revenue, borrowing, and coinage powers which together constitute the power of the purse. From this cluster of powers is derived what may be called its *fiscal function* which has been performed through the years by the several fiscal committees of the House and Senate with the aid, since 1921, of the General Accounting Office as an agent of Congress.

Here too is granted the power to regulate interstate and foreign commerce, to promote science and the useful arts, and to constitute judicial tribunals inferior to the Supreme Court. Here also is conferred the power to declare war and to provide and maintain an army and navy—the power of the sword. This potent section concludes by granting Congress power "to make all laws which shall be necessary and proper for carrying into execution the foregoing powers, and all other powers vested by this constitution in the government of the United States, or in any department or officer thereof"—the blanket clause which subsequently became "a Pandora's box of wonders," in Charles Beard's graphic phrase, "under the light shed by the expansive imagination of Chief Justice Marshall."

Having vested these vast powers in the new national legislature, the framers turned to create and implement the executive power in Article II. Here, in granting the President power to make treaties and appoint ambassadors, superior court judges, and other officers of the United States, they attached the proviso of the "advice and consent of the Senate," two-thirds of whose members present must concur in making treaties (Section 2). From these conditions expressly attached to the treaty and appointing powers of the President flows what may be called the *executive council function* of Congress, a function performed via the Senate Committee on Foreign Relations in the case of treaties and diplomatic appointments and by other appropriate Senate committees in the case of major judicial and administrative appointments.

Before completing their monumental task, the founding fathers expressly entrusted one other important function to Congress. In Article V they gave it the right, when two-thirds of those voting in both Houses approved, to propose amendments to the constitution—called the *constituent function*. In practice, amendments are proposed in the form of joint resolutions, which have their several readings and are enrolled and signed by the presiding officers of the two houses, but are not presented to the President for his approval.

Between 1791 and 1933 twenty-one amendments to the federal constitution were adopted. One of these, the twelfth amendment, directed the President of the Senate to count the vote cast in the electoral college for President and Vice President in the presence of the Senate and House of Representatives. In practice, the electoral count occurs in the Hall of the House at 1:00 P.M. on the sixth day of January following every meeting of electors. This amendment also authorized the House of Representatives to choose the President, and the Senate to choose the Vice President, in case no candidate for these offices had a majority vote in the electoral college. Congress has thrice performed this *electoral function* during its history. Thomas Jefferson and John Quincy Adams were chosen President by the House of Representatives in 1801 and 1825, and Richard M. Johnson was elected Vice President by the Senate in 1837.

Thus it will be seen that the architects of the Grand Design of 1787, keenly conscious of the incompetence of Congress under the confederation, expressly vested the primary powers of the new national and federal government in the Congress of the United States. From the place of prominence they gave it in the fundamental framework and the vast powers they conferred upon it, the framers evidently intended to make Congress the central department in the new republic. With a lively recollection both of the tyranny of the British Crown and of the weakness of the confederation, they sought at once to establish a strong central government and to avoid the dangers of dictatorship. It is not surprising, therefore, that they placed chief reliance on a powerful national legislature. On the face of the frame as originally established it is plain that the founders expected Congress, alone or in collaboration with the executive, to perform at least seven fundamental functions: the legislative, judicial, housekeeping, fiscal, executive council, constituent, and electoral functions.

PRESENT PATTERN

Manifold changes in the state of the nation and the world have occurred since 1787, imposing unpredictable new problems and responsibilities upon the government in Washington. Since the fathers framed the constitution, the nation has undergone an industrial revolution, waged six great wars, and suffered several major economic depressions. From 13 states with four million inhabitants living close to the Atlantic coastline, it has increased to 48 states and 140 million people spread from sea to shining sea. Then a regime of small farmers, planters, and petty traders, it has expanded into a unified national economy dominated by great corporate enterprises. While our annual federal budget has mounted from less than one million to one hundred billion dollars, our national wealth and income have likewise immensely multiplied. Meanwhile, our participation in two world wars within a generation has willy nilly precipitated the American nation onto the world stage as a great power, compelling the United States in its own interest and self-defense to assume heavy international responsibilities.

All these and many other developments, unforeseen by the founding fathers, have enormously magnified the volume and complexity of the public business, the size and activities of the federal government, and concomitantly the functions and tasks of Congress. The impact of more than a century and a half of turbulent history upon its role has been significant and pervasive. Some of its original functions have proved to be of a nominal character or have rarely been exercised. Others have been delegated to or taken over by the executive branch or have been frustrated by a combination of circumstances. And some important new functions, not expressly granted in the original design, have evolved under the stress of changing conditions.

As the United States attained the summit of its power and prestige midway in the twentieth century, the federal government bore slight resemblance to the infant republic or even to that of 1914. Profound changes in its economy and society had been accompanied by an equivalent transformation in the status and importance of the central government. Accelerated by depression and war, these trends were almost entirely manifest in the enhanced position and power of the executive branch and the prestige of the Presidency. Since 1789 the executive departments had grown from three in number: War, Treasury, and State—to upwards of 80 departments and agencies which appeared before Congress in 1945 seeking appropriations for their multifarious activities. In addition, between 500 and 700 committees, commissions, and boards had sprung up like mushrooms in the lush soil of wartime Washington. Under the peerless leadership of one of our greatest presidents, Franklin D. Roosevelt, the executive office had attained worldwide influence and renown.

Congress, meanwhile, had changed little in the intervening decades. For the most part, it was still operating with the same machinery and methods, the same facilities and services, that it had inherited from the era of Thomas Brackett Reed. Overworked and underpaid, often lampooned by the press and unfairly criticized by the thoughtless, our national legislature had fallen from its once high estate. Few any longer regarded it as the keystone of the federal arch. With Congress overwhelmed by its great responsibilities, operating under its ancient ritual, the streamlined age of the Giant Clipper, radar, and the atomic bomb seemed to have passed it by.

Making the Laws

Still enshrined in the altar of the constitution, Congress has come to share its legislative function more and more with the judiciary and the administration. The Supreme Court early asserted its right to review the constitutionality of federal statutes and to invalidate those deemed incompatible with the fundamental law, thus exercising a judicial veto on the acts of the people's elected representatives nowhere expressly conferred by the Philadelphia formula. Moreover, the courts, while disclaiming a lawmaking function, have repeatedly interpreted federal acts so as to alter or modify the intent of Congress and have otherwise substituted their judgment for that of the legislature. Between 1789 and 1936, 84 different provisions of federal law were declared null and void by the highest court in the land, establishing in such cases at least the fact of judicial supremacy first affirmed by Chief Justice Marshall, all notions about the twilight of the Supreme Court to the contrary notwithstanding.

Although the practice is by no means novel, there has been a growing tendency in recent decades for major legislation to originate in the executive departments. As administrative problems have become more technical, Congress has turned more and more to the Executive for guidance in drafting new laws—not from any lazy impulse to shirk its duty, but rather out of a conscientious desire to formulate workable legislation. Such guidance, indeed, is quite consistent with the constitutional directive authorizing the President from time to time to give Congress information of the state of the union and to recommend to its consideration such measures as he shall judge necessary and expedient.

This practice works both ways. On the one hand, many congressional committees automatically refer bills they receive to the departments affected for their advice and they seldom report bills favorably, if at all, unless they have received a departmental blessing. Many bills, moreover, are drawn or revised in the departments at the express request of Congressmen and committees. On the other hand, much legislation is tailor-made in the departments and sent up to the Speaker or appropriate committee chairmen for introduction in the House.

Hearings are subsequently held on such bills before subcommittees and then the legislation is revised in full committee, if necessary, so as to reflect their will. This is the usual procedure in most cases in both houses—a far cry from the attitude of the Senate in 1908 when a furore was created because the Secretary of the Interior sent to the Senate the complete draft of a proposed bill. On that occasion the Senate in high dudgeon returned the measure and resolved, on motion of Henry Cabot Lodge, not to receive thereafter any communication from an executive officer, with certain exceptions, unless transmitted by the President himself. Today the fact that a bill has been drafted "downtown" adds luster to its quality.

Many committees, in fact, refuse to consider legislation that has not been cleared by the Bureau of the Budget. During the administration of Franklin Roosevelt a Division of Legislative Reference was set up in the Budget Bureau. This division reconciles and clears recommendations of the various departments and establishments with respect to legislation proposed by them so as to make them internally consistent and compatible with the President's program. Harold D. Smith, the Budget Director, told the Joint Committee on the Organization of Congress in May, 1945, that "more and more committee chairmen are sending legislative proposals to the Bureau for comment and for the collection of the views of the affected departments and agencies. I am not unmindful," he added, "that there remains considerable room for the improvement of the consistency of legislative proposals originating within the administration and for the ironing out of intra-administration cleavages in advance of requests for legislation"—an admission justified by the conflicting proposals for postwar reconversion and other projects that still reached Capitol Hill by roundabout routes, as well as by the refusal of a few so-called independent agencies to submit to bureau censorship.

Despite this well-developed tendency for legislation to spring full-blown from departments, and lobbies too, the practice is strongly resented by some Senators and Representatives as a usurpation of their legislative function. Department bills receive a "green light" from congressional committees, they often complain, while members' own bills are pigeonholed and ignored as idle fantasies. They were bitterly opposed to the so-called "must" legislation sent up by the President during the early days of the New Deal, some of which, according to Capitol rumor, passed even before it was printed or read under the pressure of the crisis. As a legislative body Congress is being reduced, they fear, to a "rubber stamp," permitted only to review and ratify or veto Executive proposals. Departmental suggestions are entirely proper and valuable, some members concede, but Congress should draft its own laws in its own language. But how can it expect to compete with the administration in the bill-drafting business, they ask, when it allows its drafting service only 12 lawyers and $90,000 a year while the solicitor's office in one department alone, Agriculture for example, employs 204 lawyers and spends $1.6 million annually?

More serious is the protest concerning the constantly expanding body of executive or administrative law or subordinate legislation. In the early days of the republic the problems of government were comparatively simple, the economy of the country was more or less automatic and self-regulating, and the business of Congress was largely concerned with tariffs, internal improvements, monetary policy, public lands, and the like. The legislative process used to be more leisurely and a few laws sufficed to govern the economic life of the nation.

Those good old days have now passed away forever down the irreversible stream of time. Beginning in 1887, when Congress created the Interstate Commerce Commission, more and more commissions have perforce been established to protect the public interest and provide for the general welfare in many areas of economic and social activity. To these agencies Congress has usually delegated the power "to issue such regulations and orders as it may deem necessary or proper in order to carry out the purposes and provisions of this act." This practice of delegating to administrative agencies or commissions the power to issue rules and regulations spelling out the general principles of law and applying them to specific cases has grown apace since 1912 and has been accelerated by recurring wars and depressions.

Congressmen generally recognize the need for delegating legislative powers as a means of reducing their work-load and of taking care of technical matters beyond the competence of Congress. But they believe that the great growth of administrative lawmaking has become a menace to the constitutional function of Congress as the legislative branch of the national government. "With the growing emphasis upon the day-to-day application of laws," wrote Senator La Follette in 1943, "the policy-making function of government is drifting away from the point at which the laws are passed." And they are deeply dissatisfied with the manner in which some administrative agencies have exercised the powers delegated to them. Thus Congressman Howard W. Smith of Virginia, in a statement before the Joint Committee on the Organization of Congress on March 28, 1945, said in part:

Under our Constitution legislation is supposed to be enacted by the Congress. I want to call your attention to what I assert to be a fact, that we now have not only legislation by the Congress, but we have four other types of legislation. . . . We have legislation by sanctions; we have legislation by subsidies; we have legislation by executive regulations, under authority of Congress; and we have legislation by interpretation—interpretations that Congress never dreamed of when we enacted the law. I think that is of very grave moment . . . I do not think the American people realize to what extent our system of government is being changed by these innovations in the way of the four types of legislation that I have enumerated.

As an example of legislation by sanction, Representative Smith cited the notorious Montgomery Ward case, and also the case of a company which was forbidden to manufacture airplane landing lights because it refused to reinstate certain dismissed employees. The granting of livestock subsidies to those observing OPA meat and livestock prices he gave as an example of legislation by subsidy. An example of legislation by regulation was seen in an order of the Wage-Hour Division, forbidding homework under certain conditions. And the interpretation of the Stabilization Act of 1942 by executive and administrative orders in such a way as to amend the revenue laws and deny court appeal was cited by Congressman Smith as an illustration of legislation by interpretation.

Thus it will be seen that executive absorption of the legislative function has gone quite far—much farther probably than was contemplated in the original design. But it would be erroneous to conclude that Congress has completely abandoned its lawmaking role. The legislative counsel of the Senate, Charles F. Boots, told a joint committee in May, 1945, that his office had drafted fifty percent of all the bills and joint resolutions introduced in the Senate during the second session of the 78th Congress. And Middleton Beaman, veteran legislative counsel of the House of Representatives, earlier informed the same group that his staff had either drafted or done substantial work on 23 percent of all the public bills and joint resolutions during the 78th Congress, 21 percent of the private bills, 36 percent of the concurrent resolutions, and 14 percent of the simple resolutions.

As the father of the congressional bill-drafting service with which he had been associated for more than a quarter of a century since its creation in 1919, Mr. Beaman summed the situation up soundly when he said:

As far as we are concerned, we have no particular objection to a department coming down here with the draft of a bill, if the committee will take that bill, discover every question of policy which is decided one way or another in the bill, and make up its own mind whether the questions are decided correctly . . . what is to be desired is that when the legislation is enacted it express accurately, down to the last comma and word in it, the intention of Congress in passing it . . . If it meets that test 100 percent, it makes no difference where it comes from, if it comes from Heaven, from an executive department, or is written in our office or some other place.

Regardless of the theory of separated powers, on which the founding fathers were ill advised by Locke and Montesquieu, the legislative function in practice is exercised in partnership by Congress and the executive. Robert Heller, author of a well-known report on *Strengthening the Congress,* spoke wisely when he said:

Initiation of legislation may come from Congress, the executive branch, or sources outside the Federal Government. *Enactment* of legislation is a function exclusively Congressional, subject to the limitations of the Constitution. But *formulation* of legislation should be a partnership project.

In formulating legislation, Congress and the executive branch should be a team; if they do not work together, they cannot carry the load. Congress should not be criticized as a 'rubber stamp' if it approves most legislation sponsored by the executive branch, so long as Congress has participated in the formulation of that legislation . . .

Congress can contribute to the partnership (a) the will of the people, (b) its own judgment, and (c) its political wisdom. But Congress is a composite body tending to represent people as groups rather than as a whole, members are not experts, and members are not necessarily well-versed in technical administrative problems. On the other hand, the executive branch can contribute to the partnership (a) some synthesis of group points of view, (b) expert opinion, and (c) technical administrative knowledge. But the executive branch may or may not directly reflect the will of the people, and except for the President, it has no constituents. Thus in legislation formulation, the strengths of each branch compensate for the weaknesses of the other. In this, there is a true basis for partnership and a false basis for separate action.

Supervising Administration

With the decline of Congress as an original source of legislation and with the great growth of administrative activities, supervision of administration has become one of the most important congressional functions. In an oft-quoted statement John Stuart Mill once observed that "the proper office of a representative assembly is to watch and control the government," a role for which he considered it better equipped than to develop legislative proposals.

While the framers of the constitution did not explicitly assign this task to Congress, it was implicit in the power of the purse and impeachment and in the Senate's role in foreign relations and appointments. Certainly from the earliest days Congress has sought in various ways to supervise and control administrative conduct in order to prevent dishonesty or waste of public funds, observe the effects of its enactments, expose the actions of the government, and hold the executive accountable for his deeds and misdeeds. To these ends Congress has several tools in its inspection kit, all of which have been used in varying degree: (1) investigations by special committees—a device first used to inquire into the defeat of General St. Clair by the Indians in 1792; (2) detailed amendment of existing laws; (3) continuous scrutiny of administration by the standing legislative committees; (4) the requirement of periodic or special reports describing executive performance; (5) resolutions of inquiry requesting information from executive departments; and (6) the Committees on Appropriations which have been since 1921 the chief weapons in the armory of congressional supervision.

In a subsequent chapter I shall deal in detail with the oversight function of Congress, especially with reference to legislative efforts to control public expenditures.

Representing the People

In addition to enacting the laws and inspecting their administration, the modern Congress in practice also devotes much time and effort to representing the people, in all their diverse individual and group interests, in the councils of the nation. This representative function was not defined as such in the original design. But just as the various financial, commercial, agrarian, and speculative interests of the newborn nation had their spokesmen in the constitutional convention, so was it certain that the multifarious interests of the states and people would find voices to defend them in the federal assembly.

From the beginning of our national history members of Congress have conceived of themselves as ambassadors from their respective states and districts or, in their more humble moments, as the people's "hired men" or "errand boys." And as governmental activities and services have multiplied and as the impact of the state on the daily life of the citizen has quickened, the average Congressman has spent more and more of his working time running errands for his constituents. Every day brings its series of personal interviews, its stack of letters requiring reply, its time-consuming efforts to adjust conflicting interests between constituents and administrative agencies. Axe-grinding constituents keep the lawmaker from his laws much of the time. But such services help to humanize the relations between the people and the huge, impersonal, bureaucratic machine in Washington, and they are also a *sine qua non* of reelection.

Congressmen not only articulate the economic, social, and cultural interests of the people, and mediate between them and the administration in case of conflict. They also help to inform and guide public opinion on the great issues of the day. With the aid of the press and radio, public debate and newsletters home, members perform the important function of keeping public opinion in touch with the conduct of the government and government officials in touch with public opinion. Congress no longer really governs the country; the administration in all its ramifications actually governs. During the nineteenth century the great issues were legislative; today administration is nine-tenths of the law. But Congress serves as a forum through which public opinion can be enlightened, general policy discussed, and the conduct of public affairs ventilated and criticized.

In performing its representative function Congress thus reflects state and local interests, plays the part of mediator between the executive branch and the people, serving in Hamilton's phrase as "the confidential guardians of the people's rights and liberties," and helps to instruct public opinion.

Keeping House

In drawing their grand design, as we have seen, the architects of Congress did not fail to provide for its internal routine and regimen. Under the constitution Congress is required to enact necessary laws providing for its own maintenance and each house is authorized to make its own rules to regulate its procedure. Both houses of the First Congress, which met in New York on March 4, 1789, adopted rules of procedure based on those used by the Continental Congress and the several state legislatures which, in turn, had been modeled on the parliamentary practices then prevailing in the English House of Commons. As time went on, these practices were adapted to the exigencies of Congress and were gradually evolved into a distinctly American mode of procedure.

Meanwhile, Thomas Jefferson, while serving as Vice President of the United States and President of the Senate (1797–1801), gave proof of his amazing versatility by preparing the notable work which has come to be known as *Jefferson's Manual of Parliamentary Practice.* This work forms the basis of the present Senate rules and many of the House rules. In 1837 the House adopted a rule, which is still in effect, permitting the provisions of this Manual "to govern the House in all cases to which they are applicable."

When a new Congress convenes, the House of Representatives customarily adopts the rules of the preceding House, but the standing rules of the Senate remain in operation indefinitely, the Senate being a continuing body with two-thirds of its membership always in office. Both houses have frequently revised, modified, and amended their rules of procedure to meet exigencies that have arisen from time to time. A sweeping revision of the House rules was made in 1910–1911 during the parliamentary battles that deprived Speaker Cannon of his former powers. Distilled and refined by long legislative practice, the rules of the House have been described by Lewis Deschler, House parliamentarian since 1928, as "perhaps the most finely adjusted, scientifically balanced, and highly technical rules of any parliamentary body in the world. Under them a majority may work its will at all times in the face of the most determined and vigorous opposition of a minority"—a deserved encomium.

But expedition and efficiency in legislation, supervision, and service to constituents require more than a well-established system of parliamentary procedure. The constantly increasing pressure and complexity of its business over the years have induced Congress to provide itself, in a rather niggardly and dilatory fashion, with a variety of internal administrative and technical services, staff facilities, physical arrangements, and records. These services and facilities, however, have grown up like Topsy and operate quite independently of each other. They are scattered and duplicated without much co-ordination all over

Capitol Hill, each house having its separate fiscal, personnel, procurement, and other services. There is no centralized responsibility for their provision. Recent progress in methods of administrative management, made in the Executive Branch under the compulsions of the war emergency, have for the most part passed Congress by. Provision for the compensation, expenses, and retirement of the members and employees of our national legislature have also lagged behind prevailing standards in government and business. Research and informational facilities in the legislative branch are also pitifully inadequate. All these are vital aspects of its housekeeping function, for upon the quantity and quality of its underlying facilities and services depend, in a practical way, the adequacy and effectiveness with which Congress succeeds in performing its essential legislative, supervisory, and representative functions. In later chapters I shall deal more fully with this housekeeping function.

Proposing Constitutional Amendments

There has been no change since 1789 in the process of amending the constitution as prescribed in Article V. Since the first ten amendments —the Bill of Rights—were adopted in 1791, the constitution has been amended only 11 times: once every 14 years on the average. Of the two methods provided for proposing changes in the fundamental law: by a two-thirds vote of both houses of Congress, or by a convention upon the request of two-thirds of the state legislatures—the former has been used in every case. All the amendments adopted have been ratified by the legislatures of three-fourths of the states except the twenty-first, repealing prohibition, which was ratified by conventions in 36 states during 1933.

Our amending process has often been criticized by students of the American constitution as unduly slow and cumbersome. The first 10 amendments were proposed to the legislatures of the several states by the First Congress on September 25, 1789, but it was November 3, 1791, more than two years later, before two-thirds of the states had ratified them. And it has taken from nine months to four years to ratify the last 11 amendments, or about 22 months on the average. The child-labor amendment, proposed in 1924, has never been ratified by the states. In his battle to enlarge the Supreme Court in 1937 President Roosevelt rejected a constitutional amendment as the way to achieve his objective because of the delays it would involve. The process is also undemocratic, he argued, in that thirteen states which contain only five per cent of the voting population can block ratification even though the thirty-five states with ninety-five per cent of the population are in favor of it.

In order to avoid by-passing the constitution or permitting the executive to subject it to procrustean treatment, Henry Hazlitt has proposed amending the amending process by following the Australian plan.[1] Amendments to the constitution of that Commonwealth may be proposed by a majority vote of both houses and approved by direct vote of a majority of the voters in a majority of the states. Under the Australian method a nation-wide popular referendum on a proposed amendment is held on a day fixed by Parliament, and the majority rules. Hazlitt also suggests that Congress retain the right to submit amendments to the state legislatures in the case of propositions too technical for direct submission to the people, and that the state legislatures should be empowered to propose amendments when one-fourth or 12 of them have agreed within a three-year period on a particular proposition. Our present one-way system, he argues, "loads the dice" in the direction of centralizing power in Washington, for Congress is not likely to submit amendments designed to curtail federal powers or prerogatives.

Much might be said both for and against Mr. Hazlitt's suggestion for making the amendment process more simple and expeditious. Probably many observers would accept the conclusion of Lord Bryce that "the process of amending the Constitution is so troublesome that even a change which involves no party issues may remain unadopted long after the best opinion has become unanimous in its favor." But despite the strong case for a change, it seems unlikely at this late date that the people will modify a process they have tolerated for more than a century and a half.

Impeaching Public Officers

Congress also functions, we have noted, as a high court of justice for the impeachment by the House of Representatives and trial by the Senate of public officials accused of high crimes and misdemeanors. Acting as a grand jury through its Judiciary Committee, the House examines charges of misconduct by such officers and the Senate sits as a court to try them when impeached by the House. This power is important because it is one of the weapons granted Congress to control

---

[1] *A New Constitution Now* (1942), Chapter XIII.

administrative behavior. But in actual practice it has seldom been exercised because of its cumbersome and time-consuming character.

In our entire history the Senate has sat as a Court of Impeachment only 12 times and has removed only four federal judges from office: John Pickering in 1804, West H. Humphreys in 1862, Robert W. Archbald in 1913, and Halsted L. Ritter in 1936. In 1799 charges against Senator William Blount of Tennessee were dismissed for want of jurisdiction in the first impeachment trial. Justice Samuel Chase of the U. S. Supreme Court was acquitted in 1805. James H. Peck, a federal district judge, was acquitted in 1831. In the most famous impeachment case in American history, President Andrew Johnson was acquitted in 1868 after a sensational three-month trial. Secretary of War William W. Belknap was also acquitted after five months before the Senate bar in 1876. Federal district judges Charles Swayne and Harold Louderback escaped conviction in 1905 and 1933. And impeachment proceedings against Judge George W. English were dismissed in 1926 after he resigned his office. Others who perhaps should have been impeached have likewise been allowed to resign without penalty.

There are serious objections to impeachment trials under modern legislative conditions. The House can and does delegate its investigation of accused officials to a subcommittee. But if the House votes for impeachment, the Senate must interrupt its already congested schedule and try the case on the floor. In actual practice it has proved almost impossible to keep busy Senators on the floor when the Senate is sitting as a court. Consequently, many Senators are not familiar with the evidence and hesitate to vote for removal of an accused official without adequate knowledge of the case. Under these circumstances the possibility of obtaining the required two-thirds vote for conviction is slight.

The defects of the traditional impeachment procedure were glaringly illustrated in 1945 in the case of federal judge Albert W. Johnson. This case came before Congress just after victory over Germany and Japan at a time when both houses were preoccupied with far-reaching national and international problems. An overworked Senate was in no mood to lay aside the United Nations Charter and similar momentous matters for an impeachment trial, nor would it have been in the public interest to do so. In this juncture, Judge Johnson fortunately resigned and surrendered the perquisites of his office, relieving the House of the duty of instituting impeachment proceedings.

The Johnson case revived interest in a remedy often advocated by Representative Hatton W. Sumners, veteran chairman of the House

Judiciary Committee. Let Congress provide by law for the trial of a federal judge (except justices of the Supreme Court) accused of misconduct by three circuit court judges designated by the Chief Justice in a civil action instituted by the Attorney General. Upon conviction the defendant would be removed from office, but he could appeal his case to the Supreme Court. The House of Representatives has twice passed such a corrective bill, in 1937 and again in 1941, to modernize the impeachment process. But the Senate has not yet availed itself of the proffered relief.

Choosing a President

Finally, Congress has the electoral function under the constitution of determining the time for choosing electors and the day on which they shall vote for President and Vice President (Article II, Section 1), of canvassing the vote cast for these offices in the electoral college (Amendment XII), and of choosing the President and Vice President if no candidates have won a majority vote in the electoral college (Amendment XII).

Pursuant to this mandate, Congress has fixed the time for choosing electors on the Tuesday next after the first Monday in November in every fourth year, and the time at which their votes are given on the first Monday after the second Wednesday in December next following their appointment. The statutes also provide for transmitting to the President of the Senate certificates of the appointment of the electors and of their votes.

The electoral count takes place in the hall of the House at 1 P.M. on the sixth day of January succeeding the meeting of electors. By concurrent resolution the two houses provide for the meeting to count the vote, for the appointment of tellers, and for the announcement of the results. On the appointed day and hour the Senate enters the hall of the House in a body preceded by their sergeant-at-arms and headed by the Vice President accompanied by the Secretary of the Senate. The Vice President presides at the joint session and the Speaker sits upon his left. Then the tellers count and announce the electoral vote of each state in alphabetical order. Applause or other manifestations of approval are out of order during the count. When the count is completed, the Vice President announces the names of the winners and the Senate retires from the hall in a body.

If no candidate has a majority, the House immediately proceeds to the election by ballot of a President, and the Senate to the election of a

· Vice President. Under the twelfth amendment, the House chooses a President from among the top three contestants for this office in the electoral count, and the Senate selects the Vice President from among the two highest candidates on the list for this office. In choosing the President the House votes by states, each state has one vote, and a majority of all the states is necessary to a choice. In choosing the Vice President a majority of the whole number of Senators is necessary to a choice. The twentieth amendment (section 4) gives Congress power to provide by law how to proceed when death has removed one of those highest on the list of those from whom the House or Senate may choose a President or Vice President. But Congress has never provided by law for such a contingency.

Congress has had an opportunity to exercise its electoral function only four times since the founding of the Republic—in 1801 and 1825 when the electoral college failed to choose a President and Vice President, in 1837 when there was no popular choice for Vice President, and in 1876 at the time of the Hayes-Tilden controversy. This historic contest was finally decided by reference to a specially constituted commission composed of five Senators, five Representatives and five justices of the Supreme Court who awarded the presidency to Mr. Hayes by a margin of one electoral vote (185 to 184) although Mr. Tilden had received a plurality of the popular vote.

Succession to the Presidency

The vacancy in the office of Vice President, caused by the death of President Roosevelt on April 12, 1945 and by the succession of Vice President Truman to the presidency, emphasizes the great importance of the role of Congress in determining succession to the presidency. This question was considered by the Founding Fathers who provided (Article II, Section 1) that:

In case of the removal of the President from office, or of his death, resignation, or inability to discharge the powers and duties of the said office, the same shall devolve on the Vice-President, and the Congress may by law provide for the case of removal, death, resignation or inability, both of the President and Vice-President, declaring what officer shall then act as President, and such officer shall act accordingly, until the disability be removed, or a President shall be elected.

Acting under this provision, the Second Congress passed a succession law in 1792 which made the President *pro tempore* of the Senate and the Speaker of the House heirs apparent after the Vice President, in the order named. The act of 1792 also provided for a special election if a double vacancy in the executive offices occurred more than five months before the end of a presidential term. In this event, the Secretary of State was to notify the state governors who were to arrange for the appointment of presidential electors.

Many of the members of the Second Congress who had been delegates to the Constitutional Convention, including James Madison, were dubious of this solution of the succession problem. They doubted if congressional officers were officers of the United States in the constitutional sense, and they objected to the blending of legislative and executive functions that would result if a congressional officer retained his legislative station after succeeding to the presidency.

Despite these constitutional doubts, the act of 1792 remained in effect for almost a century, until it was repealed by the act of 1886. Several Vice Presidents had died in the interval at times when both the President *pro tempore* and the Speakership were vacant, presenting the serious possibility of no provision for the presidency if the incumbent of that office died. Public anxiety lest the presidency lapse finally led Congress in 1886 to pass an act transferring the succession from congressional officers to members of the Cabinet, beginning with the Secretary of State, followed in line by the Secretary of the Treasury, the Secretary of War, the Attorney General, the Postmaster General, the Secretary of the Navy, and the Secretary of the Interior. The act of 1886 also required the successor to the presidency, when a double vacancy occurred, to convene Congress in special session if it were not then meeting.

A double vacancy has fortunately never occurred in the executive offices and no Cabinet member has ever succeeded to the presidency. This would have happened, however, in 1944 if the Republicans had captured the presidency in 1940. For Charles McNary, Republican nominee for Vice President, died February 25, 1944, and Wendell Willkie on October 8. Thus, his Secretary of State would have succeeded to the office for the remainder of his term.

The next development affecting succession to the presidency occurred in 1933 when the twentieth amendment was adopted. By abolishing the "lame-duck" session of Congress and providing that a new Congress should assemble on the same day (January 3) the old one ends, the danger of an interregnum in the presidency was removed. For now there is always a Speaker of the House, barring a protracted contest for that office, and the President *pro tempore* now holds office "at the pleasure of the Senate" which is a continuing body.

Prior to the twentieth amendment to the constitution it lacked any provision to take care of a case in which the President-elect was disqualified or had died. To remedy this defect section 3 of the twentieth amendment provides that:

If, at the time fixed for the beginning of the term of the President, the President elect shall have died, the Vice President elect shall become President. If a President shall not have been chosen before the time fixed for the beginning of his term, or if the President elect shall have failed to qualify, then the Vice President elect shall act as President until a President shall have qualified; and the Congress may by law provide for the case wherein neither a President elect nor a Vice President elect shall have qualified, declaring who shall then act as President, or the manner in which one who is to act shall be selected, and such person shall act accordingly until a President or Vice President shall have qualified.

The twentieth amendment removed some of the objections to placing the line of succession in the Congress. Meanwhile, the act of 1886, which remained in operation, made the Secretary of State heir apparent in the event of a double vacancy, permitting a President, in effect, to choose his own successor.

At this juncture President Truman, who had recently succeeded to that office, sent a special message to Congress on June 19, 1945, recommending prompt revision of the act of 1886 "in the interest of orderly, democratic government." Mr. Truman proposed a reversion to the plan of 1792, except that he would make the Speaker of the House next in line after the Vice President, followed by the President *pro tempore* of the Senate: both elective officers. The Speaker should resign, he thought, as a member and officer of Congress before assuming the presidency. If neither the Speaker nor President *pro tempore* qualified, Mr. Truman suggested that the succession pass to the Cabinet as provided by the act of 1886, until a duly qualified Speaker should be elected. Under the Truman plan, the successor to the presidency would serve until the next congressional election or until a special election called for the purpose of electing a new President and Vice President, who would serve only to fill out the unexpired terms of the previously elected executive officers. "In this way," said Truman, "there would be no interference with the normal four-year interval of general elections."

After perfunctory debate the House of Representatives quickly passed the Truman proposal without the special election feature, more as a tribute perhaps to its popular Speaker, Sam Rayburn, than out of deep study of the scheme. But the Senate paused to ponder the Truman and a variety of other succession plans and the knotty constitutional questions involved, being in no hurry to displace its former member and favorite heir apparent, Secretary of State James F. Byrnes. "In view of the many constitutional obstacles to the plan of succession recommended by Truman, and the danger of a successful challenge to the right of a Speaker or President *pro tempore* to serve as President when the occasion arose, the ultimate decision of Congress may well be to abandon the House bill and seek a solution through the process of constitutional amendment." [2]

---

[2] "Succession to the Presidency" by F. M. Brewer, *Editorial Research Reports*, September 20, 1945.

2.

How Congress Is Composed

To THE FREQUENT query: "What's wrong with Congress?" a favorite retort is: "Congress itself!", meaning the members themselves. Some critics of representative government allege that its basic fault is to be found not in its antiquated machinery or archaic methods or excessive work-load, but in the personnel of the legislature. In the current discussion of the problems of Congress much attention is paid to its committee structure and procedures, to its functions and volume of business, and to its relations with the administration and constituents. But comparatively little regard is paid to the members of Congress themselves—their qualifications and characteristics, how they are selected, and how representative as a group they are of the electorate.

What qualities should voters seek in selecting Senators and Representatives? Should Congress be merely a mirror of the nation or should it be composed of persons of special experience and qualifications? Is the legal profession over-represented in Congress? How many members have had previous legislative experience? Are some interests and sections of the country over- or under-represented? How can such malrepresentation be corrected? What types of districts frequently change their representation in Congress and what types retain the same members for many years? How do members obtain and retain their seats? What have been the effects upon the quality of the membership of the expansion of the suffrage, the direct election of the United States Senators, the growing size of the constituencies, and increasing campaign expenditures? What proposals have been made with a view to securing a more representative and better-balanced national legislature? Is it possible that the inner explanation of present dissatisfaction with the workings of representative government in Washington and elsewhere lies in the quality of the personnel of our legislatures? In this chapter I shall attempt to deal with some of these neglected questions, despite the paucity of available factual information about them.

Conditions of Admission

In some ways Congress is like a rather select club. Its monumental buildings on Capitol Hill, its ornate rooms and frescoed halls, its gold-plated mirrors and chandeliers, its luxurious lounges and reception rooms, its ionic columns and domed ceilings, its paintings and statues of famous members, its privileges and perquisites, its dignified atmosphere and congenial camaraderie that seem impervious to all outside criticism—all combine to make it perhaps the finest if not the most exclusive club in the land.

Nor is it an easy club to become a member of. To gain admission here a candidate must pass many tests. He must possess the qualifications as to age, citizenship, and residence specified in the constitution. He must win the nomination in the primaries of one of the two major political parties in his state or district, although a few members of minority parties have occasionally been admitted. He must receive the votes of a majority of the voters at a general election in his political subdivision. And after an aspiring candidate has surmounted all these hurdles, he must be acceptable to Congress itself which can reject him or expel him or award his seat to an opponent in the event of a contest. For example, the House rejected Roberts in 1899 because he was a Mormon with several wives; and the Senate denied Vare a seat in 1926 on account of his excessive campaign expenditures. Humphrey Marshall was expelled from the Senate in 1796 on the charge of perjury. And scores of apparent winners in congressional elections have been deprived of their seats in the House which for many decades almost always awarded contested places to the candidates of the dominant party.

The handling of election contests, incidentally, has been one of the major scandals of congressional history. Congress should vest in the courts jurisdiction to hear and decide in the first instance contested election cases in order both to obviate the evils of the traditional method of settling such contests and to save the time, money, and labor involved. The present system causes injustice to individuals, sometimes defeats the will of the people, and tends to multiply contests. It also imposes a heavy burden upon the committees concerned, takes the time of the House, and costs about $4,000 per contest.

CHANGES IN SIZE AND REGIONAL DISTRIBUTION

As the young nation grew in population and expanded westward toward the Pacific, the membership of the national legislature increased, although not *pari passu*. During its first fifty years as a federation the people of the United States quadrupled in number, growing from 3.9 million in 1790 to 17 million in 1840, while their Representatives in Congress were increasing from 65 to 232 members of the lower House. By 1890 the population had almost quadrupled again, rising in that year to 63 million persons who were represented at Washington by 357 Congressmen. And after another half century of amazing expansion, the nation had 132 million inhabitants in 1940 and the House of Representatives had limited its size since 1910 to 435 members. Meanwhile, the Senate, in which representation is based upon the number of states, increased in size from 26[1] members in 1790 to the present number of 96 in 1912 when the forty-eighth state—Arizona— was admitted into the Union.

Since population grew more rapidly than the membership of the House of Representatives, the effect of these changes was gradually to increase the average size of the congressional districts in terms of the average number of inhabitants represented by each member. Thus, during the First Congress the constituencies averaged about 60,000 persons, compared with an average of 74,000 in 1840, 176,000 in 1890, and 303,000 in 1940. In other words, a member of Congress today has five times as many constituents to run errands for as he had 150 years ago.

It is also interesting to note the effect of these changes upon the distribution of seats in the House of Representatives among the principal geographical regions of the country. The South controlled half the seats in the House in the First Congress and accounts with 135 seats for 31 per cent of the total today. New England, which had about one-fourth of the seats in 1790, now has only 6 per cent of the total. The Middle Atlantic states, which were on a par with New England in the beginning, now have 21 per cent and more than three times as many Representatives as New England. The North Central region, whose 12

---

[1] The Senate actually had 29 members during the 1st Congress because of death and resignation.

stars did not appear upon the flag until the nineteenth century, now controls 131 seats (30 per cent) in the House—the second largest single regional bloc. And the 11 Western states, last to be admitted to the Union, account for 12 per cent of the present membership. Table I in the Appendix shows the changes in the regional distribution of seats in the House of Representatives that have occurred at half-century intervals since Congress first met.

Regional Distribution of Seats in Senate

The Constitutional Convention of 1787 was in large part a struggle between the large and small states and the political machinery it devised was a compromise between their conflicting interests which was reached only after much travail. Part of this compromise found expression in the provision for a bicameral legislature, of which the lower house was to represent the people of the whole country—the national interest, and the upper house was to be composed of two Senators from each state—the federal principle. No state, without its consent, was to be deprived of its equal suffrage in the Senate.

It is interesting to note the effect of these provisions upon the distribution of political power in the upper house as between the large and small states. According to the population census of 1940, which groups the 48 states of the union into nine regions, there was a close correspondence in the case of two regions—the East South Central and the Pacific—between their proportion of the total population of the nation and their share of Senate seats. Three other regions also had an approximate balance in this respect—the West North Central, the South Atlantic, and the West South Central. In four other regions, however, there were wide discrepancies between population and political power. The six New England states have twice the percentage of seats in the United States Senate that they have of the total population, while the five states in the East North Central region have one-tenth of the places in the Senate compared with one-fifth of the entire population. The greatest disparities are to be found in the Middle Atlantic region where New York, New Jersey, and Pennsylvania, with 21 per cent of the number of inhabitants, have only 6 per cent of the seats in the Senate; and in the Mountain states which have only 3 per cent of the people, but control one-sixth of the upper chamber. This regional balance and imbalance between population and political power in the United States Senate is measured in Table II in the Appendix.

Continuity of Tenure

Another significant aspect of the composition of Congress is the comparative continuity of service of Senators and Representatives. This factor is significant in two ways: in its effect upon the relative influence of various states and regions in the legislative process; and in the tendency of long service to reconcile members to traditional legislative practices which seem wasteful and inefficient to the newcomer.

Continuity of personnel in Congress goes back in an unbroken line to Revolutionary days. Fifty-two members of the First Congress had been members of the Continental Congress. And there has been no Congress since the first in which men did not sit who had sat in the previous one. A perusal of the Biographical Directory of the American Congress, compiled by Ansel Wold, veteran clerk of the Joint Committee on Printing, shows the links of the legislative bond running from sire to son throughout American history. The plan whereby one-third of the Senate is chosen every second year insures the continuity of the membership of the upper house. Since two-thirds of its members are always in office, the Senate has legally been in continuous existence since 1789.

Until the adoption of the Seventeenth Amendment in 1913, providing for the direct popular election of United States Senators, the state legislatures repeatedly returned the same members to the upper chamber. During the past generation the turnover has been more rapid, every session bringing new faces on the scene and seeing familiar ones disappear. Yet many veterans have survived the vicissitudes of politics in the upper house. Of the 96 Senators in office in 1945, 32 or exactly one-third had served there continuously for 10 years or more, averaging 16 years of service each; and seven of them had been members of the Senate for 20 years or longer. McKellar, dean of the Senate, had entered that body in 1917, followed two years later by Arthur Capper and by Carter Glass in 1920. Of the top 32 in point of continuous service, 14 were Southerners, eight were from the Mountain states, four were New Englanders, four represented North Central states, and two came from the Middle Atlantic region.

Thanks to its habit of reelecting the same legislators term after term, the South continued to occupy a dominant place in Senate councils. During the 79th Congress Southern Senators held the chairmanships of 18 out of 33 standing committees in the upper chamber, including the powerful Appropriations, Finance, and Foreign Relations committees. They also controlled the strategic offices of president pro tem of the Senate, majority leader, and majority whip, secretary of the Senate and sergeant-at-arms.

On the other hand, border-line states like Ohio, Illinois, and Michigan, which frequently shift their political allegiance between two strong parties, suffer a heavy turnover in their congressional representation and do not acquire seniority privileges commensurate with their importance in the life of the nation. Thus, Ohio, whose first Senators sat in the Eighth Congress (1803–1805), had 41 United States Senators, from Thomas Worthington to Harold Burton, of whom 25 served one term or less; eight served between one and two terms; and only eight served two-full terms or more. Of these last eight, only one—Senator Sherman, author of the Sherman Antitrust Act—spent a lifetime in Congress, serving six years in the House of Representatives and 34 years in the Senate, as well as five years in the cabinet.

In the House with its larger membership and biennial elections for the entire chamber, the turnover is even more rapid than in the Senate. Of the 435 members of the House during the 79th Congress, 138 had served five or more consecutive terms, 40 had served 10 or more such terms, nine had been in Congress for 30 years, and one member— Sabath of Illinois, veteran chairman of the Rules Committee—was serving his 20th term. Fifty-five of the members who had been in the House for ten years or longer, and 16 of those who had served 20 years or longer, were Southerners. Eleven of the top 40 and 31 of the 138 seniors in point of continuous service represented Middle Atlantic states. Here again continuity of service reaped its reward in the 27 chairmanships out of 48 standing committees held by Southerners, including such great committees as Banking and Currency, Judiciary, Military and Naval Affairs, and Ways and Means. New York controlled seven chairmanships, all minor save Foreign Affairs. Missouri chaired Accounts, Appropriations, and Insular Affairs. And California had to be content with Interstate and Foreign Commerce, War Claims, and the Disposition of Executive Papers—the so-called "wastebasket committee."

QUALIFICATIONS OF MEMBERS OF CONGRESS

It is also interesting to compare the membership of Congress at selected intervals in its history in respect of their qualifications for service in the national legislature. For purposes of comparison I have selected the First, 29th, 54th, and 79th Congresses, including with the first and latest ones those that met fifty and one hundred years ago. Data on the median age of members of the House of Representatives are taken for the first three Congresses covered from Stuart Rice's *Quantitative Methods in Politics* (Chapter XXI) and are calculated by the Legislative Reference Service for the 79th Congress. Data on the academic training, legal work, and previous legislative experience of members are drawn from the *Biographical Directory of the American Congress* (1774-1927) for the first three Congresses and from the *Congressional Directory* for the 79th Congress. These findings are summarized in Table III in the Appendix.

Composition of Congress Today

Since January, 1941, I have spent five years on Capitol Hill watching Congress at work. And I have been very favorably impressed with the intelligence and character of most of the Senators and Representatives whom I have met during this period. They compare very well indeed in these respects with any other legislative assembly in the land. Any large legislature, to be sure, has its quota of duds and dullards, of windbags and time-servers, of old gentlemen in their dotage; few of these have displayed a genuine interest in modernizing Congress.

It does not follow, however, that the modern Congress is "a mirror of the nation," as it is often characterized. A little reflection and analysis will show, on the contrary, that Congress today is not a microcosm of the community nor what Harold Laski calls "an average sample of ordinary men," when measured in terms either of age, sex, education, occupation, or even political opinion.

As to age, the statistics show that the average member of Congress is considerably older than the average adult member of the public. In 1944, for example, the average age of United States Senators was 59, and the median age of Representatives was 52, while the average adult was only 43 years old. When the age-distribution of members of Congress is compared with the adult population as a whole, it is found that the adult population under 40 years of age is much under-represented in the national legislature, while those over 40 are greatly over-represented. Studies made by Stuart Rice indicate that the tendency since the Civil War has been for the age of first-term members to increase, for the length of service to increase, and for the average age of all the members of the House of Representatives to rise.[2] For ex-

---

[2] Stuart A. Rice, *Quantitative Methods in Politics* (1928), Chapter XXI.

ample, in the 41st Congress (1869–1871), the median age of all members was 45, of first-term members was 42, and the average number of terms served was 1.04. But in the 68th Congress (1923–1925), the latest one covered by the Rice survey, the median age of all Representatives was 51, of first-term members was 47, and the average period of legislative service was 2½ terms. When these figures are brought up to date, they show a continuation of these long-run trends. Thus, in the 79th Congress (1945–1947), the median age of all Representatives was 52 years, of first-term members was 46, and the average number of terms served (including the 79th Congress) was 4½. Meanwhile, the median age of the potential voting population was 41. The increasing average age of members of Congress compared with that of the electorate, and their longer average tenure of office, helps to explain perhaps why Congress is more conservative than the country.

As to sex, only nine members of the 79th Congress were women, or 1.5 per cent of the total membership of 531; whereas women compose slightly more than half of the total population of the United States.

In terms of academic training, members of Congress have had more school and university education than the average citizen of the country, although there is no such close correlation between school and college education and party affiliation in Congress as there is in the House of Commons.[3] During the 70th Congress (1927–1929), for example, 65 per cent of the Senators were college graduates and 18 per cent had only graduated from high school, while 58 per cent of the Representatives were college trained and 23 per cent of the members had not gone beyond high school.

Occupationally, the American Congress, like the House of Commons, is in no sense a mirror of the nation. Some occupations are greatly over-represented in Congress, notably the "talking classes" and particularly the legal profession which had 303 or 57 per cent of the 531 members of the 79th Congress. American politics, as Charles Beard once said, has long been under bondage to lawyers. Some critics of this bondage have taken the view that, while a lawyer is peculiarly fitted by training and practice to get himself elected to public office, the same qualities do not necessarily equip him to solve national problems. In a recent analysis of legal education in the colleges as a preparation for public life, two members of the law faculty of Yale University found that the nation's law schools gave the legal neophytes an effective training for professional practice, but failed to equip them with the

---

[3] J. F. S. Ross, *Parliamentary Representation* (1944), pp. 107–110.

economic, social, and political facts of modern life deemed essential to dealing with the problems of an increasingly complex civilization.[4]

Other occupational groups such as workers in manufacturing and farming, persons employed in wholesale and retail trades, and domestic servants are greatly under-represented in Congress or not directly represented at all. Aside from lawyers, the 79th Congress included 57 businessmen, 34 editors, publishers, or journalists, 26 educators, 24 real estate and insurance men, 18 farmers, and 12 bankers. Most of the chairmen of the important standing committees were lawyers. Table IV in the Appendix shows the occupational distribution of the members of the 79th Congress.

If the territorial basis of representation in the national House of Representatives were superseded by the occupational, as some writers have proposed, the most conspicuous result would be a sensational disappearance of lawyers, most of them country lawyers from small towns. And if the 435 seats in the House were apportioned among industry groups by the method of equal proportions, on the basis of the 1940 census, manufacturing would have 104 seats, agriculture 83, wholesale and retail trade 74, and personal servants 39. A comparison of Tables IV and V (see Appendix) shows that Congress is far from being the true "mirror of the nation" as commonly claimed.

As to political opinion, voters who belong to minority parties, as well as those whose candidates were defeated, have almost no representation in Congress. There were only two Progressives (Senator La Follette and Representative Hull) and one American Laborite (Representative Marcantonio) in the 1st session of the 79th Congress. Some voters in uncontested election districts (of which there were 75 out of 435 for the 78th Congress) and in the eight Southern poll tax states are virtually disfranchised; while it is possible under our electoral system for a party with a minority of the total votes in the country to capture a majority of the seats in Congress. This actually happened, for example, in 1942 when the Republicans polled 52 per cent of the popular vote, but fell short of winning a majority of the seats in the House of Representatives. In short, there is no exact correspondence between votes cast and seats won in congressional elections. The outcome is a gamble and the results do not necessarily express "the will of the people" or give "a mandate from the country."

---

[4] H. D. Lasswell and M. S. McDougal, "Legal Education and Public Policy: Professional Training in the Public Interest," *Yale Law Journal*, April, 1943.

Personnel of Parliament

Similar conclusions have recently been reached regarding the unrepresentative character of the House of Commons in England. On the basis of an elaborate statistical analysis, Mr. J. F. S. Ross shows that the House of Commons during the inter-war years was not a microcosm of the British community in respect either to the age, education, occupation, or party affiliation of its members. It was largely recruited, he finds, from the privileged classes whose economic and social advantages enabled them to dominate the political life of the country. He found a close correlation between politics and education, occupation, parentage, and financial means. According to Ross, the influence of wealth, leisure, and the single-member majority system of voting were primarily responsible for the unrepresentative character of Parliament.[5]

Nevertheless, the character of the membership of Parliament has greatly improved during the past century. Before the Reform Act of 1832, British elections were largely controlled by bribery and corruption, especially in the boroughs which were regarded as property and advertised for sale in the papers. Between 1812 and 1832 five to six thousand pounds was the ordinary price paid for a seat in Parliament or 1.8 thousand pounds on a rental basis.[6] The personnel of the House of Commons then consisted of landed gentlemen, rich bankers, merchants, brewers and traders, and East Indian Nabobs; manufacturers and their sons were only beginning to appear. Today, as a result of secret voting and universal suffrage, Parliament presents a far different occupational picture. The occupations of the members returned at the general election of 1935 were as follows:[7]

Agriculture	13	Food, drink, tobacco	7
Mining	40	Wood and furniture	8
Non-metal products	1	Paper workers	2
Brickmakers	1	Printers	10
Metal workers	18	Builders	6
Watches and clocks	1	Painters	2
Leather workers	2	Mixed materials	6
Textile workers	10	Transport	21
Clothing makers	1	Commerce and finance	76

[5] Op. cit.
[6] Porrit, The Unreformed House of Commons, p. 358.
[7] Ross, op. cit., p. 61.

Administration and defense	.....	84	Warehousemen	1
Professional	....	196	Engine drivers	1
Entertainment	....	4	Miscellaneous	1
Personal services	....	3	Not gainfully occupied	57
Clerks and draughtsmen	....	30		
			Total	602

MIGHTY MEN OF OLD

Many historic personages have marched across the congressional stage during its 160 crowded years and passed on into the annals of history. Most of them have disappeared into the oblivion of the past, leaving only their biographies in the records of Congress. But a few famous men writ large their names on the scroll of time and linger on in political memory. Of the members of the First Congress, at least ten are remembered today for their part in the founding of the Republic. There was Fisher Ames who represented Massachusetts in the first four Congresses, who sat in the state convention that ratified the federal constitution, and who was chosen president of Harvard University in 1804, but declined because of ill health. There was Charles Carroll of Carrollton, signer of the Declaration of Independence, member of the Continental Congress, and Senator from Maryland who lived until 1832 and was the last surviving signer of the Declaration. Another was Elbridge Gerry, great-grandfather of the present Senator Gerry of Rhode Island, who also signed the Declaration, was a delegate to the constitutional convention in Philadelphia, sat in the Continental and First and Second Congresses, was twice governor of Massachusetts, and was elected Vice President in 1812 on the same ticket with James Madison.

We remember Rufus King who served in the Revolutionary War, sat in the Continental Congress and the constitutional convention, had been a member of the Massachusetts and New York assemblies, became a United States Senator from New York, and was twice minister to Great Britain. There was also Richard Henry Lee of the famous Virginia Lees, who signed the Declaration, served as president of the Continental Congress, and was the author of the first national Thanksgiving Day proclamation issued by Congress after the capture of Burgoyne's army at Saratoga. William Maclay and Robert Morris are recalled, the first Senators from Pennsylvania. After winning fame as signer and delegate, Morris established the Bank of North America, but was later imprisoned for debts incurred in unsuccessful land speculations. Frederick Muhlenberg is well remembered as first Speaker of the national House of Representatives, crowning a distinguished career. But among these immortals the most imperishable names are those of James Madison and James Monroe who, after serving the new nation in many key posts, lived to become the fourth and fifth Presidents of the United States. These were the brightest stars in the firmament of the First Congress.

A half century later found a new generation of great statesmen in the legislative halls, as the dark clouds of the irrepressible conflict between the states were gathering on the horizon. Here came Stephen A. Douglas from the supreme court of Illinois, to sit six years in the lower House and 14 years in the Senate, defeating Abraham Lincoln himself for a place in that chamber in 1859, only to be defeated by him in the presidential campaign of 1860. There was that great man, John Quincy Adams, former minister to the courts of the Czars and St. James, Secretary of State under Monroe, and President of the United States by choice of the House in 1825, who lived to serve his country as a Whig in the House of Representatives until 1848. There stood Daniel Webster, gifted son of Dartmouth—the little college he loved so well, who represented both New Hampshire and the Bay State in the lower chamber, awakened the sleeping echoes of the Senate with his matchless oratory for upwards of twenty years, and served as Secretary of State under three presidents.

That was the era of Thomas H. Benton who, representing Missouri in the Senate from 1821 to 1851, was the first man to serve thirty consecutive years there, and who won renown for persuading the Senate to expunge from its Journal a resolution censuring Andrew Jackson whose aide-de-camp Benton had been in the War of 1812. John C. Calhoun then strode upon the public stage, gracing the hall of the House for six years and of the Senate for a quarter of a century, first as Vice President under Adams and Jackson, and then as Senator until mid-century, with two intervals of absence as Secretary of War in the Monroe cabinet and Secretary of State under Tyler. One of the most versatile figures of that fateful period was Sam Houston, warrior-statesman who battled the British, Indians, and Mexicans, governed Tennessee and Texas, routed Santa Anna in the famous fight at San Jacinto, was twice president of the Republic of Texas, and served four terms in the national House of Representatives and two terms in the Senate—all in one strenuous lifetime.

In that galaxy of immutable lights were also two future Presidents— James Buchanan, who fought in the War of 1812, served a decade in the lower chamber, became minister to Russia and Great Britain, sat in the United States Senate from 1834 to 1845, and was Secretary of State under President Polk before succeeding to that high office himself in 1857 on the eve of the War between the States. And Andrew Johnson, who never attended school a day in his life, but rose from a tailor's apprentice to become successively Tennessee state legislator, Congressman for a decade, governor of his state, and United States Senator. Nominated with Lincoln in 1864 to catch votes in the South and West, Johnson became President after Lincoln's assassination, was impeached by the House of which he had once been an honored member in 1868, and was acquitted by the Senate after a three months' trial by the slim margin of a single vote, living to serve five months in the body that all but convicted him until he died in 1875. That was the age of controversy over the nature of the federal union when great personalities in Congress articulated arguments founded on fundamental differences in the economy and society of Northern and Southern states.

During the three decades that intervened between the "Second American Revolution" and the war with Spain, a host of politicians appeared upon the stage of the national capitol, played their minor parts, and soon disappeared in the wings of obscurity. The House of Representatives increased in size from 243 to 391 members, duly chosen in popular elections, while the Senate expanded with the development of the far West from 74 to 90 seats, one-third of which were filled each biennium by persons designated by state legislative caucuses. A few Senators succeeded in retaining their togas for several terms during this age of "acquisition and enjoyment," but many changes occurred in the personnel of that august body. And during most of the period between 1865 and 1900 the ship of state was guided by opposing political parties in control of the Executive Mansion and the legislative citadel.

Post-Bellum Politicians

Time casts a halo over the heads of men who to their contemporaries may have seemed comparatively undistinguished. Of the hundreds who came and went in legislative halls during post-bellum days, at least a dozen left their imprint upon the archives of history. There was Eugene Hale, first of an illustrious line of federal statesmen from Maine, who spent a decade in the House of Representatives after the Civil War, declined two cabinet posts offered by Grant and Hayes, and then served thirty years (1881-1911) in the United States Senate, a longer continuous service than any other Senator of his time. There was George Frisbie Hoar, second in a long line of Hoars who represented Massachusetts in Congress between 1835 and 1906, who served in the lower chamber from 1869 to 1877, was one of the House managers in the impeachment proceedings against Secretary of War Belknap, sat on the electoral commission that decided the Hayes-Tilden presidential contest in 1876, was an overseer of Harvard, and a member of the Senate from 1877 to 1904. Among Senators from Ohio, John Sherman achieved immortality as the author of the Sherman Antitrust Act of 1891 which sought to discipline triumphant business enterprise to the ways of free competition. Sherman served three terms in the House on the eve of the Civil War, and sat in the Senate from 1861 to 1897—broken only by his occupancy of the Treasury portfolio in the Hayes cabinet. After retiring from the Senate, he served a year as Secretary of State in the cabinet of President McKinley.

Typical of the machine politicians of the period were "Boss Platt" of the New York machine and Matthew S. Quay of Pennsylvania. After four years in the House in the mid-seventies, Thomas Collier Platt entered the Senate in 1881, but soon resigned with his colleague, Roscoe Conkling, over a disagreement with President Garfield concerning federal patronage in New York. Platt dominated the Republican Party in New York state during the last quarter of the nineteenth century, finally returning to the Senate in 1897 for two terms. Matthew Quay, who had fought in the Civil War and been a state legislator and state official, was a power in state and national Republican party politics for three decades. He served in the United States Senate from 1887 to 1899, but was rejected by that body in 1900 after receiving an appointment from the governor of Pennsylvania to fill the vacancy caused by the refusal of the state legislature to reelect him. Later he was elected to fill the vacancy and served until his death in 1904.

Nelson W. Aldrich, John Sharp Williams, and Henry Cabot Lodge were a trio of outstanding Senators whose political careers spanned the turn of the century. Aldrich represented Rhode Island in the Senate for thirty years, from 1881 to 1911, and was chairman of the National Monetary Commission. Floor leader of the Old Guard machine, Aldrich named the committees and dominated the Senate, giving his name—Aldrichism—to a system of legislative supremacy in which the floor leader was supreme. John Sharp Williams of Mississippi won a niche in the hall of fame as a scholar and orator, serving eight terms in the House between 1893 and 1909, during three of which he was minority leader, and two terms in the Senate, 1911–1923, where he is still remembered. Henry Cabot Lodge—editor, historian, author, and scholar in politics—served three terms in the House (1887–1893) from Massachusetts and five terms in the Senate (1893–1924), acting as majority leader of that body from 1918 to 1924. He was also one of the party wheel horses, having been a delegate to every Republican National Convention from 1884 to 1924 and chairman of three of them. But it was as leader of the "little group of willful men" who defeated the entry of the United States into the League of Nations in 1919, thus initiating the chain of events that culminated in the Second World War, that Lodge earned a dubious immortality.

Among the historic personages of this middle period in congressional history were four famous men: Thomas Brackett Reed, Joseph Gurney Cannon, Oscar W. Underwood, and Frederick H. Gillett. Reed, who served eleven terms in the House, is chiefly remembered as Speaker in the 51st, 54th, and 55th Congresses and for a series of decisions which, taken together, prevented obstruction of the business of the House by dilatory tactics. "Uncle Joe" Cannon served 23 terms in the House between 1873 and 1923—a fifty year span—and was Speaker from 1903 to 1911. Under Cannon the Speaker organized and dominated the House, giving his name—Cannonism—to a system of control which reached its apogee under his masterful leadership. His reign was finally ended by the sensational March revolution of 1910 in which a coalition of Democrats and insurgent Republicans clipped the powers of the presiding officer. "Uncle Joe" received 58 votes for the presidential nomination at the Republican National Convention in 1908 and lived to the ripe old age of 90 years, half of them spent in the halls of the House.

After Cannon was deposed, Oscar Underwood, who had been a member of Congress from Alabama since 1897, succeeded to the mastery of the House. Underwood and Champ Clark were rival candidates for Speaker of the House in the 62nd Congress. Clark gained the Speakership, with some of the prestige, but little of the power, that formerly went with that office. And Underwood became chairman of the Ways and Means Committee which carried with it the power to select the committees, influence the rules, dominate the caucus, and be floor leader. Clark received the shadow, Underwood the substance of power in the House. The Speaker became a figurehead, the floor leader was supreme, as he was in the Senate under the Aldrich system. Later, Underwood was elected to the United States Senate where he served two terms (1915–1927), acting as floor leader in the upper chamber from 1921 to 1923. In 1928 he was a leading candidate for the Democratic presidential nomination—the refrain of the Alabama delegation ringing still in memory—"Alabama casts 24 votes for Oscar W. Underwood." A final unforgotten political figure of this "gilded age" was Frederick H. Gillett, who represented Massachusetts in the House for 16 terms (1893–1925), rose to the Speakership for three terms after World War I, and crowned his career with a term in the Senate (1925–1931). Students of political history may recall a few other names from the period of reconstruction and expansion—Bankhead, Crisp, Watson, Curtis, Dingley, McCall, Burton, Swanson, Mondell. But the rest have been erased by the shifting sands of time.

TWENTIETH CENTURY CHANGES

Article I, section 3 of the federal constitution provided that the Senate of the United States should be composed of two Senators from each state, chosen by the legislature thereof. This indirect method of election was designed by the framers to make the Senate a conservative body that would safeguard the interests of property and serve as a check on the radicalism of the direct representatives of the people in the lower chamber. Their plans worked well in practice, for as the nation grew in wealth and power after the Civil War, the Senate resembled more and more a rich man's club.

"Though the state legislatures nominally chose in solemn assembly," write Charles and Mary Beard, "in reality the assignment was made at a party caucus held behind closed doors where pecuniary bargains were frequently consummated. Every now and then a magnate, accustomed to buying engineers, lawyers, managers, palaces, and works of art, brushed aside the decorum of constitutional propriety and bought a seat in the Senate with such disregard for refinements of easy ethics that investigations, revelations, and alarms inevitably pursued him. Indeed from year to year the country was shocked by noisy scandals connected with the elevation of plutocrats to the august body once ornamented by Calhoun, Webster, and Clay, until eventually the weary public was led to suspect that even in unknown cases the senatorial toga had been secured by something other than high and meritorious statesmanship based on patriotic principles."[8]

---

[8] From Charles A. and Mary R. Beard, *The Rise of American Civilization* (1927), Vol. II, p. 560. By permission of The Macmillan Company, publishers.

Effects of Direct Election of Senators

Meanwhile, the forces of social democracy which had been seeking to purify American politics since 1883 via civil service reform, the secret ballot, the direct primary, and the initiative, referendum, and recall, now put their weight behind the movement for the direct election of United States Senators as a means of freeing that body from the venality of the state legislatures and bringing it closer to the interests of the common man. This reform had been urged as far back as 1868 by Andrew Johnson and the House of Representatives had repeatedly passed an amendment for the purpose, only to be blocked by senatorial beneficiaries of the original design. Backed by the Populists, the movement gathered momentum after the turn of the century, was reluctantly endorsed by Taft and Woodrow Wilson, and was finally proposed to the legislatures of the several states by the 62nd Congress in 1912 and declared ratified by the necessary two-thirds on May 31, 1913. Under the Seventeenth Amendment United States Senators are now elected by direct vote of the people of each state.

It is difficult to evaluate the effects of this change in political machinery upon the composition and caliber of the Senate. By 1913 three-fourths of the candidates for the Senate were being nominated in direct primaries, so that the secret caucus had already been partly replaced by the polling booth. The terms of the Senators in office when the Seventeenth Amendment was ratified expired at biennial intervals in 1915, 1917, and 1919. Thus, the full effect of the change upon the personnel of the membership was not apparent until the 66th Congress assembled on March 4, 1919. By that time, 56 of the Senators who owed their togas originally to state legislatures had been reelected by the people, three had died, and 37 had disappeared from the scene either voluntarily or by popular verdict. In other words, more than half of those last chosen by legislative caucus were subsequently approved by the people.

Among those who passed from the political stage after adoption of the Seventeenth Amendment were DuPont of Delaware, James Hamilton Lewis of Illinois, Weeks of Massachusetts, Vardaman of Mississippi, Elihu Root of New York, Burton of Ohio, Tillman of South Carolina, Lea of Tennessee, and Goff of West Virginia. And among the new faces that appeared in the Senate, some of whom must have been beneficiaries of the new method, were Underwood of Alabama, Johnson of California, McCormick of Illinois, Curtis and Capper of

Kansas, Broussard of Louisiana, Fernald and Hale of Maine, Walsh of Massachusetts, Newberry of Michigan, Kellogg of Minnesota, Harrison of Mississippi, Moses of New Hampshire, Frelinghuysen and Edge of New Jersey, Wadsworth of New York, Harding of Ohio, McNary of Oregon, Knox of Pennsylvania, Gerry of Rhode Island, McKellar of Tennessee, and King of Utah. Whether these changes were for better or for worse will be a matter of opinion in particular cases, but there can be little doubt on net balance that the general level of senatorial intelligence and character had not declined.

Writing in 1942 out of a rich knowledge of American history, early and late, Charles Beard defended the modern Congress against allegations of decline. "In their efforts to appear wise," he said, "critics of Congress often refer to the great of old—to orators like Daniel Webster, John C. Calhoun, and Henry Clay—and assert that, in comparison, members of Congress today are of small caliber. It is true that no member now can, or chooses to, deliver orations in the grand manner. But is that proof of a decline in intelligence and character? In my opinion, it is nothing of the sort. It is pertinent to note that, in spite of their oratory, these mighty men of old could not resolve the sectional issue of their time and let the nation drift into a civil war . . . The truth is that oratory of the grand style, whatever its merits, if any, is no longer appropriate to or useful in the discussion of the complicated questions of our day, which call for highly specialized knowledge and less rhetoric."

As a close student of the Congressional Record, Beard ventured this opinion: "It is possible to pick out of the Record for the past ten years addresses (not orations) which for breadth of knowledge, technical skill, analytical acumen, close reasoning, and dignified presentation compare favorably with similar utterances made in the preceding century by the so-called great orators. . . . Considering the complexity of problems before Congress today, and taking account of the distractions which now beset Senators and Representatives, the quality of serious speeches in both houses is amazingly high." Beard concluded "after studying the operations of the first Congresses of the United States and the operations of the Seventy-sixth Congress, I am convinced that for disinterestedness, absence of corruption, and concern with the public good, the present body is of a higher order." [9] This judgment is confirmed by oldtimers who have been in the service of the Senate since pre-World War I days. On the basis of personal acquaintance with the

---
[9] Charles A. Beard, "In Defense of Congress," *American Mercury*, November, 1942.

plutocrats of yesteryear and the democrats of today, they assert that, despite a few demagogues and bigots, the modern Senate compares favorably in quality and competence with its predecessors.

Results of Woman Suffrage

Meanwhile, the campaign for woman suffrage, which had been launched in 1869 by Elizabeth Cady Stanton and Susan B. Anthony and had been successful in a dozen states by 1915, reached the national level. Charles Evans Hughes endorsed the national enfranchisement of women during his campaign for the presidency in 1916 and President Wilson personally urged its passage before a joint session of Congress on the eve of the 1918 congressional elections. Congress finally responded in June, 1919, by proposing the Nineteenth Amendment whose ratification by the requisite number of state legislatures was announced in August, 1920.

The effects of woman suffrage upon the composition and quality of Congress are conjectural. Some feared that the enfranchisement of women would demoralize American politics, while advocates of the movement believed that it would improve the personnel of representative assemblies. After the experience of a quarter of a century, most observers would probably agree that woman suffrage has increased the political literacy of the electorate, but I doubt if it has had much effect one way or the other upon the personnel of parlimentary democracy. By and large, women seem to vote much as their husbands do. "Let women look back on the quarter-century since they were enfranchised," challenged Dean Margaret Pickel of Columbia University, "and measure their performance by the promises they made when they were demanding the vote. Let them ask themselves how many, who considered themselves active politically, campaigned for a lightweight because they went to college with his wife? How many voted for a humbug because he buttered them up? How many—and let them be particularly ashamed of this—never voted at all, because they had an appointment for a permanent on registration day, or thought politics a boring or dirty business?" [10]

Of the 96 United States Senators who were in office when the 19th amendment was ratified, 50 were reelected when their terms expired and 46 were not returned for one reason or another. Some of the latter no doubt withdrew voluntarily, while others were defeated at the polls.

---

[10] Margaret Barnard Pickel, "There's Still a Lot for Women to Learn," *The New York Times Magazine*, November 11, 1945, p. 14.

To what extent woman suffrage contributed to their retirement remains hidden in the secrecy of the ballot. Most of those who disappeared from the national capitol at this time, whatever the cause, are nameless in history.

Status of Ex-Congressmen

What happens to members of Congress after their legislative careers are over? The great majority of them return to their constituencies, either to retire worn out by the fray or to resume the practice of law or business if too much time has not elapsed since they went to Washington. Some "lame ducks" receive appointments to administrative jobs in the national government and others become federal judges. A few, like South Trimble, clerk of the House, and Wall Doxey, Sergeant-at-Arms of the Senate, enter the employ of Congress, while others exploit their intimate knowledge of the legislative ropes as lobbyists in the service of special interest groups in the nation's capital. Over the passing years a goodly number of former members have received cabinet appointments. In 1945, for example, four members of the Truman cabinet—Anderson, Byrnes, Schwellenbach, and Vinson —had served in the national legislature. Some like Senators Black and Burton have been elevated to the Supreme Court. And 19 of the first 32 Presidents of the United States were formerly members of the House or Senate.

A random sample of 25 ex-Congressmen living in Washington in 1945 revealed one of them as President of the United States, four were members of the Cabinet, two were Supreme Court justices, five were federal judges, five were executive officers, four were employees of Congress, one was working for the Republican National Committee, another was a lobbyist, a third was practicing law, and one had retired.

HOW TO IMPROVE QUALITY OF MEMBERS

Several proposals have been advanced with a view to obtaining a more representative, progressive, and better-balanced membership in our national legislature. The main suggestions are as follows:

1. Lengthen the term of office of members of the House.
2. Reduce the size of the House of Representatives.
3. Make federal grants-in-aid of election expenses.
4. Increase the compensation of members.
5. Pay retirement allowances to members.
6. Continue salaries to ex-members for a limited time.

7. Organize an in-service training program for new members.
8. Educate the electorate to select better Representatives.
9. Abolish the single-member majority system of election and replace it by the proportional representative system.
10. Require candidates for Congress to submit to the electorate verified credentials.
11. Offer candidates the option of taking psychological intelligence and aptitude tests and publish the results.
12. Require previous service on state or local governmental bodies.

The arguments made for these proposed reforms may be briefly summarized. Longer terms for members of the House, which would require a constitutional amendment, would be less costly and hazardous than the present two-year term, make members less dependent on local pressures, and enable them to give more attention to national problems. A smaller House would increase the competition for seats and hence improve the quality of members. At present, there are 435 seats in the House of Representatives and the average congressional district contains 115,000 electors.

A grant-in-aid of election expenses would reduce the strain on the resources of candidates and so widen the field from which they might be drawn. Under the Corrupt Practices Act the present legal maximum expenditure per candidate for the House is $2500, or an amount equal to three cents for each vote cast at the last general election for a Representative, but not over $5000 in all. A candidate for the Senate is limited to $10,000 or three cents for each vote cast at the last general senatorial election, but not over $25,000. It is suggested that the amount of the grant might be fixed at three cents per valid vote recorded for the candidate. The grant would be in aid only of legal expenditures and in no case would exceed the actual expenditure made. No grant would be made where there was no contest for the office. This reform, it is argued, would place congressional campaigns on a more equitable basis and would encourage the candidacy of many suitable persons who cannot now afford to run for Congress.

Members of Congress are now paid $10,000 a year and in addition receive an allowance for clerk hire of $9500 plus $700 for stationery, plus 20 cents a mile for one round trip each session to their homes. These sums seem generous compared with those paid a member of the House of Commons who receives $2500 as salary and $500 for travel expenses. But they fall short of the cost of living and campaigning today. Congressional salaries should be increased in order to attract candidates from the higher-paid realms of business and the professions for whom a mere $10,000 a year makes slight appeal.

A strong case can also be made for paying retirement allowances to members of Congress who, after many years of public service, lose their seats or elect to retire. Under existing conditions, retirement means loss of livelihood for elderly members. Heavy recurring campaign expenses and the rising cost of living preclude the possibility of saving much out of salary for old age. Presumably, it was such considerations which led the 77th Congress to amend the Civil Service Retirement Act so as to make members who had attained the age of 70 years and had rendered at least 30 years of service, or who had attained the age of 60 years and rendered at least 30 years of service, or who should thereafter attain the age of 62 years and have rendered at least 15 years of service, eligible for retirement on an annuity amounting, for example, to $1428.50 in the case of a member of the House who had served five terms, and to $2857.00 for a member who had served ten terms, the maximum benefit being $3000. This amendment was approved January 24, 1942, but so great was the public outcry against this alleged "pension grab" that Congress repealed the provision less than two months later.

A possible alternative to congressional pensions would be to continue an ex-member's salary for a limited length of time, say two years, after he ceases to be a member. This arrangement would enable a member to "make ends meet" during a brief interruption in his legislative career or, if he decides not to attempt a "comeback," it would give him a chance to reestablish himself in his former occupation in case he had given it up. Members who voluntarily resigned their seats would not be eligible for "continued salary" unless they resigned because of ill-health or some similar good reason beyond their control.

Another suggestion for improving the fitness of members is to inaugurate what might be called an in-service training program for newly elected legislators on Capitol Hill, at which experienced legislators and officers of the legislative branch would give a series of talks on legislative organization and procedure and constitutional practice designed to initiate new members into the folkways of Congress. This scheme would help new congressmen "learn the legislative ropes" and familiarize them with the aids at their disposal in the Legislative Reference Service, the Office of Legislative Counsel, and elsewhere. It is surprising how many members are unaware of the existence of these services.

In the last analysis the quality of members depends, of course, upon the education of the electorate. Much has been accomplished in recent years through the better newspapers and the radio, fireside chats, and the like to stimulate public interest in politics and to promote better understanding of public affairs. Wider popular participation in politics and party activities, including the selection of candidates, would have beneficial effects upon their quality. The suggestions made elsewhere in this book for overcoming electoral ignorance and apathy and for bringing the people into closer touch with the legislative process in action—using our political institutions to develop and expand the political understanding and competence of the voters—are pertinent at this point.[11]

In his searching study of the personnel of Parliament, J. F. S. Ross traces the defects of parliamentary representation primarily to the single-member majority system of voting. Single-member constituencies, he argues, are fundamentally inconsistent with the proper representation of political opinion. Every congressional district contains both Republican and Democratic voters, "but whereas in an efficient system the contest would determine in what proportions the respective parties should *share* the representation of the constituency, in the present system the contest determines which of the parties shall have the whole of the representation." Dissatisfied with the present system, Ross seeks "some other system that will be less clumsy and less capricious in its action, will give more scope to and make better use of the native shrewdness and good sense of the electorate, will reflect more accurately the state of political feeling in the country, give a better-balanced House of Commons, and promote a higher general standard of integrity, ability, and zeal amongst candidates and members." [12] These conditions are fulfilled to his satisfaction in the method of the single transferable vote, commonly known as proportional representation. With this system, it is argued, it would no longer be possible for a minority to defeat a majority, nor for one party to monopolize representation, nor for there to be uncontested elections. This is not the place in which to rehearse the case for and against proportional representation, or to evaluate our experience with it in the American cities which have tried it. Whether or not its adoption on a continental scale as a method of voting in congressional elections is within the realm of

---

[11] See also W. Ivor Jennings, *Parliament Must Be Reformed* (1941), Chapter IX.

[12] J. F. S. Ross, *Parliamentary Representation* (Yale University Press, 1944). See also Chapters XXXIII and XXIV, *ibid*.

practical politics is a problem in the hazardous calculation of probabilities. Were it possible to give it a trial in the United States, the results would be exceedingly interesting and would test the superior merits claimed for the system.[12]

Three subsidiary reforms are also suggested: (1) require every candidate to present to his electorate verified credentials stating his age, date of birth, place of residence, any university degrees, his professional qualifications, present occupation, and the essential facts of his career; (2) have each candidate for Congress take a series of psychological intelligence and aptitude tests and publish the results officially, so as to give the voters a means of comparing their qualifications, experience, and characteristics; and (3) require previous service of candidates, say for three years, on a state or local body.[13]

The Ideal Member

Article 1, Section 2 of the constitution states that "No Person shall be a Representative who shall not have attained the Age of twenty-five Years, and been seven Years a Citizen of the United States, and who shall not, when elected, be an Inhabitant of the State in which he shall be chosen."

Section 3 of the same Article provides that "No Person shall be a Senator who shall not have attained to the Age of thirty Years, and been nine Years a Citizen of the United States, and who shall not, when elected, be an Inhabitant of that State for which he shall be chosen."

Apart from these prescriptions as to age, citizenship, and residence, the constitution is silent as to the qualities to be sought in prospective members of Congress. It is left to the voters to determine their own standards of representation. In choosing its representatives, three conceivable alternatives face the electorate: (1) They can take an apathetic, don't-care attitude and vote a straight party ticket, leaving it to the party machinery to select the candidates; (2) they may be content with Laski to have their representatives be "an average sample of ordinary men";[14] or (3) they may insist upon some special fitness for the job.

If the people really want an efficient and democratic Congress, they will reject the first alternative because the quality of the members obviously does matter, unless they are to be mere pawns for the party whips. The argument that the Congress should be an average sample

---

[13] *Ibid.*, Chapter XXV and Laski, *A Grammar of Politics*, p. 340.
[14] Harold J. Laski, *Democracy in Crisis* (1933), p. 80.

of the population does not fit the facts, as we have seen. If Congress were a representative sample of the people, it would be younger on the average, half of the members would be women, they would be less well educated than they now are, and the occupational distribution of the members would be entirely different than it is. This leaves the third alternative which holds that the voters should choose representatives who are specially qualified by experience, attainments, and aptitudes to serve in our national legislature.

In order adequately to perform the functions outlined in the first chapter, the ideal member of Congress should have a large fund of information about public affairs and an understanding of social psychology. He should have a sense of history, a sense of values, and a critical habit of thought. He should know enough about public problems to vote independently and intelligently instead of blindly following the lead of committee chairmen and the party whips. Without being an expert on all questions, he should be able to see their interrelations and ramifications and anticipate how proposed measures will actually work out in practice. He must be able to take an overall view of a problem and to weigh the long-run benefits of a proposal against its short-run drawbacks. He must be intimately acquainted with his constituents, their needs and aspirations, and with economic and social conditions in his district or state. But where conflicts of interest arise between his district or state, his party, and the country as a whole, he must remember that his primary obligation is to the general welfare. "You choose a member, indeed," wrote Edmund Burke to the electors of Bristol in 1774, "but when you have chosen him he is not a member of Bristol but is a member of Parliament."

In helping Congress fulfill its function of watchdog of the Treasury and overseer of the administration, the ideal member must be an alert, informed, and watchful critic. "If he is to play this part adequately," as Ross well puts it, "he must have an extensive fund of general knowledge, common sense, and shrewdness; he must have plenty of energy and endurance; and, above all, he must feel and respond to the trust reposed in him by his constituents; he must take his duties seriously and fulfill them scrupulously." [15]

Without neglecting the principles and policies of his political party, the ideal member will recognize the need of placing the common welfare above mere party advantage. What Ross writes of the House of

---

[15] Ross, *op. cit.*, p. 188. This thorough study of the personnel of Parliament has much comparative interest and value for students of Congress.

Commons in this connection applies with equal force to our own Congress. "It is time that the rather childish habit of treating politics as a game in which the chief object is to diddle your opponents were dropped altogether, and a more sober and adult outlook substituted. . . . A ding-dong battle between the 'ins' and the 'outs' may be amusing, but it belongs to an earlier and cruder stage of civilization and it is time it gave way altogether to a higher view of statecraft." [16]

In short, the ideal member of Congress will be a man of undoubted integrity who will not seek personal advantage or reward or indulge in nepotism, but will resist the pressures of sectional interests and functional groups and place principle above expediency and nation above party. He will be a man of intelligence, courage, and zeal, with exceptional qualities of mind and spirit, skilled in the rare art of mediating between the public services and the people, able to exercise foresight and balanced judgment. He will be fitted by temperament for a legislative career, having a real interest in human beings *per se,* with a real flair for politics and public affairs as well as tolerance, sympathy, patience, and a sense of humor to compensate him for the tedium and trivia of his task. He will have had enough education, formal or informal, to be familiar with the economic and social history of the United States, with recent political, economic, and social trends, and with the basic facts of our political and social life.

In a recent magazine article a member of Congress, who comes close to these ideal specifications, noted that Congress was more conservative than the country: "the majority is out of step with the predominant desires and opinions of the American people." [17] If this be true, the explanation may be found in the higher average age of members than that of electors and in the unrepresentative occupational character of the membership. If Congress is to be in harmony with the sentiments and attitudes of the people it represents, there ought to be a closer correspondence between their average ages, on the one hand, and a better balance of occupational experience among the members, on the other. The first condition would be obtained if members entered Congress in their thirties and retired when they had passed the prime of life and were no longer able to give efficient service. The second desideratum, to get a wider and less lopsided distribution of occupations in Congress, would be achieved if representation in the House or

---

[16] *Ibid.,* p. 189.

[17] Representative Jerry Voorhis, "Stop Kicking Congress Around!," *American Mercury,* June, 1944.

Senate were based upon professions or trades rather than places. But such a change savors too much perhaps of the Italian "corporative" system and is probably beyond the realm of practical politics in the United States.[18]

---

[18] Cf. Senator J. William Fulbright, "The Legislator," *Vital Speeches*, May 15, 1946, pp. 468–472.

3.

The Rising Burden of Congressional Business

CONGRESS AS AN institution is heavily handicapped in many ways in performing its modern functions. Of all its handicaps the rising tide of legislative and other business is undoubtedly the basic obstacle. The business of Congress—once relatively limited in scope, small in volume, and simple in nature—has now become almost unlimited in subject matter, enormous in amount, and exceedingly complex in character. The Founding Fathers had expected that Congress would confine itself, for the most part, to the external affairs of the new nation, leaving the conduct of internal affairs to the states and communities. Congress would have little to do, Alexander Hamilton thought, after the central government was firmly established and a federal code formulated. But with the steady expansion of the national domain, the rapid growth of population, and the development of commerce and industry, this expectation proved to be chimerical. As the new Republic grew greater, the demand for congressional action increased apace. From the opening day of the First Congress on March 4, 1789, to the adjournment of the 78th Congress on December 19, 1944, no less than 762,702 bills and resolutions (public and private) were introduced in both chambers—an average of 9,778 for each of the first 78 Congresses.

FIRST AND 78TH CONGRESSES COMPARED

Some conception of the enormous expansion in the business of Congress is afforded by a comparison of the work of the First (1789–1791) and the 78th (1943–1944) Congresses.

Points of Comparison	1st Congress	78th Congress
Number of Bills Introduced:	268	7,845
House of Representatives	142	5,628
Senate	126	2,217
Number of Laws Enacted:	118	1,157
Public Acts and Resolutions	108	568
Private Acts and Resolutions	10	589
Types of Statutes	10	47
Subjects Discussed	17	74
Number of Members:	91	531
Representatives	65	435
Senators	26	96
Number of Days in Session	519	695
Number of Committees (standing, select, joint):	3	106
House of Representatives	2	55
Senate	1	51
Committee Reports:	155	4,709
House of Representatives	85	3,316
Senate	70	1,393
Presidential Messages Received	12	7
Executive Department Communications Received	72	2,112
Nominations Confirmed	211	21,371
Petitions Filed	650	6,253

The foregoing figures measure the great growth in legislative business since 1789 and reflect the attendant burdens. The sheer bulk of bills introduced increased thirty-fold, while the number of committees available to receive and handle the rising flood grew from 2 to 106. Total committee reports jumped from 155 to 4,709 and the number of laws produced by the legislative mill multiplied ten-fold. Meanwhile, as the population of the country expanded from 4 to 140 million and 35 new states were admitted to the federal union, the membership of Congress available to handle the added work load multiplied almost six times. The early Congresses usually took long summer recesses and met for not more than 10 months out of the biennium, whereas today our national legislature is in almost continuous session. The 17-month session of the First Congress was exceptionally long as a result of the problems associated with the launching of the new government.

Business of First Congress

Such legislative statistics afford no measure, however, of the changes in the range and complexity of public problems facing Congress then and now. The First Congress established the State, War, and Treasury

Departments; fixed import and tonnage duties and regulated their collection; appropriated revenue and provided for public debt; admitted Kentucky and Vermont to the Union and settled certain state accounts; established courts of justice and fixed the compensation of public officers; provided for the census of 1790 and regulated trade with the Indians; and otherwise dealt with the comparatively simple problems of the federal government in that remote age. Many problems in the early days of the Republic were state and local in scope and were left to the states and localities or to the private forces of the frontier to settle. Accordingly, the legislative process in Washington was much more leisurely and the life of a congressman far more tranquil than it is today.

Of the 96 public laws approved by the First Congress, 18 dealt with foreign affairs (including tariff duties), 16 with relations between the central government and the states, and 10 with the defense of the infant nation. Eighteen were concerned with administrative matters (including salaries), 15 with questions of public finance, and nine with the judiciary. Only three were pension acts and only two were for the relief of private claimants.

Work Load of the 78th Congress

Contrast this with the work load of the 78th Congress. More than half of the laws it passed—589 out of 1,157—dealt with private and local matters which diverted its attention from national policy-making and with which it ought not to have been burdened. These included measures relating to the District of Columbia, the settlement of private claims and pensions, the building of bridges over navigable streams, and other private and local legislation.

Of the 568 public laws approved by the 78th Congress, the Senate spent 10 days and filled 263 pages of the *Congressional Record* debating the Connally peace-machinery resolution alone. Much of the work of this wartime Congress was devoted to enacting 37 appropriation bills involving a total of $182 billions—most of it for the prosecution of World War II. This Congress also spent much time on a pay-as-you-go tax program baffling in its complexity, the regulation of strikes and control of the Food Administration, federal aid to education and national war service legislation.

In anticipation of victory it debated and passed demobilization and reconversion measures, contract termination and disposal of surplus property bills, and postwar highway and public works planning programs. It authorized the renegotiation of contracts and enacted a

GI Bill of Rights. The soldier ballot bill was debated in the Senate for 10 days and filled 245 pages of the *Record,* while the House consumed 236 *Record* pages in debating extension of the price control act. Meanwhile, 21 House and 10 Senate special committees were actively investigating administrative conduct and wartime industry, taking over 100,000 pages of testimony and making many reports, while it was a rare day that did not witness eight or ten standing committees in session.

Expansion Since 1911

In volume, scope and complexity the legislative agenda of 1943–1944 was obviously a far cry from that of 1790. It was a far cry, too, from the days a century ago when Congress struggled with Andrew Jackson over the Bank of the United States and the sale of public lands. It was a far cry even from 1911 when Robert Ramspeck, Democratic whip in the 79th House, came from Georgia to Washington to work in the Capitol Post Office and serve as a congressional secretary. Congress was then in session only nine months out of 24, and the members spent the remainder of their terms at home practicing law or attending to their private business. The mail they received then dealt largely with free seed, rural routes, Spanish War pensions, and occasionally a legislative matter. Members had ample time to attend to their congressional duties. "It was a pretty nice job that a Member of Congress had in those days," Representative Ramspeck reminisced when he appeared 34 years later before a joint committee studying the burdens of legislators. "At that time the Government affected the people directly in only a minor way . . . It was an entirely different job from the job we have to do today. It was primarily a legislative job, as the constitution intended it to be."

The enormous expansion in the work load of Congress dates back, in fact, only to the first World War. A succession of crises in our national life, marked by our participation in two world wars within a single generation, plus the intervening depression of 1929–1933 and the following recovery efforts, imposed vast new responsibilities upon Congress and the administration for the conduct of national and international affairs. Making up as if for lost time, Congress delegated large powers over American economy and society to a score of regulatory commissions, credit corporations, and developmental authorities. Responding to the exigencies of events and the requirements of the times, Congress and the federal government took almost all human affairs as their province. So great, indeed, was the gradual expansion of federal authority and activity from Woodrow Wilson's administration on that no important field of human interest and endeavor failed to feel its impact.

The results of this centripetal, impersonal, and apparently inexorable trend were seen not only in the astronomical rise of federal expenditures and debt, in the reduction of once sovereign states to a relatively minor role in American government and economy, and in the tremendous growth of the power of the President, but also in the mounting burdens upon Congress itself. Still functioning for the most part with the machinery and facilities inherited from the simpler days of the mauve decade, its calendars and committees became increasingly congested, its councils confused, and its members bewildered and harassed by multiplying technical problems and local pressures. It was only natural, under these conditions, for Congress to place greater reliance upon the President and his well-staffed agencies for guidance and to delegate responsibility for policy-making, economic regulation, and social adjustment to a host of federal commissions, bureaus, and agencies.

COMMITTEE ACTIVITY

The committees are the workshops of Congress. Committee work is the core of the legislative process. Here Senators and Representatives organized in congressional microcosms hear testimony pro and con bills referred to them, study and revise them, sometimes initiate new measures, and review administrative operations. Committee work includes hearings open to press and public as well as deliberation in closed meetings. It involves contact with experts, charts, and documents. It is the center of legislative activity where the law-making and supervisory functions of Congress are largely performed.

During 1945 there were 273 of these miniature legislatures on Capitol Hill, classified as follows:

Committees	House	Senate	Total
Standing	48	33	81
Special	5	7	12
Joint	6	6	6
Standing Subcommittees*	97	34	131
Special subcommittees*	9	34	43
	165	114	273

* Not including claims.

Not all these committees, of course, were equally busy or important. Of the standing committees, about 20 in each House accounted for 90 per cent of the membership and of the public general bills reported. Ten of the House standing committees are known in party parlance as "exclusive" committees in that their members serve on no other major committee. The work load of these ten is so heavy that their members are expected to concentrate upon it alone—an arrangement which has the advantage of leaving enough vacancies on other committees to give every member of the majority party a committee assignment. These ten "exclusive" committees are: Ways and Means, Appropriations, Judiciary, Agriculture, Rivers and Harbors, Post Offices and Post Roads, Foreign Affairs, Military Affairs, Naval Affairs, and Interstate and Foreign Commerce.

There are no "exclusive" committees in the Senate where the average Senator sat on seven committees. Because the Senate has fewer members than the House and carries a heavier burden in such fields as foreign affairs, to say nothing of its predilection for unlimited debate, the average Senator probably carries a greater legislative burden than the typical Representative. On the other hand, the load of the House is heavier in the field of appropriations and in the handling of departmental business for constituents.

Standing Committees

Table VI in the Appendix provides a quantitative measure of the comparative activity of the standing committees of the House and Senate during 1943–1944 in terms of the number of bills referred to and reported by them and hearings they held. But they do not measure the actual time spent or work done in committee. Some bills require extensive committee work involving public hearings as well as long and intensive work by individual members, staff, and subcommittees. Other bills consume little or no committee time. Committees often receive several bills on the same subjects, while measures not advocated or supported by the administration are usually pigeon-holed. An analysis of Senate standing committee activity during the First Session of the 78th Congress (1943) showed the following distribution of referred bills by subject-matter fields. It will be noted that legislation relating to national defense accounted for almost one-fifth of all bills introduced in the Senate, and that the top six fields listed in the table accounted for more than four-fifths of the total.

Field	No. of Bills	Per Cent of Total
National Defense	133	19
Social Welfare	115	16
Judicial Proceedings	94	13
Natural Resources	82	12
Fiscal & Monetary Policy	79	11
Civil Service & Government Organization	75	11
Transportation	46	6
Agriculture	40	6
Commerce & Industry	16	2
Labor Problems	11	2
Public Works	9	1
Senate Administration	7	1
Foreign Affairs	6	1
	713	100

Another measure of standing committee activity is to be found in the volume of their printed hearings. During the 78th Congress (1943–1944) all the standing committees of the Senate and House together produced 120,435 type pages—the equivalent of 400 good-sized books. On the Senate side the chief producers of this vast wartime output were the committees on Military Affairs, Agriculture and Forestry, and Appropriations. On the House side the Appropriations, Naval Affairs, Merchant Marine and Fisheries, and Ways and Means committees were the leading contenders or the most long-suffering listeners.

Special Investigating Committees

The work load of Congress often overflows its regular standing committees and leads to the creation of select or special committees to investigate particular problems. Congress has set up such special committees many times in our history either to inquire into executive misconduct, as in the case of the scandals of the Grant and Harding days, or to investigate economic and social conditions in Podunk Corners or Puerto Rico, or to examine campaign expenditures or the conduct of the war or a hundred other topics of public or party interest. Between 1789 and 1925 upwards of 300 inquiries into executive acts alone were made by select committees.

Under modern conditions, select committees have proved to be useful devices for eliciting information, informing Congress and the country, scrutinizing executive performance, and illuminating public problems. They enable young and energetic members to side-step the seniority custom, to employ expert and zealous personnel rarely found on the staffs of standing committees, and to conduct vigorous and searching investigations into vital public questions. Senators and Congressmen like Truman, La Follette, O'Mahoney, Murray, Cox, Tolan, and Dies in our own time have won national fame or dubious notoriety from their chairmanships of great national inquiries. During the 78th Congress 20 special committees, 10 in each house, were investigating such subjects as small business, air accidents, national defense, campaign expenditures, un-American activities, gasoline shortages, executive agencies, postwar policies, silver purchases, and the Federal Communications Commission. Their combined appropriations for that Congress totaled $767,500.00.

Joint Committees

Unlike the state legislatures which frequently make use of joint committees representing both houses as a means of dealing with matters of mutual interest and of avoiding duplication, Congress seldom relies on this device. Joint committees are not popular in the lower chamber whose members find that they do most of the work thereon while the Senate members receive the lion's share of the credit. Both houses, moreover, are jealous of their prerogatives.

Fewer than 20 joint committees have been created by Congress during the past century. Six such committees—three standing and three select—were in use in 1945. Joint standing committees on printing, the Congressional Library, and internal revenue taxation were created by statute in 1852, 1902, and 1926, respectively. Joint select committees on reduction of nonessential federal expenditures, selective service deferments, and the organization of Congress were set up by acts and a concurrent resolution in 1941, 1943, and 1945, respectively.

Four of these committees performed housekeeping functions and were assisted by small staffs; two were inactive and rarely met. On the other hand, the revenue, expenditure, and legislative organization committees made comprehensive studies of the subjects assigned them and were a heavy drain upon the time and energy of their active members. During the spring of 1945, for example, the Joint Committee on the Organization of Congress held 39 public hearings and four executive sessions, heard 102 witnesses, and published 1,533 pages of hearings and other documents.

In actual practice much of the work load of several of the standing committees of Congress is carried by the subcommittees into which their membership is divided. Thus the Appropriations, District of Columbia, Interstate Commerce, and Merchant Marine and Fisheries committees, among others, customarily divide the labor of their business among subcommittees, a practice which permits their members to specialize in particular segments of the committees' jurisdiction. During 1945 there were 106 subcommittees in the House and 68 in the Senate— 174 all told.

WORK LOAD ON INDIVIDUAL MEMBERS

In the last analysis, of course, it is the individual congressman and his office staff who bear the real brunt of the burden of representative government today. The conscientious congressman is a plural personality. If he takes his job seriously, and most of them do, he is at once a national lawmaker, a representative of his state or district, an overseer of administration, a watchdog of the Treasury, an errand boy and counsel for his constituents, a partner in foreign policy, and a keeper of the legislative household. With all these duties and responsibilities the hard-working member obviously must be a modern Hercules. And it is small wonder if he has at times an inferiority complex.

Time and again congressional witnesses, who appeared before the Joint Committee on the Organization of Congress during its 1945 hearings, complained that they were physically unable to perform their legislative duties satisfactorily. Handling their mail, interviewing constituents and callers, visiting departments on behalf of aggrieved groups in their districts, keeping committee appointments, and attending chamber sessions left little time for the adequate study of complex legislative problems. The consensus of the testimony on this point was that the average member of Congress, especially from the larger and more populous states and districts, is now so preoccupied with trouble-shooting details and non-legislative matters that he can spend only a small fraction of his time as a legislator.

Senator Downey of California summed up the situation succinctly from an overworked Senator's angle of vision:

Each day Senators have matters come before them which could, if they could spare the time, occupy their attention for months . . . yet here we are compelled to dispose of weighty and complicated matters after being able to listen to arguments only for perhaps an hour or two . . . Observe for a moment the volume of business that is done in my office alone. It is so great as almost to break me and my whole staff down. In mail alone we receive from 200 to 300 letters every 24 hours. And this is in addition to telegrams and long-distance calls and personal visits. We do the best we can. We try to have every letter answered the day it is received. My staff is departmentalized. That is, each girl is an expert in some particular field . . . If the office were not so organized, we could not possibly begin to carry the load. Yet, Mr. Chairman, I can say to you truthfully that even if I had four times the amount of time I have I could not possibly perform adequately and fully the duties rightfully imposed on me as ambassador from my state. In the departments of the Government there are always delays or injustices or matters overlooked in which a Senator can be of very great assistance to his constituents. The flood of duties in my office has reached such proportions, and is so steadily increasing, that I am almost totally unable to enter into any study of legislative matters. That means that frequently I have to inform myself concerning matters of importance by listening to arguments on the floor of the Senate. And yet even my presence on the floor is only intermittent, so great is the burden of my office duties if I am to efficiently carry out my responsibilities with respect to the state of California.

A Typical Day

The job of an industrious Representative is just as grueling as that of a busy Senator. One day early in 1943 the editors of *Fortune* sent a reporter to the office of Congressman Everett M. Dirksen of Illinois, one of the ablest, hardworking members of the House of Representatives, to make an actual record of a typical day in his life. This is how Mr. Dirksen spent that day:

Up at 6:15 A.M., he walked to the Carlton Hotel for a seven-fifteen breakfast date with the head of the industrial relations department of an Illinois railroad. Fortunately, this visitor already knew a good many other interested Government officials, so the Congressman did not have to take time to arrange a string of interviews for him.

Delayed by the long breakfast session, Dirksen arrived at his office in the Old House Office Building at eight-forty-five, three-quarters of an hour behind his usual time. His first visitor, after a less-experienced Congressman seeking advice, was a Chicago business man. Chicago is outside Dirksen's district, but people often feel free to call on anyone in their State's congressional delegation. This one wanted to talk about home-loan financing and also about rent control on commercial properties in connection with a bill pending before the House Banking Committee. Dirksen pledged "sustained attention" to these matters. Meantime conversation, as always, was being continually interrupted by the ringing of the telephone. One after another, four other Congressmen called about items in pending bills under the jurisdiction of the Appropriations Committee, of which

Dirksen is an influential member. Betweentimes Dirksen made numerous telephone calls of his own, among them: (1) to the *New York Times* about an article it wanted him to write; (2) to the Civil Service Commission to get advance information for a constituent on her rating in a recent examination; (3) to a fellow member of the District of Columbia Committee about a pending bill that would permit Washington's charitable institutions to use oleomargarine instead of butter; (4) to the Library of Congress for some data on public power that he could expect to receive in about two weeks.

Next visitor was a college trustee worried about what would happen to the college unless the Army or Navy selected it for one of their training programs. Could the Congressman help? The Congressman would try. After the trustee came a farm organization representative concerned with price ceilings on farm commodities, who wanted to talk with Jimmy Byrnes and somebody in O.P.A. The Congressman arranged the appointments.

Normally, Dirksen spends the first hour in his office reading and answering his mail. But having lost the earlier hour, he turned now to this task and kept at it until 12:15 P.M. Then, in the outer office where secretary and stenographer work and visitors wait, he picked up two post-war planners and took them over to the Capitol for a quick lunch in the House restaurant.

The daily session of the House, which normally begins at noon, had been under way for an hour when Dirksen arrived on the floor. Debate on a merger of Western Union and Postal Telegraph was in progress. Dirksen's attendance was sporadic—the normal thing in Congress—for he was repeatedly called off the floor by visitors and telephone calls. In the course of a couple of hours messengers summoned him five times. Once was for a visitor, another college official with the same worries as the first. Two of the phone calls were from Illinois, one to announce that a college president would arrive next morning, another from a banker who wanted an appointment with Leo Crowley of the F.D.I.C. A third call was from an official of a steel company in his district, come to Washington to protest against his lend-lease quota of ingots and billets. A fourth took him to Union Station, where an entraining W.P.A. official had a post-war project that he was impatient to discuss. In addition, the Congressman had to drop in at a meeting of the Appropriations Committee, and return to his office for a little talk to a visiting college class in political science.

The telegraph debate was succeeded by a fiery one on renewing the Dies Committee for another two years. Dirksen, not much interested in hearing last year's arguments repeated, occasionally improved his time by retiring to the cloakroom to go over papers in his briefcase. After the Dies roll call, in which he voted yea, he went back to the Office Building and stopped briefly at the office of another Congressman from Illinois who was giving a little farewell party honoring his secretary's departure for the Army.

Back in his own office, Dirksen cleared up details of dictating, letter signing, and telephoning, then packed his briefcase with his evening's reading. He reached the Mayflower at seven. As usual, several people were waiting to buttonhole him in the lobby. One was still another college trustee, two more were Navy officers on confidential business. He also stopped for a chat with the new chairman of the Republican National Committee about liaison between the Committee and the G. O. P. contingent in Congress. Fed, he rolled up his sleeves, hooked on his spectacles, and settled down to read a file on the Independent Offices Appropriation Bill. After a brisk walk and a look at the evening papers, he turned out the lights at eleven-twenty, seventeen hours after he had turned them on. Except for dinner and his stop-off at the farewell party, he had been working all the time.[1]

Constituent Chores

Several years ago Representative Luther Patrick of Alabama made an amusing speech in the House in which he offered his colleagues ten simple rules of conduct for handling their constituents:

1. Entertain with a smile constituents, their wives, their sons, sons' wives, etc. Go with them to the White House, show good reason why you are unable to personally have them meet the President, take daughters to meet midshipmen at Annapolis.
2. Explain what bill is up for debate, points for discussion, how it will be passed, how you will vote and why.
3. Attend to balcony and point out Speaker Bankhead, Leaders Rayburn and Martin, Ham Fish, Dewey Short, that man Martin Dies, and name each lady Member of Congress.
4. Respond to worthy causes, make after-dinner speeches, before-dinner speeches, learn to eat anything, anywhere, any night—work all day, dictate all night, and be fresh as a rain-washed daisy for next day's duties.
5. Be a cultured gentleman, a teller of ribald stories, a profound philosopher, preserve a store of "Confucius say" gags, be a ladies' man, a man's man, a he man, a diplomat, a Democrat with a Republican slant, an admirer of the Roosevelt way, a hater of the New Deal, a New Dealer, an old dealer, and a quick dealer.
6. Learn how to attend six to eight major functions, rushing home and back during each term on one round-trip travel pay.
7. Have the dope on hot spots in town, with choice telephone numbers for

---

[1] "Congressman: A Case History," *Fortune*, April, 1943, by special permission of the editors.

the gay boys from back home, and help to contact all local moral organizations and uplift societies in Washington.

8. Learn to be an expert guide. Keep car in tip-top shape.
9. Know names and dates related to all points of interest, and be able to explain and supply information regarding public buildings and statuary about Washington.
10. Be an authority on history, travel, psychology, philosophy, education, economics, civics, finance, export trade, Government printing, international relations, neckties, and fishing tackle."

Representative Patrick continued:

A congressman has become an expanded messenger boy, an employment agency, getter-out of the Navy, Army, marines, ward healer, wound healer, trouble shooter, law explainer, bill finder, issue translator, resolution interpreter, controversy oil pourer, gladhand extender, business promoter, convention goer, civic ills skirmisher, veterans' affairs adjuster, ex-serviceman's champion, watchdog for the under dog, sympathizer with the upper dog, namer and kisser of babies, recoverer of lost baggage, soberer of delegates, adjuster for traffic violators, voters straying into Washington and into toils of the law, binder up of broken hearts, financial wet nurse, good samaritan, contributor to good causes—there are so many good causes—cornerstone layer, public building and bridge dedicator, ship christener—to be sure he does get in a little flag waving—and a little constitutional hoisting and spread-eagle work, but it is getting harder every day to find time to properly study legislation—the very business we are primarily here to discharge, and that must be done above all things.

Some idea of the extent to which routine chores divert attention from the main business of lawmaking is afforded by an analysis of the mail received by Senator Pepper of Florida during one week of September, 1945. The week's total mail (not counting newspapers) amounted to 1096 pieces, of which 896 were letters and 200 were form publications. 81 per cent of the letters came from Florida residents and 19 per cent from other states. 65 per cent of the letters dealt with personal problems—service discharges, the draft, redeployment, pensions, benefits, disability ratings, the GI bill of rights, job assistance, passport and immigration matters, and complaints about war agency regulations. 17 per cent of the letters pertained to pending or proposed legislation— full employment, labor standards, health and education, patents, and other topics. 13 per cent of the mail expressed general opinion on matters of current interest—the draft, foreign relations, labor problems, atomic energy, and the like. And the remaining 5 per cent consisted of personal communications and invitations to the Senator. Of the form mail received by Senator Pepper during the sample week, 35 per cent came from pressure groups, 20 per cent from foreign embassies, 20 per cent were government reports, 5 per cent came from Florida, and the remaining 20 per cent was miscellaneous in character. One wondered when the writers of these 896 letters expected the Senator to attend to the legislative business for which they sent him to Congress. Evidently many constituents preferred him to serve as a super chamber of commerce and not as a national legislator.

Much of the time of a Senator's busy office force is also taken with telephone calls. During one week in August, 1945, when both Senator Pepper and his secretary were out of town, 491 telephone calls were made to and from his office—an average of 82 a day. Of these, 218 were incoming and 273 outgoing calls. 59 per cent of the calls were made on behalf of constituents and dealt with their discharges, advancement in rating, change of duty, wartime regulations, veterans' problems, jobs, housing and federal work projects, passport and immigration problems. 17 per cent of the total related to Senator Pepper's trip to Europe, 13 per cent to matters of office service, and only 11 per cent to legislative topics.

Personal interviews with importunate constituents and visiting firemen are another drain on congressional time, especially in the case of members from nearby states. Senator Tydings of Maryland told the joint committee studying the problems of our federal legislature that he frequently had as many as 20 requests a day for personal interviews. Since Congressmen customarily attend committee meetings from 10 to 12 o'clock in the morning and Congress generally meets from 12 to 5 o'clock in the afternoon, the only time available for receiving visitors is from 9 to 10 o'clock in the morning or during the luncheon hour, or at the end of the day when they are busy reading and signing their mail. Callers often confer with their congressmen in the reception rooms adjoining the Senate and House chambers, sending in their cards and calling the member off the floor. Some members prefer this method for personal interviews, perhaps because it permits them for a while to escape the tedium of dull debate.

Visiting departments and bureaus "downtown" is another chore that dips deeply into the legislative day. Many members, especially of the lower House, devote long hours to appearing before federal agencies in response to constituent complaints about their rules and regulations. War agency regulations caused a tremendous increase in this "departmental business" after 1941, constituting in many congressional offices the largest single element of their work load. Problems of price and rent control, fuel oil, meat, and slaughtering quotas, sugar rationing, and W.P.B., O.D.T., F.W.A., and other regulations converted many a potential lawmaker into a lawyer appealing the case of his consumer and industrial clientele before the federal bar.

These adjustments are part of the humanizing aspect of the democratic process. Looking after local needs and interests, as D. W. Brogan reminds us in his penetrating analysis of *The American Character,* is a very proper concern of the American politician. "Not merely will he not get re-elected if he neglects the local chores, but he should not be. One of the things that hold the vast area of the United States together is the belief that the political machinery provides a means whereby local and personal interests and sentiments are really taken into account in Washington."

Committee Work

Aside from his office work and departmental business, much of the burden of which in actual practice is carried by his office staff, committee work engages a large part of every member's attention. Here the legitimate legislative job of Congress is chiefly done. The 96 Senators of the 78th Congress occupied 581 seats on its 43 standing and special committees. Sixteen served on seven, nine served on eight, and four Senators sat on nine committees, to say nothing of service on subcommittees which, as we have seen, are frequently used in both chambers.

Meanwhile, the 435 members of the House occupied 966 committee seats on its 57 standing and special committees, an average of slightly more than two committees per member. During the second session of the 78th Congress:

84	Representatives	served	on	1	committee each
120	"	"	"	2	committees each
57	"	"	"	3	" "
15	"	"	"	4	" "
11	"	"	"	5	" "
13	"	"	"	6	" "
14	"	"	"	7	" "
5	"	"	"	8	" "
1	Representative	"	"	9	"

The burden of committee work falls unevenly, of course, upon their members, varying with the activity of the committees themselves, the sense of responsibility of their personnel, and the competence of their staffs. Some committees are minor, inactive ones and seldom meet. Alvan Fuller, a former Representative from Massachusetts, resigned in disgust from the Committee on Expenditures in the Interior Department in 1918, writing Speaker Champ Clark that it was merely an "ornamental barnacle on the ship of state" and a waste of the taxpayer's money. The only excuse for existence of some committees is the extra office space and clerical allowance to which their chairmen are entitled. In each house, however, there are 12 or 15 major, active committees dealing with legislation of national significance and having a combined membership of some 400 Representatives and about 216 Senators. The committees on Appropriations, Military and Naval and Foreign Affairs, Banking and Currency, Agriculture and Labor, Finance and Ways and Means are among those that have borne the heaviest legislative burdens of these latter years.

Some conception of what service on such committees meant to the individual member was given by Senator Burton of Ohio in his ninth semi-annual report to his constituents for the first half of 1945. On the eve of taking the judicial veil, this conscientious Senator gave his Ohio friends an accounting of his stewardship unique in congressional annals. His report, dated July 26, 1945, contained a tabulation of committee and subcommittee meetings he had attended since first coming to the Senate in 1941. It showed that he had been a member of four major and three minor committees during 1941–1945 and had attended 126 of their meetings in his first year, 159 the second year, 169 the third year, 208 the fourth year, and 180 meetings during the first half of 1945—a total of 842 committee meetings in four and one-half years in the Senate. One can only conjecture what level the upward curve would have reached by arithmetical progression had President Truman not promoted his erstwhile colleague to the Supreme Court. Moreover, during the period covered by his final report, Senator Burton had been in North Africa and the Middle East on a special investigation for the Truman-Mead Committee and had also played a vigorous part in the drafting and promotion of measures for international (B_2H_2) and domestic (B_2H) stability.

Floor Attendance

Last, but not least, of the demands upon the time of individual members are the sessions of the House and Senate. Here on the floor the legislative process formally begins with the introduction of bills and resolutions, continues through the three reading stages, and finally ends with the committee report, debate, and vote. The standing rules require that every member of the House shall be present within the Hall during its sittings, unless excused or necessarily prevented; and that no Senator shall absent himself from the service of the Senate without leave—rules not always enforced, to be sure, but subject to application whenever a member insists upon it, as Senator La Follette did once during the first session of the 79th Congress.

Before Hitler attacked Poland, Congress enjoyed long recesses between sessions with an opportunity for rest and recreation and refreshment of contacts with constituents. But since January, 1939, it has been in almost continuous session. The 76th, 77th, and 78th Congresses combined ran for 2,031 calendar days, and the House of Representatives was actually in session for 1,128 days between January 3, 1939 and December 19, 1944. During the last complete Congress, the 78th, there were 300 roll calls in the House, of which 144 were quorum calls and 156 were yea and nay votes: and 728 in the Senate, of which 521 were quorum calls and 207 were yea and nay votes. Normally, it takes from 20 to 25 minutes for a quorum call in the House and from 30 to 40 minutes for a record vote. In the Senate quorum calls consume from five to 20 minutes, depending upon the attendance, while record votes in the upper chamber run 15 minutes on the average.

There are no over-all statistics of actual man-hour attendance on the floor of the House or Senate. But here again the indefatigable Senator Burton has given us a record of the Senate attendance of at least one member of that body. Out of 698 separate sessions of the Senate held during his service there, from January 3, 1941, to June 30, 1945, he attended 594 sessions. Out of 1,301 quorum calls made during the same period, he attended 1,153. And out of 468 contested roll calls made, he voted in 410. How many Senators can match this high attendance record?

Effects on Health

Under present conditions of life and labor the lot of a congressman is thus far from enviable. He may occupy a place of power and prestige in his home town or state, but seen at close range in Washington he leads a dog's life. Chosen to be a policy-making member of the national legislature, he soon becomes a glorified lobbyist for local interests and errand boy for his constituents.

Sooner or later many members of Congress become Capitol casualties, what with the stress and strain of their strenuous lives, the inescapable attentions and entertainment from well-wishers, bad eating habits, and financial worries. They wear themselves out and die before their time because of overwork. Senator Francis Maloney of Connecticut, who died of heart failure at 50 shortly after he had been elected chairman of a joint committee to devise methods of lightening legislators' burdens, was a victim of the very conditions he sought to remedy.

"When I first came to the Capitol," remarked Dr. George W. Calver, congressional physician, "it was not uncommon to pick up a member of Congress who had died in his office at the rate of about one a month. The death rate ran from 22 to 28 men per Congress, sometimes as high as 22 deaths in one session . . . With all the irons which a member of Congress has in the fire, it is difficult to see, under the present situation, where he has to visit departments, attend committee meetings, do a thousand and one other things besides his congressional duties, how he gets along as well as he does."

Representative John M. Coffee, for 10 years a member of Congress from the state of Washington, had been secretary to a United States Senator more than 20 years ago. "My office represents one-sixth of the state," said he, "but we do more work for that one district in a day than all the congressmen representing the whole state did in a week 20 years ago." Mr. Coffee reflected the attitude of his colleagues when he told the Joint Committee on the Organization of Congress that:

The public should be told that the average member of Congress and average Senator is a very hardworking, conscientious, serious-minded individual. Most of them work too hard for their own good. Most of them do not take enough time out for exercise or recreation, because they are so conscientious that they do not want to neglect the many people at home who are urging that they introduce measures in their behalf.

I have seen members here fail right in front of my eyes. I have seen—and all of us know to whom I am referring—men, because they worked so hard and so conscientiously, neglect their own health. I have in mind certain young members of the House of Representatives, who came to that body at the same time I did, who have aged 20 years in the last 8 years, all because they did not take enough time out for recreation, rest, change, or vacations. They have overdone their work, and they are today just on the verge of cracking up.

We cannot all be as resilient as Franklin D. Roosevelt, but even he died at the age of 63, although he came from a family of great longevity. The average person could not stand up for even a year or two without a sinking in his health. Most of us would not be able to do it. Most of us cannot sleep soundly at night after we go through these tremendous pressures all day long. Most of us are not built that way. We need recreation; we need a change and surcease from the grind.

REDUCING THE VOLUME OF BUSINESS

Several remedies are available to Congress if it really wants to obtain relief from the importunities of constituents and devote its attention to matters of national importance. There has been so much public discussion of suitable correctives in recent years that I shall not undertake to do more than to point out the most promising roads to reform.

Stop Errand Running

The most fundamental solution would be for Congress to formulate a Charter of Congressional Freedom, declaring by concerted action its independence of errand-running for constituents. It could by concurrent resolution forbid its members from appearing before, or intervening with, any executive agency to get a job or a concession or a priority or a favor for any constituent. And it could forbid executive officers from heeding any congressional intervention on behalf of any constituent. Congressmen could decide once and for all to stop being local lobbyists before the departments and to devote their time and energy to being national statesmen. In one courageous self-preserving ordinance, it could write "finis" to this departmental business and abolish patronage appointments in which most members find there is more grief than gain. Post office jobs and appointments to Annapolis and West Point should be placed under civil service. This solution may seem heroic, but no other single reform would do as much to liberate congressmen for their constitutional duties. Only by acting in concert, however, can such emancipation possibly be achieved.

If outright prohibition seems beyond the realm of practical politics in the present climate of opinion, Congress should equip its members with well-paid administrative assistants competent to handle their departmental work for them. Such assistants should know their members' constituencies as well as the Washington ropes. In the upper chamber they should take care only of statewide matters for their Senators, and on the House side they should coordinate the departmental work of state delegations, as Senator Downey has suggested, so as to avoid unnecessary duplication of service. The establishment on Capitol Hill of a general liaison office for the downtown departments, proposed by Representative Priest of Tennessee, through which departmental business could conveniently be handled, would be a desirable concomitant reform.

Barring abandonment of intervention in administration, this device of the administrative assistant is a less drastic method of dividing the work load than that advocated by former Representative Ramspeck of Georgia. He proposed to solve the problem by having each congressional district elect two Representatives: one a stateman and orator to sit in the House of Representatives and concentrate on legislative matters; the other a business agent and errand boy to handle the business of the district with federal agencies. The number of congressional districts and the membership of the House would be halved, under the Ramspeck plan, in order to avoid increasing the cost of government. This is an ingenious and imaginative proposal, but it is unlikely to win much favor from members of Congress or from the general public.

Eliminate the Private Calendar

In the House of Representatives the first and third Tuesdays of each month are reserved for the call of bills on the Private Calendar. Bills for the relief of individual claims against the United States for personal injuries or loss of personal property and the like are called on the first Tuesday, and omnibus bills for the relief of sundry claimants are called on the third Tuesday, at the Speaker's discretion, and considered by the House as in Committee of the Whole. Although the second Private Calendar Tuesday in the month is frequently dispensed with, much of the time of the House and of the committees concerned is consumed in the course of a session in the consideration of bills of a private character. On the average it takes about 45 minutes to call the bills on the Private Calendar on each day they are in order.

During the 78th Congress 802 committee reports were referred to the Private Calendar in the House (there is no such calendar in the Senate), of which number 795 were acted upon by the House and 589 were approved. The rules of Congress impose no limit upon the number of bills or resolutions which a member may introduce. During the 79th Congress (from January 3, 1945 to July 16, 1946), 793 private bills were introduced in the Senate and 2,849 in the House and referred as follows:

Committees	Senate	House	Total
Claims	538	2,017	2,555
Pensions	75	178	253
Military and Naval	107	176	283
Immigration	85	284	369
All others	118	194	312
Total	793	2,849	3,772

None of this private bill legislation needs to receive congressional attention. The private bill committees perform functions which, save for historical accident, would be performed by departmental officials. Their legislative consideration consumes valuable time and there is no good reason why they should not be transferred to an appropriate administrative or judicial agency.

In recent years more than 2,000 small claim bills have been introduced in each Congress, of which less than 20 per cent became law. Of all the presidential vetoes during the 75th-77th Congresses, fully one-third were of bills granting relief for property damage or personal injury resulting usually from vehicle collisions. It is estimated that the cost to the Executive and Legislative Branches involved in considering the claims bills of each Congress, not including congressional salaries, amounts to $125,000; that the printing costs alone of the claim bills which fail of passage are almost $19,000 per Congress; and that it costs almost $200 to pass a single bill, more in some cases than the amount of relief granted. In short, the procedure for relief of tort claims by special act of Congress is slow, expensive, and unfair both to the Congress and to the claimant.

The logical remedy for this condition was offered to Congress by President Roosevelt in a special message on January 14, 1942. Said he:

I suggest that the executive departments and independent establishments be authorized to adjust and determine tort claims up to $1,000, with review by the Attorney General of awards over $500. I also suggest that the United States district courts be given jurisdiction over claims of this nature up to $7,500, with a right of appeal to the Court of Claims. The passage of such legislation would be of real assistance to the Congress and to the President at a time when matters of grave national importance demand an ever-increasing share of our attention. It would also make available a means of dispensing justice simply and effectively to tort claimants against the Government and give them the same right to a day in court which claimants now enjoy in fields such as breach of contract, patent infringement, or admiralty claims.

I should point out that the Congress, if this procedure were adopted, would, of course, retain every right to enact legislation granting relief, or further relief, in the event that in any special case the Congress felt that justice had been denied.

Adoption of this oft-repeated proposal would allow the claims committees to be pruned from the legislative tree. Similarly, the handling of veterans' pensions could be simplified by referring them to the Veterans Administration, a step which would eliminate three pension committees in the House and one in the Senate. Since private claims and pensions account for practically all the business referred to the Private Calendar, it could then be dropped and the time saved for matters of major national importance. This sensible reform would probably have been achieved long ago but for the reluctance of congressmen to sacrifice such a handy procedure for making friends and influencing people, especially on election eve.

Limit on Private Member Bills

If Congress confined its attention to administration and committee bills, the congestion of its calendars would be still further relieved. Many bills and resolutions are introduced in both chambers by individual members on their own initiative or "by request" of some private group. There is also much duplication of bills on the same subjects. If the introduction of private member bills were limited or ruled out, lobbying would be correspondingly curtailed and purity in politics promoted.

In the English House of Commons the Government alone in practice introduces legislation. "The chances of a bill being introduced by a private member and passing into law are so slender," according to a veteran member of Parliament, "that it is not worth the while of any wealthy body or corporation to offer pecuniary inducements with this object. Thus, a source of corruption not unknown in some countries is avoided, as is also a great deal of "lobbying" by vested interests." [2]

During the war, in fact, private members of the House of Commons were deprived of the privilege of presenting legislation, and the new Labor Government declined to restore it after it came to power. This

[2] A. W. H. James, How Parliament Works, The Sign Post Press (1944).

led to a lively debate in the Commons on August 16, 1945, in which Sir Alan Herbert rose to defend the traditional privilege. Private bills, he argued, pertained to matters which are too difficult or too dangerous, too big or too small, for the Government to undertake. The newly elected members were full of enthusiasm, but they would be bound by party restrictions and would suffer a sense of personal frustration. Under the pre-war practice, on a private bill day, they could stand up and say "Boo" to the bosses and the Government whips. It made, indeed, for a certain camaraderie between parties. And it was a good education for all young M. P.'s to participate in these debates. But the move against restoring the right, Sir Alan asserted, suspended part of the freedom so recently fought for. The Opposition was against monopolies. Did they suggest that the Government had a monopoly of wisdom? Each member had made promises to constituents—some quite fundamental. But he might as well be in the German Reichstag if he could not introduce bills designed to carry them out. If the motion were passed now, it would no doubt deprive all future Parliaments of this privilege. Despite Sir Alan's plea, the privilege was abolished in the larger interest of parliamentary economy.

Home Rule for Washington

In addition to disposing of its departmental business and private legislation, Congress could lighten its load considerably by granting home rule to its grown-up ward, the District of Columbia, and by delegating various local and minor matters to administrative action.

For the past 70 years Congress has functioned after a fashion as city council for the District of Columbia. Each session much legislation dealing with District affairs is introduced in both chambers and referred to the District of Columbia committees. During the first seven months of the 79th Congress, for example, 47 District bills were introduced in the Senate and 85 in the House, as well as several joint resolutions. These committees find it difficult to muster a quorum for the consideration of such municipal matters, since members are naturally more interested in the affairs of their own districts.

In the fullness of time, however, much District business is reported and comes up for consideration in the House of Representatives on the second and fourth Mondays of each month which are reserved under a House rule for District of Columbia matters. Thus, during the 78th Congress 57 separate bills were reported by the District committees and acted upon by either or both of the houses. They dealt with such petty matters, trivial in comparison with the transcendant national and international issues on the agenda of that wartime Congress, as the regulation of the practice of the healing art, the sale of shad and herring, the disposal of dead human bodies, providing butter for the patients of St. Elizabeth's Hospital, and changing the name of Conduit Road to MacArthur Boulevard.

During and since the war the drain of District business on the time of the House has diminished. During the 78th Congress, for example, out of 46 potential District days, only 11 were utilized by Representative Randolph, Chairman of the District Committee, to bring up District business, which the House was able to dispose of, on the average, in about half-an-hour on each occasion. And during the first nine months of the 79th Congress, only 8 out of a possible 18 District days were claimed by Mr. Randolph who, to economize the time of the House had adopted the procedure of allowing District legislation to accumulate on his calendar until it was sufficient to merit floor consideration.

That Congress would concern itself with the "petty chicken feed of District ordinance passing" was no part of the intention of the Founding Fathers. To be sure, they gave Congress exclusive legislative authority over the area to be chosen as the seat of government, but they did not intend it to sit as a municipal council for the District or to deprive the Capitol City of home rule. Its inhabitants, wrote James Madison in the *Federalist* (No. 43), "will have . . . their voice in the election of the Government which is to exercise authority over them," and "a municipal legislature for local purposes, derived from their own suffrages, will of course be allowed them."

Consistent with this original conception, Washington enjoyed local self-government for 72 years—from 1802 to 1874 when the so-called Territorial Government was liquidated as the result of congressional displeasure with the administration of Governor Shepherd, a presidential appointee. The present system, set up in 1874 as an emergency arrangement, has continued to date by a process of drift and neglect, not in pursuance of any governmental principle or deliberate desire to deprive Washington of home rule.

The sound remedy for this situation, and one long overdue, is for Congress to follow the practice of the states and adopt a municipal charter for the city of Washington. Such a charter would grant all the ordinary municipal powers, including the taxing and appropriating power, to a local council-manager government. Congress, of course, would retain ultimate control over the District, just as New York State does over Albany. It could veto any act of the city council and withdraw at any time the authority delegated. But it should shed its present burden of being a board of aldermen and get "back on the beam" of national policy making. "It is incredibly short-sighted," affirms Merlo J. Pusey, editorial writer and columnist for the *Washington Post,* "for a great democratic nation to keep a city of roughly 900,000 residents, larger than 13 of the states, in a status of political peonage. That mistake is further magnified when we realize that this denial of political rights to residents of the Capital operates to hamper Congress in the performance of its own duties and obligations as a national policy-making body."

Delegation of Minor Law-Making

Congress could also lighten its labors in no small degree by further extending its practice, begun 60 years ago, of delegating minor law-making to administrative agencies, subject where advisable to legislative veto. Legislative energy should not be frittered away on such matters as pensions for servicemen and veterans, bridge bills, post office legislation, Indian and territorial business, the construction of highways and national cemeteries, and the erection of statues and memorials. All manner of questions that call for local or special legislation should be determined by the appropriate administrative or judicial bodies operating under general standards fixed by law. When such fateful issues as the control of atomic energy, the maintenance of full employment, and the preservation of world peace confront a national legislature, it is fatuous for its attention to be diverted by such minor and local details as granting rights-of-way over federal land or permitting seeing-eye dogs to enter public buildings. Yet a survey of the public general bills introduced during the first session of the 79th Congress prior to the August recess revealed that approximately one-half of them were of minor or local importance. Out of 808 Senate public bills, 47 were District of Columbia bills and 335 more were classified as minor. And out of 2,299 House public bills, 85 were District bills and 1,089 were of minor significance.

As a single example of such minor law-making, consider the legislation governing the construction of bridges over navigable waters of the United States. During the 76th Congress more than 100 public enactments authorized the construction or extended the permissible time of construction of bridges affecting navigation. The passage of each one of these acts undoubtedly cost the taxpayers several hundred dollars and consumed a large amount of time in the Congress, in the War Department, and at the White House. Under prevailing law, the Secretary of War and the Chief of Engineers are responsible for approving the location, engineering plans, and other important features of such bridge enterprises as Congress may authorize, so that administrative action is essential to the execution of the enterprise after Congress grants its authorization. In order to save time and money, Congress should pass an enabling act, as President Roosevelt recommended, delegating to the Secretary of War the responsibility for authorizing the construction and maintenance of bridges over navigable waters in accordance with such general policy as Congress may prescribe. The Secretary of War, of course, would submit periodic reports of his acts.

Senatorial Consent to Executive Nominations

Still another way of reducing the volume of work is suggested in the case of executive nominations. The constitution empowers the President to nominate, "and by and with the advice and consent of the Senate" to appoint ambassadors, other public ministers and consuls, judges of the Supreme Court, and all other officers of the United States whose appointments were not otherwise provided for and which should be established by law. This was not much of a chore for the First Congress when the Senate confirmed only 211 presidential nominees. But the task had multiplied one hundred-fold when the Senate had to investigate and pass upon 21,371 persons during the 78th Congress. Many of these appointments, to be sure, such as commissions and promotions of service personnel, are handled en bloc and involve only perfunctory senatorial scrutiny. But even allowing for these, there are still several hundred executive and judicial posts to be filled each year which require the attention of Senate committees. Not long ago Senator McKellar, whose appetite for patronage was hard to appease, proposed to add several thousand places to the list by conditioning the appointment to all administrative positions paying $4,500 and over upon senatorial consent. Fortunately for an already overworked Senate his effort proved abortive.

If the business of confirmation is not to become merely an automatic ceremony or degenerate into a patronage grab, and if the fitness of appointees for public office is to be adequately investigated, as the Fathers intended, then the Senate must have help in performing its "advice and consent" function. In his testimony before the Joint Committee on the Organization of Congress, Mr. George Smith, research assistant to the minority leader of the Senate, suggested that federal nominees be selected from panels of qualified persons prepared by the professional associations in the fields in which appointments are to be made. The endorsement of candidates by organizations like the American Bar Association and the Society for Public Administration, he believed, would furnish the Senate with assurance of their fitness and avoid the present danger of filling offices with incompetent men.

Lesson from Supreme Court Experience

In keeping abreast of its swelling business Congress can learn a lesson from the experience of the United States Supreme Court. As the nation expanded and conflicts over federal relations and between economic interests increased, the Supreme Court's business steadily developed. From 1789 down to 1925 our federal judicial system was the object of a continuous process of legislative tinkering. Judicial reform waited always on legislative sterility and political rivalry, while the mounting business of the courts outran their ability to dispatch it. The Supreme Court was compelled to seek relief through its control over practice, but relief from Congress was slow to come.

After the Civil War, patent, admiralty, and bankruptcy litigation, extensions of federal jurisdiction, the National Bank Acts, the Court of Claims and constitutional amendments swelled the dockets and made the influence of the federal courts all-pervasive while exhausting their resources. Between 1865 and 1891 a struggle to eliminate the circuit duties of the Justices and to establish an intermediate appellate tribunal went on against legislative inertia, political hostility, the issue of states' rights and absentee ownership, and the drift of habituation, mitigated only by increases in personnel and minor limitations upon jurisdiction in the Judiciary Acts of 1869, 1875, and 1887. But in spite of the lack of speedy justice and quick review, real relief was persistently postponed while Congress clashed over remedies and the purposes of the courts, the House favoring and the Senate resisting curtailment of power. Finally, the establishment of the nine circuit courts of appeals in 1891 brought genuine relief and the first structural modification in the federal judicial system since its creation.

The period from 1891 to 1911 also brought increased business to the Supreme Court thanks to litigation after the Spanish-American War, regulatory and social legislation, the creation of administrative commissions, and District of Columbia litigation. In 1897 finality in all criminal cases except capital offenses was given to the circuit courts of appeals. Subsequent acts since 1907 have been chiefly concerned with restricting the right of appeal to the Supreme Court. In 1912 the Court came to its own rescue by excluding from appeal the purely local laws of the District of Columbia. And in 1911 the twenty-year movement to reduce the range of the business of the federal courts succeeded in the Judicial Code in increasing the pecuniary amount necessary for resort to these courts and unified the scattered legal provisions relating to their business.

From the Judicial Code to the postwar judiciary acts the jurisdiction of the Supreme Court underwent progressive contraction, a trend interrupted in 1914 by the grant of appellate control over state courts: the only time since the Judicial Code when Congress has broadened the jurisdiction of the Court. Restriction was essential if the Court was to cope with the rising tide of litigation augmented by the legislative mills, the Fourteenth Amendment, and the flow of social and regulative legislation. The growth of the federal courts' business, stimulated by World War I and the downpour of employers' liability litigation, was accommodated in 1915 and 1916 by acts decreasing the obligatory jurisdiction of the Supreme Court in bankruptcy cases, relegating trademark and employers' liability litigation to final disposition by the circuit courts of appeal, attaching Puerto Rico to the first circuit, restricting reviews from the Philippine Islands to *certiorari,* cutting down the period for appeals, and lengthening the Court's term. *Certiorari* was also extended as the only means of securing review in certain cases.

Finally, in the Judiciary Acts of 1922 and 1925 Congress modernized an eighteenth-century judicial system that had proved inadequate to twentieth-century needs and conditions. In 1922 it consented to the assignability of judges by the Chief Justice upon certificates of need and dispensability, to the creation of a judicial council, and to an increase in the number of federal judges. The annual conference of the senior circuit judges with the Chief Justice has become a permanent and invaluable feature of the federal judicature, serving Congress as legislative counsel and the lower federal courts as promoter of effective administrative standards, and resulting in rules for the prompt dispatch of business.

The Judiciary Act of 1925, by curtailing the Supreme Court's jurisdiction, completed Chief Justice Taft's program of judicial reform. Much of the Court's business was still not germane to its prime purposes, i.e., to resolve conflicts among coordinate appellate tribunals and to determine matters of national concern. Prolific sources of such unrelated business were cases coming from the district courts, the Court of Claims, and the District of Columbia Court of Appeals. As a result of the Act of 1925, the Supreme Court now receives cases only from the district, state, and circuit courts of appeals and in only three types of cases is review free from discretion. Thus the Court can now confine itself to constitutional and national issues. "The Act of 1925 has cut the Supreme Court's jurisdiction to the bone." [3]

The lesson of this story for Congress is obvious. Congress cannot expect to catch up with its congested calendars and effectively confine itself to national policy-making unless it emulates the Court and delimits its activities.

Devolution to the States

Another proposal for lightening the legislative load is for Congress to devolve more of its work upon the states and regional authorities. Devolution to the states, advocated by Governor Bricker and others during the 1944 campaign, even were it possible, would not reduce the legislative load materially. Under our federal system certain public services have traditionally been left to state and local governments to render: police and other protection, provision of highways, health, hospitals, and sanitation, correction, education, recreation, and more recently old-age assistance and unemployment insurance. Expenditures for these functions are overwhelmingly made at the state and local levels, except those for social insurance which were about equally divided in 1941 between the federal government, on the one hand, and state and local governments, on the other. The only public services predominantly rendered or financed by the federal government in 1941 were: national defense, aids to agriculture, conservation of natural resources, and the welfare group which covers work relief, general relief, categorical assistance (includes old-age assistance, aid to the blind, and aid to dependent children), and institutional care. None of these functions could be devolved upon the states except the public welfare programs whose administration is already largely decentralized. Since 1933 the federal government has assumed the major share of financial responsibility for the public welfare programs because of the more limited fiscal resources of the states and localities and interstate differences in wealth and need.

---

[3] *The Business of the Supreme Court*, by Felix Frankfurter and James M. Landis, 1927.

The modern tendency, to be sure, is toward the expansion of federal activities as our economic and social life becomes more unified under the impact of large-scale production and cheap and rapid communication. This trend, which can hardly be reversed, is reflected in the rising federal share of all public expenditures which increased between 1913 and 1941 from one-fourth to three-fifths of the total, indicating the growth in the relative fiscal importance of the central government as an agency for providing public services. Meanwhile, however, the share of the states had also risen, though not so much as the federal, from 14 per cent of the total in 1913 to 20 per cent of the total in 1941. On the other hand, the local share of net public expenditures has suffered a marked decline since 1913, dropping from 60 per cent of the total in that year to 22 per cent in 1941. The relative positions of the federal and local governments had been almost exactly reversed in the intervening generation under the impact of war, depression, and the economic and social changes of the era. And the war accelerated this basic trend in American government and society.

Contrary to considerable popular and some congressional misapprehension,[4] however, the recent expansion of federal activities has not been accompanied by serious curtailment of local functions. By 1941, for example, 525 local housing authorities and 107 local soil conservation districts had been created at the direct solicitation of the national government and supported by substantial appropriations made by Congress to aid these new local units in their respective fields.

"It has been frequently asserted," according to the President's Commission on Recent Social Trends, "that the federal government has steadily encroached upon the domain of state activities. That the sphere of federal authority has been greatly widened in recent years is not contested, but that this encroachment has resulted in the abandonment of whole spheres of state work and their complete transfer to federal administrative agencies is by no means apparent. Federal centralization, in most cases, has proceeded by means of the institution of cooperative relationships or the imposition of varying degrees of control, both of which imply the continuance of local activity. Much of the influence recently exerted by the federal government has been in the direction of increasing rather than restricting the work done by state agencies. Information and guidance supplied by federal experts enable state officials to accomplish a notable variety of tasks to which they

[4] Representative Hatton W. Sumners, "Don't Blame the Bureaucrat," *The Reader's Digest,* September, 1943.

were previously unequal. Federal supervision and types of federal grants-in-aid act as powerful stimulants in fields both old and new. Even when federal activities have supplanted those of the states, the local agencies concerned have not, as a rule, disappeared, but have manifested a tendency to fill in the gaps left in the compass of their work by an expansion of the tasks not affected by the transfer of authority." This statement is as true now as it was when it was made.[5]

In short, devolution to the states is not the solution of our problem. Now that the nation has become an economic and social unit, a return to so-called "states' rights" would be a regressive step. "It is not disintegration through devolution that is required, but integration." [6]

Regional Decentralization

Devolution to regional authorities, on the other hand, offers more promise and is worth exploring. One federal function that might well be administered regionally is the coordinated development of the land and water resources of the great river valleys of the United States. Regional authorities have been charged by Congress with this function in the Tennessee Valley (T.V.A.) and the lower Columbia River Valley (the Bonneville Power Administration). Proposals to create valley development authorities modeled after the T.V.A. in the other great drainage basins of the country have been made by Senator Norris and were renewed by President Roosevelt. River valley development involves multiple-purpose projects for navigation, flood control, low-cost hydro-power, irrigation, pollution control, recreation, reforestation, and water supply. Development through such coordinated projects has already proved itself in the Tennessee Valley and the Columbia Valley. It is estimated that similar developments in the Arkansas, Missouri, Colorado, and other river valleys would provide enormous possibilities of industrial expansion aggregating more than $25 billion.

Although the method of administering such regional programs has been a bone of contention, there can be little doubt that the adoption of such schemes would tend to mitigate the tendency toward excessive centralization in Washington. But there is no reason to believe that they would afford much relief to Congress. For it would presumably be necessary to formulate, consider, and enact separate legislation for each of the river valley development programs, to make annual provi-

---

[5] Report of the President's Commission on Recent Social Trends (1933), pp. 1293–1294.

[6] W. Ivor Jennings, Parliamentary Reform, p. 42.

sion for the regional authorities in the appropriation bills, and to maintain continuous legislative oversight of their administration. A case can be made out for regional decentralization on other grounds, but there is little prospect of its relieving the legislative load.

Revision of Congressional Time-Table

In addition to reducing the volume of business by the processes of elimination, delegation, and devolution described in the previous pages, so as to enable Congress to concentrate upon its essential legislative, investigative, and supervisory functions, there are several time-saving steps which might be taken in the interest of economy and efficiency.

Of these, the most obvious to any observer in the galleries would be to install electric roll-call devices in both chambers in order to expedite quorum calls and record votes. Under the constitution the presence of a majority of the members is necessary to transact business in either House and it is the duty of the chair to ascertain the presence of a quorum when the point is raised. This is done by having a clerk call the roll—a slow, time-consuming procedure often used to delay action. During the 78th Congress 1,028 roll calls in both Houses consumed a total of 320 hours, on a conservative estimate, which was equivalent to $13\frac{1}{3}$ full-length days or 64 five-hour legislative days. Had the halls of Congress been equipped with automatic voting devices, two calendar months would have been saved which the members could have spent in recess at home. Eleven states, including Alabama, California, Florida, Iowa, Louisiana, Michigan, Minnesota, Nebraska, Texas, West Virginia, and Wisconsin have adopted electric voting in one or both houses to expedite roll calls. Under this procedure there is a button on each member's desk and a colored board by the Speaker's rostrum where his vote is visibly and automatically registered.

Much of the time of the Senate could be saved if it would also tighten up its rules regulating debate. Thanks to precedents established by Speaker Reed fifty years ago, the problem of obstruction or filibustering has been largely solved by the House of Representatives. In the Senate, however, where debate is unlimited and often irrelevant to the pending business, and where action is had only by unanimous consent, obstruction by various devices frequently occurs. Even under the closure rule, adopted in 1917 after President Wilson had denounced a filibuster, a determined minority can still prevent action. Successful filibusters have been conducted in our own time by one man, e.g.,

Senator Bilbo's filibuster against the Fair Employment Practices Committee and his threat in October, 1945, to hold up legislative business for 30 days in order to defeat a railroad bill.

The ability of a minority of Senators to defeat legislation desired by the majority and to compel the adoption of measures opposed by them has been ardently defended by Senators like the late George W. Norris and vigorously condemned by others like Senator George H. Moses, Speaker Cannon, Vice President Dawes, and President Wilson. Many public bills, desired by the party in power and approved by public opinion, have been defeated in the Senate by the practice of unlimited debate. The mere threat of a filibuster has often prevented or forced action.

If the Senate is unwilling to adopt a closure rule rigid enough to eliminate the filibuster, it could at least require debate to be germane to the subject under consideration. Or it could adopt Senator Downey's suggestion and set aside certain hours, say 10–12 A.M. on certain days, with advance notice of subjects and speakers, when Senators might talk to their hearts' delight on anything under the sun without interrupting the regular order of legislative business.

Members of Congress spend considerable time dashing around Capitol Hill between committee and chamber meetings often held at the same time in widely scattered rooms. Some committees have permission to meet while the legislature is in session, with the result that business on the floor is suspended until a quorum can be assembled. Senators are members of many committees which often meet simultaneously, so that they must either neglect some assignments or pay them only superficial attention. These conditions could be remedied to a considerable extent if session days and committee days were staggered, e.g., by reserving Mondays, Tuesdays and Wednesdays for committee meetings and hearings, and Thursdays, Fridays and Saturdays for chamber sessions, or by providing that no committee may meet when the Houses are in session. It would also save time and energy if all the congressional committee rooms were housed in one administration building together with the Executive Branch agency liaison offices; and if subway trolley service such as the Senators have were provided between the House Office buildings and the Capitol.

Representative Hale of Maine, latest in a distinguished line of congressmen from the Pine Tree state, has called attention to an abuse of the personal privilege procedure in the House of Representatives. In order to obtain time in debate not otherwise available or to defend one's reputation against attack, members sometimes gain the floor by making a point of personal privilege. "There is no reason," says Mr. Hale, "why some irresponsible libel by Walter Winchell or Drew Pearson should cost the House of Representatives 435 man-hours. A member's reputation and standing is generally about the same after he has addressed the House for an hour on a question of personal privilege as it was before."

Finally, if Congress were to fix in advance a certain date for adjournment of the session, by adopting a *sine die* resolution, as Representative Poage has proposed, it might well expedite the conduct of business so as to be able to conclude on schedule. It was a drawback of the Norris amendment to the constitution, abolishing the so-called "lame-duck" session, that it fixed no deadline upon a session of Congress.

Adoption of such proposals for making more effective use of its time, together with the suggested reductions in its jurisdiction, would undoubtedly allow our national legislature to take a recess for at least three months each year. Congressmen, constituents, and the country would all greatly benefit by such a revision of the legislative time-table.

Relief from Routine Chores

With the growth of the functions of the national government, with the increasing size of the constituencies, and with growing familiarity with the techniques of "working" a congressman, the claims of constituents on the legislator's time have become incessant. Correspondence and various personal services to the electorate consume a large part of every member's time, as we have seen, leaving little for the study of important legislation. Every day brings its series of personal interviews, its stack of letters requiring reply, and its varied requests. These daily trivia are not likely to diminish in the calculable future.

To relieve members as far as possible of these time-consuming chores, they should make more use of the excellent services provided by the Legislative Reference Service in the Library of Congress and by the Division of Public Inquiries in the Bureau of the Budget. Newly elected members should be informed of the availability of these services which should be strengthened and perhaps combined. A general service bureau might also be set up within the Legislative Branch for the use of members in handling especially heavy mail, to provide automobile service on public business, and duplicating and special messenger services. A high-caliber executive assistant could relieve members of many personal interviews and departmental calls. Members should also be supplied with all the stenographic and clerical help they need which varies, of course, from district to district and time to time. In short, as Robert Heller well says, "Members of Congress should not spend one working minute on anything that somebody else can do just as well." A congressman's time is not expendable and should not be so regarded.

In one of his Godkin lectures at Harvard some years ago, Robert Luce, himself a member of the House of Representatives for 20 years and a keen observer of the legislative process, summed up our theme in this chapter when he said:

The chief source of trouble in our lawmaking bodies, state and national . . . is the attempt to do more work than can be well done under present conditions. We have been blind to what has been brought about by the growth of population; by the march of science; by the triumphs of invention; by the economic and social changes of the last fifty years. We vainly try to cope with the results of the use of machinery long outgrown. Because of an exaggerated respect for precedent, or of inertia or timidity, we refuse to scrap that part of the machinery which no longer accomplishes a useful purpose and we refuse to adjust the rest of it to modern conditions.

When a manufacturer finds that he can no longer handle the work pressed upon him, he will either tune up his machinery so that with the same plant he can turn out more product, or he will add more plant. Either or both of these things can be done with the machinery of legislation. Without doing any person or any interest serious harm, the procedure of Congress could be so improved along lines already thoroughly tested by other important legislative bodies, that one-third more work could be done in the time now consumed. Or by using methods familiar in England and on the continent of Europe, enough work might be shifted from Congress to other agencies so that Congress could probably handle with ease all that would remain.[7]

Representative government in the United States can be saved only by wise and deliberate curtailment of the business of Congress.

---

[7] Robert Luce, *Congress: An Explanation*, pp. 142–143.

4.

Congressional Machinery

AS EVERY STUDENT of American government and every visitor at the Capitol knows, the Congress of the United States consists of a Senate and a House of Representatives. The framers of the federal constitution adopted a bicameral legislative system on the English and colonial model to protect the influence of the smaller states and to safeguard property rights. While this system has many theoretical disadvantages and practical drawbacks, and has recently been abandoned in one state (Nebraska), the American people are not prepared to abolish bicameralism in Washington.

Organization of the House

Under the constitution as amended, Congress assembles at least once each year beginning in January. A new House of Representatives first of all chooses its Speaker, who has always been one of its members, and its other officers—a clerk, sergeant-at-arms, doorkeeper, postmaster, and chaplain—none of whom has ever been chosen from the membership of the House, and who continue in office until their successors are chosen and qualified. After a new House has chosen its Speaker and other officers and adopted as usual the rules of the preceding House, it is organized and ready to transact business. The Senate, which is a continuing body in that two-thirds of its membership is always in office, also chooses its officers, other than the President of the Senate who is the Vice President of the United States. Officers of the Senate include a President pro tempore, chaplain, secretary, sergeant-at-arms, secretary to the majority, and secretary to the minority.

In organizing itself at the opening of a new Congress, the House proceeds under general parliamentary law until the former rules have been revised, reported, and adopted. Normally few changes are made

84

in the former code and the debate upon the rules takes place in an amiable and leisurely manner. The House is in Committee of the Whole on the state of the Union at this time and the discussion ranges far and wide. The newer members seize the opportunity to air their views on the great issues of the day and perhaps the antiquated character of the rules, while the old timers sit back in silence, confident that time and experience will bridle the new steeds to the tried and ancient ways.

In ante-bellum days, however, the organization of the House was often marked by exciting contests. During the 1840's, when the great struggle over slavery was gathering momentum, strife over the adoption of the rules or the election of officers grew increasingly violent. "For weeks or months, at the beginning of a Congress," writes McConachie, "the contest would wage with no other bridle upon vociferous radicals than the regulations compiled by British parliamentarians of the seventeenth century. In 1861, before he left the House to take part with the Confederacy, John H. Reagan declared that these passionate wrangles had been a chief cause of the disruption of the Union." [1]

ADMINISTRATIVE MACHINERY

For the performance of its functions and the conduct of its business each House of Congress has devised three types of machinery: an administrative organization, a committee system, and a political structure. Each of these mechanisms plays an important part in the legislative process and each requires more or less drastic revision if representative government is to operate effectively.

The administrative machinery of Congress has grown up like Topsy since 1789. From the beginning each House has elected a secretary or clerk, a sergeant-at-arms, and a chaplain, and the lower chamber has also chosen a doorkeeper and postmaster. The clerk of the House is its chief administrative officer. His duties do not terminate with the adjournment of Congress as do those of the Speaker. As defined in the rules and statutes, they include acting as presiding officer during the organization of the House, preparing the roll of Representatives-elect, and keeping and printing the *House Journal*. He also certifies the passage of bills and joint resolutions, attests warrants and subpoenas, and carries on the underlying administrative work of the House.

The sergeant-at-arms is charged with keeping order on the floor of

---

[1] Lauros G. McConachie, *Congressional Committees* (1898), p. 110.

the House, serves summons to witnesses to appear before its committees, and conducts the obsequies of deceased members. As disbursor
of members' salaries and travel allowances, he currently does a $12
million banking business every year. The sergeant-at-arms is also the
custodian of the mace, impressive symbol of legislative authority, which
he carries on high to quell disorders in the House. The duties of the
doorkeeper, chaplain, and postmaster are self-evident.

Each of the officers of the House and Senate has a staff appointed
largely on patronage by the party in power. But many employees of
Congress have been so long in its service as to constitute the nucleus of
a permanent career staff. Leslie C. Biffle, popular secretary of the
Senate, has served Congress continuously in various capacities since
1909. Men like John C. Crockett, sonorous chief clerk of the Senate,
Charles L. Watkins, its able parliamentarian, Edward J. Hickey,
journal clerk, Guy E. Ives, printing clerk, James D. Preston, versatile
veteran of many posts, and Carl A. Loeffler, secretary to the minority,
have served the Senate for upwards of half a century. South Trimble
has been clerk of the House at intervals since 1911. Marcellus C.
Sheild was clerk of the House Appropriations Committee from 1916 to
1945. Elmer Lewis, superintendent of the House Document Room, has
been on its staff since 1918—to mention only a few of the long-tenure
careerists in the employ of both houses.[2]

In the early days of the Republic only a handful of officials made up
the administrative staff of Congress. In 1825, for example, it had only
19 officers and employees. By 1850 the combined staff had increased
to 53 persons and by 1900 to 193, of whom 45 were employed by the
Senate and 148 by the House. At the turn of the century the office of
the secretary of the Senate had grown to 25 persons, including legislative, reading, minute and journal, financial, enrolling and other clerks
and a keeper of stationery. And document and folding rooms and a
heating and ventilating department had been added. In the House the
clerk's office now numbered 32 persons and eight new departments appeared in the *Congressional Directory:* document and folding rooms,
heating and ventilating, official reporters of debates and committee
stenographers, the office of the Architect of the Capitol, Capitol Police,
and the National Botanic Garden which probably belongs in the Department of Agriculture.

The administrative structure of Congress continues today substan-

---

[2] For other examples see Lindsay Rogers, "The Staffing of Congress," *Political Science
Quarterly,* March, 1941.

tially the same as it was a half century ago, the chief innovation in the interim having been the establishment of the Office of Legislative Counsel in 1919 with bill-drafting and legal duties. But the size of the administrative staff has multiplied tenfold since 1900, rising in 1945 to 426 Senate officers and employees and 572 on the House side, plus 887 on the permanent force of the Architect of the Capitol, the latter being concerned with the construction, operation, and maintenance of the Capitol buildings and grounds. If to these be added the clerks to members, committee employees, and various special and minority employees, the entire congressional staff (exclusive of employees of the Architect) comprised 2,987 persons as of June, 1944. (See Table VII in the Appendix.)

Charts I and II in the Appendix show the internal organization of the Senate and House of Representatives as they stood in 1945.

Cost of Operating Congress

The cost of operating the congressional machine is a mere drop in the bucket of total federal expenditures. In 1900 Congress proper[3] cost the taxpayer only $4.4 million, which was nine-tenths of one per cent of total federal expenditures in that year and equivalent to six cents per capita of the total population. By 1944 the cost of Congress had increased to $14.6 million, which was less than two-tenths of one per cent of the total cost of the federal government at that time, or 11 cents per capita. $5.5 million of this figure went for the salaries and mileage of members. Of every seven dollars spent by the federal government in 1940, a prewar year, Robert Heller estimates that only one cent was spent on Congress—an infinitesimal sum. Since 1916 the cost of maintaining our national legislature has doubled, while the cost of the whole federal government[4] has multiplied 15 times.

Table VIII in the Appendix itemizes the cost of running representative government in Washington during the fiscal year 1944.

DEVELOPMENT OF COMMITTEE SYSTEM

For the performance of its legislative, fiscal, supervisory, and housekeeping functions both houses of Congress have organized themselves into a system of committees that is unique among national representative assemblies. All bills and resolutions introduced in Congress are

---

[3] Exclusive of the Architect of the Capitol, Botanic Garden, Government Printing Office, and Library of Congress other than the Legislative Reference Service.
[4] Exclusive of interest on debt, debt retirement, and abnormal military expenditures.

first referred to these committees, considered and screened by them, and those that win favor are then reported back to the chambers with recommendations for action. Committee reports on bills raising revenue or appropriating money are referred in the House of Representatives to a Calendar of the Committee of the Whole House on the state of the Union. All other public bills are referred to the House Calendar, and all private bills to the Private Calendar. Business in the Senate is referred to the Calendar of Bills and Resolutions.

The congressional committee system has grown by fits and starts since the early days of the Republic. In the beginning Congress referred its business to a legion of select committees. For every bill and every petty claim a separate special committee was set up. At least 350 such committees, for example, were raised in the Third Congress. But as time went on the number of select committees rapidly declined. The Thirteenth Congress (1813–1815), with its three war sessions, had about 70; and by the Twenty-Third Congress (1833–1835) their number had dropped to 35. As the nineteenth century advanced, the select committees tended to group themselves into the first standing committees which gradually grew in number as the select committees fell off. The following table shows the chronology of the fall and rise of the select and standing committees of the House of Representatives:[5]

DEVELOPMENT OF CONGRESSIONAL COMMITTEES

SELECT COMMITTEES OF THE HOUSE

Congress	Period	No. of Committees
3rd	1793–1795	350
13th	1813–1815	70
23rd	1833–1835	35
33rd	1853–1855	22
43rd	1873–1875	20
78th	1943–1945	10

STANDING COMMITTEES OF THE HOUSE

Congress	Period	No. of Committees
1st	1789–1791	2
4th–7th	1795–1803	6
10th–12th	1807–1813	10
13th	1813–1815	13
14th	1815–1817	20
17th	1821–1823	26

[5] Based for the period from 1789 to 1895 on L. G. McConachie, *Congressional Committees* (1898) and thereafter on the *Congressional Directory*.

STANDING COMMITTEES OF THE HOUSE (*Continued*)

Congress	Period	No. of Committees
22nd	1831–1833	30
25th–27th	1837–1843	34
31st–35th	1849–1859	38
40th–42nd	1867–1873	45
43rd–47th	1873–1883	46
53rd	1893–1895	55
54th	1895–1897	57
61st	1909–1911	61
66th	1920–1921	60
70th	1927–1929	46
78th	1943–1944	47

As a result of this evolutionary process, responsibility for legislative action was scattered in 1945 among no less than 81 "little ministries," as Wilson once called them: 48 in the House and 33 in the Senate. From time to time both houses still resort to select or special committees for consideration of particular problems. During the 1st session of the 79th Congress, for example, there were seven such select committees in the House and eight in the Senate, as well as three joint select committees. The acts also provide for two joint standing committees: on printing (1846) and the library (1802). And a joint Committee on Internal Revenue Taxation was established by law in 1926. In addition, there were 21 congressional commissions and boards such as the Interparliamentary Union and the Boards of Visitors to the Military and Naval Academies.

These 81 "little legislatures" were by no means of equal magnitude and importance. More than half of them on both sides of the Capitol were classified as minor and relatively inactive so far as meetings, hearings, publications, and reports were concerned. Not more than 12 or 15 in each House were major committees dealing with public problems of national significance. These included some of the so-called *legislative* committees having jurisdiction, defined or customary, over the several subject-matter fields of legislation. Another group, the *fiscal* committees, dealt with revenues and appropriations and were among the most important and powerful committees of Congress. In a separate category were the committees having *supervisory* functions such as the Joint Committees on Printing and the Library, Federal Expenditures, and Administrative Acts. The committees having jurisdiction over private claims and pensions were in the *private* bill class. And half a dozen in each house dealt with matters of internal administration or *housekeeping* such as the committees on rules, audit and control, accounts, and enrolled bills. As V-Day dawned over the land most observers of the congressional committee system, both within and outside that body, agreed that it was over-ripe for revision. Few defenders could be found of the lack of effective liaison between the committees, of the splintering of public policy-making induced by the system, or of their overlapping jurisdiction and wasteful duplication of the time and energy of all concerned.

Committee Eminence in the House of Representatives

An analysis of the relative importance of the standing committees of the House of Representatives, made by John C. Eberhart of Northwestern University, reaches some interesting conclusions. His study is based on a summary of 4,841 committee appointments over a period of 27 years (1914–1941), analyzed in terms of five criteria of committee importance or desirability: (1) length of service in the House when appointed; (2) length of service on the committee; (3) the holding power of a committee; (4) the drawing power of a committee; and (5) a combination of drawing power and holding power.

Application of these criteria to almost 5,000 committee appointments in the House over almost three decades of congressional history indicates that the 13 major standing committees of the House are rated in the following order of importance:

1. Ways and Means	7. Foreign Affairs
2. Appropriations	8. Naval Affairs
3. Rules	9. Banking and Currency
4. Interstate and Foreign Commerce	10. Rivers and Harbors
5. Judiciary	11. Military Affairs
6. Agriculture	12. Post Offices and Post Roads
	13. Merchant Marine and Fisheries

"The hierarchy is really a pyramid," says Eberhart, "with the Ways and Means Committee at the peak, and a layer of very unimportant minor committees at the bottom."

The Staffing of Committees

Employment of clerical assistance by congressional committees was slow in beginning. Many a chairman kept the records of his committee during the first half century or longer. McConachie reports that the committee on the defeat of General St. Clair paid a clerk $150 in 1793 and that another clerk was allowed a like sum in 1796. In 1803 the House declined to consider a motion to employ two clerks for the committees collectively. Similar proposals were rejected in 1815 and 1817. Not until about 1835 or 1840, after repeated pleading by chairmen, was assistance allowed in emergencies on a per diem or hourly basis. Only four clerks were employed by House committees in 1853 and four more were added during the Civil War. After the middle of the nineteenth century several of the more important committees in the House and Senate began to appoint full-time clerks.[6] By 1893 forty-one House committees had annual clerks as well as a large number of session clerks and messengers.[7]

Not until around 1900, however, did the appropriation acts begin to carry items specifying funds for the standing committees in both houses and the first comprehensive legislative pay bill authorizing appropriations for all legislative employees, including committee clerks, was not enacted until 1924. That act appropriated $270,100 for 141 Senate committee clerks and $200,490 for 120 House committee employees: $470,590 for 261 clerks, assistant clerks, and janitors. Twenty-two years later the Legislative Appropriation Act for 1946 specified 356 clerks for Senate and House committees and provided $978,760 for their hire, plus the unexpended balance of the grant to the House Committee on Appropriations. Of this total, $95,620 was provided for "additional clerical assistance" at the discretion of certain chairmen, which probably raised the total number of committee employees during the 79th Congress to about 400. Table IX in the Appendix shows the staffing and total compensation for all the committees of the Senate and House of Representatives during 1945–1946.

Committee clerks are appointed on patronage by the chairmen as one of the perquisites of office, subject only to the nominal approval of the committees. When a Senator becomes chairman of a standing committee, his clerks and assistant clerks become ex-officio clerks and assistant clerks of the committee. Thus their tenure is exposed to all the political and mortal hazards surrounding the lives of their chairmen who may be appointed to bench or cabinet (e.g., Senators Burton and Byrnes), or be defeated at the polls, or be killed in an airplane

---

[6] Lindsay Rogers, *op. cit.*, p. 3n of reprint.
[7] McConachie, *op. cit.*, pp. 65–66.

accident (e.g., Senators Cutting and Lundeen), or die from overwork (e.g., Senator Maloney).[8] Turnover among the committee staffs is rapid and career appointments are few and far between. Some of the abler committee clerks, however, have served terms ranging from five to twenty-five years. John Carson was clerk of the Senate Interstate Commerce Committee from 1929 to 1934 and E. J. Layton has served as clerk of the House Committee on Interstate and Foreign Commerce since 1921.

By and large, the conditions of work on Capitol Hill compare unfavorably with those in the Executive Branch. This situation was brought out a few years ago by a joint committee appointed to investigate the numbers and compensation of the officers and employees of Congress. In recommending certain modest increases the committee said: "Service in the executive departments is of certain tenure, regular, and short hours, carries annual vacation and sick leave and retirement privileges, and is under pay schedules which permit promotion from time to time without action by Congress in changing the rates. Service under the legislative branch is of uncertain tenure under the patronage system, irregular hours of employment, no promotion possibilities, no retirement privileges, and involves travel expenses between the home district and the Capital."[9] Under these circumstances, the turnover is rapid in the legislative staff, many of whom during the war transferred to more lucrative jobs in downtown departments.

Top base salary currently paid Senate standing committee clerks is $3,900 and from $2,760 to $3,300 on the House side. A few career clerks receive additional sums "so long as the position is held by the present incumbent." The Legislative Appropriation Act for fiscal 1946 thus rewarded one House and four Senate committee clerks. The clerks of both Appropriations Committees receive $8,000 each, making them the highest paid standing committee clerks on the Hill. On the Senate side added emoluments are also received by the assistant clerks of Appropriations, Indian Affairs, and Public Lands and Surveys, and by the Finance Committee clerk. On the House side the clerks of Inter-

---

[8] An act of the 76th Congress provides that committee and members' clerks who have held their posts for four years and "whose separation from the service is involuntary and without prejudice shall acquire, upon passing such suitable noncompetitive examination as the Civil Service Commission may prescribe, a classified civil service status for transfer to a position in the classified civil service, "provided the transfer is obtained within "one year from the date of separation."

[9] 71st Congress, 1st Session, House Report No. 22, June 14, 1929, p. 3.

state and Foreign Commerce, Judiciary, un-American Activities, and Ways and Means are compensated above the norm.

At these modest prevailing rates of pay it is not surprising that few employees of the standing committees of Congress are experts in their fields. Some, of course, acquire a certain expertness after long service, like the clerks of the appropriations subcommittees. But by and large there are all too few qualified technicians on committee staffs. Lindsay Rogers has estimated that perhaps 200 congressional employees (including committee and legislative clerks and the parliamentarians) are in positions to influence policy-making.[10] But few of them would claim to be top-notch specialists in the subjects under their committees' jurisdiction. Their forte, rather, is in handling the routine administrative work of their committees, compiling the calendars, doing research, drafting reports, and handling public relations.

Legislative Counsel

In order to complete our picture of the mechanics of the committee system, several useful adjuncts to it deserve mention. One is the Office of Legislative Counsel which was established in 1919 to assist the committees (and if time permits the members) of Congress in the long and intricate process of bill drafting. This office now has some dozen lawyers directed on the House side by the veteran counsel, Middleton Beaman, and on the Senate side by the competent Stephen E. Rice. $90,000 was allowed this office for salaries and expenses during 1945-1946. The two chief counsel are independent officers, appointed by the Speaker of the House and the President *pro tempore* of the Senate, respectively. Each has the power to nominate his own staff, subject to approval by the appointing authority. The small staff of this office has been overworked in recent years and it is generally regarded as desirable that the staff of the Legislative Counsel should be strengthened and that more committees should utilize its services.

For advice on proposed legislation and aid in bill drafting, congressional committees have long looked also to administrative agencies. This practice is a desirable one not only because much modern legislation is concerned with public administration, but also because administrative officials are, on the whole, more familiar than legislators with the concrete conditions to which the statutes are to be applied. Since 1932, however, there has been an increasing tendency for executive

[10] *Op. cit.*, p. 10.

officers to go beyond giving advice on legislation in response to congressional solicitation, and to embody their proposals in the form of fully drafted bills, and to have these bills introduced in Congress by administration supporters after they have been approved by the legislative reference division in the Bureau of the Budget. This growing practice of sending tailor-made "must" legislation to Capitol Hill has aroused the ire of legislators jealous of their constitutional prerogatives.

Legislative Reference Service

Another important cog in the legislative machine is the Legislative Reference Service in the Library of Congress. Created in 1915, this agency now furnishes a variety of general information, digest, abstract, index, legal, research, and other services to the members and committees of Congress. During 1945–1946 it had an appropriation of $198,300 and a staff of 79 persons, of whom 58 were at the professional level. With congressional demands on the Service currently running in the neighborhood of 15,000 a year, it was obviously greatly understaffed and underpaid. Under these conditions, Congress was compelled largely to rely upon experts attached to the executive branch for guidance on the bewildering variety of complex problems that crowded its postwar calendars. At the same time, there was growing recognition in the House and Senate that they had in their own Library unrivalled resources for technical aid on all important public problems. There was also a growing determination that Congress should have its own independent research facilities and a research staff equal in quality to the staff and facilities available to the executive branch of the government and to special interest groups.

A typical expression of the congressional attitude toward staffing was that of Senator La Follette. Writing in the *Atlantic Monthly* of July, 1943, the Senator said: "The question of adequate and expert staff is of vital importance. Undoubtedly one of the great contributing factors to the shift of influence and power from the legislative to the executive branch in recent years is the fact that Congress has been generous in providing expert and technical personnel for the executive agencies but niggardly in providing such personnel for itself."

"One of the traditional powers of Congress over the executive," he continued, "is supposedly control over the purse strings. Obviously, that control cannot be exercised intelligently unless Congress has the facilities and the expert staff to appraise and evaluate appropriations just as the Budget Bureau does. Yet the annual appropriation for the staff of the Bureau of the Budget is 13 times as large as the appropriations for the staff of the Senate and House committees on appropriations combined."

Borrowed Personnel

This parsimony in the staffing of Congress was no doubt responsible for the expanding use by its standing and select committees of specialists borrowed from administrative agencies. The practice of borrowing government personnel is said to be a long-standing one which has attained sizable proportions in present times. Senator Wherry of Nebraska informed the Senate on January 29, 1945, that during the last quarter of 1944 ninety-five persons had been furnished by 25 Government agencies to 14 Senate committees. The total annual rate of pay received by these individuals was reported to be $253,560.

Congressmen are increasingly dubious of this practice. Under it, some think that agency lobbyists appear in the guise of committee advisers and seek to influence legislation in favor of their own agencies. They are sometimes used, it is alleged, by committee chairmen to write speeches or conduct research on subjects of personal interest to them. To curb such abuses and to encourage committees to hire their own help, the Senate adopted a resolution effective January 1, 1946, conditioning payments from its contingent fund in excess of $5,000 upon the approval by its Audit and Control Committee of itemized budgets of their contemplated expenditures to be submitted by investigating committees. The resolution also required such committees to reimburse the departments in advance for the salaries of detailed personnel, and it forbad them to use their services unless funds were available for such reimbursement. Subsequently the effective date of this resolution was postponed to April 1, 1946.

Apart from the staffs associated with the drafting and legislative reference services, and the experts temporarily detailed for special inquiries, mention should also be made of the Joint Committee on Internal Revenue Taxation. Established by the Revenue Act of 1926, this committee had a permanent staff of 17 employees under the able direction of Colin Stam, and a $71,000 expense fund during 1945–1946. The committee is composed of 10 members, of whom five are ranking members of the Senate Finance Committee and five of the House

Committee on Ways and Means. Its staff acts as a fact-finding and advisory agency for these committees in the performance of their investigatory duties concerning the operation and effects of the federal system of internal revenue taxes.

JOINT MACHINERY

Under a bicameral legislative system like ours the process of lawmaking is a dual one in that all laws must run the gauntlet of both houses and win the approval of each. In view of the differences between the two chambers in their politics, tenure, and membership, the possibility of their arriving independently at identical conclusions on legislative measures is quite remote. Obviously, therefore, some machinery and methods of co-operation had to be devised to avoid deadlock and impasse in the performance of congressional functions.

Several devices and procedures have been developed over the years to facilitate joint action. In particular, three mechanisms for the meshing of the legislative gears, unique in parliamentary practice, have been evolved by American legislatures: the joint committee, the conference committee, and the joint staffing of parallel committees.

Joint Committees

Joint committees have been used at intervals from the earliest days of the Republic, mainly for ceremonial and routine administrative purposes and for the conduct of investigations. The First Congress set up select joint committees to prepare conference rules, choose chaplains and arrange for the inauguration of President Washington, for the assignment of space in the Capitol building, and for fixing a time for adjournment. Henry Clay used a joint committee in 1821 to consummate the Missouri Compromise. Joint committees flourished during the Civil War and Reconstruction period when they were formed to investigate the conduct of the war, emancipation and reconstruction, retrenchment and Southern outrages, and the condition of the Indian tribes. During the 54th Congress the subjects of charities in the District of Columbia and free alcohol in the arts were referred to select joint committees.[11] More recent examples of their use have been on revision of the laws (1907), on the Ballinger-Pinchot controversy (1910), to investigate short-term rural credits (1920), veterans' benefits (1932), governmental reorganization (1937), federal expenditures (1941–1945), and the organization of Congress (1945–1946). And Congress has long

[11] McConachie, op. cit., pp. 240–243.

used joint standing committees on enrolled bills (1789), the library (1843), printing (1846), and the disposition of useless papers (1889).

Joint committees have certain obvious advantages. With the rising burden of the public business, they are more economical of the time and energy of busy legislators and administrators, substituting a single inquiry for two separate investigations. Moreover, they accelerate the legislative process—an important consideration in periods of national emergency. The joint committee device also helps to maintain coordinate equality with the executive branch, by preventing it from playing one house off against the other. Furthermore, when measures are matured by joint action in this way, differences between the houses are not likely to arise and require subsequent adjustment in conference with all the attendant evils. For these reasons joint committees are widely and successfully used by state legislatures and have been commended in recent times for more frequent use on war and postwar problems by Congress as well.

In actual practice, however, the House and Senate seldom cooperate in this manner on major matters of public policy, so jealous are the two houses of their independence and prerogatives. The question which house shall supply the chairman is usually answered in favor of the Senate, with the lower House naming a vice chairman. It is the custom, however, of the Joint Standing Committee on Internal Revenue Taxation to elect a chairman and vice chairman annually, alternating these offices between the chairman of Ways and Means and the chairman of Finance—a happy solution of this question and an example others could follow.

Difficulties have also arisen in joint committees over voting, the practice here being to vote per capita and not as representatives of the two houses, which makes it impossible to have an odd number of members so as to avoid ties without giving one group a plurality over the other; although the membership from the House of Representatives is usually, but not always, larger than that from the Senate. The other objections raised against joint committees: that they concentrate power in a few hands, make it difficult to punish recalcitrant witnesses, and are slow to instruct and discharge by concurrent resolution do not seem very weighty today. Nevertheless, each house apparently still prefers to preserve its own freedom of action and to run the risk of having its bills emasculated by the other body rather than to participate in a united inquiry and receive a report which might run counter to its wishes.

Conference Committees

Another main mechanism of joint House and Senate action is the conference committee. Inherited from the English Constitution, the conference committee system is an evolutionary product whose principal threads were woven on the loom of congressional practice into a unified pattern by the middle of the nineteenth century. "By 1852," writes Ada McCown, historian of the origin and development of the conference committee, "the customs of presenting identical reports from the committees of conference in both houses, of granting high privilege to these conference reports, of voting upon the conference report as a whole and permitting no amendment of it, of keeping secret the discussions carried on in the meetings of the conference committee, had become established in American parliamentary practice." [12]

Conference committees are composed of Senators and Representatives, usually three each, appointed by the presiding officers of both houses, for the purpose of adjusting differences between bills they have passed. This device has been extensively used by every Congress since 1789. Of the 1157 laws enacted by the 78th Congress, for example, 107 went through conference and, of these, 36 were appropriation bills on which the House had disagreed to Senate amendments. In practice, most important legislation goes through the conference closet and is there revised, sometimes beyond recognition, by the all-powerful conferees or managers, as they are styled. A large body of law and practice has been built up over the years governing conference procedure and reports. [13]

Suffice it to say here that serious evils have marked the development of the conference committee system. In the first place, it is highly prodigal of members' time. McConachie calculated that the average time consumed in conference was 33 days per bill. Bills are sent to conference without reading the amendments of the other chamber. Despite rules to the contrary, conferees do not confine themselves to matters in dispute, but often initiate entirely new legislation and even strike out identical provisions previously approved by both houses. This happened during the 78th Congress, for instance, when an important amendment to the surplus property bill, which had been approved by both houses, was deleted in conference.

---

[12] Ada C. McCown, *The Congressional Conference Committee* (1927), pp. 254–5.
[13] See *Cleaves' Manual of the Law and Practice in regard to Conferences and Conference Reports* printed in the Senate Manual.

Conference committees, moreover, suffer like other committees from the seniority rule. The senior members of the committees concerned, who are customarily appointed as managers on the part of the House and Senate, are not always the best informed on the questions at issue, nor do they always reflect the majority sentiment of their houses. Furthermore, conference reports must be accepted or rejected in toto without amendment and they are often so complex and obscure that they are voted upon without knowledge of their contents. What happens in practice is that Congress surrenders its legislative function to irresponsible committees of conference. The standing rules against including new and extraneous matter in conference reports have been gradually whittled away in recent years by the decisions of presiding officers. Senate riders attached to appropriation bills enable conference committees to legislate and the House usually accepts them rather than withhold supply, thus putting it, as Senator Hoar once declared, under a degrading duress.

It is also alleged that under this secret system lobbyists are able to kill legislation they dislike and that "jokers" designed to defeat the will of Congress can be inserted without detection. Senator George W. Norris once characterized the conference committee as a third house of Congress. "The members of this 'house,' " he said, "are not elected by the people. The people have no voice as to who these members shall be . . . This conference committee is many times, in very important matters of legislation, the most important branch of our legislature. There is no record kept of the workings of the conference committee. Its work is performed, in the main, in secret. No constituent has any definite knowledge as to how members of this conference committee vote, and there is no record to prove the attitude of any member of the conference committee . . . As a practical proposition we have legislation, then, not by the voice of the members of the Senate, not by the members of the House of Representatives, but we have legislation by the voice of five or six men. And for practical purposes, in most cases, it is impossible to defeat the legislation proposed by this conference committee. Every experienced legislator knows that it is the hardest thing in the world to defeat a conference report." [14]

Despite these admitted evils, impartial students of the conference committee system defend it on net balance as an essential part of the legislative process. Some mechanism for reconciling differences under

[14] "The Model Legislature," address at Lincoln, Nebraska, February 22, 1934. Reprinted in *Congressional Record,* February 27, 1934.

a bicameral system is obviously indispensable. The remedy for the defects of the device is not to abolish it, but to keep it under congressional control. This can be done by enforcing the rules which prohibit the inclusion in conference reports of matter not committed to them by either house and forbid the deletion of items approved by both bodies; by permitting conference managers to report necessary new matter separately and the houses to consider it apart from the conference report; by fixing a deadline toward the close of a session after which no bills could be sent to conference, so as to eliminate congestion at the end of the session—a suggestion made by the elder Senator La Follette in 1919; by holding conferences in sessions open to the public, letting conference reports lie over longer, and printing them in bill form (with conference changes in italics) so as to allow members more time to examine them and discover "jokers." [15]

A drastic remedy for the shortcomings of the congressional conference committee would be to follow the example of Nebraska and adopt a unicameral legislature, thus eliminating the need of conferences. But this is merely an academic suggestion, for neither house of Congress would sign its own death warrant by submitting such a constitutional amendment to the states. Within the bicameral framework perhaps the most promising remedy is to make more use of joint standing committees in the formulation of important bills. It is easier through such committees to prevent differences from arising in the initial stages of bill drafting than it is to compose them after measures have passed both houses. Persuasive testimony on this point was presented to the Joint Committee on the Organization of Congress by Representative Hale of Maine: "A committee of conference is not nearly as well adapted to framing legislation as a joint standing committee. A joint standing committee having agreed upon a bill can generally procure its passage with minor amendments through both bodies. But a committee of conference finds it much harder to get the coordinate branches of the legislature to recede from a position previously taken and concur with the other branch. All sorts of factors of pride and prestige are involved on the presentation of conference reports which are not involved in the report of a joint standing committee."

Joint Staffs

Aside from joint and conference committees, the only other joint mechanism known to congressional practice is the joint staff. Many of

---

[15] Cf. McConachie, op. cit., pp. 247–252, and McCown, op. cit., pp. 268–269.

the congressional commissions and joint committees have had staffs, usually on a temporary or part-time basis. In recent times, for example, the Temporary National Economic Committee (1939–1941), a mixed commission whose membership included three Senators and three Representatives, had a staff of 186 persons at the peak; the Joint Committee on Federal Expenditures (1941–   ) has four employees; while the Joint Committee on the Organization of Congress (1945–1946) had only two persons on its staff. The separate staffs of the corresponding or parallel committees of both houses seldom pool their resources or work together, except perhaps on the occasion of an all too infrequent joint hearing. The Joint Committee on Printing (1846) has long had a staff of three persons, while the outstanding example of joint staffing is afforded by the Joint Committee on Internal Revenue Taxation (1926) whose permanent staff of 17 includes its chief of staff, Colin F. Stam, an assistant chief of staff, executive assistant, technical assistant, two attorneys, two statisticians, three economists, and six clerks. Created by statute and appointed on merit, this joint staff has rendered invaluable service to the members of the Senate Finance Committee and the House Committee on Ways and Means. It offers a model of what a well-staffed joint standing committee can achieve when Congress overcomes its animus against them.[16]

Parallel Committees

The development of parallel or twin committees in both houses with similar functions and jurisdictions also makes for closer connections between them. During the 79th Congress 22 committees in each house had identical names (e.g., Appropriations, Banking and Currency, Civil Service, *et al.*) and nine more had kindred duties although slightly different nomenclature (e.g., those in the fields of agriculture, commerce, foreign relations). It is still true, as it was when Woodrow Wilson described congressional government as government by the standing committees of Congress, that they make little effort to act in concert. Yet there are informal contacts between the corresponding committees of the House and Senate and occasionally concurrent resolutions authorize them to hold joint hearings, a practice to be encouraged and extended.

When Congress sees fit to modernize its committee structure, it might well carry this parallel tendency to completion by creating twin committee systems in both chambers so that each pair of identically-

---

[16] The Joint Standing Committee on the Library (1802) rarely meets and has no clerk or staff.

named committees will have identically-defined jurisdiction over the corresponding area of public policy and administration. The close correlation of the two committee systems would facilitate joint action on measures of mutual interest by means of joint hearings and joint staffs: a practice with a long record of successful operation in the Massachusetts legislature. Such a system of twin committees in both houses would facilitate liaison between them, fix more definitely the responsibility for policy making, and economize the time of busy administrators and legislators alike.

If in addition the administrative branch of the national government were streamlined by a similar division of labor along functional lines, then public policy making and execution could be coordinated by "triangular links" between the great groups of administrative agencies and their opposite number committees in Congress. This ideal pattern, rendered increasingly imperative by the advent of the Atomic Age, would greatly improve the machinery for legislative-executive cooperation in governmental affairs. It would also facilitate the performance by Congress of its legislative and supervisory functions, provide direct channels of communication and cooperation between the two branches, promote more harmonious and unified action in the development of public policies, and overcome the handicap of our system of separated powers.

Procedural Links

In addition to the joint mechanisms described in the foregoing pages, the House and Senate have also been linked together by joint and concurrent resolutions, joint rules, joint sessions, and joint attendance at impeachment trials.

A *joint resolution* is a bill so far as the legislative process is concerned. All joint resolutions except those proposing constitutional amendments are sent to the President for approval and have the full force of law. They are used for incidental, unusual, or inferior legislative purposes such as extending the thanks of the nation to individuals, the invitation to Lafayette to visit America, the welcome to Kossuth, and notice to a foreign government of the abrogation of a treaty. Joint resolutions have also been used to declare our intervention in Cuba, to correct an error in an existing law, to elect managers for the national Soldiers' Home, and to make special appropriations for minor and incidental purposes.

Congress has developed the *concurrent resolution* as a means of expressing facts, principles, opinions, and the purposes of the two houses. Joint committees are authorized by this form of resolution which is binding on neither house until agreed to by both, and which is not sent to the President for approval. It was a concurrent resolution, for example, which early in 1945 launched the joint La Follette-Monroney inquiry into the defects and improvement of our national legislature.

The two houses of Congress early adopted *joint rules* to govern their procedure in matters requiring concurrent action, but they were abrogated in 1876 after a continuous existence of 87 years. Their most useful provisions continue to be observed, however, in practice.

Finally, *joint sessions* of Congress are held in the Hall of the House from time to time to hear the President deliver a message in person or for memorial or ceremonial purposes. Occasionally the House of Representatives or its managers have attended impeachment trials in the Senate chamber. It did not attend at all in the trials of Blount, Swayne, and Archbald; and after attending at the answer of Secretary of War Belknap, the House decided that it would be represented for the remainder of the trial by its managers alone. At the trial of President Andrew Johnson the House, in Committee of the Whole, attended throughout the trial, but this was exceptional.

Possible Innovations

Closer cooperation between the House and Senate in the formulation of party policy on legislative issues might be achieved in two ways: by the holding of joint caucuses or conferences of all the party members of both houses, and by the formation of a legislative council or cabinet composed of the party leaders in each chamber.

The party caucus, as is well known, is a general assembly of the membership of a political party in one house, held to choose the party's candidates for office in the chamber and to determine party policy on pending legislative questions. Each party in each house has its own separate caucus or conference. Joint caucuses of the party members in both houses apparently have never been held. The suggestion has been made that joint caucuses might be held before bills on important matters of public policy are drafted with a view to sounding out party sentiment thereon and evoking party support on both sides for a common program of action, thus reducing the likelihood of later conflicts between the chambers and the need of sending disputed bills to conference. Past experience with party caucuses, however, casts doubt on the efficacy of such a scheme. For it has been found in practice that caucuses, even within one house, tend to become mass meetings at which the party leaders give pep talks that may have some temporary inspirational and educational value, but which rarely, if ever, result in the adoption of definite party directives. Members come, listen to a babel of tongues, and return to vote their personal convictions.

A more promising proposal for promoting cooperation between the two houses calls for the creation of a joint steering committee with power to prepare and initiate a legislative program. Such a Legislative Council or Cabinet, as it is styled, would be composed of the leaders of the majority party in both chambers, including the presiding officers, floor leaders, and the chairmen of the major policy committees. The Council would be charged with the duty of developing a coherent and coordinated legislative program rather than what Roland Young has described as "a jerry-built policy formulated by a hundred different committees." [17] It would seek an organic, overall approach to public problems instead of the piecemeal, splinter approach hitherto prevalent. Composed of the majority party leaders, the Legislative Council would also fix party responsibility for its legislative program on a national level. Serviced by an expert staff, including the secretaries to the majority, such a central committee of Congress could improve coordination between the two houses in the formulation of balanced legislative programs and in the determination of the order of congressional business.

Moreover, the Council, or an executive committee thereof, might well be authorized to meet from time to time with the President and his cabinet, or members thereof, as Thomas K. Finletter has urged,[18] with a view to better liaison between the two branches in policy making and closer collaboration in the conduct of public affairs, both foreign and domestic. Since 1933 ten states, beginning with Kansas, have created similar "legislative councils," composed of a few experienced legislators from both houses, aided by an expert staff, to study and sift legislative proposals.

To be sure, we already have the nucleus of such a joint Legislative-Executive Cabinet on an informal basis in the periodic conferences at the White House which President Roosevelt used to hold with the so-called "Big Four": the Vice President, Speaker Rayburn, and Majority Leaders Barkley and McCormack. Sometimes these meetings, which

---

[17] Roland Young, *This is Congress* (1943), p. 249.
[18] Thomas K. Finletter, *Can Representative Government Do the Job?* (1945), Chapter XI.

President Truman has continued, are also attended by chairmen of committees charged with important pending legislation. Representative George Outland of California has suggested that these meetings be formalized and enlarged to include the minority leaders of both chambers.[19]

We may conclude our analysis of the joint machinery of Congress by saying that, by and large, there is little cooperation between the House and Senate in the early formulative stages of the legislative process; but very considerable collaboration via conference committees in the concluding stages. Yet behind the scenes there is much friendly and informal intercourse between their members and employees, as well as a spirit of mutual respect and deference, which belie superficial signs of separatism.

POLITICAL MECHANISMS

To complete our picture of the machinery of Congress, it remains to consider the political party mechanisms that operate behind the legislative scenes. Although there is no reference to them in the federal constitution or in the rules of the House and Senate, congressional elections have been controlled by political parties ever since Thomas Jefferson and Alexander Hamilton fought over the relative roles of state and national governments in the early days of the new Republic.

From the origin of the two-party system in late seventeenth century England down to today, experience has taught Anglo-Saxon peoples that parliamentary democracy depends for its effective functioning upon the presence of two major political parties. On almost all significant public questions there are in general two main schools of thought —liberal and conservative. In order that these different ideas on matters requiring governmental action may be formulated and enacted into law, the members of a legislative body tend to group themselves into two parties and to evolve some form of party organization, leadership, and voluntary discipline. From time to time third parties, voicing discontent with existing party programs and seeking some change, have made a brief appearance on the American political stage. The Free Soil Party of 1845 and the Progressive Party of 1924 still linger in political memory. But these minor movements are absorbed in time by the major parties and eventually disappear into the wings of obscurity. The presidency is the great prize of American politics. Unless they

---

[19] George E. Outland, "We *Must* Modernize Congress," *Reader's Digest*, February, 1945.

can make a serious bid for the presidency, third parties in the United States soon wither away. Since the dissolution of the insurgent Republicans after World War I, no attempt has been made to build up a third party bloc in Congress. Experience with multiple parties abroad indicates that they are a curse. Leadership becomes impossible and the pursuit of a stable policy unattainable when a ministry has to depend upon shifting coalitions.

For many years political control of the United States Congress has been divided between the Democratic and Republican parties.[20] Both parties have developed machinery for their governance consisting in each house of a caucus or conference, a Committee on Committees, a Committee on Patronage, a Steering Committee, a floor leader, and a party whip.

The Party Caucus

What the Democrats call a "caucus" and the Republicans style a "conference" is the cornerstone of the party organization. It is composed, as we have seen, of all the party members in the chamber. Several days before a new Congress convenes, these organizations hold meetings of their own at which they select their party candidates for important House offices and discuss party policies for the coming session. Since the Senate is a continuing body, its officers remain in office until there is a change in party control of the upper chamber.

For example, early in the second session of the 78th Congress the 38 Republican Senators met and organized themselves into a Minority Conference. They chose Senator Vandenberg as chairman of the conference, Senator Taft as chairman of their Steering Committee, Senator White as their floor leader, and Senator Wherry as party whip. They also appointed a Steering Committee of nine members, including Senators Taft, White, and Wherry and six other members, and named Mr. George H. E. Smith, research assistant to the floor leader, as secretary of the committee. The Steering Committee of the Senate Minority Conference holds weekly meetings while the Senate is in session at which its members discuss problems of party policy, consider their legislative program, and plan their floor tactics. Members of the Minority Conference do not consider themselves bound, however, by decisions of their Steering Committee, and each Republican Senator feels free to take an independent stand on legislative questions according to his

---

[20] Only one Senator and two Representatives belonged to minor parties during the 1st session of the 79th Congress.

personal convictions and the local and group pressures which impinge upon him.

As an instrument of party control the caucus has waxed and waned with the passing years. Under Cannon's regime as Speaker of the House (1903–1911), the Speaker was omnipotent and the majority party caucus was rarely needed or used. But after "Czar" Cannon was shorn of his power in the parliamentary revolution of 1910, the majority caucus became the dominant factor. The Democrats, who captured control of the House in the congressional elections of that year, promptly erected on the ruins of Cannonism a new political structure based on the secret caucus. In a vivid account of the party battles of the 62nd Congress, an astute eye-witness described this shift from "Czar" Cannon to "King Caucus." "Shorn of all pretence," he declared, "the caucus is a cowardly contrivance to manacle the majority and enable a minority to control. Every member who participates in a caucus is bound to abide by the decisions of that caucus, and to carry out its decrees . . . Without the power to bind its members to unanimity, a caucus becomes only a conference." A bare majority (115 members) of the caucus, he concluded, could bind, gag, and deliver not only its own minority, but the House itself. One hundred and fifteen members were more powerful than the other 278 members of the House. A majority of the democratic caucus controlled all legislation. The secret caucus not only decided the issue in advance, but also the exact form in which it should be voted on in the House. Control of Congress was completely in the hands of a minority of representatives from the South.[21] The caucus is still the cornerstone of the political structure of the Democratic Party in the House of Representatives, but it has fallen into disuse during latter years as a weapon of party control. And it was entirely abandoned soon after Cannon's overthrow by the Republican Party, which adopted instead in both houses the conference system for discussing party policy and action without attempting to control the votes of its members.

The Committee on Committees

In each house both major parties also have a Committee on Committees. In the House of Representatives the Republican Committee on Committees is composed of one representative from each state having Republican representation in the House, each state delegation selecting its member on the committee; while the Democratic members of the

[21] Lynn Haines, *Law Making in America* (1912), pp. 9–15.

Ways and Means Committee serve as the Democratic Committee on Committees. These two committees nominate the parties' candidates for the House offices of Speaker, Clerk, Sergeant-at-Arms, and floor leader, for the Committee on Patronage, and for the standing committees of the House. These nominations are later approved by the party caucuses and the majority party candidates are elected by the House. A similar procedure is followed in the Senate, except that nominations of party candidates for elective Senate offices are made only when party control of the upper house changes hands or vacancies occur, and that nominations to the standing committees of the Senate are made only to fill vacancies caused by death, defeat, transfer, or resignation.

The elder Senator La Follette, in the days when "Aldrichism" flourished in the Senate, thus characterized the "committee on committees" system:[22]

Under the present system of choosing the standing committees of the United States Senate a party caucus is called. A chairman is authorized to appoint a committee on committees. The caucus adjourns. The committee on committees is thereafter appointed by the chairman of the caucus. It proceeds to determine the committee assignments of Senators. This places the selection of the membership of the standing committees completely in the hands of a majority of the committee on committees, because in practice the caucus ratifies the action of the committee, and the Senate ratifies the action of the caucus. See now what has happened: The people have delegated us to represent them in the Senate. The Senate, in effect, has delegated its authority to party caucuses upon either side. The party caucus delegates its authority to a chairman to select a committee on committees. The committee on committees largely defers to the chairman of the committee on committees in the final decision as to committee assignments. The standing committees of the Senate as selected, Mr. President, determine the fate of all bills; they report, shape, or suppress legislation practically at will.

The Patronage Committee

In addition to organizing the House, electing its officers, the chairmen of all standing committees and a majority of their members, the party in power controls the patronage through its Patronage Committees. In the House the Committee on Patronage, composed of three members of the majority party, appointed by the Speaker, distributes

---

[22] Quoted by Haines, *op. cit.*, p. 7.

some 200 minor jobs, e.g., doorkeepers and pages, among party members on the basis of seniority. Each majority party member, except committee chairmen, is allowed one patronage employee. The chairmen receive their patronage in the appointment of committee clerks. The ordinary congressman applies to the patronage committee for a job and is assigned one on the basis of seniority. The most popular jobs are those of doorkeepers and pages. During the manpower shortage, Republican appointees were accepted for some positions. No supervision of appointees is undertaken by the Patronage Committee, but if an employee is incompetent, the Patronage Committee will usually discharge him upon the recommendation of his supervisor. The system gives jobs to those (i.e., older men) who might not otherwise be employed. All patronage employees know that they may lose their jobs if a change in party occurs.

In the Senate 99 per cent of all Senate employees in the offices of the Sergeant-at-Arms and the Secretary of the Senate are patronage positions under the Patronage Committee's jurisdiction. All applications for patronage by Senators are addressed to the chairman of the Patronage Committee who refers them to the appropriate office, the committee serving only as a central clearinghouse. Senate patronage jobs include warehouse, telegram office, folding room, and postoffice employees, as well as the Capitol police. The total allotment for patronage jobs on the Senate side is about $360,000. Because of low salaries and insecure tenure, the turnover is heavy. Each majority party Senator is allowed approximately $6,600 worth of patronage. This usually results in four jobs to a Senator with no stipulation about chairmen of committees. Dismissal of Senate patronage employees is analogous to that on the House side.

One hundred and seventeen patronage jobs are allowed in the Office of the Architect. These positions are filled upon the recommendations of the House and Senate Patronage Committees. Of the 117 employees, 92 are elevator operators, 24 are laborers, and one is a clerk. Their total compensation amounts to $139,620. There is a high turnover in patronage positions, and the Architect is anxious to place all employment in his office on a merit basis.

Political patronage includes not only most of the employees of Congress, but also postmasters, rural mail carriers, and many other federal workers scattered throughout the country. In filling these inferior positions as well as the more important posts, it has long been a practice of "senatorial courtesy" for the President to consult the members of his party in both the Senate and House. These spoils of office help to lubricate the extra-constitutional party machinery that links the legislative and executive branches of the national government.

The Steering Committee

Another tool in the congressional political kit is the steering committee. In the House the Democratic Steering Committee has been composed since 1933 of the Speaker, the majority floor leader, the chairman of the caucus, the party whip, the chairmen of Ways and Means, Appropriations, and Rules, and one representative from each of the 15 zones into which the country is divided for party purposes, each such representative being elected by the Democratic delegation from the zone. The Democratic Steering Committee elects its chairman, vice chairman, and secretary and cooperates with the party leaders in the planning and execution of Administration policy.

Since 1933 the Republican Steering Committee in the House has been appointed by the minority leader, who serves as its chairman, with the approval of the Republican Committee on Committees. It has eight members including the minority leader and presently one member each from Iowa, Kansas, Kentucky, Minnesota, Ohio, Pennsylvania and Washington. The chairman of the party conference, the party whip, and the four Republican members of the Committee on Rules sometimes meet with their steering committee.

In the Senate the Democratic Steering Committee is composed of 17 Senators. The majority leader, the party whip, and the secretary of the caucus are ex-officio members. The Republican Steering Committee in the Senate, as noted above, has nine members, including the chairman of the party conference, the floor leader, and the party whip.

According to ex-Senator Byrnes, "these committees seldom meet and never steer." This observation is probably a half-truth, for we know that they do meet from time to time at the call of their chairmen. But it is probably true that they seldom steer—for reasons soon to be noted. These steering committees in the two houses are in reality legislative program or "order of business" committees. They examine the bills pending on the calendars and recommend to the party membership the order in which the unfinished business of the chamber should be considered, subject of course to appropriation bills, conference reports, and executive business—all of which have priority.

Other important cogs in the party machine are the floor leaders, the

party whips, and the House Committee on Rules. The floor leaders—
two in each chamber—are chosen by their respective party caucuses, act
as party leaders on the floor of the house, and have no standing committee assignments in the lower chamber. After the fall of Speaker
Cannon in 1910, the majority floor leader—Oscar Underwood at the
time—became the real leader of the House. He dominated the party
caucus, influenced the rules, and selected the committees as chairman of
Ways and Means. The party whips, who are selected by their floor
leaders, keep the party membership and leadership informed of each
other's wishes, and round up party members for important divisions.

Committee on Rules

Last but far from least in the political hierarchy is the House Committee on Rules whose jurisdiction and powers make it an effective
instrument of majority party control of legislative action. This political
committee, which owes its existence to the constitutional right of the
House to "determine the rules of its proceedings," was a select committee from 1789 to 1849, a standing committee during the 31st and
32nd Congresses (1849–1853), and again select from 1853 to 1880 when
it converted itself rather covertly into a standing committee for the
second time and has so continued ever since. The Rules Committee
has varied in size from five to 14 members. At present (1945) it has
12 members of whom eight are Democrats and four are Republicans.
Six of its members are Southerners, two come from Illinois, and one
each from Michigan, Indiana, Ohio and New York. Rarely has the
region beyond the Rocky Mountains been represented on Rules. The
Speaker was first made a member in 1858 and remained as such until
his removal in 1910.

After the Speaker became a member of Rules in 1858, it gradually
rose to a preeminent position in the congressional committee system.
Thanks to a series of favorable rulings by the Speaker, the Committee
on Rules acquired the power (a) to consider and report special orders,
(b) to sit during sessions of the House, (c) to report matters not
previously committed to it, and (d) to have its reports immediately
considered. By the exercise of these powers the Rules Committee can
sift the business coming from the other 47 committees of the House
and decide which bills shall have the right of way to consideration on
the floor and the order in which they shall be taken up. Through its
power to report new business, it has original as well as secondary

jurisdiction over the legislative agenda. By amending their measures as a condition of giving them a "green light" to the floor, Rules can substitute its own judgment for that of the great legislative committees of the House on matters of substantive policy. It can also determine the duration of debate on a controversial measure and restrict the opportunity to amend it, thus expediting or delaying a final decision.

Moreover, since the Rules Committee is the only channel through which first-degree amendments of the rules can reach the House, it is able to prevent changes in the rules and so prevent parliamentary reform. It can also add to or subtract from the size, jurisdiction, and privileges of the other committees as they win or lose its favor. In short, the Committee on Rules is to a large degree the governing committee of the House. To it the House has largely delegated the power vested in itself by the constitution to regulate its procedure.

Under Cannonism the House Rules Committee was a "sleeping giant," in Haines' apt phrase. But after Cannon was dethroned and the majority floor leader succeeded to the scepter, Rules became an active power. If a majority (7) of its members refuse to report a bill to the House, the other 428 are impotent to compel action. Only by the laborious discharge petition procedure, which requires 218 signatures, can the House force the Rules Committee to act upon any subject over which it has jurisdiction. It can dispose as it pleases, for example, of resolutions for special investigations and of proposed innovations in parliamentary practice. Thus the Kefauver resolution, providing for a report and question period similar to the question hour in the House of Commons, was smothered by this committee, despite a nationwide demand for its trial. On the other hand, the Cox resolution for an investigation of the Federal Communications Commission, introduced by the ranking majority member of Rules after that agency had revealed his receipt of a fee from an Atlanta radio station, won the committee's approval.

Through special rules this powerful committee is able to advance directly, or to retard indirectly, any measure which it selects for passage or slaughter. Three kinds of special rules are handed down by the Rules Committee: (1) "gag rules" limiting amendment of pending measures; (2) rules permitting certain favored legislation to come before the House; and (3) rules which make certain bills the next order of business in order to obstruct others which otherwise would come up for consideration via the usual calendar route. By the exercise of its powers the Rules Committee can also function as a steering committee, steering the House in whatever direction the exigencies of the hour appear to demand.[23]

Whether such concentration of political power in one committee is good or evil depends upon whose ox is gored. By some the practice is defended as a legitimate means for clearly fixing party responsibility and obtaining able and energetic guidance of legislative affairs. In his thorough, readable, and objective history of congressional committees written after a century of their evolution, McConachie penned the following encomium to the Committee on Rules: "Their skill as parliamentarians versed in the peculiar environment, traditions, character, customs, and rules of the House cannot be matched within or without Congress. They know how to gauge accurately and finely the sentiments of the body which they lead, whether on subjects political or non-political, so as to avoid a vote which shows want of confidence. Rarely, if ever, do they make the slip of even introducing a special order which will fail of success. They have come through long personal acquaintance to that frame of political mind wherein, though of different parties, they will much more readily and frequently cooperate than will any five Representatives of opposing faiths whose careers are just beginning. Hence, they often stand shoulder to shoulder in preserving peace where discord would otherwise run rampant between the two large heterogeneous crowds of followers upon the floor. But where word is given for battle upon planks of party creed, the committee of five dwindles to a triumvirate which guides and voices the will of the majority; which works for the maintenance of party unity; which conciliates rebels of its own side of the House when it cannot overawe them, and, if overruled on some rare occasion, submits with good grace that brings the Speaker out of his sanctuary to walk between the tellers and be counted as when he was an ordinary Representative a score of years ago; which arbitrates among great committees of equal privilege, arranging the programme for consideration of their bills by the House; finally, which brings together the chiefs in daily council to hold its touch with the majority within the Congressional Hall and to turn the search-lights out beyond the Capitol over the drifting currents of public opinion. Despotic power cannot build itself upon a two years' tenure . . . This better legislative machinery has come in the rise of the Committee on Rules and of the informal steering committee of which it is the nucleus . . . Here is a revival and perpetuation of that unity of lawmaking which characterized those

---

[23] Haines, *op. cit.*, pp. 22–27.

first years when the Committee of the Whole on the State of the Union held the primacy for the formulation of laws. A better century has begun, wherein the American House of Representatives will express more readily and truly the more easily known will of the people." [24]

Those who in our own time believe in more definite fixation of party responsibility and in more effective legislative leadership, as means both of holding political parties accountable for the performance of campaign pledges and of correcting the existing dispersion of leadership in Congress, will presumably take a complacent view of the situation. Willoughby, for example, has suggested strengthening the Rules Committee by making its Republican and Democratic members the executive committee of the two caucuses in the House, with the power of selecting the chairmen of committees and making all committee assignments.[25] If it were also given the function of formulating the parties' legislative programs, its collective responsibility would be complete and the legislative command would be unified.

There are those like Senator O'Mahoney, on the other hand, who fear concentrated authority in any form and who would, therefore, be vehemently opposed to any further steps in that direction. Others, like Representative Herter, former Speaker of the Massachusetts Legislature, think that the Rules Committee should function only as a traffic director on the legislative highway, deciding the order of business but without authority to pass upon the merits of bills or to block the presentation of favorable committee reports to the House. Congressman Adams of New Hampshire, former Speaker of its House—the largest legislative body in the land—believes that unanimous committee reports should automatically have the right of way to the House floor. And advocates of progressive social legislation, such as the Fair Employment Practices Committee, have denounced the House Rules Committee as "cartelism in Congress" and a bottleneck operated by "reactionary" Southerners. Of the 12 members of Rules, six are Democrats from Southern or border states. For all practical purposes that is a working majority. And two of the six are veteran masters of parliamentary manipulation. They stand guard at the legislative gates and test all applicants for admission by their own political and sectional predilections.[26]

---

[24] McConachie, *Congressional Committees* (1898), pp. 204–207.

[25] W. F. Willoughby, *Principles of Legislative Organization and Administration* (1934), p. 554.

[26] See "D-Day on Capitol Hill" by Senator Wayne L. Morse, *Collier's*, June 15, 1946.

The Senate Committee on Rules resembles its namesake in the House in name only. It is essentially a housekeeping committee, having jurisdiction under standing orders over the Senate wing of the United States Capitol and the Senate Office Building. It issues rules for the regulation of these buildings which are carried out by the Architect of the Capitol, the Sergeant-at-Arms, and other Senate officers and employees. So far as the organization and parliamentary practice of the Senate is concerned, this committee has the reputation of being little more than a graveyard for proposed parliamentary reforms. Its 13 members average 64 years of age and are quite wedded to the good old ways of doing things. The conservatism of old age has apparently long controlled the Senate Rules Committee. Fifty years ago McConachie remarked that the older members "are upon the inside of the Rules Committee room, braced against the doors, and only death carries them away." [27]

Speaker of the House

No account of the political machinery of Congress would be complete without a description of that outstanding figure—the Speaker of the House of Representatives.

Under the constitution the Speaker is one of the elective officers of the House. Incumbents of this office since 1789 have been both presiding officers and political leaders of the lower chamber, as the colonial speakers were before them. The speakership is an office of great honor and influence and is always held by a member of the House. Each of the major political parties nominates a candidate for the office in caucus and the House elects the candidate of the majority party at the opening of each new Congress. The nominees for this coveted place are usually men who have served in the House for many years, have learned the legislative ropes, and have won the esteem and confidence of their colleagues.

Forty-six Speakers and Speakers pro tem have presided over the House since 1789. Fourteen had formerly been speakers of their state legislatures and 23 others had prior state legislative experience. Muhlenberg, Clay, and Pennington were elected to the office in their first terms in the House. Every other Speaker served in the House from one to 14 terms before his election. Since 1900 no Speaker has served less than

[27] In 1946, however, the Senate Rules Committee approved the creation of a special committee to consider legislative reorganization which brought in the La Follette reform bill.

eight terms before his elevation. Many famous men have occupied the chair: among them Clay, Polk, Colfax, Blaine, Reed, Cannon, Clark, Gillett, and Longworth. Henry Clay served as Speaker for 12 years throughout his entire career in the House, holding the record for the longest period in the chair.

Eight of the first 46 Speakers were New England members, nine represented Middle Atlantic states, ten came from the Middle West, and 19 were Southerners. Every Democratic Speaker since the Civil War, except Rainey of Illinois, has been from the South. Unlike the Northern and Western states, the South tends to return its representatives to Congress term after term, thus building up seniority and power in party councils.

The Speaker of the House derives his powers and duties from the constitution, the rules of the House, previous decisions of the chair, and general parliamentary law. He presides at sessions of the House, announces the order of business, puts questions and reports the vote. He also decides points of order and can prevent dilatory tactics, thanks to the earlier rulings of Speaker Reed. He appoints the chairmen of the Committee of the Whole and the members of select and conference committees. He chooses Speakers pro tem and refers bills and reports to the appropriate committees and calendars. He also enjoys the privileges of an ordinary member of the House and may vote and participate in debate on the floor.

But the Speaker is more than a mere presiding officer. He is also the political leader of the party in power in the lower chamber and wields great influence behind the scenes upon the character and conduct of the legislative business. His political powers gradually evolved during the nineteenth century, reaching their zenith under the masterful leadership of Speakers Reed and Cannon. Finally in 1910 the House rebelled against the despotism of "Czar" Cannon and a coalition of Democrats and insurgents Republicans led by George W. Norris combined to clip his powers in the famous March revolution of that year. They removed the Speaker from the Rules Committee of which he had formerly been chairman. They stripped him of the power to appoint the standing committees of the House and their chairmen which he had previously possessed and exercised as a powerful weapon of party discipline. And they restricted his former right to recognize or refuse to recognize members seeking to address the House.

In the event, however, these reforms have proved to be less drastic than they seemed at the time they were achieved. Although the Speaker is no longer a member of the Rules Committee, he still dominates it. He cannot compel it to act, but he can thwart it when it does act. For its majority members are not appointed unless they are *persona grata* to him, and he can prevent the adoption of any rule reported by that committee of which he disapproves by getting one of his trusted lieutenants to make a point of order against the rule on some technicality and by sustaining it. There is no effective appeal from decisions of the chair on points of order under the existing rules of the House. When it is recalled that no legislative business can be considered by the House until it has approved a rule reported by the Rules Committee granting such business the right of way to the floor, it will be realized what a potent whip hand the Speaker holds over both the Committee on Rules and the House itself. The only way to liberate Rules from its subservience to the Speaker would be to amend the rules of the House so as to provide for the decision of points of order by majority vote of its members. And the only chance to make such a change in the rules would be during the brief interval at the opening of a new Congress after the House has convened and before the election of the Speaker.

Although the Speaker lost his power in the revolution of 1910-11 of appointing the standing committees of the House, he still appoints the select committees, the House members of conference committees at the suggestion of the chairmen of the committees in charge of the bills, and the chairman of the Committee of the Whole. His power of recognition was then reduced, but he still has a discretionary power of recognition over motions to suspend the rules and on days other than consent calendar days. Prior to 1910 the Speaker controlled the House in collaboration with a coterie of trusted party lieutenants. Since 1910 the leadership of the House has been in commission. The chief difference between the old oligarchy and the new is that control of the House was formerly open, centralized, and responsible, whereas today it is invisible, dispersed, and irresponsible. Formerly the country could see the wheels go round, but now it cannot. Despite the overthrow of Cannonism, the speakership thus continues to be the most powerful office in Congress.

PARTY RESPONSIBILITY

In the foregoing pages I have described the several cogs in the party machinery of Congress. But this machinery will not propel itself like a modern rocket bomb. It is merely a set of mechanisms for the selection of party leaders, the development of party policies, the discussion and crystallization of party programs, the determination of party strategy, and the enforcement of party discipline. When, as in recent times, there are diverse schools of thought on public policies within a party, when political parties are merely loose coalitions of autonomous elements, and when party members refuse to abide by group decisions, then party machinery fails to achieve its full potentialities.

The development of greater party responsibility and accountability is being emphasized as a prime desideratum of a more effective democracy.[28] Witnesses who testified at the hearings of the Joint Committee on the Organization of Congress in 1945 declared that our party machinery could be more effectively used to ascertain party sentiment, to formulate more consistent legislative programs, and to integrate the various parts of the legislative structure. Political parties are obligated, it was argued, to carry out the promises made in the platforms of the victors, as well as the identical or equivalent pledges set forth in the platforms of the vanquished. And this obligation was held to rest especially upon party officers in Congress, including not only the titular leaders but also the chairmen of influential committees.

It is easier to declare such a duty than it is to enforce it, for several reasons. To hold political parties responsible for their acts or failure to act is difficult when, as at present, both major parties are split into liberal and conservative factions. Nowadays, moreover, members of Congress are the focus of many conflicting pressures from their states and districts as well as elsewhere. The general platitudes of party platforms and political philosophies afford no infallible guidance to the politician beset by complex, concrete issues. Meanwhile, the onward sweep of science and technology has been dissolving, with a psychological lag to be sure, the traditional sectional divisions and political alignments of the American people. Regions once predominantly agricultural and mineral, like the South and West, are becoming industrialized, with resulting admixtures of new social elements and political ideas. Hereditary voting, though still a potent form of "American ancestor worship," as Brogan says, is on the wane; and independent voting, which makes for fickle party allegiance in Congress, is increasing. Under a system where both major parties stand for everything and are not sharply divided along class or economic lines, party responsibility for specific programs of action is difficult to

---

[28] Cf. Robert Heller, *Strengthening the Congress* (1945), p. 3. And *Hearings* before the Joint Committee on the Organization of Congress, *passim*.

attain. It is further weakened when, as in the United States, national elections are held by the calendar at biennial and quadrennial intervals rather than, as in England, when some great controversy has precipitated a general referendum.

While party irresponsibility seems an evil to those seeking the prompt performance of campaign promises, it has been a fortunate feature of American politics that our two major parties have traditionally divided along vertical and not horizontal lines, having their Right and Left "lunatic fringes," but meeting at the center upon almost common ground on matters of fundamental principle. It may be, as some observers suggest, that a new alignment of American political forces is in the making, with conservatives and liberals tending to coalesce in opposing camps. If such a readjustment of the American party structure materializes, it may make for greater party responsibility and accountability. But as the economic and social bases of party composition became more distinct, the chances of compromise between conflicting interests, which has been the happy alembic of our political life, might correspondingly diminish.

Proposed Innovations

There are several conceivable ways in which party government in Congress could be strengthened. One way would be to abandon the usage which prohibits anyone from seeking to represent in the House of Representatives a district in which he does not himself reside. The constitution requires that a Representative must, when elected, be an inhabitant of the state in which he is chosen, but beyond that it imposes no geographical limitation. This medieval practice, a survival of the intense localism of colonial days, has caused incalculable loss to the public life of America and has set local above national interests. It has also discouraged the candidacy of our ablest citizens and has facilitated local raids on the national treasury. Now that Washington has become the political capital of the world, the result of this ancient usage is to bring the vision of a parish to the politics of a planet. In England party discipline is more effective because the party directorates control the distribution of constituencies. If a member of Parliament does not follow the party line in the House, he can be deprived of a place to represent at the next general election. Abolition of the residence requirement here would probably strengthen party control, but the usage is so long-standing that there is little likelihood of its abandonment.

Another way would be to arm party leaders in Congress with sanctions to discipline recalcitrant members. Those who refused to abide by party decisions might be deprived of patronage or, which would be a worse penalty, of their committee assignments. This happened in 1925 when the insurgent Republicans, who had bolted their party to support La Follette for President in 1924, were read out of the party and denied their former committee posts when the Republicans organized the House in the 69th Congress.[29]

Party government in Congress could also be fortified by the creation of a joint or single caucus, as Willoughby has suggested, composed of all the members of a party in both chambers. The joint caucus would be a mechanism making possible united action on party policies and programs, as well as common counsel with the Executive. But it would be cumbersome in size, probably difficult to manage, and would impair the cherished independence of the two houses.

The most promising remedy for the diffusion of party responsibility in our national legislature is the proposal to establish a Legislative Cabinet or Council. Let the party in power in Congress through its caucus appoint a group of its recognized leaders—the Vice President and Speaker, the two floor leaders, and the chairmen of the major committees—and let it hold them collectively responsible for formulating the party's legislative program, in consultation with the President, and for pushing it to adoption. The Legislative Cabinet would include the leaders of the majority party in both houses. If the Senate and House were controlled by opposing parties, the Legislative Cabinet would be bipartisan. The Cabinet would be collectively and publicly responsible to the Congress, the party in power, and the country for the conduct of legislative business. It would formalize the existing informal and secret steering committees, bringing them out from behind the scenes into a place of public prominence. If defeated in either house on any important party measure, the Legislative Cabinet would resign and the party caucus would elect a new floor leader who in turn would select new committee chairmen.[30]

The Legislative Cabinet idea has won wide support both within and without Congress. It was endorsed by many Congressmen who testified before the Joint Committee on the Organization of Congress. It has been recommended by the Committee on Congress of the American

---

[29] See Henry A. Wallace, "Party Responsibility," *Colliers*, June 22, 1946.

[30] This feature is not an indispensable part of the proposal, but it would make for responsible party government within Congress.

Political Science Association and many writers. James F. Byrnes advocated it in a notable article on "Streamlining Congress" in the *American* magazine. Robert Heller made an equivalent proposal for "majority and minority policy committees" in his well known report on strengthening Congress, conceiving these committees as devices by which the voters could test the performance of party promises made in election campaigns. And Lawrence H. Chamberlain, in a thoughtful analysis of the problem, summed up the arguments in its favor as follows:[31]

The party assumes the responsibility of selecting its acknowledged leaders to represent it; the leaders accept the responsibility of formulating a program which represents the national interest as they see it and which they in their political wisdom believe to be within the limits of practical attainment; they present this program to the country and defend it to the best of their ability. The voters, convinced of the integrity of these leaders, whether they agree with their point of view or not, are in a much better position to judge the issues and pass judgment upon the final decisions of the Congress. Our political system will not have been changed; demagoguery will not have been eliminated; individual congressmen will still vote their convictions or record the wishes of those who dominate their constituency. But it will be easier to judge the party in power by its works, as distinguished from its promises, and, perhaps, even its promises will be more significant than formerly.

Strengthening Party Government and Responsibility

One of the avowed aims of the recommendation for majority and minority policy committees is to strengthen party responsibility and accountability. Creation of such policy committees will go far to achieve this objective.

But a basic obstacle to party unity will still remain: the uncoordinated terms and timing of the election of President, Vice President, and members of both houses of Congress. The fact that two-thirds of the Senate are not up for reelection in the presidential year, that all the members of the House are up for election for only half the President's term, and that the rival major party may capture control of the House in the mid-term elections—is not conducive to party unity. For opposing parties to control the White House and either or both houses of Congress is the very negation of party responsibility. Here is

---

[31] Lawrence H. Chamberlain, "Congress—Diagnosis and Prescription," *Political Science Quarterly,* September, 1945, p. 445.

a defect in the national scheme of elections that cannot really benefit either party, that is destructive of the principle of party responsibility, and that can be very detrimental to the country—as was clearly shown in Mr. Hoover's last two years as President.

Professor William Anderson has suggested that the way to avoid this potential destruction of party responsibility and to improve legislative-executive relations is to synchronize the election of the President, Vice President, and all members of both houses by giving them all four-year terms and electing them all at once.[32] If all the members of a major party who seek election to a national office had to stand together in each campaign, all would have a common interest in and responsibility for the success of the administration. They would swim or sink together, instead of each member having his own little safety raft and a corresponding lack of responsibility for the party as a whole. They would have a full four years in office to prove their capacity, because there would be no off-year elections.

The rival party could come up once in four years with all the members of its best team seeking office at the same time against the party in power. Each party would find it more necessary, both when in and out of power, to retain a united front. The executive would have to consult more with the party leaders in Congress, and they with him. The party members in both houses would have to take a greater interest in the nominee for President, in the party platform, and in the success of the party as a whole. In the campaign more attention and support would have to be given to the candidates for seats in Congress.

This step forward could be taken, it is argued, without any change in the constitutional provisions that govern the powers and the relations of Congress and the President. Each would have the same constitutional powers and position as at present. The change would consist simply in the creation of conditions that would conduce to a greater sense of joint responsibility on the part of the President and the majority in the two houses of Congress.

---

[32] *Suggestions for Strengthening Congress,* a print of the Joint Committee on the Organization of Congress, June, 1946, pp. 34–39.

5.

Reorganizations in the Past

RECENT EFFORTS TO improve the machinery and methods of Congress have encountered surprisingly little overt opposition. Formidable if hidden resistance may be expected, however, from the beneficiaries of the seniority custom. This is the custom under which the chairmanships of the standing committees automatically go to the majority party members who have had the longest, uninterrupted service on them; a custom which dates back to the earliest years in the Senate, but only to 1910 in the House. Committee chairmen, and ranking minority members who expect to become chairmen when the minority of today becomes the majority of tomorrow, are naturally not enthusiastic about changes in the committee system which might clip their privileges and powers. And the ranking majority members who would become chairmen if the latter died or resigned probably feel the same way. With 81 standing committees at present (1946), there is thus a strong bloc of 243 of the older Senators and Representatives who have a vested interest in the status quo.

These gentlemen have sometimes been heard to say that Congress has gotten along pretty well with practically the same setup for 150 years, so why change now?

There are three obvious answers to this line of argument. In the first place, the country has experienced an industrial revolution since 1789 which has radically altered and complicated the conditions facing Congress. In the second place, the contemporary decline in the efficiency and prestige of Congress indicate that the time has come for another reorganization. And, in the third place, Congress has reorganized itself several times in the course of its history to cope with changing conditions. Agitation for the reorganization of Congress is no new thing; and, if the present agitation results in such a reorganization, this also will not be out of line with precedent.[1]

From its very earliest days, Congress, especially the House, has many times altered its organization and procedure. Some of these reorganizations were relatively minor, consisting merely in the addition or dropping of a single committee. On the other hand, there have been other reorganizations which have profoundly altered the previously established equilibrium of power, bringing far-reaching changes in their train. An institution such as Congress is a living thing, possessing, it is true, an underlying permanent role under the Constitution, but with an ever-changing sphere of activity. Like any social organism, growth and change are of its very essence, always providing that the organism is not false to its fundamental purpose.

Causes of Organizational Change

The changes in organization, and even more those in procedure, have chiefly been changes made necessary by the steady and of late the tremendously rapid growth in the magnitude, complexity, and number of problems which Congress must face. In many instances, these changes have taken the form of additional committees, especially of late a greater use of the select, special, or investigating committee. Procedural changes designed to render more orderly and more effective the use of the time of members and of the houses as a whole have also been frequent. Apart from procedural changes, the growing congestion of business has resulted in some increase in the staff facilities of Congress and even more in greater reliance on the part of Congress upon research and advice from the executive branch.

Besides the changes in congressional organization caused by the growth in its responsibilities, the greatest other single factor producing organizational change has undoubtedly been the search for an acceptable equilibrium between strong leadership verging on dictatorship, on the one hand, and a democracy approaching disorganization on the other. Somewhere in between these two poles, the House (and to a lesser extent, the Senate) has sought to find a combination of responsible leadership and orderly democratic participation which would realize the ideal of our system of government. The pendulum has swung back and forth. When democracy in Congress became too

---

[1] For the remainder of this chapter I am indebted to an unpublished manuscript in the files of the Legislative Reference Service, Library of Congress, prepared by Ernest S. Griffith and A. D. Sarkissian.

splintered and dispersive, controls, chiefly of party, have been reflected in organizational and procedural changes looking toward a stronger leadership. When the hand of such leadership became too heavy, a revolt has come which has expressed itself in the democratization of organization and procedure.

In recent decades, a new factor making toward organizational change has entered the picture. This is the tremendous growth in function, power, and responsibility of the Executive. This growth goes far beyond anything associated merely with war. Ultimately it is the result of the complexities of a technological age—an age which is also an age in which the common man has demanded that his voice be heard. Much of the current discussion of proposals for the reorganization of Congress arises consciously or unconsciously out of the desire to recover the earlier position of Congress as a more effective instrument in the American system. The Select Committee of the House to Investigate Executive Agencies in a recent report put the matter as follows:[2]

Today a large percentage of the most important legislation which is introduced in, and eventually passed by, the Congress does not truly originate there. In fact, a very large percentage of so-called administrative measures are painstakingly drafted after thorough study and briefing by the very executive officials who are intended to be the recipients of the powers which the legislation delegates. Furthermore, these same officials are generally the only expert and fully informed witnesses to testify before the legislative committees of the Congress having jurisdiction over the proposed bills. If there are opposing witnesses, they do not, as a rule, represent the Congress or the people generally but rather some special interest group. . . .

It may well be added that not only are the scales tipped in favor of the passage of all administrative proposals but are also heavily weighted in opposition to any congressional move to retract and recall powers previously delegated to executive agencies and officials. Nor, in case of sharp disagreement with the Executive on the part of Congress, is there adequate means of developing the constructive congressional program to meet the problem in question which the American form of government certainly contemplates in such instances.

The framers and ratifiers of the constitution never contemplated that the legislative branch of the Government which they set up would become a mere ratifying body of a supreme executive will. It is, of course, entirely proper that the executive branch of Government should make known its

---

[2] House Report No. 1912, 78th Congress, 2d Session, p. 2.

needs and its program to the Congress. The constitution so provides. However, it is highly improper for the Congress to enact legislation, no matter what its source, without having fully considered it from every point of view, particularly that of the general public interest.

Thus far the chief organizational change which Congress has developed in response to this situation has been to increase the number of investigations conducted either by special committees or by the standing committees or subcommittees thereof. Other changes in organization and procedure have been suggested, such as bringing the cabinet members on the floor of the House, arranging for regular appearances of members of the executive before the standing committees, and an increase in the staff aids available to Congress. In this latter connection, the staff of the Joint Committee on Internal Revenue Taxation, the temporary additions to the staffs of the Appropriations Committees, and the actual and proposed increases in the Legislative Reference Service illustrate possible further changes of this character.

Changes in organization have been made more frequently in the House than in the Senate. The former, as the larger body, is more complex and offers potentially more opportunity to divide up the work. Not only in procedure, which is much more formalized in the House than in the Senate, but in organization as well, a more detailed and complex structure has evolved.

This chapter deals ostensibly with changes in organization. However, the line between changes in organization and changes in procedure is difficult to draw. For example, some of the most important alterations in the power and place of the Rules Committee in the functioning of the House have been made by procedural changes. Procedural changes such as these must necessarily be included if they form an integral part of a given reorganization. Changes in both organization and procedure are part of a common development concerned sometimes with smoother functioning, sometimes with the location of power, sometimes with the reassertion of the authority of Congress itself.

Efforts at reorganization are not the peculiar bent of any one political party. Reorganizations have been proposed and carried through, not only by both of the two great parties of the present day, but also by the Whigs and Federalists during their time in power. Both Republicans and Democrats have concerned themselves with the more effective operation of the Congress and its party leadership, and not infrequently the actual move resulting in reorganization has had bipartisan support. The story that follows is essentially chronological.

REORGANIZATION IN THE HOUSE OF REPRESENTATIVES

The organization of Congress during its early years was quite simple. Precedents for the most part seem to have been unconsciously established rather than consciously thought out. Some of those dating from this period are with us to this day.[3]

1789–1812

It seems to have been the idea at the outset that most of the significant deliberations of the House would be in its general sessions. Only gradually did the advantage appear of thorough consideration of measures in their initial stages through the medium of committees. Yet this advantage did appear, and the further advantage of designating certain committees as standing committees to handle all related measures had resulted in the establishment of six standing committees by 1800, and ten by 1810. Nevertheless the special committee remained the characteristic method of handling legislation till after the War of 1812. These committees were numbered in the hundreds in most sessions.

During its first year, the House balloted for its more important committees. The Speaker appointed those with three or less members. However, in 1790 the rule was passed that all committees should be appointed by the Speaker unless the House especially directed otherwise. In 1796 the Speaker was also given the power to appoint the chairman of the Committee of the Whole, the early custom of nominating and electing him having failed to work satisfactorily.

Many of the standing committees were associated with the emergence of special problems. The Louisiana purchase was shortly followed by making the Public Lands Committee a standing committee. In 1808 the Committee on the District of Columbia entered the same category, and the development of highways elevated the Post Office and Post Roads Committee to the same status in the same year.

At first it was customary to give representation to each state on the

[3] Information concerning this period has been obtained chiefly from the following sources: McConachie, L. G., Congressional Committees (New York, 1898), pp. 133f., 349ff.; Willoughby, W. F., Principles of Legislative Organization and Administration (Washington, 1934), pp. 332, 345; Wilson, W., Congressional Government (Boston, 1900), p. 104f.; McCown, A. C., The Congressional Conference Committee (New York, 1927), p. 38.

important committees. This eventually made the committees unwieldy, and the practice gradually faded. However, geographic representation on committees has remained a factor in committee assignments down to the present time.

So far as one can judge, the use of rules and changes in organization as devices to obtain or retain power had not as yet put in its appearance. The structure was simple, and it was not yet clear even at the end of the period that the standing committee would dominate. From the very outset a conference committee of representatives of the two houses was appointed as the method of adjusting differences, and this procedure has continued to the present day.

1812–1860

During this period, the standing committee became the established device for consideration of congressional business. It was also a period in which the struggle for power expressed itself occasionally in changes or attempted changes in rules and organization. The structure of Congress was becoming more complex, but this complexity had not as yet reached the point at which it could be used by obstructionists as a method of reducing the legislative body to a position approaching impotence.[4]

The era of good feeling under President Monroe witnessed the establishment of a number of additional standing committees, enough collectively to constitute an important reorganization of the structure of the House. In 1814 a standing committee on national expenditures was created, and in 1816 six additional committees on expenditures were established for the various departments. This was in response to the current clamor for a general house cleaning of the executive branch. By 1820, the Committee on Commerce, Industry and Agriculture was replaced by three committees representing the three constituent parts of the committee's work. In 1822, committees were set up on military and naval affairs and foreign affairs. The standing committees on Indian affairs and territories dated from about the same time.

Between 1825 and 1860 there were virtually no organizational changes of any consequence. The Roads and Canals Committee was established in 1831, and Patents and Public Buildings and Grounds in

---

[4] Information concerning this period has been obtained chiefly from the following sources: McConachie, *op. cit.*, p. 134; Alexander, D. S., History and Procedure of the House of Representatives (Boston, 1916), pp. 32, 190; Atkinson, D. R., Committee on Rules and the Overthrow of Speaker Cannon (New York, 1911), pp. 17, 20, 28.

1837. There were also a number of minor changes, some sporadic and some permanent, which might be regarded as straws in the wind. For instance, in 1841 the Rules Committee, which hitherto had been without special privileges, was given power to report "at all times." This made the majority potentially the master of the House. From 1849 to 1853 the Rules Committee was made a standing committee, but in the latter year it reverted again to its more temporary status. In 1849 a protracted struggle over the Speaker had led temporarily to provision for his election by plurality vote, if a majority was unobtainable after three ballots. However, the House subsequently reverted to the early practice of selection of the Speaker by majority vote, and this practice has remained with only occasional deviations ever since. In 1853 the rules were amended to give the Rules Committee priority in its reports, although it was no longer a standing committee. In 1858 the Speaker became its chairman. It later became apparent that this move was one of the most important developments in House organization, although it was quite casually introduced at the time.

1860–1889

This period was characterized by a growing complexity in the economic and social organization of the nation which in turn was reflected in a more intricate organization of the House. It was a period characterized by intense resistances within Congress both to organizational change and, for that matter, to legislation of any sort. The minority became adept in utilization of rules to block the will of the majority, and the end of the period found an extremely decentralized power system prevailing within the House.[5]

The Civil War period witnessed the establishment of one of the most important joint select committees of the two houses Congress has ever known. This was the so-called committee on the conduct of the Civil War. It originated primarily to investigate the disaster of Ball's Bluff, but exercised a roving commission thereafter to look into all sorts of matters connected with the war effort. A similar assertion of congressional interest in the Executive was the Joint Select Committee on Retrenchment (1866–1872), a forerunner incidentally of Civil Service reform.

1865 brought an important reorganization of the committee system.

---

[5] Information (other than that specially cited) concerning this period has been obtained chiefly from the following sources: Alexander, op. cit., pp. 128, 196, 235; McConachie, op. cit., pp. 233, 243; Wilson, op. cit., p. 114.

Hitherto the Ways and Means Committee had united within itself both revenue and appropriation. The dual job had become far too onerous for the same people to handle, and the Appropriations Committee was formed as an offshoot. By 1876 the Appropriations Committee itself was given an enormous increase in its functions by a change in rules which declared "any general legislation that was germane to a bill to be in order if retrenching expenditure." [6] This left the door wide open for the committee to deal with legislation of a general nature. During the next four years the committee became so powerful that a reaction inevitably set in. In 1880 the Committee on Commerce and the Committee on Agriculture were given power to report appropriation proposals directly to the House, and in 1885 the functions of the Appropriations Committee were still more widely dispersed by the setting up of eight independent appropriations committees corresponding generally to the executive departments. This dispersion was the final outcome of the resentment against its chairman's (Randall) alleged arbitrary conduct.

. . . Randall's high tariff views had prevented his reelection as Speaker on the return of his party to power, but he could not be denied his former committee chairmanship, the post of power on the floor. There he successfully opposed his own party on the tariff and was accused even of overriding the Senate by holding back appropriation bills. He certainly used these bills to control other legislation in the House. It was not enough for a member to arrange with the Speaker for recognition on his pet bill. He must also "see" Randall, or a privileged appropriation bill would be clapped in the way. In revolt against this dictatorship, the following Congress broke the single control of appropriation bills by Randall's committee and distributed them among thirteen committees. . . . [7]

There were other evidences of the prevalent dispersive action which was scattering the earlier concentration of leadership. The selection of committees by the Speaker was threatened in 1881 by the proposal to substitute selection of committees by a committee chosen by the caucus. This move failed because the motivation of the member proposing it was suspect, even though many sympathized with his allegation that the Speaker used his power to favor particular points of view in particular committee assignments. In 1883 the growth of internal im-

---

[6] Luce, R., Legislative Problems (Boston, 1935), p. 373.
[7] Rowell, C. H., "The Next Step in Washington." World's Work, Dec. 1924, v. 49, p. 161.

provements had reached the point at which jealousy of the power of the Committee on Commerce resulted in setting up the separate Committee on Rivers and Harbors. All these devices were in the direction of dispersion of responsibility.

In the direction of greater authority, a proposal was made in the early 80's to establish an executive committee empowered to examine and sort the bills reported by the other standing committees. This was lost. However, in 1883 the Committee on Rules was given a potentially important power to report so-called special orders which provided times and methods for consideration of particular bills.

. . . In 1883, the exceedingly important power was conferred upon the Committee on Rules to report what are known as "special orders" providing times and methods for consideration of particular bills. This grant of power, or, to speak more correctly, assumption of power by the committee, had three important results; one, to place it within the power of the House to suspend the rules for the purpose of taking up a bill out of order by a majority vote, since the special rule reported by the committee could be adopted by such a vote; two, to increase the power of the majority party to control legislative proceedings and order of business, since such party could usually command a majority, but often not a two-thirds vote of the House; and, three, greatly to increase the power and influence of the Committee on Rules.[8]

In spite of these attempts at some measure of correlation, the period as a whole represented the most extreme decentralization of power and responsibility in the House reached during modern times.

1889-1910

This was the era of the "special orders." It was marked by the use of the powers of the Rules Committee by the Speaker to govern the time of the House.[9]

A reaction against the earlier decentralization was inevitable and this reaction took the form of a tremendous growth in the power of the Speaker of the House. The period ended with signs of an approaching revolt against this extreme concentration of power. From the elevation of Thomas B. Reed to the speakership in 1889 dates the ascendancy of the incumbent of this office.

---

[8] Willoughby, op. cit., p. 452.
[9] For a good account of the period (other than those otherwise cited) see: Atkinson, op. cit.

Reed stated at the very outset that it was his intention to protect majority rights over against the minority obstructionists.

In the beginning of Reed's reign as Speaker, the House was characterized by more of mobbishness than ever before or since. Members were ungoverned and ungovernable. Students of that parliamentary period will remember the "no quorum" difficulties that so often completely obstructed the public business; and that under certain privileged motions a half dozen men could filibuster for hours, days or weeks, whenever the spirit moved them.

In this crisis came Reed and the Reed rules. The situation seemed to justify an extreme remedy, and that was the kind provided. Reed ruled over the refractious few with an iron hand. He enlarged the powers of the Speakership. He broke ground and sowed seeds which later ripened into Cannonism.[10]

Reed's rulings were eminently designed to prevent anarchistic filibustering. Reed's successor, Crisp, for the most part continued the same trend. Under the first real test of the priority to be accorded the special orders from the Rules Committee, the rule was vindicated. In 1893 the Rules Committee was given power itself to originate special rules and orders and was allowed to meet at any time. This gave the committee by far the largest role at the time in the control of the House.

In 1893 four regularly selected committees became standing committees in a minor reorganization. The most important of these was on the reform of the Civil Service.

Speaker Cannon continued the Reed tradition when he assumed the speakership in 1903. Wilson, writing just prior to this, gives the trend as follows:

A more important matter—at any rate, a thing more concrete and visible —is the gradual integration of the organization of the House of Representatives. The power of the Speaker has of late years taken on new phases. He is now, more than ever, expected to guide and control the whole course of business in the House,—if not alone, at any rate through the instrumentality of the small Committee on Rules, of which he is chairman. That committee is expected not only to reformulate and revise from time to time the permanent Rules of the House, but also to look closely to the course of its business from day to day, make its programme, and virtually control its

---

[10] Haines, Lynn, Law Making in America (1912), p. 5.

use of its time. The committee consists of five members; but the Speaker and the two other members of the committee who represent the majority in the House determine its action; and its action is allowed to govern the House. It in effect regulates the precedence of measures. Whenever occasion requires, it determines what shall, and what shall not, be undertaken. It is like a steering ministry,—without a ministry's public responsibility, and without a ministry's right to speak for both houses. It is a private piece of party machinery within the single chamber for which it acts. The Speaker himself—not as a member of the Committee on Rules, but by the exercise of his right to "recognize" on the floor—undertakes to determine very absolutely what bills individual members shall be allowed to bring to a vote, out of the regular order fixed by the rules or arranged by the Committee on Rules.

This obviously creates, in germ at least, a recognized and sufficiently concentrated leadership within the House. The country is beginning to know that the Speaker and the Committee on Rules must be held responsible in all ordinary seasons for the success or failure of the session, so far as the House is concerned. The congressional caucus has fallen a little into the background. It is not often necessary to call it together, except when the majority is impatient or recalcitrant under the guidance of the Committee on Rules. To this new leadership, however, as to everything else connected with committee government, the taint of privacy attaches. It is not leadership upon the open floor, avowed, defended in public debate, set before the view and criticism of the country. It integrates the House alone, not the Senate; does not unite the two houses in policy; affects only the chamber in which there is the least opportunity for debate, the least chance that responsibility may be properly and effectively lodged and avowed. It has only a very remote and partial resemblance to genuine party leadership.[11]

By 1909 the power of the Speaker had been extended to a quasidictatorship, and the Rules Committee had become the chief instrument of this control.

If the attempt is now made to sum up the powers that the speaker in his threefold capacity as a member of the House, as its presiding officer, and as the person selected by the majority party to lead it in the congressional arena, had come to have in 1909; that is, immediately prior to the momentous occurrences shortly to be narrated, it will be seen to how great an extent the problem of leadership had found its solution by the vesting in the hands of this officer the general power of direction and control over the House and its proceedings. Through his power to appoint committees, and,

---

[11] Wilson, *op. cit.*, pp. ix–xi.

in so doing, to designate who should hold the strategically powerful positions of committee chairmanships, he determined the whole organization of the House in its most essential aspect and in no small degree the legislative opportunities of the individual members. Through his untrammeled power to grant or withhold recognition for the purpose of making the motions through which members might avail themselves of the special procedures of unanimous consent and suspension of the rules for securing consideration of bills in which they were interested, which procedures, in many cases, offered the only opportunity that existed for securing the passage of these bills, he not only could determine what measures would or would not be enacted, but had a weapon by which he could discipline members who failed in any respect to make their action conform to his will. And, through his position as chairman of the Committee on Rules and the fact that the other representatives of his party on that committee held office by his selection, he had to a large extent the still greater power of determining at any time when the House should lay aside all other business and proceed to the consideration of a bill which he desired to have passed, and, in so doing, to determine the character of action that might be taken on such bill. Combined with this last positive power was that of preventing resort to this procedure on any initiative other than his own. This resulted from the fact that any proposal in the form of a resolution directing the Committee on Rules to report a special rule had to be referred to that committee, and the speaker, as chairman of that committee, could prevent action upon it by refusing to have the resolution reported, or by the more simple expedient of not calling the committee together for its consideration. Taken in conjunction, these several powers thus placed in the hands of the speaker both positive and negative powers of the most far-reaching character. To such an extent was this true that, both in Congress and throughout the country, the speaker came to be considered as an officer second only in power and influence to the President of the United States himself and so far as the enactment of legislation was concerned to exercise powers superior to his.[12]

This, then, was the situation with which those who sought to curb the power of the Committee on Rules were confronted, after the failure of the insurrection at the opening of the Sixty-first Congress:

(1) The speaker, as a member of the Committee on Rules, could use all the power of his great office to execute the program which he, as the leading member of that committee, had arranged.

(2) The committee had the right to report at any time.

(3) The consideration of the reports of the committee could not be put aside.

---

[12] Willoughby, *op. cit.*, p. 539–540.

(4) Debate on the report of the committee could be curtailed to forty minutes by the moving of the previous question.

(5) Action on the report could not be evaded by the breaking of a quorum.

(6) The dilatory motion had been robbed of its terrors.

(7) The Committee on Rules, alone of the committees of the House, could hold meetings during a sitting of the House without special leave.

(8) No proposition for a change in the rules could be brought before the House except through a report from the Committee on Rules.[13]

Here and there insurgency had become evident, but Speaker Cannon used his great powers to impose penalties on those showing signs of revolt. For the most part these penalties consisted in unattractive committee assignments and failure to recognize the offending member. Party responsibility had become absolute, and that responsibility was concentrated in a minority of the members and eventually in the Speaker himself.

A change in committees amounting to a minor reorganization should be recorded. In 1909 six minor committees were dropped. It is conjectured that their dropping was accounted for actually by the opening of the House Office Building. Previous to this date a committee chairmanship was virtually necessary, if a member was to have an office of his own. The spending committees remained divided. Nevertheless the tendency was toward the concentration of all that was vital in the hands of the most prominent.

1910–1946

The period opened with a successful attack on the powers of the Speaker. This brought a certain dispersion of leadership, although by and large sufficient concentration remained to ensure a measure of party responsibility. The passing of the Budget and Accounting Act of 1921 represented the greatest single subsequent change. Since 1921 modest progress has been made in the direction of greater maturity and effectiveness of organization.[14]

The reorganizations of 1910 and 1911 are the most spectacular and best known of any associated with Congress.

Some signs of insurgency had appeared previously, and minor con-

---

[13] *Political Science Quarterly,* September 1911, v. 26, no. 3:395.

[14] For accounts of the period, see: Hasbrouck, P. D., Party Government in the House of Representatives (New York, 1927), esp. Intro.; Willoughby, *op. cit.,* pp. 332–333, 503–508.

cessions had been made. The immediate episode was not in itself of great importance, and the position assumed by the Speaker was probably justified by precedent.

In the contest for the mastery of the House, thus opened, the solid strength of the Democrats and Insurgents was pitted against the regular Republicans. The regulars, warned by recent defections, deemed it prudent to play for time, in the hope of being able to summon enough absent members to prevent the reversal of the speaker's decision. Speaker Cannon, therefore, withheld his decision for an unprecedented time, while his lieutenants vainly sought to secure an adjournment or recess. The Insurgent and Democratic allies on their part grimly held the House in session all night; and it was not until twenty minutes after two o'clock on the afternoon of the 18th that a recess was taken until four o'clock. This recess of less than two hours was agreed to, it is said, on the understanding that the speaker would be ready to give his ruling on the point of order at its conclusion.

When the House met at four o'clock the speaker expressed his readiness to rule. The House, conscious of another struggle impending, decided to prepare itself for the trial of strength by a night's rest and postponed the announcement of the ruling to 12:05 P.M. on the next day; but this was done only after the allies had satisfied themselves that no unfair advantage would be taken of their concession. Their attitude of suspicion was justified, on the following afternoon, by the reprehensible conduct of Mr. Mann, one of the parliamentary experts of the House, in attempting to deprive Mr. Norris of his hard-earned privilege of presenting his resolution for a vote.

In the long hours of the night of March 17 and the morning following, much was said and done that was irrelevant and disorderly. For once in the recent history of the House of Representatives every member said what he wanted to say and took as long as he desired to say it. . . .

Although seventy-six pages of the *Record* are filled with discussion ostensibly held for the speaker's enlightenment, everyone knew from the beginning what position he would take. Everyone knew, too, that Mr. Norris would appeal from the decision and move the previous question, and that Mr. Dalzell would move to lay the appeal on the table. These expected things happened, together with an attempt to defeat action through a motion to adjourn, which was promptly voted down. The House refused to lay the appeal on the table, and under the operation of the previous question the decision of the chair was overruled by a vote of 162 to 182, after which the speaker, without comment, placed the Norris rule before the House. . . .[15]

---

[15] Atkinson and Beard, *op. cit.*, pp. 402, 408.

The underlying causes of Cannon's overthrow must be sought partly in the background of progressivism under Theodore Roosevelt and partly in the inevitable swing of the pendulum away from autocracy of any sort. Cannon had grown more and more tyrannical and arbitrary and the contrast between the democratic mood of the nation and his conduct as Speaker had become far too pronounced to be ignored.

The major change effected was in the power of the Speaker himself. No longer was he to be a member of the Rules Committee. A new Rules Committee, composed of ten members instead of five, was elected by the House, the chairman to be chosen from this number by the committee members themselves. In actual practice this meant selection by party caucus; within the party caucuses by a committee on committees of the Republicans and by Democratic members of the Ways and Means Committee serving for that party. The Rules Committee remained very much under Cannon's control so long as the Republicans were in power.

However, in 1911 the Democrats obtained a majority and carried the reorganization somewhat further.

Besides adopting the several new arrangements which they had helped to force upon the Republicans in the last two Congresses, the Democrats made five concessions to the reform sentiment of the House, and included two measures for their own protection:

1. They abolished six superfluous committees.

2. They took away from the Speaker the last of his three great powers, which had been recognition, membership on Rules, and the appointment of committees. Of these, the third was perhaps the most important. The new rule provided for the election of standing committees by the House.

3. The Fitzgerald rule establishing a Unanimous Consent Calendar was changed, by requiring that a bill be on that Calendar at least three days, thus giving Members a chance to study it, before it could be called up. A second chance was also allowed on a succeeding Monday for a bill to which objection had been made.

4. Fridays were designated as the days on which the Private Calendar would be in order, although this order of business was not made mandatory, as were the other calendars. This provision wrote into the permanent rules of the House a practice that had been followed by means of special orders for a number of Congresses. It contained the added refinement of assigning second and fourth Fridays to pension claims, and all other Fridays to the residue of private claims. (Rule XXIV, cl. 6.)

5. An attempt was made to strengthen the discharge rule against its abuse by Mr. Mann.

6. The so-called Holman rule, dropped when the Republicans came into power in 1895, was restored. Ordinarily, general legislation is not allowed on appropriation bills. The Holman rule (rule XXI, clause 2, second sentence) makes certain exceptions, however, in the case of changes which tend to retrench expenditures, particularly amendments having the approval of the committee with jurisdiction over the subject matter.

7. A new paragraph (clause 3) was added to rule XXI, as follows:

"No amendment shall be in order to any bill affecting revenue which is not germane to the subject matter in the bill; nor shall any amendment to any item of such bill be in order which does not directly relate to the item to which the amendment is proposed." [16]

By the middle of the decade, the pendulum again swung back a bit and expressions of dissatisfaction with the absence of any center of responsibility, especially in the matter of appropriations, began to be heard. Moreover, there was a general feeling, coming to a focus in a letter of Representative Fuller of Massachusetts,[17] that Congress as a whole was not organized and functioning in accordance with the demands of the age.

Out of the general desire for reform in the decade 1910–1920 came a Legislative Drafting Service, and the Legislative Reference Service in the Library of Congress.

The major development of this period came with the passage of the Budget and Accounting Act of 1921. This in itself had a profound and far-reaching effect upon congressional organization.

That the full purport of the new procedural system for the handling of appropriation bills may be seen it is necessary that a brief account be given of the system that existed prior to its adoption. The basic defect of the old system was that it made no attempt to consider the problem of financing the government as a whole; indeed, not even was the attempt made to consider at one time, and through the instrumentality of a single appropriation bill, the needs of the several administrative services of the government. In the House, the work of framing appropriation bills for the support of the government was distributed among no less than eight committees, each acting independently of the others, no one of them having responsibility for seeing that the totals recommended to be appropriated would bear a

---

[16] Hasbrouck, op. cit., p. 11–12.
[17] Hasbrouck, op. cit., p. 15.

proper relation to available resources and prospective income. This division of responsibility, moreover, was not in accordance with any logical or consistent classification of the fields of activities of the government. In no case were all the expenditure needs of a department considered by a single committee or provided for by a single appropriation bill. . . .[18]

The Committee on Appropriations was now given the exclusive function of appropriating and at the same time was forbidden to include legislative matters in the appropriation acts. Similarly, the general legislative committees were assigned the function of substantive legislation, but they in their turn were forbidden to sponsor measures for the appropriation of funds.

Changes took place in 1923, when the World War Veterans' Legislation Committee was created and the "pocket veto" power of the chairman of the Rules Committee curbed; and in 1926 when the important Joint Committee on Internal Revenue Taxation was set up.

A further reorganization took place in 1927. This was sponsored by the Republican party organization then in power. Sixteen committees, most of which had become moribund, were abolished.[19]

Since 1927, during a period which included the great depression and the second world war, only procedural or minor organizational changes have occurred.

REORGANIZATION IN THE SENATE

Both branches of the federal legislature are subject to some formal and routine organization at the beginning of each Congress. This step is more thorough in the House than in the Senate because at each Congress the House is a "new" body while the Senate, having only a third of its membership composed of newly elected members, retains its character as a continuous body. Moreover, House members themselves elect their officers at each Congress, while the Senate has no choice in the selection of its presiding officer, unless there is a vacancy in the office of Vice President when it chooses a President *pro tem.*

In the following summary only the more important and successful attempts at reorganization of the Senate are enumerated. Changes in procedure as well as points of parliamentary detail have been omitted. Special emphasis is placed upon the committee system and its evolution through the course of Senate history, for as President Wilson observed,

---

[18] Willoughby, *op. cit.*, p. 503–504.
[19] Congressional Record, Dec. 5, 1927, p. 12.

"Congress in session is Congress in public exhibition, while Congress in its committee rooms is Congress at work."[20]

In the early history of the Senate when it was reluctant to delegate power and responsibility, working through committees was not considered a necessary expedient. The relatively light work of the Senate at the time, compared with its work today, also accounted for the small number of committees. Only slowly and hesitantly, as the volume of its work multiplied with the passing years, did the Senate begin to devolve a large part of its work upon committees.

Development of Committee System

The select or special committee system, as opposed to the standing committee system, was much in vogue in the early days of the Senate. "Prior to December 1816, all bills and joint resolutions, and other matters requiring such consideration, were referred to and reported upon by special committees appointed for the purpose. The different subjects treated of in the messages from the President and the general appropriation bills were included in the measures thus referred."[21] According to William Hickey, at one time chief clerk of the Senate, resort to special or select committees was so common that, in the first session of the 14th Congress (1815–1816), between 90 and 100 such committees were created.[22]

The appointment of so many select committees at each session of the Senate "had become inconvenient," and on December 5, 1816, when Senator James Barbour of Virginia submitted a motion to add eleven more standing committees to the four already established, many of the Senators were for the motion. Five days later this motion, in the form of a resolution, was passed. The resolution provided for the appointment of the following standing committees at each session:[23]

> A Committee on Foreign Relations
> A Committee on Finance
> A Committee on Commerce and Manufactures
> A Committee on Military Affairs
> A Committee on the Militia

[20] Quoted by George B. Haynes, *The Senate of the United States*, p. 270.

[21] *Precedents: Decisions on Points of Order with Phraseology in the United States Senate*, compiled by Henry H. Gilfry, p. 194.

[22] *Statement of the Rules and Practice of the Senate of the United States in Appointment of Committees from March 4, 1789, to March 14, 1863*, 62nd Congress, 3rd Session, Sen. Doc. 1122, p. 4.

[23] *Ibid.*, p. 5.

A Committee on Naval Affairs
A Committee on Public Lands
A Committee on the Judiciary
A Committee on the Post Office and Post Roads
A Committee on Pensions

To this list was added on December 16 a Committee on the District of Columbia.

In 1820 two of the four original committees, the Committee on Engrossed Bills and the Joint Committee on Enrolled Bills, were combined. The Joint Library Committee was dropped and a new standing Committee on Indian Affairs was appointed. Thus the total number stood at fifteen in 1820. In the course of the next thirty odd years some other standing committees were created and a few were eliminated, so that by 1853 there were twenty-five standing committees in the Senate.

In 1889, when the Senate passed the century mark of its career, its standing committees numbered forty-two. During the next quarter century this number almost doubled. In 1884 five select committees attained the rank of standing committees. In 1896 this process of "graduation" proceeded and three more standing committees were created. Nine new standing committees were created in 1909 and it was also resolved that all select committees constitute themselves standing committees. Three more standing committees were created in 1913, bringing the total number in the Senate to the record high of seventy-four.

This expansion increased work on committees to such an extent that some Senators were often prevented from attending regularly the sessions of the Senate. Probably there was also some duplication of work in certain committees. At any rate, in 1921 a radical step was taken when the number of standing committees was cut to less than half. In April of that year Senator Brandegee introduced a resolution the adoption of which reduced the number from 74 to 34. He explained that "the object of the changes was to increase the size of the major committees and to place upon them some of the younger men." This move was a decisive step in the direction of reorganization.

The following tabulation indicates the extent of the change:

SENATE STANDING COMMITTEES BEFORE AND AFTER THE
CHANGE OF 1921

Before

1. Additional Accommodations for the Library of Congress
2. Agriculture and Forestry
3. Appropriations
4. Audit and Control of the Contingent Expenses of the Senate
5. Banking and Currency
6. Canadian Relations
7. The Census
8. Civil Service and Retirement
9. Claims
10. Coast and Insular Survey
11. Coast Defense
12. Commerce
13. Conservation of National Resources
14. Corporations Organized in the District of Columbia
15. Cuban Relations
16. Disposition of Useless Papers in the Executive Departments
17. District of Columbia
18. Education and Labor
19. Engrossed Bills
20. Enrolled Bills
21. Examine the Several Branches of the Civil Service
22. Expenditures in the Department of Agriculture
23. Expenditures in the Department of Commerce
24. Expenditures in the Department of Justice
25. Expenditures in the Department of the Interior
26. Expenditures in the Department of Labor
27. Expenditures in the Navy Department
28. Expenditures in the Post Office Department
29. Expenditures in the Department of State

After

1. Agriculture and Forestry
2. Appropriations
3. Audit and Control of the Contingent Expenses of the Senate
4. Banking and Currency
5. Civil Service
6. Claims
7. Commerce
8. District of Columbia
9. Education and Labor
10. Enrolled Bills
11. Expenditures in the Executive Departments
12. Finance
13. Foreign Relations
14. Immigration
15. Indian Affairs
16. Interoceanic Canals
17. Interstate Commerce
18. Irrigation and Reclamation
19. Judiciary
20. Library
21. Manufactures
22. Military Affairs
23. Mines and Mining
24. Naval Affairs
25. Patents
26. Pensions
27. Post Offices and Roads
28. Printing
29. Privileges and Elections
30. Public Buildings and Grounds
31. Public Lands and Surveys
32. Revision of the Laws
33. Rules
34. Territories and Insular Possessions

Before

30. Expenditures in the Treasury Department
31. Expenditures in the War Department
32. Finance
33. Fisheries
34. Five Civilized Tribes of Indians
35. Foreign Relations
36. Forest Reservations and the Protection of Game
37. Geological Survey
38. Immigration
39. Indian Affairs
40. Indian Depredations
41. Industrial Expositions
42. Interoceanic Canals
43. Interstate Commerce
44. Investigate Trespassers upon Indian Lands
45. Irrigation and Reclamation of Arid Lands
46. Judiciary
47. Library
48. Manufactures
49. Military Affairs
50. Mines and Mining
51. Mississippi River and its Tributaries
52. National Banks
53. Naval Affairs
54. Pacific Islands, Porto Rico, and the Virgin Islands
55. Pacific Railroads
56. Patents
57. Pensions
58. Philippines
59. Post Offices and Post Roads
60. Printing
61. Private Land Claims
62. Privileges and Elections
63. Public Buildings and Grounds
64. Public Health and National Quarantine
65. Public Lands
66. Railroads
67. Revolutionary Claims

68. Rules
69. Standards, Weights, and Measures
70. Territories
71. Transportation Routes to the Sea-
    board
72. Transportation and Sale of Meat
    Products
73. University of the United States
74. Women Suffrage

Selection of Committeemen

During the early years of the Senate the members of its select and standing committees were elected under a rule which provided that "all committees shall be appointed by ballot, and a plurality of votes shall make a choice." [24] This method of selecting committeemen was in force for over thirty years. In 1822 the following resolution was adopted: "All committees shall be appointed by the presiding officer of this House unless especially ordered otherwise by the Senate." [25] This practice was followed for only a few years, and in 1826 the Senate reverted to choice by ballot. Two years later the appointment of Senate committees was assigned to the President *pro tempore,* but in 1833 the old rule of choice by ballot was revived. The subsequent history of this procedure is summarized in the following statement from Haynes: [26]

In the history of Senate organization few periods have been of more interest and significance than the ten days at the opening of the second session of the twenty-ninth Congress, December 7–17, 1846. The motion to entrust to the Vice-President the appointment of committees was promptly defeated. In accordance with the regular rule, the Senate began balloting for chairmen. After the chairmen of six committees had been elected, there developed a long debate over the method of choosing the other members. Vice-President Dallas advocated the method formerly in vogue by naming lay members of a committee in order, from the one receiving the most to the one receiving the fewest votes. The Democratic leader, Sevier, came forward with motions which arranged the names and safeguarded the majority's succession to chairmanships which might become vacant. After several committees had been filled by this method, by unanimous consent Rule 34 was suspended, and the Senate proceeded to elect upon one ballot a list

---

[24] Rule XV, *Annals of Congress,* I, pp. 21–22.
[25] 62nd Congress, 3rd Session, Sen. Doc. 1122, p. 8.
[26] Haynes, *op. cit.,* p. 277.

of candidates for all the remaining vacancies presented by Senators Sevier and Speight. This list gave to each committee thus filled its chairman and the majority of its members from the same party which held a majority in the Senate. From that day to this, the appointment of Senate committees in most cases has been a perfunctory affair: by unanimous consent the portions of the rules requiring election by ballot and separate majority choice of chairmen have been suspended and the election has taken place by yea-and-nay vote upon the resolution for the adoption of a list which has usually been mutually agreed upon by representatives of the caucus or conference of each of the two parties.

The size of standing and select committees has gradually increased through the years. Membership was first limited to three. One of the rules of 1806 provided that "at the commencement of each session a committee, consisting of three members, shall be appointed." The organization ushered in by the new standing committees in 1816 also brought in changes in membership. All the standing committees appointed in that year were made up of five members. In the middle of the century membership was raised to seven; by 1900 most of the standing committees were composed of nine members, and in recent years the committees have varied from about ten to twenty-five members, in accordance with the importance or difficulty of their fields.

The practice of setting up and making use of select joint committees dates from the opening weeks of the First Congress, but this was not common; such committees were "used to adjust interests of the moment between the two houses." Certain select joint committees gradually grew into standing committees and have continued to function as such through the years. In 1926 a joint standing committee on internal revenue taxation was created by statute and provided with an expert staff.

The Legislative Drafting Service Act of 1919 provided the Senate with a Legislative Counsel who is "appointed by the President of the Senate." This act marked the first step in making available to the Senate the services of specialists in legislative processes. Priority in the services of this officer and his assistants is apportioned among committees requesting assistance, individual Senators being accommodated as time and opportunity permit.

6.

Making the Laws

DURING THE FEDERALIST period of American history, when Congress was small in size and volume of business, it deliberated typically in the Committee of the Whole on the State of the Union. This parliamentary device, which dates from the reign of James I, is merely the House itself under another name with the same procedure, but with unlimited debate and with a chairman other than the Speaker. Here, in Committee of the Whole, the early Congresses first discusssed their problems, hammered their laws into shape, heard election contests, and laid the foundations of national policy. After 1800, as the House grew in size and business, Congress gradually developed the habit of referring new matters for first consideration to small committees which had previously been used to review the work of the Committee on the Whole. Their positions were now reversed and the bulk of the business of Congress came in time to be handled initially in committee instead of on the floor.

In the Early Days

At first, the business of law making was handled by hosts of select committees. At least 350 such committees, for example, were raised in the Third Congress. A special committee had to be formed for every petty claim. But the number of select committees rapidly declined. The Thirteenth Congress (1813–1815), with its three war sessions, had about 70; and by the Twenty-third Congress (1833–1835) their number had dropped to 35. Meanwhile, as time went on, the select committees tended to group themselves into the first standing committees which gradually grew in number as the select committees fell off. Ten standing committees had been set up in the House of Representatives by 1809, 20 by 1817, 30 by 1833, 45 by 1867, 55 by 1895, and 61 by 1911. As the business of Congress accumulated in particular areas of internal administration and public policy, such as the election of members, House accounts, revenues and expenditures, interstate commerce, private claims to land, and the like, committees were set up to consider and advise the House with respect to their disposition.

The development of lawmaking machinery on the Senate side followed a similar pattern. Select committees were largely relied upon until 1816 when 12 standing committees were created to handle legislation dealing with claims, commerce, the District of Columbia, finance, foreign relations, judiciary, manufactures, military and naval affairs, pensions, post offices and post roads, and public lands and surveys. Thereafter new subject-matter fields were gradually assigned to new standing committees until 1891 when the committee structure in the upper house reached its present pattern. The following table shows the origin and development of all the present standing committees of Congress.

Increase in Legislation

The business of lawmaking has waxed and waned through the years with changes in the state of the Union. During the First Congress, for example, the legislative mills ground out a total of 118 acts, all but 10 of which were public laws. The output gradually increased during the first half-century of the federal Congress, passing the 500-mark for the first time in the 25th Congress when 532 laws were enacted in the last biennium of the Jacksonian period. Thereafter legislative activity subsided in volume until the swelling business of Civil War and Reconstruction days pushed the output to 1,012 laws produced by the second Congress of the Grant administration. An even century after it first met found our national legislature reaching new levels of productivity with 2,251 acts passed by the 51st Congress, almost three-fourths of which were private bills.

Sixteen years later the 59th Congress reached an all-time peak, pouring out a torrent of 7,024 laws, nine-tenths of which were private bills stimulated probably by the late war with Spain. From 1907 to 1925 the business of lawmaking declined to less than a thousand acts a biennium, despite many important measures passed during the Wilsonian era. Since 1925 the legislative output has levelled off at about 1,500 laws per Congress, on the average, approximately evenly divided between public and private measures. Over the whole period of the first 78 Congresses, a total of 64,446 laws were passed between 1789 and 1945, of which

CHRONOLOGY OF CONGRESSIONAL COMMITTEES*

Established	House	Senate	Joint
1789	Elections No. 1 Enrolled Bills	Enrolled Bills	
1794	Claims		
1795	Agriculture Interstate & Foreign Commerce Revision of the Laws Ways and Means		
1804	Accounts		
1805	Public Lands		
1806	Library	Library	Library
1807		Contingent Expenses	
1808	District of Columbia Post Office & Post Roads		
1813	Judiciary War Claims		
1816	Expenditures in Executive Departments	Claims District of Columbia Commerce and Manufactures† Finance Foreign Relations Judiciary Military Affairs Naval Affairs Pensions Post Offices & Post Roads Public Lands & Surveys	
1820		Indian Affairs	
1821	Indian Affairs		
1822	Military Affairs Naval Affairs Foreign Affairs		
1825	Pensions Territories	Agriculture & Forestry	
1831	Invalid Pensions		
1837	Patents Public Bldgs. & Grounds	Patents Public Buildings & Grounds	
1841		Printing	
1842		Expenditures in Executive Depts.	
1844		Territories & Insular Affairs	
1846	Printing		Printing
1849	Rules		

Established	House	Senate	Joint
1864	Coinage, Weights, & Measures		
1865	Appropriations		
	Banking & Currency		
	Mines & Mining	Mines and Mining	
1867	Education	Appropriations	
	Labor		
1869		Education & Labor	
1871		Privileges & Elections	
1873		Civil Service	
1874		Rules	
1883	Rivers & Harbors		
1887	Merchant Marine and Fisheries	Interstate Commerce	
1889		Immigration	
1891		Irrigation and Reclamation	
1893	Election of Pres., V. Pres. and Representatives		
	Immigration & Naturalization		
	Irrigation & Reclamation		
	Civil Service		
1895	Elections No. 2		
	Elections No. 3		
1899	Insular Affairs	Interoceanic Canals	
1903	Census		
1913	Roads	Banking and Currency	
	Disposition of Exec. Papers		
1915	Flood Control		
1923	World War Veterans' Legislation		
1926			Internal Revenue Taxation
1929	Memorials		
1945	Un-American Activities		

* Includes all standing committees in existence in 1945.
† Separated in 1825.

28,237 were public and 36,209 were private bills. Certainly from the standpoint of productivity the workers in the legislative vineyard are above reproach, unless it be from some Bruce Barton who objects to quantity production in the field of lawmaking.

Of all the measures that are introduced in the modern Congress, nine-tenths are pigeon-holed in committee and forgotten and not more than three per cent pass both houses and are signed by the President.

Most of those that survive the travail of the legislative process are private bills or trivial public measures. Few matters of major importance finally clear all the legislative hurdles and are enacted into law. "The sins of Congress," as Luce remarked, "are far more those of omission than of commission."

ORIGINS OF LEGISLATION

The formulation of legislation, as we saw in Chapter One, is no longer exclusively a congressional concern. For most bills introduced members are merely conduits for the executive departments, private organizations, and individual constituents. More than half of the bills dropped into the "hopper" originate in the federal departments and bureaus and are later revised in committee to accord with congressional views. In the simpler economy and society of the nineteenth century almost any member of Congress was competent to prepare and draft legislative proposals. But under the complex conditions of modern society intelligent legislation can neither be conceived nor drafted without expert knowledge which few Congressmen claim to possess. The executive departments, on the other hand, are well staffed with experts in all fields of public policy-making and most new legislation in modern times has originated with them. Thus, American legislative practice has tended to resemble the English system under which all public bills are introduced by the government of the day, but with these differences: that in the United States administration measures are not introduced by Cabinet members but by their spokesmen in the House and Senate; and that in England public bills are considered as to their general principles by the whole House before reference to standing committees for detailed analysis, whereas here they are first referred to standing committees for review, revision, and report.

Executive initiative in lawmaking under the American system finds its fundamental warrant in the constitutional provision that the President "shall from time to time give to the Congress information on the state of the Union, and recommend to their consideration such measures as he shall judge necessary and expedient." This he does in his message to Congress at the opening of a session in which he discusses the general problems of the day and recommends legislation on many subjects, as President Truman did in his 21-point program submitted to the first session of the 79th Congress; and in special messages suggesting legislation on specific subjects such as Pearl Harbor or the control of atomic energy. Administrative officers also submit legislative proposals to Congress in their periodic departmental reports and in response to requests from congressional committees. Such departmental suggestions, as we have seen, are usually routed through the Legislative Reference Division in the Bureau of the Budget as a check upon their compatibility with the President's program.[1] The President's messages are referred to House and Senate committees having jurisdiction over the subjects covered and the supporting legislation, which has probably been drafted in the departments concerned, is promptly introduced in both chambers by the chairmen of the committees in charge.

All bills for raising revenue must originate in the House of Representatives, under the constitution. And the general appropriation bills, which provide the funds for carrying on the activities of the government, also customarily originate in the House.

Although little legislation originates in Congress today, that body is still responsible for sifting, testing, and debating all legislative proposals wherever they come from and for determining the final shape of public policy. Congress must decide what bills are to be considered and approved and what the legislative policies of the nation are to be. The Executive Branch formulates and executes. The Legislature determines policy and evaluates its performance.

Executive Assistance

In performing their share of the lawmaking function the members and committees of Congress draw facts and figures from many official and unofficial sources. There are three principal sources of congressional information: executive agencies, private groups, and legislative aids within Congress itself.

The primary source of legislative data is in the federal departments. In the formulation of legislative policy Congress leans heavily upon periodic and special reports from administrative agencies, and upon the testimony of experts from the administrative branch before its committees. Special inquiries are frequently made by executive agencies at the request of congressional committees. This is particularly true of offices like the General Accounting Office, the Federal Trade Commission, and the Tariff Commission which are agents of the legislative branch. Many departments maintain congressional inquiry sections

---

[1] For a good account of the role of the executive departments and the Budget Bureau in this connection, see Carl R. Sapp, "Executive Assistance in the Legislative Process," *Public Administration Review*, Winter 1946, pp. 10–19.

which devote full time to furnishing information requested by legislators or their secretaries, not only for use in lawmaking but also on matters of interest to constituents. The Congressional Inquiry Section in the Department of Agriculture is perhaps the best known on Capitol Hill for its efficient service. Less favorably regarded are the liaison offices which several wartime agencies established at the Capitol. These offices were sometimes less helpful than they might have been to Congressmen, depending upon the nature of their requests and their political affiliation.

Many congressional offices find the facilities of the United States Information Center useful, particularly in getting information on difficult problems when the usual sources fail. Operated by the Division of Public Inquiries of the Office of War Information during the war and of the Bureau of the Budget afterwards, this division functions as the central information center covering all federal agencies. It renders a referral service for congressional correspondence, compiles the *United States Government Manual* and several specialized directory lists, and publishes useful handbooks and reference lists which are available to congressional offices. During 1945 the division had a staff of 43 people and cost $130,000 to operate. Its director testified that every Senator and 390 Representatives had used its facilities. The services of the division might well be more fully used by Congressmen in handling their correspondence, and its constituent inquiry services, which account for less than five per cent of all inquiries handled, might well be transferred to the Legislative Reference Service in the Library of Congress.

Several improvements in methods of obtaining information from the executive branch should be made. The annual appropriation to the General Accounting Office for the making of investigations requested by congressional committees should be increased, and the staff of its Investigation Division should be expanded with qualified accountants and specialists in expenditure analysis who should be available on call to the revenue, appropriating, and expenditure committees in both houses. More, if not all, of the major administrative agencies should establish branch liaison offices at the Capitol to serve the convenience of Congressmen and their constituents. One general liaison office for the entire executive branch, with appropriate functional subdivisions, might better serve this purpose. Deputy departmental secretaries should be placed in charge of these liaison offices and devote their full time to the work of mediation—an arrangement which worked well in the field of foreign affairs while Dean Acheson was Assistant Secretary of State in charge of congressional relations. Greater use of the staff facilities of the Budget Bureau, Treasury Department, and General Accounting Office might well be made by the fiscal committees of Congress. There are rich veins of unmined data here waiting legislative exploration. And finally, it would be very helpful both to Congressmen and citizens if the various agencies would present their reports in a more concise, intelligible, and nontechnical fashion with visual aids, cross-references, and brief summaries. Busy legislators have no time to read the bulky, dryasdust documents turned out by the authors of annual reports. Happily some agencies have already begun to modernize their style of reporting.

Private Organizations

Private groups are also a prolific source of information—good, bad, and indifferent—bearing upon the business of lawmaking. The spokesmen of special interest groups with every sort of axe to grind buttonhole Congressmen in the corridors of the Capitol, importune them in their offices, and press their claims in committee rooms. The number of these groups and their lobbyists is legion, and most of them are listened to with at least feigned respect, for legislators learn by listening and desire to be reelected. It is also their high function to work out compromises between conflicting pressure groups and so help to preserve domestic tranquillity. But when the clamor of the greedy claimants becomes too strident, many a member privately invokes a plague on all their houses.

Not all the testimony and telegrams from unofficial sources, however, are of the self-seeking variety. In 1945, for example, the United States Chamber of Commerce began to issue to every Congressman a *Legislative Daily* bulletin telling what congressional committees met yesterday, who appeared, what committees will meet today and who will appear before them, and what happened on the House and Senate floors. This bulletin, and the Chamber's daily report on *Governmental Affairs*, are very helpful short-cuts to congressional knowledge on current developments in both branches of the national government. Similar information might well be published in the daily *Congressional Record*. Much useful and disinterested information on contemporary public problems is also furnished by private research foundations like the Brookings Institution and the Twentieth Century Fund, and by civic groups such as the National League of Women Voters and the National Planning Association. The reports of presidential commissions like the Committee on Economic Security,[2] model bills drafted by groups such as the National Conference of Commissioners on Uniform State Laws, and the publications of the Public Administration Clearing House and other professional organizations are invaluable aids in lawmaking at all levels of American government.

LEGISLATIVE STAFF AIDS

Despite increased reliance upon executive leadership in the field of legislation, Congress does not lack aids of its own in the formulation of legislative policy. There are the clerks and secretaries who work in the offices of the members, some of whom become quite adept in digging up facts and figures and preparing memoranda on legislative questions. The Congressional Secretaries' Club, which was formed in 1935 and has 450 members, publishes a *Congressional Handbook* containing much valuable information and data of special use and interest to Congressmen and their staffs, and an *Information Bulletin* including references to various departmental publications. There are the clerks of the standing committees—over 300 of them during fiscal 1946 with a total payroll of almost one million dollars—who do research and administrative work for the committees and their chairmen. As a rule, few standing committees have expert staffs, but the Appropriations Committees, the Joint Committee on Internal Revenue Taxation, and the Senate Committees on Education and Labor and Military Affairs are current exceptions to this rule.

There are also the expert staffs of special investigating committees— a device frequently used by Congress throughout its history for informative purposes—many of whose employees in latter days have been borrowed from administrative agencies as a means of supplementing modest committee appropriations. During October, 1945, for example, Senate committees reported that 61 persons in their employ whose annual compensation aggregated $238,031 were on the payrolls of downtown departments. Regardless of criticisms of this practice on the grounds that it evades congressional control of investigating committee expenditures and provides departments with an argument for larger appropriations to cover the cost of loaned personnel, it has made much valuable information available to Congress. It has also provided a "sabbatical spree" and fresh experience for civil servants. The borrowing of administrative personnel by congressional committees is not a

---

[2] For an able study of the use of fact-finding commissions for legislative purposes, see Carl Marcy, *Presidential Commissions* (1945), especially pp. 25–35.

new practice, but it was extensively used after 1933 and contributed much to the success of such investigations as the civil liberties, migratory labor, national defense, wartime health, postwar planning, and small business inquiries. And, as McGeary points out, the practice has often been specifically authorized by House and Senate resolutions.[3]

To assist the members and committees of Congress in the long and intricate process of bill drafting, there is the Office of the Legislative Counsel which includes four lawyers, one law assistant, and two clerks for each chamber: 14 in all. Salaries and expenses of the office come to $90,000. Bill drafting is a technical task which calls for experience and judgment. The small staff of this office has been overworked in recent years and it is generally regarded as desirable that the staff of the Legislative Counsel should be strengthened. The usefulness of the Legislative Counsel depends on the personal confidence which the committee members have in him as their legal drafting counsel. He should work in close association with all the experts on the legislative staff, but be an independent officer appointed by the Speaker of the House or the President Pro Tem of the Senate and have the power to nominate his own staff subject to approval by the appointing officer. The independence of the Office of Legislative Counsel is essential to its success and that independence depends upon the direct relationship between the Counsel, the appointing officer, and the committees.

Legislative Reference Service

Apart from the staffs associated with the drafting services, the appropriations committees and the Joint Committee on Internal Revenue Taxation, and the experts temporarily employed for special committee inquiries, the only technical aids hitherto available to Congress within the Legislative Establishment are those supplied by the Legislative Reference Service. Created by Congress in 1915, this Service suffered serious personnel losses during the war to the armed forces and to administrative agencies.

Prior to 1945 the salaries were lamentably inadequate and qualified persons were obtained and retained with great difficulty. Specialists on subjects such as money and banking and social welfare were paid only $2600. Nevertheless, despite these deficiencies congressional use of the

[3] M. Nelson McGeary, *The Developments of Congressional Investigative Power* (1940), pp. 63–66.

service steadily increased since its reorganization in 1939 under the able direction of Luther Evans. By 1945 demands for service, both qualitative and quantitative, within Congress itself had grown so great that the present director, Ernest Griffith, presented plans to the Appropriations Committees for an expanded and adequate Service. The number of inquiries handled had more than doubled in five years with little increase of staff. Currently they were running about 16,000 a year. The plans in general met with favor and a small additional sum was made immediately available to permit a salary scale commensurate with the importance of the work and to increase somewhat the very small number of specialists on the staff. Strong sentiment for a more substantial increase was evident, but it was thought best to await the report on the role recommended for the Service by the Joint Committee on the Organization of Congress which was holding hearings on this subject as well as others.

The report of this committee contained important recommendations for the Legislative Reference Service, assigning to it the task of meeting the research demands of all individual members of Congress and serving as a reserve research pool for committees. The response of Congress was to grant an initial substantial increase to a total appropriation of $425,000 (not including a separate increased appropriation for the State Law Section of $88,000). These figures were subsequently increased July 1, 1946 under the new increased pay scales to approximately $480,000 and $96,000, respectively. By January 1, 1947 it is anticipated that the Service will have at least one qualified specialist in a majority of the fields of importance to Congress, and at salaries comparable to those in the Executive branch. This will still leave the Service somewhat understaffed quantitatively, but Congress is now alert to its needs in this regard and seems determined to make eventual adequate provision.

Present demands absorb all of the time of the staff. Its valuable services include: the assembly of special collections of reference works, statutes, bills, reports, and documents useful in framing legislation; the preparation of indexes, digests, and compilations; special services to certain members on particular topics; consultation with members on problems in which they are interested; the preparation of material for speeches; digests of arguments pro and con various bills; assistance in the organization of committee hearings; and basic data studies of problems likely to come before Congress for committee deliberation. Such studies, for example, have been made of procedures of the peace settlement, strikes in war industries, the future of the Civilian Conservation Corps, federal aid to education, federal field offices, workmen's compensation for federal employees, the federal role in child welfare, the control of atomic energy, and the Reciprocal Trade Agreements Act. The Service also prepares and distributes to members abstracts of significant books and articles in the whole field of public affairs, and maintains an extensive collection of pamphlets, reports, releases, and clippings from many magazines and newspapers. Congress now possesses in its Library the largest collection of research materials ever assembled. It thus enjoys unrivalled resources for technical aid on all important public problems. All that is required to make these resources fully effective is an adequate research staff to use them.

The average member of Congress has no time for research and few can afford to employ competent research assistants. It is no criticism of the committee and members' clerks to say that, with few exceptions, they are not technical experts on fiscal and monetary policy, foreign trade, and the like. One of the functions of Congress is to inform its own members with unbiased information on any topic. For this purpose, there is a growing consensus of opinion that the Congress should have independent research facilities and a research staff equal in quality to the staff and facilities available to the executive branch of the government and to special interest groups.

A typical expression of the congressional attitude toward staffing is that of Senator La Follette. Writing in the *Alantic Monthly* of July, 1943, the Senator said: "The question of adequate and expert staff is of vital importance. Undoubtedly one of the great contributing factors to the shift of influence and power from the legislative to the executive branch in recent years is the fact that Congress has been generous in providing expert and technical personnel for the executive agencies but niggardly in providing such personnel for itself."

"One of the traditional powers of Congress over the Executive," he continued, "is supposedly control over the purse strings. Obviously, that control cannot be exercised intelligently unless Congress has the facilities and the expert staff to appraise and evaluate appropriations just as the Budget Bureau does. Yet the annual appropriation for the staff of the Bureau of the Budget is 13 times as large as the appropriations for the staff of the Senate and House Committees on Appropriations combined."

Location of Legislative Staff

The question arises whether the major standing committees of Congress should have their own separate staffs, like that of the Joint Committee on Internal Revenue Taxation, or whether such aids should be drawn from a permanent pool of trained and qualified researchers located, say, in the Legislative Reference Service in the Congressional Library.

The arguments in favor of committee staffing are chiefly these: (1) Experts attached to particular committees become specialists in their fields; (2) they are free to give committee members their own personal appraisal of pending proposals; and (3) they are able to anticipate problems which will be coming to the committee's attention and to prepare members in advance for their consideration. On the other hand, the following objections are raised to separate committee staffs:

(1) Permanent staffs composed of qualified experts attached to the standing committees might develop hostility to the Executive departments under their jurisdiction and create rival legislative and administrative staffs. An example of this possibility is seen in the occasional conflict between the Treasury Department and the staff of the Joint Committee on Internal Revenue. (2) Appointments to such staffs might be used by committee chairmen for patronage purposes and would not be available to the minority members of the committees. (3) This arrangement would require duplicate staffing of House and Senate committees, unless the committee system were reorganized along identical lines in both chambers, in which case joint staffs could be used. (4) If the major standing committees were staffed on the scale of the Joint Committee on Internal Revenue, which has 15 employees, it would greatly increase the cost of the Legislative Establishment.

The arguments for establishing a central staff pool are briefly these: (1) The traditional attitude of the Legislative Reference Service on controversial questions is one of scientific impartiality, which would obviate friction with the experts from the Administration. (2) Appointments to the staff of the Service are non-partisan in accordance with the requirements of the merit system. (3) The Director of the Service, in consultation with committee chairmen, could assign one or more members of his staff to each important standing committee under arrangements that would ensure close physical proximity and continuing confidential service. (4) The ultimate cost of an adequately staffed congressional research bureau would run close to half a million dollars, while permanent staffs attached to the major standing committees might cost four times as much. On the other hand, it is argued that staff aides drawn from a central pool might be good generalists, but would lack special knowledge of particular problems of interest to members and committees, and that they would not be at liberty to express their own point of view on controversial questions.

Opinion varies as to the proper location of the staff function in the legislative structure. Some prefer a central staff pool; others believe that the committees should have their own separate staffs. Some think that in actual practice Senators and Representatives will want their staff aids close at hand and will depend upon their positive counsel. Others believe that staff experts should refrain from expressing personal preferences as to alternative legislative policies. Some are confident that committee chairmen will appoint qualified personnel to their staffs. Others hold that the temptation to use a larger and better paid staff for patronage purposes might prove irresistible if their appointment were left to the committees; that the provision of Congress with truly independent and adequate technical staff aids would be defeated unless trained and qualified experts were appointed who knew Congress and its needs as well as their specialties; and that, in expanding the legislative staff, the best way to avoid patronage appointments is to establish a joint staff service by statute and place its personnel under the merit system. They argue that the Office of Legislative Counsel was set up by statute and has not become a political plum. Whether or not reliance is placed upon a central staff pool, the Legislative Reference Service has rendered outstanding service to the members and committees of Congress and it should be given an increased appropriation so as to permit it to employ top-flight professional experts on all the major economic and social problems of the day.

It should be the duty of the legislative staff, wherever located, not to determine policy, nor necessarily to oppose the departmental experts, but to advise and assist the committees of both houses in the analysis, appraisal, and evaluation of recommendations submitted to Congress by the President or any executive agency; to aid legislative and conference committees of Congress in analyzing proposed legislation before them; and to assist congressional committees by marshalling the arguments pro and con alternative courses of action. A competent and independent legislative staff will not dispense, however, with Congress' need of expert advice from the departments. Trained and experienced men in administrative agencies will continue to be of special use to Congress and no legislative staff service could fully take their place.

Proposed Improvements in Legislative Staff Aids

In order to improve the information services and facilities to the members and committees of Congress upon which intelligent lawmaking depends, several steps should promptly be taken. Each member should be authorized to employ a high-caliber assistant at $8,000 a year to assist him in his office work. Many congressional offices now lack persons who are familiar with the tools of the research trade and who know how to analyze and digest materials on modern public problems. Lecture courses for congressional secretaries should be arranged to familiarize them with departmental policies and programs, for much of the departmental business of Congressmen is handled for them by their secretaries. Since the volume of office work varies with the size of the congressional districts, some system of flexible clerk-hire allowances should be adopted according to the size of constituencies, or a stenographic pool should be provided upon which members could draw at busy seasons.

The committees of Congress should greatly expand their staffs with trained investigators and research technicians qualified by adequate training and experience in the fields covered by the committees which employ them. A model committee staff would include a staff director, a specialist and assistant in each main branch of the committee's province, a chief clerk and file clerk, one liaison man for each agency under the committee's jurisdiction, and a sufficient number of secretaries and typists. The committees should hire their own staff personnel on merit and not borrow them from federal departments except under unusual circumstances and then only for brief periods. A graded schedule of staff salaries should be established high enough to attract and keep persons of competence, integrity, and expertise.

A weekly or biweekly bulletin might well be issued to all members summarizing the activities of each of the major committees of Congress. Such a bulletin would not only keep the members posted on committee work, but it would also show which committees were relatively inactive and which ones were carrying more than an average work load. The House and Senate Small Business Committees, chaired by Representative Patman and Senator Murray, have adopted this practice which has received widespread congressional commendation.

A detailed analysis of legislative positions and their duties should be made and a job classification plan developed for all the employees of Congress covering their titles, qualifications, employment, promotion, tenure, leave, and retirement.

The majority and minority caucus or conference in each chamber should each be equipped with an adequate secretariat to assist the party leaders on both sides of the aisle in planning the legislative program and formulating party policy.

Members of Congress should be invited to participate in both the formulation and negotiation of international agreements which will require either the advice and consent of the Senate or the provision of funds. Influential members of both houses of Congress participated in the actual negotiations of the Bretton Woods program and the United Nations Organization—an arrangement which won widespread legislative approval and greatly improved the climate of congressional opinion, as well as understanding, of international political and economic problems.

In order to keep Congress as a whole better informed of legislative developments and of economic and social conditions, it is suggested: (1) that a daily calendar or bulletin be issued to all members showing the business scheduled to come before the committees and houses on the current and following days; (2) that an information service on sources of information be furnished all members; (3) that Congress should make more frequent formal and organized inquiries into basic national affairs, preferably by creating ad hoc mixed commissions like the Temporary National Economic Committee rather than special investigating committees; (4) that members of Congress should make more field inspection trips in order to obtain more first-hand information concerning the state of the nation; and (5) that committee hearings and documents be fully indexed so as to increase their usefulness and expedite quick reference.

THE BIOGRAPHY OF A BILL[4]

To the reader unfamiliar with the legislative process it may be of interest to trace the biography of a bill, after it has been conceived and

---

[4] Adapted from an outline of congressional procedure for passing legislation prepared by Hon. William Tyler Page, Clerk of the House of Representatives, 1919–1931.

born, from the moment of its introduction to the day, perhaps months later, when the President signs it.

In the House the bill is first dropped by the member into a basket on the clerk's desk known as "the hopper." The Speaker's clerk goes through the batch of new bills and assigns the bill to the committee having jurisdiction under the rules. The bill is numbered, proper records are made of its introduction, date on which it was submitted, etc. and it is then printed.

In the Senate, a Senator desiring to introduce a bill, having first been recognized by the presiding officer, sends it to the Secretary's desk. If there is no objection, the Legislative Clerk reads the bill by title. If objection is made to its second reading, it must be postponed for one day. It cannot be referred until it has been read twice. The desired reference to committee is frequently indicated on the bill by its author; otherwise, the presiding officer announces the committee to which it will be referred. In the event a question arises as to its reference, the author, or any other Senator, may make a motion to refer it to a certain committee.

Bills sometimes are ordered to lie on the table temporarily, to be taken up at a later date for reference or consideration without being referred. Reference of a Senate bill is not mandatory. After being referred the bill is numbered and entered in the bill book and in the Senate Journal of the proceedings of that day.

On the following morning, printed copies of the bill are delivered to the Secretary's Office, and to the Senate and House document rooms, the original being returned and placed in the files of the Senate.

Considered in Committee

When printed copies are received by the clerk of the committee to which the bill has been referred, the bill is placed on the list of bills before that committee and is then ready for consideration by the committee.

Some committees have regular meeting days, while others meet only at the call of the chairman. When the committee meets, the calendar is called by the clerk, and a particular bill taken up for consideration. If the bill is one of importance, it may be referred to a subcommittee, appointed by the chairman, for study. Where a matter is deemed to be of sufficient importance, and the committee or subcommittee desires information on the subject, hearings are held and witnesses are called, or may request to be heard, to give testimony. A day is appointed for the hearings and both sides are notified. If the opposition presents arguments strong enough and the committee is convinced that the bill should not be passed, the committee may adopt one of two courses of action.

1. Vote to report the bill to the House (or Senate) with the recommendation that it do not pass. This is called an adverse report and is seldom made.

2. Vote to lay the bill on the table. This means that the committee merely lays the bill aside without reporting it favorably or adversely. This is commonly known as "pigeon-holing" a bill. This term comes from the old-fashioned desks with pigeon holes, wherein papers were put away and forgotten.

But if the opposition does not present a strong enough case, and the committee votes to approve the bill, it is reported favorably to the House (or Senate), with or without amendment, with a recommendation that it be passed. Sometimes a detailed report from the committee containing the majority and minority views of the members is filed with the bill. These reports are printed.

In the Senate, if the committee fails to report a bill within what may be deemed to be a reasonable time, any Senator has the privilege, under the rules, of entering a motion to discharge the committee from its further consideration. If the motion is agreed to, the bill is thereby taken out of the jurisdiction of the committee. Only by unanimous consent can it be considered at that time; otherwise it must lie over a day. In the meantime it is placed on the calendar of bills under Rule VIII.

In the House, if a member wishes to discharge a committee from consideration of a bill he may, after the committee has had the bill at least 30 days, file a motion to discharge which must be signed by a majority (218 members) of the House. If the motion prevails, the bill may then be considered directly by the House, either immediately if so decided, or from the calendar where it is then referred.

Takes Its Place on the Calendar

When a bill is reported from a committee to the House (or Senate), it is referred to a calendar. The House and Senate calendars are actually lists on which bills and resolutions are recorded in numerical order to be considered under given circumstances at periods fixed in advance. The House has five different calendars, whereas the Senate has but one, although the Senate Calendar is supplemented by orders of business which are, in effect, special calendars.

The House Calendars, as provided for in House Rule XIII, are as follows:

1. The Union Calendar: A calendar of the Committee of the Whole House on the State of the Union, to which are referred bills raising revenue, general appropriation bills, and bills of a public character directly or indirectly appropriating money or property.

2. The House Calendar: A calendar to which are referred all bills of a public character not raising revenue nor directly or indirectly appropriating money or property.

3. The Private Calendar: A calendar of the Committee of the Whole House, to which are referred all bills of a private character.

4. The Consent Calendar: A special calendar subject to call on the first and third Mondays of each month when a bill requested to be placed thereon may be considered under unanimous consent.

5. The Discharge Calendar: A special calendar where motions to discharge a committee from consideration of bills are placed.

Is Taken Up for Consideration

Numerous ways are provided by the House and Senate rules for taking up a bill once it is on a calendar. The particular method will depend upon the nature of the bill, whether privileged or not. In the House, it may be considered under the regular order of business. It may be taken up by unanimous consent. It may be called up on "Calendar Wednesday" by direction of the committee reporting it. It may be passed under suspension of the rules, which requires a two-thirds vote. It may come up on certain days if it is a private bill. It may take precedence over other bills if it is an appropriation or revenue bill. And if, in the view of the Rules Committee, the bill deserves prompt and special consideration, that committee may bring in a rule for its immediate consideration and prescribe the terms under which it may be considered, including a time limit on debate, over-riding all rules save the rule for a motion to recommit. A motion to recommit means to return it to committee for further consideration.

Neither house can take action on a bill unless there is a quorum present. The rules declare that a quorum is a majority of its members. Thus in the Senate 49 Senators constitute a quorum of that body and in the House a quorum is 218 members. Votes are decided by a majority of those present. Absentees' votes are usually paired.

May Be Debated

Ordinarily the duration of the debate in the House is determined by the importance of the measure and the amount of controversy involved. The discussion is generally opened by the chairman of the committee in charge, and, unless a specified time has been set for debate, it is ended by a motion for the "previous question" and the vote is taken. Owing to its size the House has various rules for limiting debate. In certain circumstances debate is limited to forty, twenty, or ten minutes. In the case of important bills a debate limit of one or two days is fixed in advance, with the time equally divided between the proponents and opponents.

A majority vote of those present and voting is required to pass an ordinary bill. A two-thirds vote is required to suspend the rules and for certain measures specified in the constitution such as a resolution to amend the constitution.

Considered by the Senate

When a bill is passed by the House, that fact is certified by the Clerk of the House. The certified copy is then carried to the Senate, where, after certain formalities, it is received by the presiding officer who refers it to the Senate committee having jurisdiction of the subject matter. Here it undergoes another process of examination.

The Senate committee, in turn, is at liberty to hold hearings, to shelve or "pigeon-hole" the bill, to approve it as it stands, or to make amendments of its own. If approved or amended, the bill is reported in due time to the Senate, where it takes its place on the Senate calendar.

A Senator, when reporting a bill, may request unanimous consent for its present consideration. Upon objection the bill goes to the calendar. If granted, the bill is usually passed with little or no debate. It may or may not be amended, depending upon the recommendation of the committee. It is, however, within the right of any Senator to propose amendments to any bill under consideration.

Senate Rule VIII, which governs the consideration of the calendar bills, states (in part):

At the conclusion of the morning business for each day, unless upon motion the Senate shall at any time otherwise order, the Senate will proceed to the consideration of the Calendar of Bills and Resolutions, and continue such consideration until 2 o'clock; and bills and resolutions that are not objected to shall be taken up in their order, and each Senator shall be entitled to speak once and for 5 minutes only upon any question.

On Mondays in the Senate, when there is a morning hour, the call of the calendar can be dispensed with only by unanimous consent; but on any other day, following the announcement of the close of morning business, it is in order for a Senator obtaining recognition to move to take up any bill on the calendar out of its regular order, and the consideration of the bill may continue until the expiration of the morning hour at 2 o'clock, when the presiding officer lays before the Senate the unfinished business of the previous day. A bill taken up is open to amendment, the amendments reported by a committee usually being first considered. The next step, after the amendment stage, is the engrossment and third reading of the bill. This reading is usually by title only, but, upon demand, it must be read in full. The question is then put upon its passage, which is carried by a majority vote. At any time before its passage, a bill may be laid on the table; postponed indefinitely (either of these motions having the effect of killing the bill); made a special order for a certain day; laid aside temporarily; or recommitted or referred to a different committee.

Most bills are passed by a viva voce vote only; that is to say, without a roll call; but, under the constitution, a yea-and-nay vote may be had upon demand of one-fifth of the Senators present.

A bill of major importance is never considered under the 5-minute rule, provided in Senate Rule VIII, but is taken up on motion, which, after 2 o'clock, is debatable, and thereby acquires a preferred status as unfinished business. This status gives it priority, after the morning hour, over other measures except those privileged in their nature, such as conference reports and amendments between the houses. Its consideration may be continued over a period of several days; but it may be displaced as unfinished business at any time by affirmative action upon a motion to take up another bill.

After its passage, the bill is attested by the secretary as having passed the Senate. It is then messaged to the House of Representatives. If amendments have been made, they accompany the Senate engrossed bill, and the concurrence of the House is requested in the amendments.

The House amendments in due course are laid before the Senate. They are read and may, by unanimous consent, be considered en bloc.

Some of the House amendments may be agreed to, others agreed to with amendments, and still others sent to conference. The concurrence of the Senate in the House amendments completes the legislative steps. If a House bill is passed by the Senate with any new revisions, it is returned to the House. If the bill as amended by the Senate is accepted by the House, that ends the matter. The bill is signed by the Speaker and the Vice President or President pro tem and is presented by the Committee on Enrolled Bills to the President for his approval or rejection.

May Go to Conference

But if, on the other hand, the House disagrees to the Senate amendments, the Senate is so informed, and if it still insists upon its amendments, each branch appoints representatives to a joint conference committee, which is charged with the duty of composing the differences between the two bills. The committee nearly always reaches an agreement, and then resubmits the bill to each house for a majority vote. The report of the conference committee is almost invariably confirmed by the vote of the two branches. It sometimes happens that the Senate and House committees are far apart in their final conclusions as to the details of grave measures, and in such cases a heavy responsibility is intrusted to the conference committee.

Debate in the Senate

In the Senate debate is unlimited. There is, however, a rule under which debate may be brought to a close and a vote forced. This is Senate Rule XXII, adopted in 1917, which provides for "cloture," i.e., closing of debate. It was designed to bring to an end what is known as a "filibuster," or the continuous speech-making by one or more Senators to prevent a bill's coming to a vote. The rule provides that a motion to close debate shall be signed by 16 Senators and adopted by two-thirds vote. Only four times since 1917 has the rule been invoked, since Senators are extremely alert to the preservation of their right to free and unlimited debate. It was first invoked on November 15, 1919, on the peace treaty with Germany. The second occasion was during the debate on the World Court on January 25, 1926. Cloture was also invoked on February 15, 1927, to permit a vote on the bill to establish national bank branches, and again on February 28 of the same year on the bill to establish a Bureau of Prohibition in the Treasury Department.

Goes to the President

After a bill has been duly considered and passed by both houses of Congress, it must still be passed upon by the President. If he approves it and signs it, the bill becomes law, is numbered and placed in the files of the State Department.

If, however, the President does not approve it, he is empowered by the constitution to veto it. If he vetoes it, the bill is returned to the house in which it originated. If a two-thirds majoriy of each house votes to override the presidential veto, the bill becomes law without the President's signature. If either house fails to register a two-thirds vote for the bill, the presidential veto stands and the bill does not become law.

The President, under the constitution, has 10 days (Sundays excepted) after the bill has been presented to him, in which to act upon it.

In the event the President does not desire affirmatively to approve the bill, and, on the other hand, is unwilling, for what he deems sufficient reason, to veto it, he may, by not returning it to Congress within the 10-day period after it is presented to him, permit it to become a law without his approval. But if the Congress should adjourn prior to the expiration of the 10-day limit, it fails to become a law. This is what is known as a "pocket veto."

A joint resolution proposing an amendment to the constitution, which requires a two-thirds vote of both branches, does not require the approval of the President. It must be ratified by three-fourths of the states.

A bill, as described above, has a happy fate compared with the great mass of bills submitted. Much of the time of committees is given to the rejection of bills. But once a bill escapes from committee it is disposed of as outlined. All legislation not disposed of, except treaties, which are referred to the Senate only for approval, dies with the Congress and must be reintroduced in the new Congress and start at the beginning of the line again.

MAKING AN ACT OF PARLIAMENT

It is interesting to compare the process of law making in the American Congress with the making of an act of Parliament in England, from which we inherited so many of our legislative practices, and to note the differences. As described by one who has sat in the House of Commons since 1931, the life story of an English law is as follows.[5]

Preparation

A considerable urge is felt, or is supposed to be felt, in the country for, say (to take an imaginary example), pensions for spinsters at thirty. At a general election this project has been included in the program of one of the parties and that party has been returned to power. In due course, at the beginning of a session the matter will be included in the tentative program for that year's work, known as the "Speech from the Throne." This is the warning for all interests, both for and against, to gird their loins. It means that the Cabinet have decided to include a measure to give effect to their promise in their program, and the Minister concerned (in this case, the Minister of Health) has been told approximately when the time-table will permit the introduction of the bill and that he and his staff of permanent officials (civil servants) must prepare it. Until an Act of Parliament is passed and becomes law, it is called a bill.

The Minister will have already started conversations and enquiries. He will have found out from the Chancellor of the Exchequer within what financial limits he must work. All sorts of organizations and societies and individuals will put in memoranda. When the outline of his intention is clear enough, the Minister will call in some extremely able gentlemen (barristers specialising in such work, who have become civil servants and are known as parliamentary draftsmen) who will put into the legal form of a bill, ready for presentation to Parliament, proposals that the Minister has arrived at.

At a convenient stage a Cabinet committee will have examined the draft proposals and later the whole Cabinet will have had an opportunity to examine the proposed bill.

In due course, a formality will be gone through, the Minister "presenting" the bill and the House of Commons automatically granting it "first reading." (A bill may be first introduced in the House of Lords and come afterwards to the Commons, but one of a financial character such as our imaginary example would start in the Commons.)

The life and troubles of a bill ordinarily begin, publicly at least, with the "second reading." If the subject is a complicated one, the Government, either in advance or when the bill is introduced, may publish a "White Paper" to expound its ideas, or it may publish an explanatory

[5] A. W. H. James, *How Parliament Works* (1944), pp. 21–24.

memorandum accompanying the bill. A White Paper published in advance of the bill may be debated and voted upon before the bill is presented and thus act as a sort of *ballon d'essai*.

Second Reading

A "second reading" debate is the examination of the general principles of the bill and permits a wide discussion. Arguments for and against the bill including alternative methods of dealing with the problem are ventilated, and, in accordance with the size and importance of the measure, the debate may last for one, two or three days. This marks the vital distinctions between the British and foreign parliamentary systems. In the British system the bill must win the victory in a discussion on general principles. In most other systems a bill must sustain examination by a committee before the regulative assembly is allowed to see it. At the end of a second reading debate a division usually takes place following party lines.

The Financial Resolution

In the eighteenth century the main danger to the working of Parliament was corruption by the Crown of the individual member of Parliament. That has gone, but there is still a danger that the individual member might attempt to divert more than his fair share of the national income to those who elect him. Therefore, all expenditure has to be initiated by the Government who prescribe the limits of expenditure for each bill by means of a financial resolution. The modern practice is to draw such resolutions widely so that there is reasonable scope for improving the bill, but it is not possible for the member for Muddlehampton to propose a Muddlehamptonian Utopia when the rest of the country merely gets a reasonable improvement.

Committee Stage

Assuming that a bill receives a "second reading" (and, as has been explained, in fact Governments do not introduce legislation without making sure it is likely to receive sufficient and necessary support to ensure its passage), the bill then goes through a "committee stage." This may be taken in one of two ways (or occasionally by a combination of the two) : either the bill is considered by the whole House, which for this purpose resolves itself into a committee, or else it is referred to a standing committee from the House, which sits in a committee room upstairs. A standing committee consists of a proportionate number of Government and Opposition supporters, and is presided over by a chairman selected from a small all-party panel of experienced members. Standing committees consist of not more than 85 or less than 40 members, 20 forming a quorum. In either case, the procedure of the committee stage of a bill is to go through it line by line and clause by clause, amendments being moved and debated, rejected or accepted, and each clause voted upon. The Government may accept amendments and incorporate them in the bill, or it may itself propose amendments. Whether the bill is taken through its committee stage upstairs, or on the floor of the House, depends upon its importance, its length and complexity, and so forth.

A bill may also be referred to a select committee. Such bills are mainly those upon which the House as a whole desires information because they affect particular interests. Select committees may be set up to consider other questions or to consider proposals embodied in a bill. A select committee has power to send for papers and to examine witnesses on oath. It considers the matter referred to it, and then reports back to the House. Thus, it does not exactly take the place of an ordinary committee of the House.

Upon some great constitutional issue, as in the case of the Government of India Bill of 1935, a joint select committee of both houses may be set up to examine and to report.

Report and Third Reading

Next, the bill returns to the House for a "report and third reading," which are usually taken on the same day.

When the bill has been through the lively seas of a committee stage, new aspects have become apparent and new points of view have arisen. For some of these the Minister has been ready. Others demand fresh consideration which he has promised to give. The report stage shows the results of his promises in new amendments which he puts down, and also gives the Opposition a chance to raise points which they do not think have been adequately discussed during committee. As this stage takes place in the House, the Speaker or his deputy keeps a watchful eye to see that there is not mere repetition of the debates in committee.

The third reading is again a general debate, but only upon what the bill now contains after alteration by the committee. The bill then goes to the House of Lords.

The House of Lords not only has certain powers of rejection and revision, but it also performs a valuable routine function. As the bill has left the Commons it may well have got into a tangle, legally speaking, owing to the acceptance or insertion of amendments. The bill may, therefore, be "tidied up" in the Lords and returned to the Commons for what are then, in fact, agreed verbal changes. Thereafter, the bill will receive the Royal Assent and become a law.

Different Kinds of Bills

Money bills must originate in the Commons and are not sent to committees upstairs, but are taken by a committee of the whole House.

Ordinarily, the passage of bills introduced by private members, that is, not by the Government acting through a Minister, is so discouraged by lack of time as to be practically impossible. In this way, collective Cabinet (and party) responsibility for legislation is preserved and crank legislation is held in check. Private members are also protected from pressure upon them from outside interests.

Rare exceptions are when there is a real general urge for some change in the law, but of such a nature that no party will willingly commit itself to the issue. An example of this was the reform of the divorce law introduced by Mr. A. P. Herbert. Once it had become apparent to the Government of the day that there was a general all-party desire to see this bill become law, facilities were afforded for its passage. No party likes to touch certain topics—religion and betting are the best examples—that cut right across party lines while at the same time arousing strong prejudices. In the example referred to, Mr. A. P. Herbert's temerity in introducing the bill resulted in such strong support from the majority of all parties that the Cabinet of the day could afford, and felt in duty bound, to take the risk of allotting parliamentary time for the passage of the measure upon a non-party vote.

There is another class of bill to which reference must be made—a private bill, which is a very different thing from a private member's bill. Local authorities and statutory undertakers are not allowed to execute public works beyond certain defined limits without parliamentary sanction. For example, a municipality wishes to develop a water or electricity supply scheme, or a railway wants to build a new line. It has to secure the passage of a bill to obtain permission. These bills, if given a "second reading," as they commonly are, are then referred to a "private bill committee." Such a committee consists of three or four members sitting in a room upstairs under the chairmanship of an experienced member. No party interest or alignment is involved. The committee really sits as a quasi-judicial body. Counsel, members of the parliamentary bar, argue the case upon its merits before the committee.

It may be, for example, that a neighboring town considers that its interests will be affected, perhaps that some future scheme of its own might be prejudiced, and it will, therefore, employ counsel to oppose the bill.

The bill, if passed by the "private bill committee," then receives approval by the House.

It will be seen that an act of Parliament, if it be a large and complex one, involves a great amount of parliamentary time. The Government of India Bill of 1935 occupied 40 days of the House's time, besides months, indeed years, of preparation.

SIMPLIFYING THE COMMITTEE STRUCTURE

The legislative function of Congress is largely performed, as we have seen, by its standing committee system which, it is generally agreed, needs to be completely modernized. There are far too many standing committees. Many committees have overlapping and duplicating jurisdictions which give rise to competition among them for preference and power and make it difficult to fix responsibility for the formulation of legislative policy. Other committees are inactive, seldom meet, and are merely ornamental barnacles on the ship of state. Each committee "goes its own way at its own pace" without much effort to act in concert. There is no effective coordination of committee work within or between the two houses. A dozen committees carried on independent investigations of the conduct of the war, and half a dozen are presently studying various postwar problems.

This splitting up of the legislative function, to be sure, enables the members of standing committees to become specialists in particular fields. They acquire familiarity with the history of a subject and with the men who administer the agencies under their jurisdiction. "Sometimes they become better informed than the heads of departments themselves. Often they make wiser judgments in matters of policy because they have a broader outlook, a better understanding of the needs of the country as a whole, more sense of proportion." [6] But this splinter approach also militates against the dovetailing of interrelated policies and the development of consistent legislative programs. Specialism has manifest advantages, but the division of labor among committees, especially in the Senate, is very unequal. Minor committees

[6] Robert Luce, *Congress: An Explanation* (1926), p. 5.

have a sinecure. The designation of 10 House committees as "exclusive" was a partial corrective of this condition. Moreover, many members have so many committee assignments that they find it impossible to attend their meetings because of conflicts and appear by proxy: a criticism more applicable to the Senate than the House.

The La Follette Proposal

These and similar complaints have led to a series of proposals for committee consolidation and the Joint Committee on the Organization of Congress was authorized to make recommendations to this end. Among these proposals three are especially noteworthy. Writing in the *Atlantic Monthly* for July, 1943, Senator La Follette suggested that the number of standing committees in the upper house be reduced from 33 to 13. Of the 13 new committees, eight would deal with substantive policy and five would have administrative functions. The eight substantive policy committees would be: Agriculture, Armed Forces, Finance and Monetary Affairs, Foreign Relations, Interior, Natural Resources and Public Works, Interstate Commerce, Judiciary, and Labor and Public Welfare. The five administrative committees would be: Appropriations, Expenditures in Executive Departments, Rules and Administration, Claims, and District of Columbia. Under the La Follette proposal, each of the policy committees would have 12 members and would be an exclusive committee in the sense that its members would have no other major committee assignment. The policy committees would be empowered to act jointly with corresponding committees of the House of Representatives. "No person familiar with the situation in the Senate today," said Senator La Follette in introducing his proposal in the Senate, "can deny that there is a pressing need for committee reorganization and for the streamlining of the legislative branch of the Government if it is to survive in the struggle for power which is bound to continue."

The Wadsworth Plan

The second proposal was made by Congressman Wadsworth of New York, member of Congress since 1915, in testimony before the Joint Committee on the Organization of Congress in March, 1945. Speaking of the committee system in the lower chamber, Mr. Wadsworth said that it had "grown like Topsy" in a planless manner since the early days of the Republic, with the result that legislative matters are today scattered over some 48 committees, of which not more than 16 were important. The other committees rarely meet, he said, but have been continued to provide perquisites for their chairmen and assignments for new members. New members come to Washington with fresh enthusiasm, hoping to play a useful part in the legislative process, but their enthusiasm is soon dampened by assignments to unimportant committees. In order to correct these conditions, Mr. Wadsworth recommended a sweeping reorganization of the committee system in the House of Representatives. He proposed to reduce the number of standing committees in that chamber from 48 to 17 each of which would have 25 members, on the average, except Appropriations which would have 35, thus giving each Representative one important committee assignment. Under the Wadsworth proposal the line-up of House committees would be as follows:

Agriculture	Labor
Appropriations	Merchant Marine & Fisheries
Banking & Currency	Armed Services
Civil Service	Veterans' Affairs
Public Works	Public Lands
Interstate & Foreign Commerce	Ways and Means
Judiciary	Rules
Foreign Affairs	House Administration

Un-American Activities[7]

A Parallel Pattern

The third suggestion, made by the writer, proposes to eliminate the inactive committees and merge those with overlapping jurisdictions so that each house would have one committee in each of 12 broad areas of public policy, with clearly defined jurisdiction over legislation in each field and over the administrative agencies responsible for its execution. The 12 areas, which cover the domain of public policy-making in modern America, are agriculture, commerce and industry, labor, foreign affairs, national defense, fiscal and monetary policy, social welfare, natural resources, public works, transportation, governmental machinery and services, and the judiciary. Thus there would be twin committees in

---

[7] This committee, sequel to a select committee by the same name which won dubious fame for its witch-hunting antics, was reincarnated as a standing committee in 1945 at the behest of Representative Rankin after the political demise of its former chairman, Martin Dies. It should be abolished and its functions transferred to the Department of Justice.

each chamber with broad jurisdictions rather than narrow specialized fields of responsibility, an arrangement which would facilitate joint action on matters of mutual interest by means of joint hearings and joint staffs: a practice with a long record of successful operation in the Massachusetts legislature.

Such a system of parallel committees in both houses would increase the efficiency of the committee structure, avoid jurisdictional disputes, and fix more definite responsibility for legislative policy. It would also facilitate liaison between the chambers and economize the time of busy legislators and administrators alike. By setting up twin committees in broad areas of public policy, correlated with the pattern of the administrative structure along functional rather than departmental lines, this plan, I believe, would greatly facilitate the performance by Congress of its legislative and oversight functions, provide direct channels of communication and cooperation between the Legislature and the Executive, and overcome the handicap of our system of separated powers.

Such a coordinate scheme of arrangements already exists, to a certain extent, in the fields of agriculture, civil service, foreign relations, military and naval affairs, Indian affairs, and other areas. The process and machinery of integration and consolidation might well be further extended into fields now lacking it. In addition to the 12 policy committees, each house would also have a Committee on Administration, charged with general oversight of its rules, accounts, and internal housekeeping activities.

Under each of these proposals the functions of the existing Joint Committees on Printing and the Library would be absorbed by the new Committees on House and Senate Administration, but the Joint Committee on Internal Revenue Taxation would continue without change. In addition, it has been suggested that four new joint standing committees be established: (1) a Joint Committee on Appropriations with investigative and research functions in the field of appropriations analogous to those performed by the Joint Committee on Internal Revenue in the field of taxation; (2) a Joint Committee on Public Accounts to supervise the General Accounting Office and review the Comptroller General's reports; (3) a Joint Committee on Executive Agencies to conduct investigations and studies into the practices and procedures of administrative agencies; and (4) a Joint Committee on the National Budget to study and report its findings and recommendations with respect to the national budget to be transmitted to Congress by the President under the Employment Act.[8] I shall have occasion to deal more fully with these proposed new joint standing committees in the next chapter.

Streamlining of the congressional committee system along the lines outlined above is the heart and *sine qua non* of legislative reform. Little overt opposition to this reform has been heard in the halls of Congress. Instead, the proposal for fewer and smaller policy committees has been endorsed by many Senators and Representatives, despite the sacrifices of seniority and chairmanships it would entail. But there are powerful vested interests in the existing outmoded committee structure which may be expected behind the scenes to resist any sweeping change by every parliamentary weapon at their command. Each of the 55 committees that would be abolished or absorbed under the proposed reform has a chairman and ranking majority and minority members who would lose prized places of power and prestige, and the patronage that goes therewith. Here is a strong nucleus of 165 senior members most of whom will probably vote "nay" when the role is called on the resolution to modernize the committee system. And they will probably be joined by the chairmen of the several special committees in both houses whose functions would be absorbed within the comprehensively defined jurisdictions of the new standing committees.

In Defense of the Status Quo

One can anticipate the arguments that will be made by the apologists of the present committee system. The dispersal of legislative power among 81 committee chairmen is more democratic, they will say, than to concentrate it in the hands of one man as the House did before 1911 when the Speaker chose the chairmen. To this the answer is that it is not proposed to return to one-man rule, but to make 12 or 15 men in each house collectively responsible for legislative leadership: a number large enough to avoid one-man dictation, but small enough to correct current centrifugal tendencies.

It will also be argued that the present system provides incentive to a legislative career by offering one member out of every six or seven the chance of a chairmanship and that this incentive would be removed in proportion to the reduction in the number of standing committees. The reply here is that there will be as many, if not more, opportunities for legislative influence and usefulness as chairman of a major active

---

[8] Since this was written, a Joint Committee on the Economic Report has been established for this purpose.

committee or important subcommittee than there are today in the empty honor of chairing some minor committee that seldom meets and cuts little legislative ice.

Others may argue that the existing system, under which Senators serve on half a dozen different committees, gives wide experience of legislative problems and so avoids the dangers of narrow specialization. In actual practice, however, there is a limit to the span of human attention and when a member sits on several committees which are simultaneously active, he tends either to focus on one of them and skimp the others or to spread himself superficially over them all. Under the proposed reform there will still be many opportunities for a variety of experience through service on several subcommittees, but it will be more pertinent and useful experience within the framework of an integrated committee pattern.

Some will also say that the proposed reform will not lead to any real reduction in the total number of congressional committees because subcommittees will take the place of many of the existing committees. That remains to be seen, but the new committee structure will be more logically organized with more clearly defined jurisdictions, permitting more effective meshing of the legislative gears, and the rash of special committees will be eliminated.

Finally, it will be argued against streamlining the committees of Congress that the present duplicating system allows a choice of reference of measures to friendly or hostile committees according to the attitude of the leadership toward particular legislative proposals. To this the answer is that "the power to pigeon-hole is a dangerous power" as Luce said twenty years ago. No committee should be used as a graveyard for the burial of bills in which there is widespread public interest. It is a travesty on representative government to let any little group of legislators, however bigoted or benighted, deny the whole House the right to discuss and debate important measures like poll tax repeal or fair employment practices.

IMPROVING COMMITTEE OPERATION

The effectiveness of congressional committee procedure depends in large part upon the character of the testimony presented and upon the time and interest devoted by committee members to hearings, meetings, and deliberations. If hearings are well planned and conducted, if relevant evidence is clearly presented and succinctly summarized, and if committeemen carefully consider matters referred to them, then the process should yield fruitful results. This was the experience of such recent committees as the La Follette civil liberties, the Tolan interstate migration, and the Truman-Mead national defense committees. In other cases, however, congressmen, witnesses, and detached observers have found fault with committee procedure. Irregular and infrequent meetings, inadequate staff aids, poorly organized agenda, no advance planning or efficient conduct of hearings, lack of the subpoena power, mistreatment of witnesses, repetitious, lopsided, and irrelevant testimony, hearings published without summary or index, poor attendance by committeemen, incomplete and unsystematic records, and defective reports are the principal shortcomings attributed by contemporary critics of the way some congressional committees operate.

Membership and Organization

Committee operations could be improved in several ways. First, as to their *membership:* by assigning members to committees on the basis of their special knowledge, experience, and interest in the various legislative fields; and by making certain members of each legislative committee (e.g., the chairman and ranking minority member) ex officio members of the Committee on Appropriations, to meet with it when the bill making appropriations for the departments and agencies under their jurisdiction is being considered by that committee. The quality of committee performance will be improved when members are chosen on the basis of special aptitude for its work, and appropriations will be more wisely made if considered in the light of the experience of those whose duty it is to keep constant watch over departmental operations. The latter suggestion is merely an extension of the Senate practice since 1931 whereby, under Rule XVI, paragraph 6, three members of each of seven legislative committees (Agriculture and Forestry, Post Offices and Post Roads, Military Affairs, Naval Affairs, District of Columbia, Commerce, and Foreign Relations) are ex officio members of the Senate Appropriations Committee.

Second, as to internal *organization:* by dividing the committee into as many subcommittees as there are principal functional or geographic subdivisions of its province and by clearly delimiting the area each subcommittee is to cover. Thus, the Foreign Affairs Committees would have subcommittees for each of the principal geographical regions of the world (as the Foreign Affairs Committee of the House now has) or for each of the principal policy problems (trade, investment, migration, reconstruction, etc.) in the international field. And, to give another example, the Transportation Committees would have subcommittees on the merchant marine, public roads, inland waterways, aviation, and railroads. This scheme would insure that each phase of the committee's province would receive special attention, with the full committee dovetailing the several parts of the picture and taking an overall view of its entire field.

Meetings and Staffing

Third, as to meetings: by having regular weekly committee meeting days so timed as not to conflict with other important committee meetings; or by requiring chairmen to call committee meetings on the petition of a majority of the members. Some have also suggested that committee meetings should be open to the public, but this, I think, would be undesirable. For in executive committee sessions members cannot talk to the press or the galleries, partisanship disappears behind closed doors, and secrecy improves the chances of compromise.

Fourth, as to committee staffing: by the expert staffing of the standing committees, by the segregation of committee staffs from the personnel in the private offices of their chairmen, by not using committee staffs to do the purely personal office work of their chairmen, by making the services of the staff equally available to minority as well as majority members of the committee, by the development of close working relations between the chairman and staff director, by the systematic organization and distribution of staff work, and by the much greater use of joint staffing—a practice which has worked well in the case of the Joint Committee on Internal Revenue Taxation and which helps to bridge the gap between the two chambers. Effective committee operation has seriously suffered from failure to satisfy these conditions. Joint staffing alone would go far to replace joint committees, to which many members are averse. It would also reduce the necessity of referring differences to conference committees. Surprising as it seems, there was little collaboration between the houses at the staff level on postwar reconversion and full employment legislation.

"It is rather asinine," said Congressman La Follette to a group of his Indiana constituents, "for the Congress to appropriate millions of dollars, yes, even billions of dollars, for the staffing of the executive branch of the government with lawyers, statisticians, engineers, and economists, and fail to have the courage to set up a similar body for themselves and to appropriate ample funds for obtaining the best impartial body of experts in America upon any and all legislative subjects. If Congress takes this step," he continued, "then article I, section 1 of the constitution . . . will again become a living, vital section of the constitution. If it is not done, you could chisel the words of that article and section in letters a hundred feet high and 20 feet deep across the face of the greatest mountain in America and they would no more preserve the constitutional mandate that laws and policies shall be made by the Congress than if they had never been expressed or written into it." [9]

Agenda and Hearings

Fifth, as to committee *agenda:* by publishing monthly legislative calendars showing the legislative history and current status of all bills and resolutions referred to the committee, hearings held, reports made, laws enacted, nominations referred, action taken, communications received, subcommittee assignments, and minutes of committee meetings. Of the 84 standing committees of the 79th Congress (including three joint ones) only seven Senate committees, 10 House committees, and the Joint Committee on Printing published calendars. A model worth emulating is the calendar of the Senate Committee on Military Affairs prepared by W. I. Smalley, its able special assistant. Furthermore, each committee should schedule at least once a month a docket day when members of the House or Senate could appear before the committee and plead for a hearing on legislation they had introduced. This suggestion was made by Representative Herter of Massachusetts on behalf of what he called the "submerged element of the Congress," meaning the new members. "They file bills which they consider of considerable importance, but through perfectly arbitrary rulings of the chairman of the committee, they never have a chance to say why they consider they are important either to their districts or to the nation. The bill is dead and gone." [10] This device, he thought, would reduce the objections to the seniority custom. Moreover, referred bills and resolutions should be considered upon the petition of one-third of the members of the committee—a procedure designed to prevent the pigeon-holing of legislation in which several members are interested.

Sixth, as to committee *hearings:* by setting standards in the rules for

[9] Speech by Rep. Charles M. La Follette on "The Functions of Congress in Today's and Tomorrow's Problems" before the Rotary Club of Evansville, Indiana, August 3, 1943. Printed in the *Congressional Record*, September 23, 1943 (appendix), pp. A4278–9.

[10] Hearings before the Joint Committee on the Organization of Congress, March 19, 1945, p. 101.

hearings before all congressional committees on the following points:
by giving adequate advance notice of hearings to all interested parties;
by obtaining from witnesses advance copies of statements to be submitted and briefly digesting them for the information of committee
members; by informing prospective witnesses what the committee
would like them to cover in their testimony; by encouraging the assembly and disclosure of all pertinent information; by advance planning
of the order in which witnesses shall be called so as to promote a logical
development of the case; by briefing committee members on the objectives of the hearing, the testimony to be heard, and the pertinent questions to be asked so as to elicit all relevant information; by not asking
irrelevant questions if members are not adequately prepared, allowing
counsel to develop the case; by submitting weekly previews of pending
hearings to the press; and by the greater use of joint hearings held by
parallel committees of the two houses on common problems so as to
avoid duplicating testimony and save the time of all concerned.

All citizens have the democratic right to present their views to their
representatives in Congress. This right should not be abridged; neither
should it be abused by tedious and irrelevant harangues. Congress also
has a right to secure the disclosure of all pertinent facts bearing on
proposed legislation, including not only the arguments of special interest groups with axes to grind, but also the testimony of disinterested
experts and spokesmen for the public interest. Care should be taken
by committee counsel in planning hearings to invite persons qualified
to speak for the general welfare as well as lobbyists for pressure groups.
Otherwise the legislative product of the hearing process may have a
strong sectional or group bias.

Too often committee hearings are held without adequate advance
preparation on the part of the members, the witnesses, or the staff. The
staff may have failed to choose the witnesses well or coach them wisely;
the witnesses may not have filed advance copies of their statements with
the committee or their testimony may not be succinct, lucid, and
pertinent; the committeemen may lack the requisite background information or fail to study the hearing briefs and ask intelligent questions. The hearings held by the Truman-Mead Committee, which
investigated the conduct of World War II, were among the best
managed hearings on the "Hill" in recent years; but even they fell
short sometimes of these ideal standards.

An able summary of the way in which committee hearings should be
planned and conducted was given by Robert K. Lamb who served

between 1938 and 1943 as a special investigator and staff director of four outstanding Senate and House investigating committees.[11]

Every set of hearings should be based upon the most careful advance preparation by the chairmen and committee members in conjunction with the staff. For this purpose I suggest that committee members rotate responsibility for certain hearings or divide up the witnesses whom they are to question.

In reading this statement today I am violating one of the rules I have in mind. As far as possible no witness should be allowed to read a prepared statement to a committee. It takes valuable time when the committee might better be questioning the witness. Generally speaking all expert witnesses should be asked to submit statements well in advance of their appearance. Wherever possible these statements should be based upon questions submitted by the committee to the witness. In the case of nonexperts all witnesses should (if possible) be interviewed in advance by committee investigators. These interviews should be recorded at least in brief form. The committee member who is to lead off in questioning a witness should use a digest of the expert's prepared statement or the nonexpert's interview. From these materials, a limited number of questions—enough to hit the high lights of any witness's knowledge—should be prepared by or for the committee member who leads in the questioning. Thus the other committee members can familiarize themselves with the problem in the shortest space of time.

For the use of the committee the chairman and staff should prepare and the committee should meet and consider a memorandum describing the objective of each set of hearings, and showing how each witness is expected to contribute to the development of an over-all picture of the problem being investigated. (The committee will note here the contrast with standing committee hearings in which, so far as possible, the committee undertakes to hear all comers, with little attempt at selectivity.) Every effort should be made to hear all parties necessary to a rounded presentation, but in the interests of speed and efficiency the committee should ask all witnesses who have only a limited contribution to submit written statements and not ask to appear. The press should be furnished with a brief preview each week on pending hearings.

By requiring all witnesses who appear before special committees to file statements or be interviewed in advance, by making available these statements or a digest of the statement or interview to each member of the committee, and by having one member of the committee responsible for preparing in advance to question each witness, the work of the committee can

---

[11] Hearings before the Joint Committee on the Organization of Congress, June 29, 1945, pp. 1019–20.

be greatly expedited. Furthermore the record as presented to Congress, the press, and the public will be greatly improved.

Powers and Witnesses

Seventh, as to committee *powers:* by making the committees of Congress responsible for their acts and omissions to the Legislative Council proposed below.[12] Traditionally, congressional committees have lacked any definite responsibility. Their control over legislation referred to them has been almost unlimited. They can amend or re-write bills to suit themselves. They can report bills or pigeon-hole them. They can initiate measures they desire and bury or emasculate those they dislike. They can proceed with dispatch or stall indefinitely. Their powers are enhanced by the privacy of their proceedings, their irresponsibility, and the absence of a responsible opposition. In short, congressional government is government by the standing committees of Congress, as Woodrow Wilson wrote sixty years ago. The real locus of the legislative power is not in the House or the Senate; it is in the committees. What Miss Follett observed fifty years ago is still true: "Congress no longer exercises its lawful function of lawmaking; that has gone to the committees as completely as in England it has passed to the cabinet." [13] At a time when the business of Congress was small and simple, continuous supervision of committee activity was unnecessary. But now that the national safety and the common welfare depend in so many ways upon the speed, unity, and coherence of legislative action, some machinery must be devised to keep the important committees on the job. *Quis custodiet custodes?* So far as their finances and staffing are concerned, inspection of committee conduct is the task of the Audit and Control and Accounts committees of Congress. But oversight of their legislative performance would be the proper office of a Legislative Council or Congressional Cabinet. Furthermore, full investigative powers should be granted the standing committees of Congress to allow them to study and investigate fully all matters properly within their jurisdiction. This could be done either by amending the House and Senate rules to provide such power or by simple resolution at the opening of each Congress.[14]

Eighth, as to *witnesses:* by inviting independent experts as well as the pressure boys to testify or comment upon pending legislation; by

---

[12] See page 195.

[13] Mary P. Follett, *The Speaker of the House of Representatives* (1896), p. 246.

[14] See Senate Resolution 9, 79th Congress, 1st Session.

requiring prospective witnesses to submit advance transcripts of their testimony and to confine their oral statements to brief summaries thereof instead of reading a prepared statement which could be filed with the committee; and by giving witnesses a respectful and courteous hearing. "There is no reason," says Mrs. Harold Stone of the National League of Women Voters, "why witnesses should be treated like defendants on trial for an offense against society." In most cases congressional committees have conducted their investigations with due consideration of the public interest and with fairness to the organizations and individuals under inquiry. Unfortunately, however, there have recently been conspicuous departures from this pattern: notably the Dies investigation of so-called un-American activities, and the Cox vendetta against the Federal Communications Commission.[15] Under the present rules of Congress there is no automatic guarantee against abuse of the investigatory power to suit the caprice or prejudice of committeemen. Representative Hook of Michigan has introduced a bill (79th Congress, 1st Session, H. R. 1834) which would go far to correct this situation by prescribing the activities of committees in such a way as to protect the rights of witnesses and serve the public good. The unwritten code of courteous congressional conduct does not always suffice to protect citizens and officials from intemperate attacks or punitive expeditions by a small minority which lower Congress in public esteem.

Records and Reports

Ninth, as to committee *records:* by keeping systematic calendars and up-to-date records of committee activity separately from the personal papers of the chairman and individual members of the committee; and by preserving important correspondence and documents. When chairmanships change, valuable committee records of historic interest are sometimes lost or discarded. Arrangements should be made for their deposit in the Library of Congress or the National Archives. The records of special committees should also be preserved.

Tenth, as to committee *reports:* by submitting monthly progress reports of their current activities as a means of keeping the membership informed, such reports to be published in the *Congressional Record;* by requiring committee chairmen to report bills within ten days after favorable committee action; by including in favorable reports on bills

---

[15] For a full account of the struggle between Congress and the FCC, see "Politicans vs. Bureaucrats" by Robert D. Leigh, *Harper's* Magazine, January, 1945.

a brief statement of the supporting reasons and of the national interest at stake in their passage, together with estimates of the cost of the legislation and analyses of the distribution of resulting burdens and benefits; by submitting with reports on bills a record of the committee members present when the final vote on the bill was taken in committee and how each present member voted, so that the house will know whether the report is being made by a majority or minority of the members of the committee; or, alternatively, by requiring all bills to be disposed of by majority vote of all committee members; by prohibiting the Rules Committee from preventing floor consideration of any favorable committee report; by requiring all committees to file reports on all Administration-sponsored measures not later than 60 or 90 days after their introduction; and by reducing the number of signatures on a petition to discharge a House committee from consideration of a public bill from 218 (a majority of the House) to 145 (one-third).

CHOOSING COMMITTEE CHAIRMEN AND MEMBERS

From 1789 to 1910 the Speaker appointed the members of all House committees, but since the overthrow of Speaker Cannon the selection has been made by the Committee on Committees of the Republican Party and the Democratic members of the Committee on Ways and Means, approved by the party caucus, and ratified by the House itself at the opening of each new Congress. Senate committee assignments are made by the Committee on Committees of the two major parties. The members of special and conference committees are customarily appointed by the Speaker of the House and the President of the Senate. The political composition of the committees corresponds roughly to that of the chamber itself, the majority party having a majority of the seats on each standing committee, the minority being represented in proportion to its strength in the chamber.

An attempt is made to give as wide a representation as possible on the more important committees to the several geographical divisions of the country. Thus, an analysis of the regional distribution of the membership of 15 major Senate standing committees in the 78th Congress showed that each of the nine principal geographical subdivisions of the country was represented on six committees: appropriations, banking and currency, commerce, education and labor, foreign relations, and interstate commerce; eight of the regions were represented on two committees: finance and post offices and post roads; seven regions were represented on agriculture and forestry; six were represented on immi-

gration, military affairs, mines and mining, naval affairs, and public
lands; and five were found on Indian affairs. This commendable
principal of broad regional representation also appears to operate in
the composition of the major standing committees of the House. Certain states are customarily represented on certain committees according to their major economic interests, but no state has more than two places
on an important Senate committee and three places on a major
House committee. During the 78th Congress, for example, New
York state had three representatives each on the House committees
on interstate and foreign commerce, labor, merchant marine and
fisheries, post office and post roads, and rivers and harbors; Pennsylvania had three on the education committee and California had
three on public lands. With these exceptions, no state had more
than two places on the important committees of the House.

In addition to geography, party regularity was long a leading
criterion of committee appointments. Members who failed to support
the party organization and follow the party leadership ran the risk of
losing their seats on important committees. Speaker Cannon removed
or demoted the insurgent Republicans to minor committees in the 61st
Congress because they "failed to enter and abide by a Republican
caucus . . . as well as for other sufficient reasons." And the Wisconsin
members were ousted from their places on the key committees of the
House in the 69th Congress because they bolted the Republican Party
in 1924 and supported Senator La Follette for the presidency. Ordinarily, however, members retain their committee assignments as long as
they remain in Congress.[16] And since 1932 there has been a noticeable
decline of party discipline among the Democrats.

The Seniority Rule

Seniority in point of service has been the prevailing principle governing both committee assignments and the selection of chairmen since
1846 in the Senate and 1910 in the House. Speaking to the "Baby
Congressmen" on "The Making of a Representative," Speaker Clark
once said: "A man has to learn to be a Representative just as he must
learn to be a blacksmith, a carpenter, a farmer, an engineer, a lawyer,
or a doctor." And "as a rule," he continued, "the big places (on the
committees) go to old and experienced members" of the House.[17]

---

[16] Chang-Wei Chiu, *The Speaker of the House of Representatives Since 1896* (1928),
pp. 81 et seq.

[17] Congressional Record, 64th Congress, 1st Session (appendix), p. 559. Cited by
Chiu, *op. cit.*, p. 81.

Earlier Speaker Cannon said: "A man comes here for his first term, and although he may be a man of great ability and high character, how is any one to know it? He must prove it, and until he does prove it he must serve his probation and be put, not on the Ways and Means Committee to frame a tariff bill or on the Appropriations Committee, but on an unimportant committee, where he can show what he has in him and learn the business of government." [18]

Once appointed to a committee, the custom is for a member to remain upon it as long as he desires or until he loses his seat in Congress. This custom has obvious advantages. Long service on a committee develops a certain expertness on particular problems. The older members have acquired an acquaintance with most subjects likely to come before the committee and with the personalities and private interests with whom it has to deal. There is also the gain which comes from members becoming acquainted with one another and learning how to work together. The committee becomes more of a unit as its membership becomes more stable, and it is easier to develop a nonpartisan attitude toward legislative projects.

Congressional convention further prescribes, under the so-called "seniority rule" or the "senility rule" as it is derisively called by younger members, that the member of the majority party having the longest *uninterrupted* service on the committee shall be its chairman. There may be other men on the committee of almost equal experience—in fact there may be one or two of longer, but not continuous, experience on the committee. A Senate committee may have members who have had long service on the corresponding committee of the House; but the seniority rule ignores all other qualifications except that of technical seniority on the committee. As a result, the more powerful committees of Congress are filled, and the chairmanships of all the major committees are held, by members having the longest continuous service, i.e., by members from "safe" districts or states who are repeatedly returned to Congress and who thus acquire the requisite seniority. This means in practice that the South controls the key places in both houses when the Democrats are in power, and that New England and the Middle West supply the chairmen when the Republicans prevail, while the borderline states and districts seldom win important committee chairmanships because of the frequent turnover in their congressional delegations. "Congress is probably alone among all private or governmental bodies charged with any kind of responsibility," says Alexander

[18] *Ibid.*, 61st Congress, 1st Session (appendix), p. 108.

Hehmeyer, "which let leadership depend exclusively on the accident of tenure." [19]

In Defense of Seniority

Apologists for the seniority method of selecting committee chairmen argue that the custom provides a kind of automatic protocol, like one's place at table at a state dinner or the order of appearance of counsel before the Supreme Court, which settles harmoniously the problem of priority without dispute or controversy and without jeopardizing morale. Abolition of the rule, it is alleged, would be followed by logrolling, factional fights, and political trading on a grand scale. "The danger," writes Professor J. P. Chamberlain, "that committee places would go to those who were chosen with specific bills or policies in mind would be real, and would be suspected even where it did not exist. The bitter personal feelings engendered by an open contest for committee places would complicate party management, and there would be delay in beginning work . . . until personal and sectional quarrels could be smoothed out." [20]

"Political leaders," writes Roland Young, "have developed certain stratagems to lessen the power of committee chairmen to operate independently . . . The importance of the committee chairman is now often lessened by giving careful attention to the appointment of new members to committees; by selectivity in referring bills to committees; by allowing members of Congress who are not members of the legislative committees to handle bills; and, in extreme cases, by forcibly discharging a committee from the consideration of a bill." [21] Moreover, special committees are often used to circumvent the consequences of the seniority rule. Committee chairmen are often reelected to Congress because their constituents desire to retain the power and prestige of their office. Long and continued service in Congress, it is argued, would be discouraged by abolition of the seniority system.

Robert Luce, member of Congress for twenty years from Massachusetts and the author of several books on the legislative process, considered the seniority system defective in that it holds no one responsible for seeing to it that important chairmanships are held by qualified men. "On the whole," however, he concluded, "promotion by seniority conduces most to contentment and least endangers morale. Exceptions

[19] Alexander Hehmeyer, *Time for Change* (1943), pp. 100–101.
[20] Joseph P. Chamberlain, *Legislative Processes: National and State* (1936), p. 54 et seq.
[21] Roland Young, *This is Congress* (1943), p. 114.

must at times be made, but the rarer the better for peace and harmony
. . . Though not the only factor in deciding merit, experience is the
most important factor." [22]

Defects of Seniority Custom

On the other hand, critics of the seniority custom condemn it as
seriously defective in the following respects:[23]

1. The protection given a chairman because of his seniority enables him
to be arbitrary with impunity.

2. The seniority rule practically eliminates the possibility of with-holding
a committee chairmanship from the senior man, even though he may be
unqualified for the job.

3. The reasons for re-election may have no correlation with competency
for a chairmanship. Thus, the basis for selection of chairmen is one not
necessarily related to the factors which should control.

4. Those sections of the country which regularly re-elect their members
of Congress tend to obtain overbalanced control when their party comes
into power because their members accumulate seniority even when their
party is not in power. Other sections of the country reflect changes in
public sentiment by electing new members. But the latter have little chance
to hold the positions where the changed public sentiment could receive
appropriate recognition.

One of the greatest drawbacks of the seniority system is that it de-
stroys party responsibility or prevents political parties from performing
their campaign promises. For if the chairmen of committees owe their
places not to their political parties but to the accident of tenure, then
they can follow their own inclinations on legislative matters and disregard the platform pledges and legislative program of the party
leaders. A majority of the membership of the House may come fresh
from the people with a clear mandate for a program of social action,
only to see their attempts to keep their promises frustrated and their
bills whittled away or pigeonholed by a little group of committee chairmen who were first elected to Congress a generation ago on issues now
settled or forgotten and who have risen to dominate the key committees. Thus, much of the legislative program of the New Deal era,
to which the Democratic Party was pledged, was defeated, delayed, or
diluted by the old-timers who were in control of its legislative machinery.

[22] Robert Luce, *Congress: An Explanation*, p. 9.
[23] Robert Heller, *Strengthening the Congress* (1945), p. 30.

'A quantitative analysis of the effect of the seniority rule upon the legislative history of the fair labor standards bill led E. L. Oliver, executive vice president of Labor's Non-Partisan League, to conclude that:

the seniority line is also the line of cleavage between progressives and conservatives within the Democratic Party. Following of the seniority line, in committee appointments and in 'chairmanships, greatly accentuates this cleavage, and puts effective control of the House—and to a very great extent the Senate also—into the hands of men wholly out of sympathy with the party platform, with the national administration, and with the clear majority of the Congressmen elected upon the party ticket.

It becomes obvious that if either of the two major parties is to serve as a vehicle for social action—the condition within the Republican Party is much the same as within the Democratic—the control of the congressional machinery will have to be placed in the hands of leaders really representing the majority of the party. The seniority rule will have to be scrapped. Committees and their chairmen will have to be made responsive to the decisions of the party within the nation, and of the elected representatives of the party within both houses of Congress. Unless such a change is made, the expressed attitudes of the people will not be embodied in legislation . . . the people of the country should not permit their political expression to be thwarted, and their political decisions to be set aside, by men whose power results from an archaic procedure within the party organizations of the two houses of Congress.[24]

In short, as Roland Young well says, the seniority rule "flaunts established political principles: that of party government; of a legislature responsible to the electoral mandate; and of the utilization of the best material for the most important offices. The criterion of ability is much more important than the criterion of seniority, and if a chairman has both seniority and ability, it is the result of chance rather than of design. Tenure and ability are not the same thing; indeed, seniority may often reflect the ability to stay elected rather than the ability to decide important public policy . . . The present method of selecting . . . chairmen does not reflect the election returns in any manner."[25]

---

[24] E. L. Oliver, "The Responsibility of Political Parties for Social Action," address before the National Conference of Social Work, Seattle, June 28, 1938. Printed in *Symposium on Congress* by the Joint Committee on the Organization of Congress, August, 1945, pp. 152–161.

[25] Young, *op. cit.*, pp. 108–109.

Substitutes for Seniority

The preponderant judgment of legislators, political scientists, and critics of the congressional committee system is that the seniority custom is an archaic method of selection and ought to be abolished. What are the alternatives? Let us first consider possible methods of selecting committeemen and then the chairmen.

In assigning the membership to the various standing committees we have noted that seniority, geography, and party regularity have been the traditional criteria, although the principle of party regularity has not been enforced by the Democrats since 1932 because of the deep internal schisms between the conservative and progressive wings of that party. The geographical principle seems sound provided that all the main regions of the country are represented on each committee and that no one section or economic interest (e.g., mining or farming) is allowed to dominate a committee. Assuming that the national interest is achieved by a process of interplay and compromise among the various sectional and economic interests of the nation, it is suggested that the standing committees of Congress should be composed so as to represent both the principal regions of the country and the chief interests affected by lawmaking, e.g., the consumer, labor, business and agricultural interests. Under this suggestion, made by Senator White of Maine,[26] the Committees on Agriculture, for example, would be composed of members from urban as well as rural districts and states and of spokesmen for the consumers of farm products, the producers of farm machinery and manufactured foodstuffs, and farm labor, as well as farmers themselves.

In addition to the tests of geography and economic interest, it is suggested that the composition of committees should reflect recent changes in public opinion as revealed in the last congressional election. This might be done, as Ted F. Silvey has proposed,[27] by dividing the entire membership of the House and Senate into three classes: first-termers, second-termers, and third-termers or longer and by giving each class representation on the standing committees of both houses in proportion to its share of the entire membership. Thus, if one-third of the members of the House of Representatives were first-termers, they would be entitled to one-third of the places on each standing com-

[26] See Hearings before the Joint Committee on the Organization of Congress, p. 882.
[27] Ibid., pp. 881–882.

mittee.[28] Some such formula would ensure that current changes in public opinion could find expression in the committee rooms as well as the obsolescent viewpoints of bygone days. If the committees on committees would modify the seniority principle in this manner and substitute the tests of geographical and economic balance in making their committee assignments, then the legislative results of committee work would be more representative of the country as a whole and of the current sentiments of all the people.

What qualifications has the country a right to expect of the chairmen of congressional committees? I suggest three basic prerequisites: ability, which embraces knowledge, training, and experience; loyalty to the national interest rather than to local or sectional interests; and a sense of political responsibility to execute party covenants with the people.

Possible Alternatives

What method of selecting committee chairmen would be most likely to insure the choice of persons possessing these qualifications? There are seven conceivable methods of selection:

1. Appointment by the Speaker of the House and the presiding officer of the Senate (or the majority leaders in each chamber).

2. Secret election by committee members.

3. Secret election by party caucus.

4. Selection by a committee on committees (or the Rules Committee).

5. Automatic elevation by seniority.

6. Automatic rotation in office at periodic intervals.

7. Election from the floor.

Of the seven possible methods listed above, the only ones that seem most likely to result in the selection of chairmen of ability, public interest, and party accountability are selection by party caucus, by the committee on committees, or by the presiding officer or majority leader. Men of undoubted ability and devotion to the public interest might be chosen by the other methods, but they fail to satisfy the important test of party responsibility. Major importance is attached to this test because, unless political parties can be held responsible for fidelity to their

---

[28] 49 Senators and 68 Representatives were serving their first terms during the first session of the 79th Congress (1945).

campaign pledges, then party platforms are a snare and a delusion and public confidence in the party system will wither away.

Of the three methods of selecting committee chairmen that seem calculated to strengthen party responsibility, election by party caucus is the least advantageous because of the cumbersome size of that body, especially in the House, and because of the opportunities it would afford for electioneering and logrolling. Moreover, it would be difficult for a party caucus or conference to hold chairmen accountable for failure to adhere to the party program.

Selection by the committee on committees of the majority party, which now makes the other committee assignments, would appear to meet our postulated requirements. Freed from the incubus of seniority, the committee on committees could be counted upon to appoint the majority party's ablest men to the chairmanships; and it should be armed with the power to remove at any time recalcitrant chairmen who refuse to cooperate with the party's legislative program.

Perhaps the best method of selection in the final analysis would be appointment of committee chairmen by the majority leaders in each house. These men are responsible for steering their party's legislative program through the stormy waters of floor debate to the safe harbor of final passage. They receive legislative proposals from the committees and determine the order of business on the floor. To vest the power of appointing committee chairmen in the floor leaders would greatly strengthen party responsibility and the authority of the majority leaders in both houses. They should also be empowered by the party caucus to remove chairmen who refuse to cooperate in the execution of the party's legislative program. In this way the line of party responsibility and accountability for legislative action would be clearly drawn—from the electorate to the majority party caucuses in Congress to the floor leaders to the chairmen of the legislative committees whose majority members could be demoted or removed by the committee on committees if they failed to cooperate with the chairmen.

Collaboration in Lawmaking

One of the inevitable results of our multiple-committee system is the diffusion of legislative leadership among 81 "little legislatures" whose chairmen compete for jurisdiction and power. Congress is a body without a head. There is no unity of command.

A remedy for this condition, which has won wide support, lies in the creation of a joint steering committee with power to formulate a legislative program. Such a Legislative Council or Cabinet or Policy Committee, as it is variously styled, would be composed of the majority leaders and the chairmen of the new streamlined committees. It would be responsible for developing a coherent and coordinated program of legislation "rather than a jerry-built policy formulated by a hundred different committees." It would seek an organic, overall approach to public problems instead of the piecemeal, splinter approach now prevalent. Assisted by an expert staff, this central committee of Congress would be a vehicle of collaboration between the committees and houses of Congress and between the legislative and executive branches in the development of balanced legislative programs and in the determination of legislative priorities. Chaired by the majority leader in each chamber, it would provide informed, responsible legislative leadership and promote coherence and continuity in lawmaking. The Legislative Council would also serve to focus party responsibility on the national level in a partisan body which the people could hold accountable for legislative action designed to carry out platform pledges. And by conferring from time to time with the President's Cabinet, as several writers have suggested, it would provide a means by which the leaders in Congress and the President could consult and collaborate in the shaping of national policy. In times of crisis, measures of major importance requiring prompt action could, upon introduction, be referred directly to the Legislative Council and, if the Council approved of them, they could be simultaneously considered in identical form by the House and Senate without reference to the standing committees. The legislative process could be greatly expedited in this way.[29]

One of the most serious defects in the machinery of Congress is the lack of cooperation between the House and Senate. Each chamber goes its own way at its own gait. Located on opposite sides of the Capitol, Senators and Representatives seldom meet and confer, and there is little collaboration between the corresponding committees of the two houses. It is academic to suppose that bicameralism in Washington could be abolished. It is too deeply imbedded in the marble of the constitution. But some of its defects could be corrected by the greater use of joint committees. Collaboration in the early stages of lawmaking via joint devices would reduce the need of reconciling differences between the two houses via conference committees in the closing stage of the legislative process.

---

[29] Cf. Alexander Hehmeyer, *Time for Change* (1943), pp. 96–97.

THE FLOOR STAGE

One significant aspect of lawmaking in recent sessions of Congress has been the comparative decline of debate and deliberation. While there has been a plethora of committee hearings on a thousand topics, there has been a minimum of assimilation and genuine deliberation upon the mass of testimony heard and facts marshalled by diligent staffs. It has been the not uncommon experience of committee counsel and clerks in recent years that their committees seldom meet and rarely function as deliberative bodies. This condition may be attributed to the high rate of absenteeism, conflicting engagements, pressure-fatigue, inertia, and to a deep indisposition on the part of the legislative mind to undergo the discipline of sustained mental effort. It is much more interesting to make an inspection trip abroad or to participate in a Pearl Harbor inquiry than it is to wrestle with the hard facts of a full employment or government reorganization bill. Calling attention to the numerous "empty benches" in the Senate chamber during the debate on the government reorganization bill in November, 1945, Senator Murdock said that one of the causes was "that Congress is more interested, and has been for some time, in investigations than it is in its legislative functions. There are not as many headlines," he observed, "in the burdensome task of writing legislation as there are in connection with certain investigations. The way to bring proper procedure back to Congress," he added, "is for Congress to exhibit more interest in its legislative functions."

Data compiled by Floyd M. Riddick, legislative analyst of the United States Chamber of Commerce, for the 77th and 78th Congresses show that "fewer and fewer bills have been debated by either House long enough to involve three or more printed pages." More than 900 bills and resolutions were passed by the House and Senate during the second session of the 78th Congress, for example, but only 86 in the House and 47 in the Senate stirred any real discussion. The others were presented with little or no discussion of their contents and passed by a voice vote or "without objections." Riddick's figures also show that less than three-fifths of the pages of the *Congressional Record* devoted to House preceedings during this session were used to debate legislative measures, and only half of the space was thus taken up by the Senate. With a few exceptions, Senators were not active in debate and unanimous-consent agreements were used to limit debate on less than half a dozen bills. The Senate's once proud boast that it was "the greatest deliberative assembly in the world" no longer seems to fit the facts.[30]

Minority Rule

It is not generally realized, I think, to what extent minority rule prevails in the making of our national laws. There are many points on the legislative highways and byways where a few legislators can lurk, like the pirates of Tripoli, and take toll of the passing traffic. After you have introduced your bill, it may be referred to an unfriendly committee whose chairman may pigeon-hole it and refuse to let the committee even consider it. If the bill gets a hearing, it may be tabled by the committee only a minority of whose members may be present. If the bill receives a favorable committee report and is placed on the calendar, it may never be reached owing to the pressure of other business or because a few men on the Rules Committee will not give it the right-of-way. If it is placed on the House calendar, the majority leader may block its consideration by moving to skip Calendar Wednesday and the call of the committees. The Speaker can decline to recognize the would-be mover of the necessary motion to take it up or, in the Senate, some opponent can start a filibuster against it. Minor measures are considered only by unanimous consent, so that one man can block any of them he dislikes.

If your bill finally reaches the vote stage, it may be adopted or rejected by a minority of the total membership of the chamber, owing to the lack of attendance on the floor. It has, indeed, been a rare occasion in recent Congresses for a majority of the membership of either House to be present at divisions on outstanding bills where no roll call vote was demanded. Much of the important legislation of the past decade has been enacted by less than a majority of the membership. Evidently this is not a new condition, for Champ Clark, when Speaker of the House, once expressed the wish that the founding fathers had made a majority affirmative vote of the total membership a constitutional condition of the passage of laws instead of merely requiring a majority of those present. And, finally, if your bill has surmounted all these legislative hurdles, it may be vetoed by the President.

Thus, the fate of every measure is at the mercy of one or a few men who, through ignorance or prejudice or bias or stupidity, may frustrate the will of the majority. Insofar as minority rule is due to absenteeism,

---

[30] Floyd M. Riddick, "The Second Session of the Seventy-eighth Congress," *American Political Science Review*, April, 1945, Table I.

it could be corrected (1) by designating different days for chamber sessions and committee meetings and (2) by permitting proxy voting, the record showing those present for and against, and those absent for and against who have voted by proxies, the sums thereof determining the vote.

Dilatory Tactics

A difficult problem of legislative procedure, with a long and dramatic history, is that of obstruction or filibustering. In the Senate, where debate is unlimited and action is had only by unanimous consent, obstruction by various devices is unchecked. Under the so-called privilege of "freedom of debate" a group of Senators can hold up any measure indefinitely by endless talk in relays and by the use of dilatory motions, making the point of "no quorum," moving to "adjourn," moving to "take a recess," moving to "adjourn to a day certain," and moving to go into "executive session." Under the pretense of freedom of debate, minority obstruction and the personal veto are possible. Even under the cloture rule (Rule XXII), adopted in 1917 after President Wilson had denounced a filibuster, a determined minority can still prevent action and successful filibusters have been conducted.

Cloture motions have been rejected fourteen times during the past 25 years: twice each on tariff measures, anti-lynching bills, and anti-poll tax bills; and once each on bills for migratory bird refuges, boulder canyon dam, retirement of disabled world war emergency officers, public building sites in the District of Columbia, and the national banking act of 1933. Three attempts to apply cloture failed during 1946: on the fair employment practices bill, on the British loan, and on the Case labor disputes bill. Cloture motions have been withdrawn or not acted upon in seven cases. Thus experience has demonstrated the inadequacy of the cloture rule as a means of limiting obstruction in the Senate. Many public bills, desired by the party in power and supported by public opinion, have been defeated in the Senate by the practice of unlimited debate. The mere threat of a filibuster has often prevented or forced action.

The practice of obstruction in the upper chamber has not only been tolerated; it has also been defended as a legitimate weapon of parliamentary procedure on the following grounds. (1) The widest possible debate upon public questions is desirable. There should be some place where the merits of a measure may be thoroughly aired in debate and where, through such debate, the public can be educated regarding the desirability of proposed action. Since extended debate is no longer possible in the House, the Senate is the only forum where free and fair debate upon proposed legislation can be had. "If we adopted majority cloture in the Senate as they have in the House," said Senator Norris, "the last vestige of fair and honest parliamentary consideration would entirely vanish." (2) In obstruction the minority finds its only defense against an arbitrary or tyrannical use of power by the majority.

On the other hand, obstruction is condemned on the grounds that (1) it permits a minority to make its will prevail over that of the majority and thus negates the principle of majority rule which is the cornerstone of representative government. (2) Obstructive tactics have frequently been used in congressional history by individual members and small groups to secure purely personal or sectional advantages at the expense of the national welfare. By the threat of a filibuster, remarked Senator Underwood of Alabama, "I have been compelled to accept minor amendments to great bills that I will not say were graft, but they were put there for the purpose of magnifying the importance of one man with his own constituency at the point of jeopardizing good legislation in America." Great public injury results, it is argued, from the threat of the use of the filibuster unless bills are passed or defeated in which Senators have a sectional or political interest or legislation is changed to suit individuals and minorities.

From time to time various proposals have been advanced to limit obstruction in the Senate. These include: (1) enforcement of Rule XIX that "no Senator shall speak more than twice upon any one question in debate on the same day without leave of the Senate, which shall be determined without debate"; (2) use of the motion for the previous question by which all further debate upon a matter may be terminated by a majority vote of the chamber; (3) adoption of a rule that amendments and debate must be germane to the subject under consideration; and (4) the application of cloture by a majority instead of a two-thirds vote of those present as now required.

The real issue involved in obstruction in the Senate is simply this: shall majority rule and responsible party government prevail? Impartial students of the question have concluded "that it is desirable that the Senate should provide by its rules for greater freedom of debate than obtains in the House, but that it should at the same time provide means by which an abuse of this freedom may be prevented . . . obstruction which goes beyond that of legitimate debate is an evil that should be brought under control both because it consumes the time of the chamber and because it places undue obstacles in the way of the proper working of party government . . . as in all cases where power is granted, the opportunity for its abuse exists and . . . reasonable safeguards against such abuse should be provided. Such safeguards, however, should not go so far as to enable the minority, in an open contest, to make its will prevail over the majority. While a majority can use its powers in an illegitimate way, the same is true of the minority, and as between the two, the former . . . (is) the lesser evil." [31]

Improvements in Floor Procedure

With the great growth in the volume of legislative business, the House of Representatives gradually developed procedural devices for expediting its work. By the grouping of committee reports in calendars, the assignment of certain days for floor consideration of certain classes of business, the treatment of certain committee reports as privileged, and by the direction of legislative traffic by the Rules Committee via special rules, the House has been more successful than the Senate in keeping abreast of its business. Much precious time is wasted in long-winded Senate speeches consisting largely of long quotations from putative authorities made to empty seats and galleries. Arguments which could be summed up in thirty minutes or less are stretched out tediously to three and four hours until all but a small handful of members have retreated in boredom to the privacy of their offices, leaving the loquacious orator to bellow almost alone. Senatorial insistence upon the right of unlimited debate might be remedied by broadcasting the proceedings, leading demagogues and bores to condense their remarks into the allotted radio time or run the risk of being retired from Congress by an outraged public. Another corrective would be to enforce the rule of parliamentary procedure requiring debate to be germane to the subject under discussion.

Perhaps the basic fault in congressional lawmaking today is the waste of time that is caused by the hangover of habits of procedure and archaic practices from the simpler days when the volume of business was small, such as the oral reading of bills in full by the reading clerks, time-consuming quorum calls that electric voting would dispense with, the patient tolerance of irrelevant debate, and the protracted discussion of points of order. As a result, sessions are longer than they need be and much business is left unfinished when Congress adjourns, including

---

[31] W. F. Willoughby, *Principles of Legislative Organization and Administration* (1934), pp. 495, 499.

most of the proposals for improvement in legislative machinery. Saving the time now wasted in these ways would shorten the hours of legislative work and the sessions of Congress, allowing members more time for recreation, recess, and refreshment of contacts with constituents.

Another serious defect in the parliamentary practice of Congress is the hasty drafting on the floor of ill-considered amendments by which much legislation is badly mangled. This could be corrected, as Representative Herter suggests, by following the Massachusetts practice where amendments are reviewed and clarified by legislative counsel before final approval at the third reading stage.

Codifying the Laws

There is room for improvement not only in the substantive content of federal law, but also in its form. There has been no general codification of federal law since the Revised Statutes of 1874 codified under 74 titles all the public general laws of the United States. The criminal laws were codified in 1909, the Judicial Code was issued in 1911, and the Internal Revenue Code is kept currently up to date by the Joint Committee on Internal Revenue Taxation. In 1925 Congress authorized the adoption of the United States Code which classifies all the permanent and general laws under 50 separate titles. By 1945 seven of these titles had been codified by the House Committee on the Revision of the Laws with the technical aid of two publishing companies, but had not yet been ratified by Congress. Under these circumstances, it is necessary for lawyers, judges, and citizens to search through many volumes of the federal statutes in order to discover what the law is on any subject not yet codified. Their search is complicated by the congressional practice of indefinitely repealing inconsistent laws and parts thereof without specific and exact reference to the earlier acts intended to be repealed. Moreover, any codified title or class of law becomes progressively obsolete with the passage of subsequent laws on the same subject.

In order to give the country a clear and understandable picture of what the law of the land actually is, Congress should set up a law revision service in the Office of Legislative Counsel, as Representative Eugene J. Keogh, chairman of the House Committee on the Revision of the Laws, has repeatedly recommended. Under Mr. Keogh's bill,[32] the law revision counsel would examine all the public acts of Congress and recommend the repeal of obsolete, superfluous, and superseded

[33] H. R. 471, 79th Congress, 1st Session.

provisions. He would also prepare a complete compilation, restatement, and revision of the general and permanent laws of the United States, one title at a time, in conformity with the original policy and intent of Congress, with such corrections and amendments as would remove ambiguities, contradictions, and other imperfections of form and substance. This reform has been endorsed by many members of the American bar and bench and is long overdue.

Acts of Congress may be classified in several ways.[33] There are the public general laws which apply uniformly throughout the country, e.g., the Selective Service Act. There are local or special acts which apply to particular communities or individuals such as the District of Columbia or World War veterans. There are private acts such as those for the relief of particular individuals who have claims against the federal government. There are retroactive laws which attempt to correct or mitigate existing conditions, e.g., the capital gains and losses provisions of the income tax laws. There are remedial laws which are designed to eliminate defects or make improvements in existing statutes. There is penal legislation which defines certain conduct as a public offense and imposes a penalty for so doing, such as the Mann Act forbidding the transportation of women in interstate commerce for immoral purposes. And there are three classes of resolutions: (1) simple resolutions which deal with matters exclusively within the jurisdiction of the respective houses and require no action thereon by the other body; (2) concurrent resolutions which deal with matters of internal administration, have no effect beyond the confines of the Capitol, and must be passed by both houses, but do not require the signature of the President; and (3) joint resolutions which are bills within the meaning of the rules and must be signed by the President, with the exception of proposed amendments to the constitution.

Of all these congressional enactments, the most important from the viewpoint of society at large are the public general laws. Digests of all public general bills (including joint resolutions) introduced in Congress have been published from time to time since the second session of the 74th Congress by the Legislative Reference Service in the Library of Congress. These very useful digests give a brief synopsis of the essential features of public bills and resolutions and a fuller digest of reported measures, and show the status of all bills acted upon.

---

[33] Cf. Frank E. Horack, Jr., *Cases and Materials on Legislation* (1940), Chapter IV.

The Legislative Product

In the end, the statutes that emerge from the travail of the legislative process reflect the influence of many forces. For better or for worse, they are affected by the way in which Congress is organized and by its rules of procedure. They show the influence of executive proposals and private pressures. They reflect the legislators' own judgment and the attitude of their constituents. The legislator's judgment, as Justice Cardozo once put it, "will be shaped by his experience of life; his understanding of the prevailing canons of justice and morality; his study of social sciences; at times, in the end, by his intuitions, his guesses, even his ignorance or prejudice. The web is tangled and obscure, shot through with a multitude of shades and colors, the skeins irregular and broken. Many hues that seem to be simple are found, when analyzed, to be a complex and uncertain blend."[34] Legislative action is also influenced by the Congressman's hope of reelection and fear of social insecurity, making him vote for measures he might otherwise oppose; by the newspapers he reads and the public opinion polls; by private group and governmental lobbyists; and, last but not least, by the intelligence and character of the legislative staff who play a large but unsung part in the legislative process. The final fabric is thus a network of many threads which it would be almost impossible to unravel and trace back into the loom of history.[35]

---

[34] Benjamin N. Cordozo, *The Growth of the Law* (1924), p. 85.

[35] For an analysis of the relative influence of Congress and the President upon 90 major laws in the last 50 years, see "The President, Congress, and Legislation," by Lawrence H. Chamberlain, *Political Science Quarterly*, March, 1946, pp. 42–60.

7.

Legislative-Executive Liaison

ONE OF THE basic problems involved in the modernization of Congress is that of building a better bridge over the gulf between the legislative and executive branches of the national government. Created by our inherited system of separated powers, this gap has caused rivalry, suspicion, and hostility between Congress and the President at intervals throughout our national history. Solution of this basic problem is essential to better understanding, mutual respect, and effective cooperation between the two branches in the heavy tasks that lie ahead.

SEPARATION OF POWERS

The American constitution in its basic features was conceived and written in the latter part of the eighteenth century. Naturally it was a product of the ideas and conditions of that time.

Students of our intellectual history will recall that the climate of opinion in the eighteenth century was deeply influenced by the writings, among others, of the great English philosopher and physicist, Isaac Newton. According to the Newtonian cosmogony, the planets of the heavens were held in balance, and celestial collisions avoided, by the operation of large-scale forces acting at a distance. This concept of an equilibrium of forces captured the imagination of the seventeenth and eighteenth centuries and was used both as a polemic against the existing social order and as a pattern for new theories and arrangements which would supersede the older scheme of things.

Thus, when political theorists began to attack absolute power and divine right and to demand political freedom, they invoked the doctrine of natural law and proposed a scheme of government on the Newtonian model. In place of royal and ecclesiastical authority, they asserted that a government of political rights and duties should be established as a self-regulating, equilibrating system. This was the model which the English adopted early in the eighteenth century, but gave up after a brief trial. And this was the model which the Founding Fathers embodied in our own constitution with its system of checks and balances and its tripartite separation of powers. They were also influenced by the French political philosopher, Montesquieu, who, misinterpreting transitional constitutional developments in Great Britain, prescribed the separation of governmental powers to prevent tyranny. Consequently, Congress and the Executive were made independent of each other.

But the framers did not contemplate a complete separation. For they expressly conferred upon the President the right to recommend to the Congress "such measures as he shall judge necessary and expedient." And it was originally expected that the heads of the executive departments would continue to present their proposals directly to Congress as the practice had been under the Confederation. But influenced by Montesquieu's erroneous idea, Congress excluded them and the result has been recurring friction and deadlock between the two branches and in recent times the decline of the legislature in power and dignity.

During the two and one-half centuries since Newton wrote his *Principia,* the science of physics has progressed and his basic assumptions and their derivative political and economic theories have become obsolescent. New discoveries by Einstein and others and the new concepts of space-time, of relativity, of quantum and nuclear physics have replaced or modified the old Newtonian theories. And it has come to be realized that the classical political and economic ideas derived from Newton, which view the social order as a part of nature, as a system or mechanism operated by massive, impersonal, and inexorable forces, are simply an elaborate metaphor based upon gratuitous and misleading assumptions.

The political, economic, and social theories based on these outmoded Newtonian concepts served a useful purpose, to be sure, in releasing the new Republic from the British crown and the surviving institutions of medieval England. But the doctrine of the separation of powers and the system of checks and balances have become a serious handicap to that constant, confident collaboration between Congress and the Executive required by the new circumstances of public affairs in the middle of the twentieth century.

Difficulties of the American System

Under our system legislative-executive relations are often embarrassed and confused. Conflicts between Congress and the President have arisen in almost every major crisis of American history. Henry Clay and Andrew Jackson fought over the distribution of governmental powers. Abraham Lincoln struggled with the legislature over the conduct of the Civil War. Theodore Roosevelt was constantly in hot water with Congress over his policies. Woodrow Wilson's valiant fight for a League of Nations designed to make the world safe for democracy was sabotaged by a minority of the Senate. Herbert Hoover and the House of Representatives reached a stalemate during the last two years of his term. Franklin D. Roosevelt's leadership toward new goals of social policy gave rise to frequent clashes with Congress. And President Truman's honeymoon with Congress, favored by his appointment of four ex-legislators (Byrnes, Vinson, Anderson, and Schwellenbach) to the Cabinet and fortified by his friendly congressional connections, was soon followed by the usual "family quarrels." A story is told of President Truman that, when congratulated on the length of his honeymoon with Congress, he replied: "If this is a honeymoon, God help marriage."

The causes of conflict between President and Congress are multiple. The constitution does not clearly limit and define the powers of each, and some duplication of functions has inevitably developed. The President has traditionally represented the American people as a whole, while individual Congressmen conceive themselves primarily as representatives of their states and districts. Relations have been confused by the increased influence and activity of pressure groups, particularly in the fields of agriculture and labor, which have over the years found Congress a more fertile field for lobbying than the executive branch. Failure of the legislature to organize and equip itself to meet modern requirements has compelled the executive to assume more rather than fewer functions in order to compensate for the delays and ineptitudes of Congress. Rival theories as to the proper functions of the President (whether leader of the government or a mere administrator of legislative policies) have again emerged. Shifts in the distribution of party power in Congress, and accumulated personal and political animosities, have exacerbated relations. Internecine strife between the northern and southern wings of the Democratic party has reduced the President's support and further embittered the running fight between the executive and legislature.

The growing pattern of government by executive order, based on broad delegations of power; the encouragement of group pressures and demands; the development of a vast and sprawling bureaucracy; the effort to manage public opinion by government "propaganda"; the submission of "must" legislation and the attempt to "pack" the Supreme Court; attacks upon the integrity of the lawmakers in executive messages; efforts to circumvent Congress and to by-pass the courts—all contributed to the growing cleavage between Congress and the Roosevelt administration. The increasing number and the technical and emotional character of the issues of the day: rationing, foreign policy, taxation and war finance, third and fourth terms, poll tax, fair employment practices, military training, strikes, foreign relief, full employment, unemployment compensation, control of atomic energy, bureaucracy, further complicated legislative-executive relations and raised the states-rights question afresh.

Thus, many complex factors enter into the perennial struggle between these two great branches of the American government. Their traditional rivalry is not personal; it is functional, flowing from the lack of an organic relationship between the legislature and the executive. Frustration, disappointment, and defeat have been the fate of every President who has tried to be a strong leader. Lag, leak, and friction have marred their relations since the beginning of our national history. Brief honeymoons have invariably been followed by bitter "family quarrels," as Senator George Wharton Pepper once described them. This chronic antagonism is evidently not merely a matter of personalities. It is an institutional conflict the root of which is to be found in a defective governmental structure, i.e., in the separation of powers and the cleavage between the personnel of the two branches. Legislators and administrators seldom come in contact with each other. Cabinet members are rarely drawn from Congress, the Truman cabinet being exceptional in this respect. Wendell Willkie had never met Senator McNary, his running mate on the 1940 Republican presidential ticket, before their nomination.

That such monastic separation is not a prerequisite of representative government is evident from the British system. Parliament comes face to face with the Cabinet. A British prime minister can crack the whip of dissolution over the House of Commons to hold it in line. And the

Commons can force the resignation of the Cabinet by defeating it on a question of confidence. But when deadlocks develop between Congress and the President, he cannot appeal to the country in general election to decide the dispute. He can only resort to political patronage, press conferences, radio talks, and pressure politics or abdicate national leadership. A stalemate ensues in which the country is the chief loser.

Present Methods of Liaison

A variety of informal devices and usages have developed to overcome the handicap imposed by this artificial separation of powers. At the top level, for example, there are the weekly meetings at the White House between the President and the "Big Four": the Vice President (or President pro tem of the Senate), the Speaker, and the two majority leaders, at which legislative program and strategy are discussed. Occasionally, there are also the personal appearances of the President or the Secretary of State before joint sessions of Congress, like that of Secretary Hull after his return from the Moscow conference. Less visible are the contacts between members of the White House secretariat and Capitol Hill. One of the President's administrative assistants, the so-called "anonymity boys," is supposed to aid the Chief Executive in his legislative relationships. There are also occasional contacts between the clerks of the appropriations committees and Budget Bureau personnel, especially when the annual budget is submitted.

Several channels of contact and communication have also developed between Congress and administrative agencies at the departmental level. There are the annual hearings before the subcommittees of the House Committee on Appropriations, each lasting several weeks, at which departmental budget officers and their aides appear and defend their estimates for the coming fiscal year. Frequent hearings are held by the numerous legislative and special committees of both chambers at which administrative officials testify. Several agencies, moreover, maintain full-time contact men on the Hill, with offices in the House and Senate Office Buildings to handle their legislative relationships. Among them, for example, are the Civil Service Commission, the Office of Price Administration, and the War and Navy Departments. In a recent reorganization the Department of State assigned the task of congressional relations to an Assistant Secretary.

In at least one instance better teamwork has been facilitated in recent years by the informal monthly conferences held by the House Committee on Public Buildings and Grounds with the National Housing

Administrator and members of his staff. This arrangement, according to former Administrator Blandford, "has worked because it has provided both the committee and the Agency an opportunity for discussion on the basis of the same set of facts. It has provided an occasion for the speedy resolving of complaints or misunderstandings and generally has developed an environment in which we have found a closer acquaintanceship and have built up a foundation of mutual respect and confidence. From our viewpoint, I think the arrangement has been especially satisfactory because Chairman Lanham has always effectively distinguished between the legislative responsibilities of his committee and the administrative tasks of the National Housing Agency." Mr. Blandford added that "we have supplemented this conference device in the past by sending to every member of the committees with which we have legislative or appropriation relationships a quarterly or semi-annual statement giving in summary form the current housing picture and a tentative look at the problems in the months ahead." [1]

Committee chairmen and individual members of Congress are also in constant communication, by correspondence and telephone, with administrative agencies on pending legislation and matters of concern to their constituents. Departmental advice is regularly sought and received on bills and resolutions and, from time to time, informal conferences on high policy are held between departmental officials and the majority and minority leaders of both houses. After October, 1940, for example, there were frequent conversations between State Department officials and members of the foreign affairs committees of Congress on questions of foreign policy.

One of the divisions in the Bureau of the Budget—the Division of Legislative Reference—undertakes to reconcile and clear recommendations of the various departments and establishments with respect to proposed legislation, enrolled bills, executive orders, and other executive documents. This division also tries to reduce the work load on Congressmen by drafting executive orders rather than bills wherever possible, and by suggesting the passage of general enabling acts to cover standard operations.[2] If there were such an enabling act on the subject of bridge building, for example, Congress would not have to concern itself with the details of every new bridge to be built.

[1] Statement of John B. Blandford, Jr., National Housing Administrator, before the Joint Committee on the Organization of Congress, May 14, 1945.

[2] For a statement of the functions and duties of this division, see Hearings before the House Committee on Civil Service pursuant to H. Res. 16, 78th Congress, p. 360.

Several of the departments maintain legislative coordination services which prepare daily digests of congressional proceedings of interest to them, receive requests for witnesses at hearings before legislative committees, and otherwise handle congressional relations for their departments.[3]

Legislative Use of Borrowed Personnel

In addition to the contacts between Congress and the administration at the top and departmental levels, there is also considerable collaboration between the two branches at the staff level through the development of the practice of staffing congressional committees by borrowing administrative personnel. Most of the committees of Congress have at one time or another had the services of experts and clerical assistants loaned to them by government departments. These persons, who remain on their departmental payrolls, often serve the committees for extended periods. In this way committees obtain expert help without direct expense to themselves. But the practice is a questionable one when administrative personnel are used to aid legislative investigations of administrative action, for how can one serve two masters? And it also deprives the departments of their services for months at a time.

How extensive this long-standing practice has recently become was revealed by Senator Wherry who reported, on the basis of a rough check, that during the last four months of 1944 a total of 14 Senate committees, of which 10 were standing committees, had borrowed from 25 government and one private agency 97 individuals whose average total annual rate of pay was $263,560. On a monthly average, there were 72 persons from outside agencies at work with Senate committees at that time.[4]

Need for Better Executive-Legislative Teamwork

The administration seems to be satisfied, for the most part, with a continuation of these informal and flexible contacts with Congress. But congressional sentiment appears to favor more formal and regular methods of liaison with the executive branch. Judging by the number of suggestions that have recently been made in Congress, many members believe that our governmental machinery has not been well designed to facilitate cooperation between the two branches.

Devised for a simple agricultural society, our political machinery is

---

[3] One of the best of these is the Legislative Reports and Service Section in the Department of Agriculture, headed by Carl R. Sapp.

[4] *Congressional Record*, January 29, 1945, pp. 545–549.

no longer competent to resolve efficiently the issues imposed on government by the needs of a great industrial nation. This problem does not arise, of course, under the parliamentary form of government where, as in England, members of the Cabinet are also members of the House of Commons and daily come face to face with the legislature. One-quarter of the membership of the House of Commons today consists of the Ministers, the under-secretaries, and the Parliamentary private secretaries. Begun by Gladstone, the custom for a Minister to have a "P.P.S." has grown with the burdens of the Ministry until now it is an accepted convenience for busy Ministers to have such assistants. Under the British system, in Bagehot's classic phrase, "the Cabinet is the hyphen that joins, the buckle that fastens, the executive to the legislature."

But under our form of government with its artificial separation of powers and mixture of functions, teamwork between Congress and the administration is difficult at any time. During the war it became increasingly apparent that methods must be found to bridge the gap between the two great divisions of our federal government. The doctrine of the separation of powers was never meant to mean that Congress and the Executive should live as suspicious rivals in separate worlds. For our government cannot be efficiently conducted, especially in time of great stress and urgency, unless there is constant, confident collaboration between the two branches.

The need for closer collaboration between Congress and the Administration has frequently been felt and voiced in the course of our national history. So long as the United States was half empty, prosperous, and well protected by broad oceans, the balance-of-power system was tolerable. But now that the nation is crowded, harassed by serious social and economic problems, and deeply involved in world affairs, better teamwork between the legislative and executive branches of our national government is essential to our welfare and security. "No item on the present agenda of democracy has a higher priority," writes Congressman Kefauver, "than that of inducing closer, stronger, steadier cooperation between the President and Congress in promoting the welfare of the people of the United States and the United Nations ... Ten years ago President Roosevelt said to the Congress: 'The letter of the Constitution wisely declared a separation, but the impulse of common purpose declares a union.'"[5]

From the bureaucratic angle of vision the need of better congressional

---

[5] Estes Kefauver, "The Need for Better Executive-Legislative Teamwork in the National Government," *American Political Science Review*, April, 1944, p. 318.

relations is also recognized. According to Paul H. Appleby, Acting Director of the Budget, the attitude within the departments toward Congress arises from a feeling of dependence, respect for the law-making function, and fear. Contact between the two branches "is poor because it is between different levels of power." Discussions relate not so much to policy or program as to administrative details which excite suspicion, irritation, and strain on both sides. Conferences at times when legislators were not after specific things which their constituents want would result in "common ground, common purpose, and mutual respect." "Congressmen," Appleby believes, "do not adequately appreciate that the bureaucrats actually do function in their own field in a way basically political and that responsible bureaucrats are more broadly—that is, more nationally—exposed politically than members of Congress, even though they function in a way different from Congressmen." [6]

Hitherto the tendency has been, after a brief honeymoon, for Congress to obstruct the Executive and for the Executive to attempt to dominate or bypass Congress, even when the same political party controlled both branches. Hereafter, it is widely agreed, Executive and Legislature should act as partners in policy making, not as antagonists in a struggle for power. This may seem like a counsel of perfection, but national safety in the atomic age demands cooperation between them. Each has certain peculiar assets to contribute to the partnership, as Robert Heller points out. "Congress can contribute . . . (a) the will of the people, (b) its own judgment, and (c) its political wisdom . . . the executive branch can contribute to the partnership (a) some synthesis of group points of view, (b) expert opinion, and (c) technical administrative knowledge." [7] Between them the two branches have what it takes to make an effective team. All that is needed are devices to harness their talents.

PROPOSED INNOVATIONS

A dozen devices have recently been proposed to span the chasm between the White House and Capitol Hill. Prominent among them is the so-called question period. Representative Kefauver and Senator Fulbright have suggested that the rules of the House and Senate be amended to provide for a fortnightly report and question period at which the heads of executive departments and independent agencies

[6] Paul H. Appleby, *Big Democracy* (Alfred A. Knopf, 1945), p. 159.
[7] Robert Heller, *Strengthening the Congress*, pp. 6–7.

would be requested to appear on the floor of Congress and answer questions. Two hours would be set aside at least once every two weeks, but not oftener than once a week, when members of the House could question administrative officials on the floor. Half of the time would be devoted to written questions that had previously been approved by the proper legislative committee, submitted to the official, and printed in the *Congressional Record*. The latter half of the question period would be reserved for oral questions by members of the House, control of this time being divided equally between the chairman and ranking minority member of the committee which issued the invitation and had approved the written questions. The proceedings during the question period would be printed in the *Record* for all to read, except for executive sessions. Questions would have to be germane, not capricious or picayune. Although this proposal has won widespread editorial and popular approval, it lies pigeon-holed in the Rules Committees, perhaps because their members are reluctant to experiment with new devices, perhaps because the administration sees in the question period an apparatus for disciplining the executive.

Question Period

The Kefauver-Fulbright proposal is modelled on question-time in the House of Commons. Members may interrogate ministers on the floor of the House from 3:00 to 3:45 P.M. four days each week, asking three questions each for oral reply and an unlimited number for written answer. The questions appear on the daily calendar and must be filed a day in advance. From 70 to 100 oral questions, and as many written ones, are asked each day and about 50 are answered. All the answers are published in the *Parliamentary Debates*. Any member may ask three supplementary questions suggested by the answers given. Ministers come with answers which have been prepared for them in their departments. Most of the questions originate among the leaders of the Opposition, but many come from the Government benches. Certain days are reserved for questions on particular subjects, although each day has a miscellaneous collection. Question-time is both informative and disciplinary in purpose. It is used both to obtain information about the daily conduct of governmental affairs and to criticize administrative activities.

Every imaginable phase of the British Government comes under surveillance during question-time. Herman Finer gives a vivid description of this device. "Starting no bigger than a man's hand, any question may develop into a crackling, intense storm, with thunder and lightning, and may even lead beyond the question hour into a full debate on government policy at a later day. There is a contingent, tense relationship, a kind of menace underneath the purring, which is exciting for the lions, for the gladiators, and for the public. There is real mental strife." The Minister's "reputation with his party, with his Cabinet colleagues, with his constituency, will depend upon the showing he makes at question-time. He is on incessant trial for the future of his own career under questioning by any of six hundred members who believe that they could do the job better than he can. It is a serious ordeal. Moreover, it is a continuous one. He might get by with an evasion on Monday, but he is in the ring again on Tuesday. He may be witty and escape in a gust of laughter on Wednesday, but the questioner may catch him on Thursday. He cannot escape all his questions all the time. Oftentimes members will gang up on him with integrated questions, so that he cannot escape a barrage." [8]

As it works in the English Parliament, question-time has several beneficial results. It keeps the ministry alert to the temper of the Commons and keeps the civil service on its toes. It provides a safety-valve for the daily escape of parliamentary steam which might otherwise accumulate and explode in sensational investigations. It directs the attention of the Cabinet to inconsistent or conflicting departmental policies and programs and to instances of administratvie inefficiency or private grievance. A daily question period in Congress might well have warned the administration and the country in time to prevent or neutralize the Pearl Harbor attack.

Question-time works well in England chiefly because, under their form of government, Cabinet and Commons come face to face with each other. The members of the Cabinet are members of the House of Commons; they are the leaders of the party in power and they hold office only as long as they have the confidence of the House. Ministers are on the floor at question-time, facing the House en bloc. There is no separation of powers or personnel. The House controls the Government whose tenure of office depends upon its retention of the confidence of the House. Questions and answers are fully reported in the press and an atmosphere of watchful alertness pervades public affairs. While

---

[8] "Questions to the Cabinet in the British House of Commons." Paper submitted on request to the Joint Committee on the Organization of Congress by Herman Finer, formerly Professor of Political Science, University of London. See committee print, *Suggestions for Strengthening Congress*, June, 1946, pp. 49–58.

the English Cabinet is the creature of the Commons and holds office at its pleasure, it acts as a steering committee of that body, lays out its agenda, appoints its committees, controls all major legislation, and rules the nation. Under such a system, the right to question on the floor and, by vote of want of confidence, to dismiss the ministry, is a vital and indispensable part of the governmental machinery.

American Substitutes for Question-Time

Under our form of government, where Congress and the Cabinet do not meet face to face, other devices have been developed to obtain information from the departments. One of these is the resolution of inquiry. Under section 5 of House rule XXII, any member of the House may submit a resolution requesting information from the head of any of the executive departments and the committee having jurisdiction is required to report it within one week. If the committee refuses or neglects to report it within the week or reports it adversely, a motion to discharge the committee is privileged. The President or department head may decline to transmit the information requested or required if, in his opinion, it would be inconsistent with the public welfare or incompatible with the public interest. Such resolutions are usually complied with, even to the transmittal of minutes of Cabinet meetings.[9] But this method is seldom used.

Hearings before the standing and select committees of the House and Senate provide another instrument of congressional inquiry. Here government officials can be interrogated without limit of time or subject matter and confidential information can be elicited in executive sessions which could not be divulged on the floor. This method has the disadvantage, however, of requiring busy executives frequently to repeat the same testimony before several committees (a condition which could be corrected by joint hearings and by clearly defining and delimiting committee jurisdictions). It also limits the knowledge gained to the members of the committee present at the hearings. Of course, any Congressman can read the testimony when the hearings are printed weeks or months afterwards. But in actual practice printed hearings are seldom read by busy legislators, even the hearings of their own committees; and interest in a question wanes with the passage of time between testimony and its publication.

Additional facilities available to members of Congress in quest of

---

[9] *Cannon's Procedure in the House of Representatives*, pp. 207–211 (fourth edition). See also his speech in the House, *Congressional Record*, March 23, 1944, pp. 3014–16.

departmental information include personal interviews and correspondence with executive officers who are usually quite accessible, and the periodical and special reports which each governmental department and agency issues, if one has and will take the time to study them. There are also the weekly conferences at the White House which the President holds with House and Senate leaders, and the regular press conferences of the President and department heads. According to Representative Cannon of Missouri, these devices "comprise the American substitute for the British parliamentary question period and are a much more effective medium for disseminating information."

Objections to Question Hour

The most powerful arguments against the institution of a question hour in the House of Representatives were presented to that body by Mr. Cannon, former Parliamentarian of the House, in a vigorous attack on the Kefauver proposal. After conceding that it had met everywhere with universal acquiescence and acclaim and describing the alternative means available to Congress for obtaining information from the departments, Mr. Cannon asserted that "this radical innovation in our system of government" would result in the abandonment of the traditional doctrine of the separation of powers. Public sentiment would force the attendance of Cabinet officers on the will of the House. "Such a question hour would degenerate immediately and inevitably into a political fencing match . . . The sergeant at arms would have to recruit a special force to preserve order . . . The device would be used for partisan political advantage . . . The questions submitted from the floor . . . would probe excruciatingly into the depths of the rawest nerve centers of current campaign issues . . . Controversies would be engendered which would bring friends to the defense and foes to the attack and the result would be bedlam and pandemonium. It would give rise to bad taste, bad manners, and bad blood . . . Instead of bringing about better teamwork between the Congress and the executive departments, it would drive a wedge of discord between the legislative and executive branches of the government and controversies kindled in the question hour would spread through the nation until they involved the remotest cross-road hamlet in the country." [10]

Mr. Cannon also foresaw insuperable mechanical difficulties in the plan. It would precipitate field days in Congress, with members com-

[10] Ibid.

peting for the limelight of publicity, and cause unprecedented traffic jams on the floor. Committees would be overburdened with reviewing the questions to be asked. The Committee on Rules would be swamped with making allotments of time, determining priorities, setting dates and duration of question periods. The routine of the Cabinet would be materially upset. Forensic rather than executive ability would become the test of Cabinet appointment. The program of the House would become more congested than ever and the *Congressional Record* would be loaded with questions and answers. In short, concluded the gentleman from Missouri, this proposal is "impracticable, obstructive, and unworkable."

Defense of the Plan

A few days later Mr. Kefauver rose on the floor of the House to reply to Cannon's attack on his proposal. Suggesting that the latter's arguments smacked of a bureaucratic origin, Mr. Kefauver asserted that the fact that the American Cabinet is responsible to the President rather than directly to Congress, unlike the British system, makes it all the more important that Congress as a whole should have ways and means to inform itself as to how its acts are being carried out. The methods of inquiry and investigation available to Congress, while appropriate and effective within limits, suffer from various defects which he described. Moreover, the system of separated powers had been intentionally and profoundly modified from the outset by the constitutional system of checks and balances providing legislative control of the executive. Question-hour would not result in a Roman holiday if Congress behaved in a responsible manner. The attendant publicity, by focusing public attention on the role of Congress in the American scheme of government, would be a good thing. If a given hour each fortnight were set aside for the question period, the Rules Committee would not be burdened. The proceedings might even save space in the *Congressional Record* by eliminating much debate now carried on in the dark as regards departmental conduct. The fact that similar proposals have frequently been made during our national history indicates that there must be some fundamental weakness in legislative-executive relationships which statesmen and scholars have repeatedly sought to remedy. Adoption of his proposal, Mr. Kefauver believed, would reduce the number of special investigating committees, establish the importance of Congress in the public mind, secure better Cabinet appointments and make them more responsive to the public will, give officials an opportunity to answer unjust criticisms, and clarify administration policy.[11]

Evidently there is much to be said on both sides of this proposed innovation. Whether question-time would be a success or failure in Congress will never be known without a trial. It is impossible to predict the results of such an experiment with scientific assurance. Political science is not in the enviable position of physics and chemistry whose practitioners can forecast the results of their experiments with precision. But no fatal effects are anticipated from a trial of the proposal. It works well in England. Informed opinion here apparently favors the experiment. Obviously there is need of better channels of communication between Congress and the Cabinet. Legislative-executive relations might flower or wither through the question hour. If they flowered, it could be continued. If they withered, it could be abandoned. You never can tell until you try.

Conditions of Success

If the experiment is made, its chances of success would probably be enhanced, judging by British experience, if the following conditions were met:

1. Question hour should be held frequently before both houses of Congress in joint session. Unless questions are asked and answered several times a week, they are apt to become superficial and sporadic. The informative and disciplinary value of question-time lies in its continuity, in the searching character of the inquiries, and in their comprehensive coverage. If questions are asked in committee, their value to the entire membership and to the public is lost. If they are asked on the floor of only one house, it might benefit by the publicity at the expense of the other house. If both houses held separate question periods, they might involve duplication and unseemly rivalry. Perhaps the best arrangement at the outset would be to experiment with questions before joint sessions for a limited period two or three days a week.

2. Questions should be scheduled so that the different Cabinet officers would come up on rotation at regular intervals. Thus, at any one question period, all the inquiries would relate to the work of one or two departments whose heads would know when their turn was coming and would have time to prepare their answers.

3. Question-time should be equally divided between Senators and Representatives and between Republicans and Democrats. Fair division

---

[11] *Congressional Record*, March 29, 1944, pp. 3314-16.

of the time between the houses and the parties seems an obvious condition of success.

4. Questions and answers should be written and printed in the *Congressional Record* to avoid misunderstanding and the number of supplementary oral questions asked on the floor should be limited. Cabinet officers should have the privilege of postponing their answers to oral questions.

5. Questions should be constructive and deal with broad matters of departmental policy and program rather than with the minutiae of administration. To this end they should be screened by the appropriate legislative committees.

6. All questions should be addressed to the President and assigned by him to the proper executive officer for reply, except in the case of the independent agencies. In this way questions will be referred to the appropriate departments and the answers will be consistent with the President's policy.[12]

Subject to these conditions and safeguards, a question period might well have beneficial results both for Congress, the executive departments, and the general public. Congress would be more fully and reliably informed. Cabinet officers would have a grand opportunity to defend their programs and win public recognition for their achievements. And public interest would be stimulated and instructed on the vital issues of the day. The success of the experiment would depend, in the final analysis, upon executive cooperation. If department heads gave frank and full replies to congressional questions in a spirit of comity, the technique could be very helpful. But if they chose to evade or refused to answer unpleasant questions, little would be gained. Congress could not discipline an evasive or hostile official except indirectly by curtailing his funds, nor would the President be bound by the statements of his Cabinet officers. In short, question-time in Congress might be much less effective than in Commons because of the lack of sanctions under our system. But if the experiment were tried in a spirit of mutual cooperation, it might yield unexpected returns.

Cabinet Government

For many years critics of our presidential-congressional system have urged that it be abandoned and that parliamentary government be introduced in the United States. In his *Congressional Government* (1885) Woodrow Wilson proposed the gradual development of the

---

[12] Cf. Finer, *op. cit.* and Heller, *op. cit.*, p. 27.

practice of having the Cabinet resign when it lost the confidence of the House of Representatives. This would tend to strengthen the Cabinet at the expense of the President, and the House at the expense of the Senate, since a cabinet cannot serve two masters. More recently Henry Hazlitt has argued cogently for the adoption of the cabinet form of responsible government in his book *A New Constitution Now* (1942). Congressional committees in 1864 and 1882 recommended admitting members of the Cabinet to the two houses to take part in debate, in the making of motions, and in the general transaction of business, but without the right to vote or the duty of resigning if their proposals were rejected or their acts censured. Such privileges are now enjoyed by the delegates from Alaska and Hawaii. The constitution of the Confederacy provided for it. And many thoughtful writers have proposed similar constitutional reforms.[13] But none of them has won sufficient support either in Congress or in the executive branch. Congress fears that the presence of the Cabinet would encroach upon legislative prerogatives, while executive officers are reluctant to expose themselves to the annoyance and possible harassment of congressional appearances.

Under the parliamentary system, the chief executive and the cabinet officers are the leaders of the majority party in the legislature in which one house is supreme. The members of the legislature and the executive do not hold office for fixed terms. At any time the legislature may dismiss the executive for want of confidence or the executive may refuse to resign and advise the Crown or President to dissolve the legislature and call a new election. Thus there can be no prolonged deadlocks between the legislature and the executive such as occur from time to time under the American system. All major legislation originates with the executive which can focus debate on matters of national policy and may be questioned upon its conduct of administration. Under this "hairtrigger" form of government, as Charles Beard calls it, the executive is responsible to the legislature which controls the conduct of governmental affairs.

Despite the strong appeal which the parliamentary system makes to logical minds, it seems very doubtful whether the American people could be persuaded to adopt it at this late date in our constitutional history. In his recent book, *The Republic,* our ace historian, Charles Beard, has given the most effective answer to advocates of such a

---

[13] W. Y. Elliott, *The Need for Constitutional Reform* (1935); Samuel W. McCall, *The Business of Congress* (1911), pp. 192–197; William Macdonald, *A New Constitution for a New America* (1921).

change. "To be workable, even in a limited sense," he says, "any form
of government must be adapted to the traditions, political experience
and habits, the prevailing economic interests, and the intellectual and
moral values of the people for whom it is devised . . . Civilization in
the United States is by no means identical with civilization in Great
Britain or any other country, despite similarities in specific features.
Our history, our experience, have been in many ways unique. Our
form of government has been adapted to our character and circumstances . . . To expect that the British parliamentary system, if adopted
here, would work as it does in Great Britain, or indeed accomplish here
the wonders attributed to it, is in my view . . . a fantasy . . . delays,
bickerings, and deadlocks in politics may be the price we have to pay
for such liberty, justice, and happiness as we have. I suspect also,"
Beard goes on to say, "in view of our political habits, that parliamentary
government here would put a premium on factious opposition tactics.
It would spur ambitious men in a restless quest for power to intrigues
and maneuvers designed to oust the President and the cabinet chosen
by Congress and to put members of the opposition in the vacant places
of power and patronage." [14]

A Joint Executive-Legislative Council

If the parliamentary system is not for us, how can executive-legislative
relations be improved within the framework of the American constitution as it stands today? Of the various proposals made to this end, that
for a joint legislative-executive council seems the most promising and
practical. Created by joint resolution and executive order, this council
would consist of the leaders of the majority party in the Senate and the
House of Representatives (i.e., their majority policy committees), on
the one hand, and of the President and designated members of his
Cabinet, on the other. The members of the joint council would meet
at regular intervals and would collaborate in the formulation and carrying out of national policy. Serviced by a competent secretariat, the
council would serve as a mediating mechanism between Congress and
the Executive at the top level of policy making.

Such a council would provide a medium for consultation among its
members before legislation is introduced to carry out pledged party

---

[14] Charles A. Beard, *The Republic* (The Viking Press, 1943), pp. 251–254. For a
penetrating comparison of the parliamentary and presidential systems, see the article on
the subject by Don K. Price in the *Public Administration Review*, Autumn 1943, and
Harold J. Laski's annotations thereon, *ibid.*, Autumn 1944.

promises and on matters of high administration policy. By giving congressional leaders a part in the formulation of policy, instead of being asked to put through measures in the preparation of which they have had no share, better cooperation between the Legislature and the Executive could be obtained. The council would also enable Congress to deal more directly with difficulties and complaints arising out of administrative action. Minority leaders in both houses might well be included from time to time in these joint conferences as a further means of promoting mutual understanding and harmony between the two branches. Formalizing the relationships between Congress and the President in this way should improve and strengthen the performance of each.

The joint council idea has won impressive support in recent years. It was first suggested by Senator La Follette in July, 1943, in an article in the *Atlantic Monthly*. His native state of Wisconsin had been the first state to create such a body in 1931. The Wisconsin executive council, as it was called, gave representation not only to the legislative and executive branches of the state government, but to private groups as well. It had the functions both of formulating a legislative program, of supervising administration, and of conducting general inquiries.[15] The idea has also been endorsed by political scientists like Beard and Elliott, by practical statesmen like Secretary Byrnes, and by writers like Hehmeyer and Finletter.

The Finletter Plan

The fullest and most challenging case for creation of a joint legislative-executive council or cabinet was made by Thomas K. Finletter in his recent book—*Can Representative Government Do the Job?* During the nineteenth century, according to Mr. Finletter, representative government was adequate to protect our political liberties. The means and ends of American government were in balance. But they cannot be balanced today, he believes, without basic changes in legislative-executive relationships. Unless means are devised to bridge the gap between Congress and the Executive, the attainment of "our new national objectives"—world peace and full employment—will be jeopardized.

Mr. Finletter reviews our alternating experience since 1900 with "orthodox" and "strong" presidents. The "weak" presidents—Taft, Hard-

<hr />

[15] John Gaus, "The Wisconsin Executive Council," *American Political Science Review,* October, 1932. See also his chapter on "The Planning Process in Government" in *Problems of the Postwar World* (1945), edited by T. C. McCormick.

ing, Coolidge, and Hoover—respected the system of checks and balances imbedded in the constitution and did not try to dominate Congress. But the strong "popular-leader" presidents, Wilson and the two Roosevelts, struggled to convert this system into a government of steady and positive power. The result has been "a government of fits and starts" marked by long periods of internal struggle and stalemate, such as the last two years of the Taft, Wilson, and Hoover administrations in which "the people as well as the President were the losers."

In order to prevent the dead hand of the constitution from frustrating our postwar objectives, Mr. Finletter concludes that the procedures of the federal government must be changed "so as to eliminate the causes of conflict between the two branches, to centralize the affirmative powers of government in the Executive, and to do so in such a way as to preserve the authority of Congress." Current trends are already moving, he observes, toward better communications between the two branches, internal reform of both, and closer collaboration between them in the field of foreign policy. Creation of a joint executive-legislative cabinet would be a next step in the current evolution.

To complete the evolution and insure that the Joint Cabinet be composed of members of the same party, Mr. Finletter also recommends amending the constitution so as, first, to give the President the right to dissolve Congress and the Presidency and to call a general election whenever a deadlock arises between Congress and the Joint Cabinet; and, second, to make the terms of Senators, Representatives, and President of the same length—say six years. The power of dissolution, he believes, would break deadlocks, make for a united government, weaken group pressures and provincialism, strengthen the national parties, and make government more responsive to the popular will. Congress could force a dissolution by declining to enact Joint Cabinet proposals. The present need of Congress to defeat the President in order to maintain its place in the federal scheme would be removed and party solidarity promoted. Unless these changes are made, representative government in the United States will be endangered. So runs the argument.

Mr. Finletter makes a persuasive case for his proposed reforms. The Joint Cabinet idea certainly deserves a fair trial. It would institutionalize the relations of Congress and the President and overcome the cleavage between legislators and administrators. Regular, open conferences have produced beneficial results in housing and international relations. The technique might well be extended and generalized. I am dubious, however, about the proposed power of dissolution. Unlike the cabinet idea, it would constitute a drastic departure from our political experience, traditions, and habits. Unless accompanied by the "balancing, compensating right" of Congress to "hire and fire" its "agent," the Executive—a practice Mr. Finletter approves in private business— the supremacy of Congress would not be preserved by giving the President the right to dissolve it. Nevertheless, these proposals present a constructive challenge to practitioners of the political art who are responsible for keeping the means and ends of American government in balance.[16]

Departmental Advisory Councils

In addition to joint conferences of congressional party leaders and members of the President's Cabinet on matters of overall foreign and domestic policy, Congress might also create advisory councils at the departmental level in particular functional fields, e.g., fiscal affairs, diplomacy and defense, social welfare, commercial policy, natural resources and the like. These councils would be composed of the chairmen and members of the appropriate standing committees in the House and Senate and of executive officials engaged in administering programs of action in these fields. They would be staffed with specialists in their particular provinces drawn from the staffs of the committees and the departments. And they would hold periodic conferences to review agency operations, consider constituent complaints, and discuss amendments of the laws governing departmental activities.

Precedents for such joint advisory councils are seen in the Temporary National Economic Committee of pre-war fame which consisted of six members of Congress and six administrative officials; the Joint Committee on Reduction of Nonessential Federal Expenditures which includes six senators, six representatives, the Secretary of the Treasury, and the Director of the Budget; the conferences of State Department officials and members of the congressional foreign affairs committees held in recent years; and the monthly meetings of National Housing Agency officials with the House Committee on Public Buildings and Grounds held during the Blandford-Lanham days.

Sympathetic collaboration between departments and congressional

---

[16] See also "Can Representative Government Do the Job?" A radio discussion by Thomas K. Finletter, Walter Johnson, and Robert M. La Follette, Jr., The University of Chicago Round Table, No. 428, June 2, 1946.

committees in these and other instances has been of great value to Congress in determining its policy and to the departments as well. Such joint meetings at regular intervals serve to keep the committees informed of agency activities and programs. They also afford agency officials an opportunity to justify their actions, explain their problems, and reply to criticisms. The proposal is to extend and regularize this practice by utilizing the standing committees of the House and Senate as vehicles of communication and collaboration between Congress and the administrative agencies within their respective defined jurisdictions.

At present there is no regular machinery of cooperation between them, aside from informal conversations and correspondence, by which the common problems of governmental policy can be surveyed. Vast powers are often delegated to governmental agencies. Sometimes laws are not clear and specific and sometimes problems defy precise legal description and definite limitation. A clear and continuing understanding of the purposes and methods of the departments is obviously desirable. This could best be gained, it is believed, by directing the regular standing committees of the House and Senate, whose jurisdiction covers such matters, to conduct a continuing review of the agencies that administer laws originally reported by the committees. Frequent consultation and reporting would greatly improve relationships at the departmental level.

Such review might well include a fortnightly question period before the committee in open session at which complaints of agency shortcomings or abuses of authority could be brought to the attention of administrators through the proper legislative committees. Congressmen with complaints from their constituents concerning agency policies and practices would refer them to the appropriate standing committees instead of to the agencies themselves. In this way special investigations of administrative conduct by select committees would be avoided, complaints could be more efficiently aired and adjusted, and the regular standing committees would become informed by continuing study and oversight concerning agency activities and needs.[17]

Success of this proposal will depend upon simplification of the congressional committee structure and its correlation with the pattern of the administrative branch, and upon the expert staffing of the committees. Otherwise, liaison links would be tangled and confused and the real work of contact and review would be desultory and fortuitous.

---

[17] Cf. J. P. Chamberlain, Noel T. Dowling, and Paul R. Hays, *The Judicial Function in Federal Administrative Agencies* (1942), pp. 231–232.

Review by Appropriation Committees

A variant of this proposal would entrust this function of liaison and oversight to the subcommittees of the House Committee on Appropriations on the ground that they are now organized along departmental lines, closely paralleling the administrative structure, and are inclined to exercise stricter supervision of administrative performance than the legislative committees which are said to have developed a paternalistic and protective attitude toward the departments over the years. As presented by Robert D. Leigh, a well-known political scientist and experienced administrator, "the proposal is briefly that the House develop its subcommittees on appropriations into compact, relatively small committees or commissions of administrative review, and that the House schedule provide for regular periodic meetings of each of the subcommittees with the heads of the executive agencies, these meeting to be open hearings with newspapermen and other interested Congressmen present, and to be concerned with questions and conference on the activities of the agencies concerned." [18]

Under existing conditions in the House of Representatives, the legislative committees authorize, the appropriations committee implements the legislation, and the Committee on Expenditures in the Executive Departments is supposed to examine accounts and scrutinize performance. In actual practice, however, the follow-up function is largely performed by the staff of the appropriations committee, with occasional inspection of selected items by subcommittee members. Appropriation hearings are based upon voluminous justifications prepared in advance by the departments, showing the planned employment of funds by projects. Subcommittees have before them a comparison of past expenditures, present programs, and future estimates. It is generally understood that expenditure programs set forth in the justifications will be quite closely adhered to, and any departure from them is disclosed at succeeding hearings. No wide departure from approved programs is made without conferring with the House and Senate Committees on Appropriations.

Members of the House Committee on Appropriations now carry a heavy work-load. In many cases they must spend eight or more weeks in attendance upon committee hearings and additional time in making studies and holding interviews; they must be present on the floor when their committee bills are under consideration, and participate later in

---

[18] Hearings before the Joint Committee on the Organization of Congress, pp. 1073–76.

conferences with the Senate Appropriations Committee. It is questionable whether the members of this busy committee would also have time to attend fortnightly meetings throughout the congressional session for the review of administrative activity unless they were assigned to only one subcommittee. If the subcommittees of the appropriations committee were enlarged in number to include seven members each for each of the 50 or more administrative units requiring separate consideration, as Dr. Leigh suggests, the Committee on Appropriations would have 350 members which seems out of the question.

Other Links

In addition to the coordinating mechanisms discussed above, another possible channel of communication and cooperation would be for each Cabinet officer and agency head to appoint a Deputy Secretary who would maintain an office at the Capitol (as several agencies now do) and devote his full time to liaison work between his department and Congress. The head of a department should have one man on his staff with the general duty of keeping in contact with Congress, and especially with the committees concerned with the work of his department. He should become acquainted with the members and gain their confidence, so that he could not only be influential in advancing the policies and piloting the bills of the department at hearings, but also keep the head of the department in touch with opinion in Congress, thus permitting the department to take steps to meet any criticism that might be developing, but which had not yet come into the open. This liaison officer would represent the opinion and policy of the department. He would promote the department's bills and to this end he would bring into hearings and conferences on departmental bills the legal, technical, and administrative officers of the department who were particularly familiar with the matters under consideration. Prior to his appointment as Undersecretary of State, Dean Acheson served for a time as Assistant Secretary in charge of congressional relations and contributed much to better teamwork between the two branches in the field of foreign affairs.

Appointment of congressional advisers or boards of visitors for major administrative agencies has also been suggested as another means of bringing the executive and legislative branches into more effective mutual collaboration. Each adviser or visitor would spend part of his time in his assigned agency; he would have full access to its personnel and activities; and would become especially informed by observation and experience concerning its programs and problems. He would become a special champion of the public interest in relation to the work of that agency and would learn to view its activities in national rather than local terms. Among his colleagues in Congress he would become a recognized and trusted authority concerning conditions in the agency, mediating between them, adjusting disputes, clarifying issues, and developing cooperative attitudes and arrangements.

Conclusion

The basic issue discussed in this chapter is whether the relationships between Congress and the administration are to be formalized or to continue to depend upon informal and flexible contacts between the President and party leaders in Congress and between the heads of administrative agencies and their opposite committees in the legislature. On the side of the administration, the preference seems to be for the present informal relationships, whereas congressional sentiment appears to favor the creation of some permanent machinery through which departments could inform Congress regularly about policy in the making and, in turn, be informed by Congress as to the attitude of public opinion. My own view is that greater success is likely to be achieved in the long run if executive-legislative relationships are institutionalized on a continuing basis.

Support for this view is found in a unique experiment in legislative trail-blazing that was carried on at Albany after 1938. During its seven years of experience the New York State Joint Legislative Committee on Industrial and Labor Conditions (the Ives Committee) had remarkable success in promoting close and cordial cooperation between the state legislature and many administrative agencies and in taking industrial and labor relations "out of politics." Phillips Bradley, Director of Education and Research of the Ives Committee, attributes its success in large part to the techniques employed by the joint committee: its bipartisan composition equally divided between the parties; its practice of having committee bills introduced in one chamber by a member from one party and in the other by a member of the other party; its operation on the principle of unanimity; its employment of a full-time research staff which studied anticipated problems and the operation of existing laws; the preparation by the staff of materials for committee members; continuous, off-the-record conference and collaboration between the staffs of the committee and the administrative agencies; the holding of a four-day informal committee session with the heads of the administrative services concerned in advance of each legislative session; the conduct of its proceedings in closed, informal sessions; and the fact that the ranking majority and minority leaders of both houses were *ex officio* members of the committee.[19]

---

[19] Phillips Bradley, "Blazing New Legislative Trails," *Survey Graphic*, May, 1944.

8.

Supervising the Administration

ONE OF THE most important functions of Congress is to inspect and review the performance by the executive branch of the government of its constitutional duties and its exercise of the powers delegated to it by the legislature. Political thought in English-speaking countries has assigned this oversight function to the elected representatives of the people for more than 250 years. "Instead of the function of governing, for which it is radically unfit," said John Stuart Mill, "the proper office of a representative assembly is to watch and control the government; to throw the light of publicity on its acts; to compel a full exposition and justification of all of them which any one considers questionable; to censure them if found condemnable, and, if the men who compose the government abuse their trust, or fulfill it in a manner which conflicts with the deliberate sense of the nation, to expel them from office, and either expressly or virtually appoint their successors. This is surely ample power, and security enough for the liberty of the nation . . ."[1]

Henry Jones Ford held it to be a fundamental condition of a representative system "that the supervision and control of the representative assembly shall extend over the whole field of government."[2]

In his analysis of the functions of the legislative branch of government, W. F. Willoughby asserted that "in some respects the most important function of a properly constituted legislature is that of acting, in effect, as the board of directors of the government viewed as a business corporation . . . the source of all administrative authority is the legislature. The legislature is the body that, subject to constitutional limitations, determines what activities shall be engaged in by the gov-

---

[1] *Considerations on Representative Government* (1875), p. 99.
[2] *Representative Government* (1924), p. 158.

230

ernment; how the administrative branch shall be organized for the performance of these activities; what sums of money shall be applied to such purposes; how this money shall be raised and disbursed; and the rules of procedure that shall be followed in performing the work to be done . . . An examination of the work of Congress and of our state legislatures will show the dominating importance of this function. Its performance certainly makes much the largest demand upon the time and energies of these legislatures." [2]

"Notwithstanding the theory of the separation of powers," writes Charles Beard, "Congress may to some extent control the various executive departments by statutes regulating even the minutest duties of the cabinet officers. The constitution merely hints at the existence of the executive departments; but the power to determine the number of such departments and to provide for the internal organization of each is, nevertheless, exercised by Congress . . . it may exercise a substantial dominion over executive departments under its power to fix salaries, define duties, and appropriate money for designated purposes." [3]

"Since the English Revolution of 1688, it has been a part of the Anglo-American tradition that elected representative assemblies control the policies and acts of the executive branch of the government," according to former President Leonard D. White of the American Political Science Association. "This doctrine was firmly embedded in the American state and federal constitutions. With some wartime reservations, it has been universally accepted throughout our country." [4]

CONFLICTING THEORIES OF CONTROL

Despite this impressive testimony in support of the doctrine of legislative control, differences concerning the proper role of Congress and the President in the realm of administrative action have at times seriously disturbed their relations. Responsibility for administration of the reconstruction program in the South after the Civil War, for example, was a bone of bitter controversy between President Johnson and the national legislature. And today the theory of legislative surveillance is being challenged by the theory of presidential responsibility for the control of administration. According to the latter theory, the President should be responsible for controlling administrative performance; the

---

[2] *Principles of Legislative Organization and Administration* (1934), pp. 24–25.

[3] *American Government and Politics* (1924), p. 252.

[4] "Congressional Control of the Public Service," *American Political Science Review*, February, 1945, p. 1.

lines of control run up vertically through the administrative hierarchy to the administrator-in-chief at the top of the pyramid; and the central control agencies (Civil Service Commission, Budget Bureau, General Accounting Office) are staff aides of the President by means of which he exercises his control over personnel, administrative and fiscal management.[5] According to the theory of congressional oversight, on the other hand, the proper office of Congress is to supervise the government; the lines of control and accountability should run horizontally from the administrative agencies directly to Congress; and the agencies of control should be attached to the legislative branch or should exercise independent judgment in dealing with administrative officials.

In actual practice, of course, the control of administration does not fall into any neat and tidy pattern. Lines of responsibility and influence criss-cross each other in a bewildering maze between the President and Congress, the numerous departments, commissions, and corporations, the political parties and pressure groups, and local and sectional interests. Administrative officials operate under the push and pull of many conflicting pressures. Historically, the pendulum of power has swung back and forth between Congress and the President, with the Chief Executive dominant during wars and domestic crises and the legislature usually ascendant afterwards, reflecting popular reaction to wartime concentration of power in the Presidency or a period of presidential defeasance such as followed World War I. "Under our present system," as Pendleton Herring points out, "presidential responsibility for the great mass of administration is often a fiction . . . In their aggregate effect, 'politics'—on the one hand in the sense of localism, personal favoritism, and partisanship, and on the other in terms of bureaucratic resistance, narrow agency loyalties, and the influence of special interests—makes the central coordination and control of administrative activity very difficult indeed." [6]

Advocates of presidential responsibility argue that congressional government has been more amenable to control by minority interests and pressure groups; and that presidential leadership is needed to counteract the centrifugal trends in our political life and to coordinate the administration of public policy at home and abroad. The theory of congressional control, they say, expects civil servants to serve two masters and permits a dangerous lack of coordination. While conceding the

[5] Pendleton Herring, "Executive-Legislative Responsibilities," *American Political Science Review*, December, 1944.
[6] *Ibid.*

propriety of legislators bringing the grievances of their constituents to administrative attention, Herring insists that "it must not take the form of congressional direction of administration. Congressmen can investigate whatever phases of bureaucratic behavior they choose; they can press for the redress of grievances felt by their constituencies. [But] they should not expect officials to serve two masters; nor should they set up special agencies accountable directly to the Congress. Experience shows clearly that effective surveillance by the National Legislature is impracticable. Congress is not organized to do such a job, and even if it were, it would run head-on into the President in his distinctive role as administrator in chief." [7]

The Conflict Reconciled

I submit that these apparently conflicting theories concerning the control of administration are not incompatible and that they can be reconciled. Under the constitution Congress has certain powers and responsibilities in connection with the appointment and removal of public officials, the safeguarding of delegated powers, the raising and expenditure of public funds, and the approval of treaties. And the President has power to make treaties and appoint certain officers and the duty to take care that the laws are faithfully executed. In performing its constitutional functions Congress must necessarily examine the credentials of presidential appointees and the conduct of accused officials; establish and maintain an administrative structure conducive to the efficient conduct of public affairs; enact the necessary revenue laws, authorize activities which require the expenditure of funds, and make the necessary appropriations; advise and consent or withhold its consent to the ratification of treaties; and in general hold the Executive accountable for the faithful and effective execution of the laws. Congress would be negligent if it failed to inspect the qualifications of persons nominated to high public posts, to review the efficiency and economy of administrative management, to guard against unsympathetic or over-zealous administration, to check dishonesty and waste, to weigh our foreign engagements, and to see that law enforcement complies with the legislative intent.

If the President is to fulfill the responsibility of his office under the constitution, however, he must have undivided executive powers and adequate means with which to exercise them. He should have a White House secretariat composed of highly qualified aides to assist him in

[7] *Ibid.*

dealing with the managerial and administrative agencies of the government. He should have adequate tools of personnel, administrative, fiscal, and planning management. He should have a well organized and integrated departmental structure free from overlapping and duplication and capable of rendering efficient public service, of effective coordination, and of democratic control. And the executive branch should be staffed throughout with civil servants selected by the merit system.[8]

Conflict between the legislative and executive branches would be greatly reduced if each branch would confine itself to its own essential functions. On the one hand, it is the function of Congress to determine the broad policies of the national government, to enact them into law, to provide the necessary funds, and to exercise general oversight of executive performance. Congress should limit its inspection and review to the operation of broad, general policies and refrain from interfering with the details of administrative action and from intervening in individual cases. Political influence in appointments to civil service posts should be outlawed and criticisms of particular agencies or regulations should be referred to the appropriate supervisory committees. "Members of Congress are always glad to help a constituent place his opinions or wishes before the right official; but when it comes to the use of influence for upsetting the normal administrative procedure, interfering with discipline, getting special favors, or otherwise infringing on the responsibilities of the executive branch, the congressman who has respect for the principles of good government hesitates."[9] On the other hand, it is the function of the President to give Congress information of the state of the Union, to recommend to its consideration such measures as he shall judge necessary and expedient, and to execute the laws. In so doing he should take care not to usurp or by-pass the lawmaking function of Congress or to issue rules and regulations contrary to legislative intent. This division of authority under the American constitution was well stated by President Wilson in a message to Congress on May 13, 1920:

The Congress and the Executive should function within their respective spheres. Otherwise efficient and responsible management will be impossible and progress impeded by wasteful forces of disorganization and obstruc-

[8] For a full account of these requirements, see *Report of the President's Committee on Administrative Management* (1937).

[9] Robert Luce, *Congress—An Explanation*, p. 89.

tion. The Congress has the power and the right to grant or deny an appropriation, or to enact or refuse to enact a law; but once an appropriation is made or a law is passed, the appropriation should be administered or the law executed by the executive branch of the Government. In no other way can the Government be efficiently managed and responsibility definitely fixed.

OVERSIGHT OF APPOINTMENTS AND REMOVALS

One of the areas in which Congress exercises oversight of administration is in the appointment of numerous officials and employees of the executive branch of the national government. In normal times about 26,000 positions in the executive branch are subject to appointment by the President by and with the advice and consent of the Senate. Section 2 of Article 2 of the constitution gives the President power to nominate, "and by and with the advice and consent of the Senate," to appoint ambassadors, other public ministers and consuls, judges of the Supreme Court, and all other officers of the United States whose appointments shall be established by law. These include department heads, members of boards and commissions, federal marshals and attorneys, collectors of internal revenue, postmasters of the first three classes, and commissioned officers in the Army, Navy, and Coast Guard. The number and type of presidential civil positions subject to senatorial confirmation in January, 1946, were approximately as follows:

> 22,100—Postmasters, first-, second-, and third-class post offices.
> 2,550—State Department Foreign Service.
> 800—Public Health Service (regular commissioned officers).
> 1,100—All other (internal revenue and customs collectors, U. S. attorneys, U. S. marshals, judges, engineers, Coast and Geodetic Survey, heads of departments and agencies, etc.)
>
> ———
> 26,550—Civil Position Subject to Confirmation.[10]

Of the positions listed above, the most important individually are located at Washington, but the great majority of them are administrative posts in the field services, including the Postal and Custom Services,

———
[10] This summary is for the executive and judicial branches only and is exclusive of military personnel of War and Navy departments, positions in District of Columbia government, and positions not requiring Senate confirmation of appointees. Employment outside continental United States is included. All told, less than one per cent of federal jobs are filled on a patronage basis.

the Internal Revenue and Immigration and Naturalization Services, the mints and assay offices, the land offices, and the United States marshals and attorneys.

Presidential nominations to these positions are sent to the Senate and are at once referred by its presiding officer to the appropriate committees having jurisdiction over the offices concerned. The committees give due consideration to the nominations made by the President and sometimes hold public hearings in the case of the higher offices when sufficient interest develops. Thus, the Foreign Relations Committee held open hearings on the nominations of Messrs. Stettinius, Clayton, Grew, MacLeish, Rockefeller, and Dunn to top posts in the State Department. Routine administrative appointments are usually approved automatically and en bloc.

Under the practice known as "senatorial courtesy," the President or the department head concerned, before submitting certain nominations to the Senate, usually ascertains if they will be *persona grata* to the Senators of the party in power of the states in which the vacancies are located or of which the prospective nominees are residents; and Senate committees customarily refer nominations to positions in the field services to the Senators from the states in which such positions are located. They seldom object to the persons proposed, but when they do object, such nominations are usually not submitted or they are rejected by the Senate. When a first, second, or third-class postmaster is to be appointed, the Post Office Department customarily submits the names of the three highest candidates on the list to the local congressman, giving him an opportunity to express his preference, unless the postmastership to be filled is in the home town of a Senator, in which case the Senator is consulted. To the extent that confirmation depends upon the approval of individual Senators, the positions involved are evidently regarded as political plums. Most patronage appointments are made on the basis of recommendations from individual Senators and congressmen rather than through party committees. The Senate usually follows the recommendation of its committees in confirming or rejecting presidential nominations, but under the standing rules final action is never taken on the same day on which a nomination is received or reported, except by unanimous consent.

Congress also exercises oversight of federal personnel administration through its Committees on the Civil Service, which report matters relating to the Civil Service Commission and alleged violations of the law, and the status of officers, clerks, and employees of the civil branches of the government, including their reclassification, compensation, and retirement. Three principal statutes govern personnel administration in large areas of the service: the Civil Service Act of 1883, the Retirement Act of 1920, and the Classification Act of 1923. Important amendments to these acts relating to the selection, promotion, compensation, hours of duty, vacations and sick leaves, and retirement of federal employees have been introduced and considered in every recent Congress. As a result, existing federal personnel legislation has been described as a "patchwork with many large holes."

Proposed Reforms

After an intensive study of personnel administration in the federal service by Floyd W. Reeves and Paul T. David, the President's Committee on Administrative Management found it to be in need of thoroughgoing modernization. "The merit system should be extended upward, outward, and downward to include all positions in the Executive Branch of the Government except those which are policy-determining in character. At the same time the civil service administration should be reorganized into a central personnel agency under a single head and a nonpartisan citizen board appointed to serve as a watchdog of the merit system." [11] The ravages wrought in the civil service by the second world war and the heavy postwar responsibilities imposed upon the federal government in national and international administration underline the urgency of executive-legislative cooperation in the development of a highly qualified and adequately compensated career service.

In extending the merit system to the entire civil service and modernizing the machinery of personnel management, Congress should restrict senatorial approval of presidential appointments to those officers enumerated in the constitution. The power to appoint to all positions of a purely administrative character should be lodged in the heads of the respective agencies and the positions should be placed in the competitive classified service. Transfer of these positions to a merit basis would make for security of tenure and greatly improve the morale of the civil service.

Despite the extension of the merit system, most congressional offices have repeated demands made upon them for help in obtaining civil service positions. This practice violates the principles of the merit system and brings more grief than gain to the congressmen. For every

[11] Report of the President's Committee on Administrative Management, p. 7.

successful applicant, there are ten disappointed office seekers who hold their representative responsible. "Gratitude," as Luce remarked, "is far weaker than ingratitude." Since V-J Day demands for help in finding government jobs have greatly multiplied. Congress should deal with this situation by adopting legislation providing for the disqualification of any applicant for civil service employment who has sought to use political influence.

Upon the role of Congress in the removal of public officers the constitution is silent, except for the impeachment power. But after much controversy over the power of the Senate to limit the President's dismissal power, the question was definitely settled in the famous Myers case in 1926 when the Supreme Court finally held that the President has an exclusive power to dismiss administrative officers as an essential incident of the executive power and his duty to see that the laws are faithfully executed. There are more ways than one, however, of getting rid of objectionable officials. If Congress cannot fire them, it can abolish their positions or cut off their salaries. Limitations were inserted in the Urgent Deficiency Appropriation Act of 1943, for example, that prevented the employment of two specified employees of the Federal Communications Commission: William E. Dodd, Jr. and Goodwin Watson, and Robert Morse Lovett of the Virgin Islands administration.[12] And in the Humphreys case the Court held that Congress may regulate the tenure of members of regulatory boards and commissions and so remove the legal basis of the President's general power of direction.[13] Harvey Walker has suggested that incompetent administrative officers might be removed by joint address of both houses of Congress.

As for impeachment trials by the Senate, experience has shown that this is a cumbersome procedure which should be replaced by a special court trial in the case of federal judges. Representative Sumners of Texas, chairman of the House Judiciary Committee, proposed that, whenever the House of Representatives resolves that the behavior of a federal judge has been other than good within the meaning of the constitution, the Chief Justice shall designate a special court of three circuit judges in which the Attorney General shall bring a civil action to determine the right of such judge to remain in office. If the court finds against the judge, he would be removed from office, but he could

---

[12] For a severe condemnation of this and similar actions, see Arthur W. Macmahon, "Congressional Oversight of Administration: The Power of the Purse," *Political Science Quarterly*, June, 1943, pp. 166–173. The proscription of Messrs. Dodd, Watson, and Lovett was invalidated as a bill of attainder by the Supreme Court in June, 1946.

[13] Humphrey's Executor vs. U. S., 295 U. S. 602 (1935).

appeal his case to the United States Supreme Court. Legislation embodying this proposal passed the House of Representatives in 1937 and 1941, but the Senate has not yet approved of this modernized impeachment plan.[14]

SAFEGUARDING DELEGATED POWERS

In the simpler days of the nineteenth century, before the rise of industrialism, Congress customarily spelled out the rules for the conduct of governmental operations in the form of specific and detailed statutes which left little or no room for administrative discretion. But with the coming of the industrial age and the growth of the regulatory and service functions of the federal government, problems calling for governmental action became too complex and technical to deal with in the statutes alone. Under these circumstances, Congress began to define the general principles of policy in the law and to delegate to administrative officials the power to issue uniform rules and regulations applying the general principles equally to concrete situations. Although delegations of rule-making powers date back to the administration of President Washington, they were most frequently made during five periods of national emergency: 1789–1815—when the young nation was trying to protect its neutral trade against British orders in council and Napoleonic decrees; 1861–1875—the Civil War and Reconstruction period; 1917–1918 during our participation in the first World War; 1933–1935—the period of the Great Depression; and 1941–1945 during the second World War. But the practice is such a long-standing one, even apart from emergency delegations, that it has become a normal technique of democratic government and has been sanctioned within broad limits by the Supreme Court of the United States in a long series of decisions. Congress still attempts, to be sure, to legislate in detail, but it has long since recognized the need of delegating the rule-making power as a means both of meeting novel and rapidly changing situations and of reducing its own burdens. Thus there is no serious doubt at this late date as to the constitutionality or necessity of the practice.

Administrative regulations in fields in which public opinion has demanded governmental action or the general welfare requires it have several noteworthy advantages over minute statutory specifications. They permit legislators to concentrate on questions of basic public policy and avoid confusion and conflict over petty details. They facilitate administration of the law by not freezing unworkable pro-

---

[14] See H. R. 1201, 79th Congress, 1st Session.

visions into the statute. They enable administrators, who are more familiar perhaps with conditions in the field, to adapt the enforcement of the law flexibly to varying situations. "Legislative details often multiply administrative difficulties and tie the hands of the administrator in red tape." And they combine the special competence of legislators and administrators: the former's superior sense of the purposes of public opinion and the latter's technical knowledge and administrative "know-how." [15]

For surveillance of the manner in which these delegated powers are exercised by the departments and commissions, Congress has traditionally depended upon several safeguards. It requires administrative agencies to submit periodic and special reports giving an account of their activities. It may pass resolutions of inquiry formally requesting information. Committees of Congress may summon administrators to testify at hearings concerning their acts. They may carry on searching investigations of administrative agencies and activities. The law may provide for the limitation of executive discretion by uniform rules and for appeal to independent tribunals authorized to protect the individual citizen against orders that do not conform to those rules. Members of Congress may voice criticisms of particular regulations upon the House or Senate floor. And Congress may withdraw the powers it has delegated or supersede the rules and regulations issued under them by its own statutes.

Prenatal and Postnatal Safeguards

James Hart describes five "prenatal" procedural safeguards. Congress may provide for the creation of advisory committees composed of representatives of groups affected by administrative regulations and require administrators to consult them. The National Industrial Recovery Act of 1933 and the War Mobilization and Reconversion Act of 1944 contained provisions for such advisory boards. The statute may require that the issuance of regulations be preceded by public hearing held after due notice, such as the hearings held under the Trade Agreements Act. Draft regulations may be published in advance and distributed to selected mailing lists for criticism and revision. Most federal regulatory agencies consult informally with the representatives of groups affected

---

[15] For an excellent study of this whole subject, see "The Exercise of Rule-Making Power" by James Hart in the Report of the President's Committee on Administrative Management, pp. 310–355.

by their rule-making powers. And the way may be prepared for the acceptance of compulsory controls by prior experimentation with voluntary regulations.[16]

Judicial review, adequate publicity, and central publication have been the principal "postnatal" safeguards of the rule-making power. In three famous cases in the middle thirties the Supreme Court for the first time condemned "delegation running riot." [17] According to these decisions, the tests of a valid delegation seem to be that "Congress must itself have the power to regulate; must define the subject to be regulated; must declare a policy with respect to that subject and set up a standard or criterion for executive action; must require a finding, at least in contingent legislation; and must delegate rule-making powers to public officials and not to private persons." [18] The courts may also invalidate regulations as being *ultra vires* for various reasons. Departmental rules and regulations have been published in the *Federal Register*.

Sterner postnatal remedies for the abuse of delegated powers include the curtailment of appropriations to offending agencies, the prosecution of officials accused of misconduct, and the reserve power of impeachment. Congress may also provide for the automatic expiration of powers granted by emergency acts upon the termination of the war or emergency, or at a stated period thereafter, as it did in the War Powers Acts. Or it may reserve the right to terminate granted powers by concurrent resolution, as it did in the Lend-Lease Act, the Service Extension Act, and the Emergency Price Control Act.

Legislative Veto

Another safeguard of granted powers which Congress has recently used in authorizing reorganization of the executive branch, and may use in the future, is to require the President to submit plans before a given date which will take effect after the lapse of a, specified period unless in the meantime Congress has passed a concurrent resolution disapproving them. The Reorganization Act of 1945, for example, provides that no reorganization shall take effect unless the plan is transmitted to Congress before April 1, 1948, or if, within 60 days after transmittal, the two houses have passed a concurrent resolution stating

---

[16] *Ibid.*, pp. 339–342.

[17] Panama Refining Co. *v.* Ryan, 293 U. S. 388 (1935); Schechter *v.* United States, 295 U. S. 495 (1935); Carter *v.* Carter Coal Co., 298 U. S. 238 (1936).

[18] Hart, *op. cit.*, p. 343.

that the Congress does not favor the reorganization plan. The same act also exempts certain agencies from its operation and circumscribes the powers granted in several other respects.[19]

This use of the concurrent resolution as a device for limiting the exercise of delegated powers resembles the British system of provisional orders under which rules issued under the authority of delegated power are classified in four ways: (1) rules on trivial matters which are subject to the complete control of the departments; (2) rules which are effective at once, but which may be annulled by Parliament within a specified time; (3) rules which become effective within a specified time provided Parliament takes no action to the contrary; and (4) rules which become effective only upon the consent of Parliament.[20] Congress might well adopt the provisional-order technique as a means of reviewing administrative rules imposing duties upon citizens which would be referred to the appropriate committees and would become effective within a given period, subject to legislative veto.[21]

Proposed Improvements

Despite the variety of weapons in the armory of congressional oversight of delegated powers, these methods of inspection and review have proved inadequate, especially under the emergency conditions of the past decade. Recurring complaints from private citizens with regard to federal administrative law and procedure have led to a widespread demand for some simple and standard plan of administrative procedure. There is no recognizable body of administrative law as there is for the courts in the judicial code. There are no clearly recognized legal guides for either the public or administrative officials. Even the ordinary operations of administrative agencies are a *terra incognita* to the uninitiated. Each agency has been free to prescribe its own pro-

---

[19] See Howard White, "Executive Responsibility to Congress via Concurrent Resolution," *American Political Science Review,* October, 1942, pp. 895–900. A similar technique was used in acts of 1934 and 1940 authorizing the Supreme Court to prescribe procedural rules for federal courts, subject to congressional veto.

[20] Provisional orders have gradually been giving way to "special orders," i.e., those which are made by Ministers and laid before Parliament and take effect when confirmed by a mere resolution of the two houses. In 1946 Parliament passed the Statutory Instruments Act to standardize the mechanics of printing and publishing delegated legislation and the processes of parliamentary control.

[21] Cf. Leonard White, "Congressional Control of the Public Service," *ibid.,* February, 1945, pp. 5–6. Robert Heller, *Strengthening the Congress,* pp. 22–23. And the testimony of W. Y. Elliott before the Joint Committee on the Organization of Congress, p. 970 of its Hearings.

cedures. Abuse of the rule-making power evidently calls for more than piece-meal investigations of individual complaints. The fundamental need is for a general code of administrative conduct prescribing the minimum requirements of fair administrative procedure for the guidance of all the rule-makers and all private interests.

Search for such a code has been the subject of intensive study in recent years by congressional committees, presidential commissions, professional organizations, legal scholars, and individual practitioners. In 1937 the President's Committee on Administrative Management wrestled with the problem in special studies of the exercise of rule-making power and of the independent regulatory commissions. In 1938 the Senate Judiciary Committee held hearings on a proposal for the creation of an administrative court. In 1939 the Attorney General appointed a Committee on Administrative Procedure which made a thorough investigation of administrative practices and procedures and recommended corrections in the rule-making and adjudicatory aspects of the administrative process.[22] In 1940 Congress passed the Walter-Logan administrative procedure bill, but the President vetoed it. Several bills were introduced in 1941 and hearings were held on them, but further action was delayed by the international crisis. In 1943 the House of Representatives set up a Select Committee to Investigate Acts of Executive Agencies beyond the scope of their authority, chaired by Representative Howard Smith of Virginia. The Smith committee received thousands of complaints concerning administrative rules and regulations and made hundreds of inquiries. In a series of reports it severely criticized the administrative regulations and procedures of the Office of Price Administration, the War Food Administration, the War Labor Board, and the National Labor Relations Board. And it embodied its recommendations for reform in a bill introduced in the House on August 24, 1944, and reintroduced on January 3, 1945.[23] Meanwhile, studies were made and hearings held by the Judiciary Committees of both houses which finally led to the introduction by their chairmen of identical bills "to improve the administration of justice by prescribing fair administrative procedures."[24]

Profiting by the earlier studies and purporting to reconcile the views

---

[22] *Administrative Procedure in Government Agencies,* Sen. Doc. No. 8, 77th Congress, 1st Session.

[23] H. R. 339, 79th Congress, 1st Session. See also the testimony of Rep. Smith before the Joint Committee on the Organization of Congress, pp. 186–199.

[24] S. 7 and H. R. 4941, 79th Congress, 1st Session.

of public and private interests concerned, which were fully consulted, the McCarran-Sumners bill has been favorably acted on by the Congress and endorsed by the Attorney General. "The bill appears to offer a hopeful prospect," he said, "of achieving reasonable uniformity and fairness in administrative procedures without at the same time interfering unduly with the efficient and economical operation of the Government." As approved on June 11, 1946, the McCarran- Sumners Act requires administrative agencies to publish or make available to the public an increased measure of information concerning their organization, functions, and procedures. It gives to that portion of the public to be affected by administrative regulations an opportunity to express its views before the regulations become effective. It prescribes, in instances in which existing statutes afford opportunity for hearing in connection with the formulation and issuance of administrative rules and orders, the procedures which shall govern such hearings. It provides for the selection of hearing officers on a basis designed to obtain highly qualified and impartial personnel and to insure their security of tenure. It also restates the law governing judicial review of administrative action. Such is the latest, if not the last, move in the long effort to discipline administration to democratic ends.[24a]

In order to assist it in the immense and continuing task of unifying and simplifying the administrative system, Congress might well create an office within the legislative branch comparable to the Administrative Office of the United States Courts. As proposed by Frederick F. Blachly, staff member of the Brookings Institution since 1925 and a leading authority in this field, such an agency would be an arm of Congress and directly responsible to it. It would have a large, well-paid staff and the right to subpoena witnesses and documents. The proposed office would make studies and recommendations with a view to the revamping of the sprawling organization and perplexing procedures of the administrative branch and would assist in the process of fitting in new legislation. It would be composed of a board representing the great regulatory agencies and the courts of appeal, a director, and advisory committees representing private, professional, civic, and research organizations. "Just as Congress has had to give up the work of detailed auditing to the Comptroller General and the settlement of contract claims to the Court of Claims, it should now give up the details

---

[24a] For a good discussion of the social "adjustment" function of the administrative process, see Ernest S. Griffith, *The Impasse of Democracy* (1939), pp. 109–111 and 166–167; and his *Modern Government in Action* (1942), pp. 69–78.

of investigation and planning for the administrative machine to an expert investigating, advisory, and recommending authority." [25]

Such an office as Blachly proposes might function under the immediate supervision of a new joint standing committee of Congress on executive agencies and procedures. As proposed by Congressmen Smith and Voorhis, this committee would report to the Congress all executive acts exceeding statutory or constitutional bounds and recommend appropriate legislative measures either to prohibit such encroachments as it discovered or to grant specific powers shown to be necessary for proper administration.[26] The establishment of a standing committee to keep watch on administrative lawmaking might obviate the need for many special investigating committees. To maintain oversight of the flood of rules and regulations issued by federal agencies might seem too large an order for a single congressional committee. In practice, however, the work would be done by an expert staff such as Blachly has proposed, and would be confined to complaints brought to the committee's attention. The committee would not concern itself with regulations pertaining to the internal business operations of the administrative departments and commissions.

PROSPECTIVE CONTROL OF EXPENDITURES

Federal expenditure is the third great area of congressional control of administration. Perhaps nine-tenths of the work of Congress is concerned, directly or indirectly, with the spending of public money. The spending power is the constitutional birthright of Congress, for that document provides that "no money shall be drawn from the Treasury, but in consequence of appropriations made by law" and that "all bills for raising revenue shall originate in the House of Representatives; but the Senate may propose or concur with amendments as on other bills." The phrase "bills for raising revenue" has been interpreted to include appropriation bills as well as tax bills. Despite earlier disagreements between the houses, the Senate has acquiesced in the sole right of the House to originate general appropriation bills, leaving its own committee on appropriations to sit in an appellate capacity.[27]

Control of spending breaks down upon analysis into (1) efforts

---

[25] Hearings before the Joint Committee on the Organization of Congress, pp. 923–929.

[26] H. R. 5484, 78th Congress, 2d Session, Sections 5 and 6.

[27] For an authoritative history of the controversy over the power of the House to originate supply bills, see Sen. Doc. No. 872, 62d Congress, 2d Session, by John Sharp Williams.

to control before the money is actually spent and (2) measures of control after expenditure. The sources of control in each case are both administrative and legislative. But the following discussion will focus primarily upon the present and proposed role of Congress in fiscal control since the legislative phase of the subject is more pertinent to our inquiry.

Since 1921 federal expenditures have been controlled by the Budget and Accounting Act of that year which provided a national budget system and an independent audit of government accounts. This act was based upon 150 years of European and American experiment with efforts to strengthen legislative control of the executive and was the product of long legislative deliberations. Title II of the act directs the President to transmit to Congress on the first day of each regular session a budget setting forth in summary and in detail: estimates of expenditures, appropriations and receipts for the ensuing fiscal year, expenditures and receipts during the last completed fiscal year, and estimates of expenditures and receipts of the current year. The act also created a Bureau of the Budget to prepare the budget and to this end empowered it to assemble, correlate, revise, reduce or increase the estimates of the several departments and establishments. Operating under the President's direction, the bureau is authorized to make detailed studies of the organization and activities of the departments and agencies with a view of securing greater economy and efficiency in the conduct of the public service. Department heads are directed by the act to appoint budget officers who are to prepare the departmental estimates which are to be submitted to the bureau on or before September 15 of each year. And the bureau is to submit information upon request to the revenue and appropriating committees of Congress.

After the budget has been prepared in the executive branch[28] and submitted to Congress, it is referred to the House Committee on Appropriations. This is the most powerful and hardest working committee on Capitol Hill. Created in 1865, the Appropriations Committee now has 45 members and 12 subcommittees, all but two of which have seven members each. Each member sits on two subcommittees except the chairman who sits on three. The pattern of the subcommittee structure corresponds closely with that of the executive branch,

---

[28] For a good description of the administrative phase of the budget process, see Fritz M. Marx, "The Bureau of the Budget: Its Evolution and Present Role, II," *American Political Science Review*, October, 1945, pp. 871–878.

facilitating performance of the committee's supervisory function.[29] Since its establishment in 1865 the committee has had only four chief clerks: Robert J. Stevens, James C. Courts, Marcellus C. Sheild, and John C. Pugh—each of whom served with distinction and continuously, irrespective of changes in political control, for more than 20 years. In addition to its chief clerk, the committee had eight assistant clerks in 1945 and 12 clerk-stenographers at a total annual cost of $80,140. The Senate Committee on Appropriations, created in 1867, now has 25 members, 10 subcommittees, one clerk, and eight assistant clerks with a total annual payroll of $38,140. It has had six clerks in 79 years. Through these two over-worked committees and their small but capable staffs, Congress has exercised its power of the purse for a quarter of a century.

Legislative Phase of Budget Process

In the legislative phase of the budget process there are four main steps: the subcommittee hearings on the departmental estimates, their report to the full committee, the main committee reports to the House, and floor consideration of the committee reports.

Hearings on the departmental estimates begin early in the session and run for several weeks in the case of major bills. The Independent Offices and Treasury and Post Office subcommittees usually commence their hearings early in December on the basis of advance proofs of the budget which they have received. Department heads are heard first, followed by the bureau chiefs, members of Congress, and private citizens who desire to testify. All appropriation hearings are held in secret sessions to which only the members of the subcommittee and the scheduled witnesses are admitted. Committeemen cross-examine the departmental officers as to their past expenditures, present activities, and future needs. The questions tend to be of a random, impromptu character, picking on this or that item in a spot-check quest for information. Committeemen are faced by departmental experts, schooled in the art of justifying their requests. Burdened with many other duties, committee members are seldom prepared to make a penetrating analysis of the estimates and tend to appropriate blindly.

---

[29] The twelve subcommittees are: Deficiencies; Independent Offices; Treasury and Post Office; Agriculture; Interior; War; Legislative; State, Justice, Commerce, and Judiciary; Navy; District of Columbia; Labor-Federal Security; and Government Corporations. The Deficiencies subcommittee handled appropriations for the war agencies. A new subcommittee was created in 1946 to handle the financing of government corporations.

Each subcommittee has only one clerk. Although the clerks are conscientious, hardworking men, the staff is inadequate to keep the committee fully informed of departmental administration and needs. Lacking sufficient information, committeemen cannot always ask searching questions and are likely to make arbitrary decisions. To be sure, the House Committee on Appropriations was authorized by the 78th Congress to borrow special investigators from time to time to assist its subcommittees in making particular studies. But investigation of one agency by personnel from another raises a question of party loyalty and has not proved of great value in the few cases where it has been tried. For the administrators who appear, these annual inquisitions are more or less of an ordeal and have real disciplinary value. But officials soon become adept in the arts of caution, evasion, and concealment. Legislators can disturb but seldom fathom the deeper waters of the federal service.

Upon concluding its hearings, the subcommittee starts "marking up" the bill, going through it item by item until they have agreed upon the amount to be appropriated for each item. Then the bill is reported to the full committee which generally accepts the subcommittee report after an hour's casual deliberation. The bill is then reported to the House and the printed hearings on it (which aggregate more than 20,000 pages on all bills during the session) are simultaneously released so that legislators who are not members of the committee have had no opportunity to study the bill, the report, or the hearings before they have to vote on the measure. As a result, floor debate on appropriation bills, which generally takes place on the same day on which they are considered and reported by the main committee, ranges far and wide and is often irrelevant to their contents. Under these circumstances, few members are present on the floor and the bills go through to passage substantially without change or with minor amendments under the watchful guidance of the subcommittees in charge. Having passed the House, an appropriation bill then goes to the Senate where it is subjected to the same process of committee hearing, consideration, report, debate, and passage all over again. Disagreements between the two houses are adjusted in conferences between the appropriation committees and usually accepted by the two chambers.[30]

---

[30] For fuller accounts of the legislative phase of the budget process, see Arthur W. Macmahon, "Congressional Oversight of Administration: The Power of the Purse," *Political Science Quarterly,* June and September, 1943; and the testimony of Representative Ben F. Jensen before the Joint Committee on the Organization of Congress.

Such, in sketchy outline, is the process by which Congress exercises prospective control over federal expenditures. At least a dozen general appropriation bills, including the departmental and deficiency bills, are ground out by the legislative mills in this manner at each regular session of Congress. During the war there were also supplemental appropriation bills for national defense and a national war agencies appropriation bill to provide for the needs of the temporary war agencies. If the money made available to an agency for a fiscal year is insufficient for its needs, it will come back—this time to the Deficiencies subcommittee—and ask for a deficiency appropriation to cover its unanticipated expenses. Some idea of the tremendous growth in the work-load of the appropriation committees is afforded by the increase in annual appropriations since 1865—the first year of the committee's existence. In that year the total expenditures of the government, including the extraordinary expenditures incident to the Civil War, were $536 million. During 1943 Congress enacted 21 appropriation bills involving a total of $115 billion of direct appropriations, compared with $58 billion in 1941 and $147 billion in 1942.[31]

Legislative oversight of administrative expenditures is not confined to the annual hearings on the estimates. When circumstances require an agency to depart from the strict letter of a specific appropriation, discreet officials customarily consult the chairman and clerk of the subcommittee in charge in order to obtain their approval of the change and avoid subsequent criticism. Some subcommittees also require the submission of quarterly or periodical reports. There is a tendency, according to Macmahon, for "administrators to meet with appropriations subcommittees in *ad hoc* sessions during the year" and for interim supervisory relationships to increase.[32]

Recent Developments

Several recent developments reflect the growing feeling in congressional circles that appropriation procedures need to be strengthened. Mention has already been made of the use of special investigators by the House Committee on Appropriations. Armed by the 78th Congress with authority to employ them and allotted $100,000 for the purpose, the committee's chief investigator compiled a roster of qualified employees of various administrative agencies who could be borrowed from time

[31] Edward T. Taylor, *A History of the Committee on Appropriations, House of Representatives,* House Doc. No. 299, 77th Congress, 1st Session, p. 11.
[32] *Op. cit.,* pp. 401–7.

to time at the committee's expense to assist it or its subcommittees in making special studies. Several such studies have since been made in this way, including one of the Rural Electrification Administration and one of the field offices of the Bureau of Foreign and Domestic Commerce. When the examinations are finished, the temporary investigators return to their posts in the departments which are remunerated by the committee for the time spent in its employ. The committee has been careful to select investigators from agencies other than those to be examined. "We call the proper operative from the department," explained Chairman Cannon in describing the arrangement to the House, "we put him on the job—a new face, a new man, a new enthusiasm, and when the job is done we send him back." [33]

It has long been the practice of the appropriation subcommittees (other than the Legislative and District of Columbia committees) to make extensive field trips in order to gain first-hand knowledge of the activities for which they are making appropriations. With the expansion of American operations overseas, subcommittees are now going to Central and South America, Europe, and the Far East, inspecting the far-flung activities of the State, War and Navy Departments. And one conscientious committeeman, Representative Albert Engel of Michigan, has kept the Labor Department and Federal Security Agency on the alert by his unexpected visitations at departmental offices and army camps. A day of personal inspection is often worth a week of committee hearings.

More than 100 governmental corporations have been created in recent years as a device for managing "big government." These corporations have been wholly outside the orbit of congressional control. Once created and capitalized, they have loaned, borrowed, spent, and operated as their managers pleased. In many cases their charters have been complete secrets to Congress. And in those instances where they were known, they were so broad as to permit the management to engage in almost every conceivable field. Their operations, fiscal or otherwise, were not under the supervision of any check except that of the prudence and common sense of the management. Few, if any of them, were required or even bothered to report to Congress on their activities.

Passage of the Byrd-Butler bill by the 79th Congress went far to remedy this condition. This act brings government corporations under the operation of the budget system and directs the General

---

[33] *Congressional Record,* December 6, 1944, p. 8915.

Accounting Office to audit their transactions annually and report thereon to Congress. Moreover, the act forbids any new government corporation to be created except by congressional authorization. There seems to be no valid reason why such corporations should not be placed under the supervision of appropriate departments or agencies in the executive branch of the government where Congress can maintain proper and adequate oversight of them. Furthermore, government corporations should discontinue the practice of making loans or advances to the regular establishments or other agencies or corporations of the government which should obtain their operating funds only by means of congressional appropriations.[33a]

Congressional oversight of the spending power has also been relaxed in recent years by the growth of so-called permanent appropriations. The practice has developed of appropriating amounts for an indefinite period without further action by Congress. Such acts remain in effect until repealed or amended. These permanent appropriations totalled $3.5 billion in 1944, exclusive of permanent trust appropriations, and had increased to $5.6 billion in 1946. $5.3 billion of this sum was for interest and retirement of the public debt and $100,000,000 was for excess-profits tax refund bonds. In 1935 a permanent appropriation of 30 per cent of the annual customs duties, which amounted to $113 million in 1946, was made to encourage the exportation and domestic consumption of American farm products. Although the war put an end to agricultural gluts, this appropriation was neither repealed nor modified, but $50 million of it was diverted in one year to finance school lunch programs. Efforts are constantly being made to add to this list and thus put other appropriations beyond annual congressional review.

Criteria and Critique of Legislative Control

The success of congressional efforts to control the spending power can be tested in terms of certain historical budget principles which have been developed during 150 years of legislative struggle to tighten the purse strings. As defined by Harold D. Smith, director of the Budget Bureau since 1939, these principles are substantially as follows:[34]

[33a] This was recommended by Herbert Emmerich in his study of Government Corporations and Independent Supervisory Agencies. See *Report of the President's Committee on Administrative Management* (1937), pp. 299–303.

[34] Harold D. Smith, "The Budget as an Instrument of Legislative Control and Executive Management," *Public Administration Review*, Summer, 1944, pp. 181–188.

1. *Publicity.* The main stages of the budget process, which include executive recommendation, legislative consideration and action, and budget execution, should be made public.

2. *Clarity.* The budget should be understandable to every citizen. As was said by a British writer in 1764: 'The administration has condescended . . . to explain the budget to the meanest capacity.'

3. *Comprehensiveness.* The budget should contain expenditures and revenues on a gross basis, reflecting all governmental activities without exception, and should show the surplus available for debt retirement or the deficit to be met by new revenue legislation or borrowing.

4. *Budget Unity.* All receipts should be recovered into one general fund for financing all expenditures. This principle condemns earmarking of revenues for specific purposes of expenditure, except in cases of trust accounts, or in cases where a special and direct relationship exists between receipts and expenditures.

5. *Detailed Specification.* Receipts and appropriations should be expressed in detailed specification; transfer of items should be permitted only in exceptional cases.

6. *Prior Authorization.* The budget should be submitted, considered, and acted upon in advance of the period during which the expenditures are to be made; it should include estimates for all foreseeable needs, thus reducing as far as possible requests for supplemental and deficiency appropriations. Budget execution should stay strictly within the legislative authorization and should be checked by an auditing agency reporting to the legislature.

7. *Periodicity.* Appropriations should be authorized for a definite period of time. An appropriation not used at the end of the period should generally lapse or be reappropriated with the specific amount and purpose detailed.

8. *Accuracy.* Budget estimates should be as accurate as possible and there should be no 'padding' of expenditure estimates or providing for hidden reserves by underestimating revenues.

Comparison of these "budgetary commandments" with actual contemporary practice led Director Smith to conclude that "budgeteers are hopeless sinners. Each one of these principles is frequently violated by those who prepare the budget, those who enact it, or those who execute it." [35] And he cited chapter and verse to prove his charge.

Moreover, the budget is not only an instrument of legislative control; it is also a tool of executive management from the point of view of which it must be tested by a different set of evolving principles.

---

[35] *Ibid.,* p. 182.

Mr. Smith sets forth eight such principles under the heads of executive programming, executive responsibility, reporting, adequate tools, multiple procedures, executive discretion, flexibility in timing, and two-way budget organization. Between the historical principles of legislative control and the new principles of executive management are certain apparent contradictions; for example, the conflict between the legislative control principle of detailed budget specification and the executive management principle of executive budget discretion. It is possible, however, as Mr. Smith shows, to reconcile these apparently conflicting principles and to make them supplement and reinforce each other. In fact, effective legislative budget control and executive budget management are mutually interdependent. Democratic budgeting and better government depend upon their reconciliation—an objective toward the attainment of which notable progress has been made in recent years under the enlightened guidance of the Budget Director in cooperation with the House and Senate Appropriations Committees.

When the efforts of Congress to control before expenditures are viewed by the detached scholar in the long perspective of American history, the conclusion is reached that the attempts of Congress to compel compliance with the laws making specific appropriations have been "in large measure, self-defeating." [36] After describing the conventions which govern the appropriation of congressional grants and the methods by which control has been loosened in practice, Lucius Wilmerding in his admirable history of the spending power concludes that Congress has permitted transfers between appropriations, authorized the unlimited use of departmental receipts, and set up credit corporations with separate budgets. And the executive has mingled appropriations, brought forward and backward unexpended and anticipated balances, incurred coercive deficiencies, and otherwise escaped the rigors of congressional control. Responsibility for this continuing state of affairs is attributed to "the carelessness of Congress in protecting its own rights and . . . to the stubborn obstinacy of executive officers who . . . pay lip service to the financial supremacy of Congress while disregarding it in practice." [37] But the basic cause, according to Wilmerding, lies in the incompatibility between extremely detailed itemization of appropriations and the needs of administration.

[36] Lucius Wilmerding, Jr., *The Spending Power: A History of the Efforts of Congress to Control Expenditures* (1943), pp. 193-195.

[37] *Ibid.*, p. 194.

An Overall Congressional Budget

With the public debt approaching $275 billion and with the annual postwar operating expenditures of the federal government running around $30 billion, there is a widespread public demand that Congress strengthen its control over the public purse. A whole battery of devices for obtaining more effective performance of its fiscal function was offered by experts who testified during 1945 before the Joint Committee on the Organization of Congress. A review of their proposals reveals a wide area of agreement among students of the appropriation process as to the steps that need to be taken.

First, congressional budget planning must be modernized. At present there is no mechanism in either house for taking an over-all view of federal finances. Receipts and expenditures are considered by separate committees in each chamber. Spending programs are split up among a dozen different subcommittees. There is no attempt to impose a ceiling on total appropriations or to keep expenditures within the limits of income. This splinter approach to fiscal policy making could be corrected by joint action of the revenue-raising and appropriating committees of the House and Senate. Early in each regular session, after receiving the President's budget message, the revenue and appropriation committees of each house, acting jointly, should submit to Congress a concurrent resolution setting forth the total estimated receipts and total anticipated federal expenditures for the next fiscal year. If total expected expenditures exceeded estimated income, the Congress should be required by record vote to authorize creation of additional federal debt for the amount of the excess. Adoption of the budget resolution by both houses would be required before any appropriation for the next fiscal year would be valid. Should total appropriations later be found to have exceeded the ceiling set by Congress, all general government appropriations (exclusive of permanent appropriations and those for servicing the public debt, for veterans' pensions and benefits and trust expenditures) would be automatically scaled down accordingly by a uniform percentage designed to bring total appropriations within the ceiling previously agreed upon. This action would be taken by the appropriations committees before the enactment of the appropriation bills for the coming fiscal year. The basic legislation for over-all budget control should provide, however, that these limitations would not apply during times of war emergency.

By setting annual budget totals in this way, Congress would create a framework for obtaining a coordinated picture of revenues and expenditures and keeping them in balance. In order to maintain continuing oversight of fiscal affairs, Congress might also create a joint committee on fiscal policy or a joint subcommittee in each house of their revenue and appropriation committees.

The appropriations committees of the House and Senate should also establish new standing subcommittees on federal aid to review annually all federal grants-in-aid to the states and set standards for their proper presentation. At present, federal aid grants are handled by various subcommittees according to the type of aid involved, but there is no unified consideration of all federal aid appropriations as a class. A new subcommittee to handle appropriations for government corporations was appointed by Chairman Cannon early in 1946.

Organization and Staffing of Appropriations Committees

Second, in order to lighten the load on the overworked appropriations committeemen, both these committees and each of their subcommittees should be exclusive committees and there should be a separate subcommittee for each of the major departments and agencies. At present, membership on the House Appropriations Committee is exclusive, but its members serve on two of its subcommittees, while members of the Senate Committee on Appropriations have several other committee assignments as well. And two of the Senate subcommittees and three of the House subcommittees presently handle appropriations for from two to six departments apiece. One subcommittee assignment should permit all its members to give more attention to, and have a better understanding of, the components of a single measure.

Members of the House Appropriations Committee receive their subcommittee assignments from the chairman of the full committee. Except in cases of removal by the chairman, members remain on their subcommittees indefinitely, advancing toward subcommittee chairmanship by the rule of seniority. Here, as in the whole congressional committee system, there appears to be need for some limit on the length of subcommittee chairmanships. Rotation of membership on these appropriation subcommittees at four-year intervals would not only increase the knowledge and inquisitiveness of the entire committee membership, but would also give individual members wider opportunity for service than the present system affords. On the other hand, it would sacrifice the advantage of the special acquaintance they acquire with particular federal agencies.

So vital, in the third place, is the role of the appropriations committees in the budget process that they should be the best equipped of any congressional committees, for upon their judgment hangs the expenditure of billions of public money. At present, however, these committees have only nine overworked clerks each. In addition, a few investigators and accountants are borrowed from time to time to augment this meager staff on a part-time basis. Everyone who has studied the work of these important committees agrees that they should have adequate permanent staffs to aid in careful scrutiny of budget requests and for "spot checking" government expenditures. Each subcommittee of the appropriations committee of the two houses should have not less than four expertly trained and well paid staff assistants, of whom two would be assigned to the chairman and two to the ranking minority member. And as a step toward closer cooperation with the Budget Bureau at the staff level, the committee clerks might attend the annual hearings before the estimates division of the Bureau.

Improved Reporting

In the fourth place, there is room for improvement in the form and content of the Budget and appropriation acts and reports. In spite of recent progress, the Budget still fails fully to meet the test of clarity. The breakdown of appropriation items varies from agency to agency and the language of the law lacks precision. "It has been the accretion of practice, for the most part stubbornly repetitive, but shaped in the past by countless forgotten situations." [38] A standard appropriation classification schedule should be devised which will clearly define in concise and uniform accounts the funds asked by agencies for their operation. Uniform classification of agency estimates should permit comparisions of expenditures by character and object as well as by organization units. What Congressman Monroney calls a "show-case accounting" schedule should precede each agency's request for funds in the printed hearings. It is recommended that estimates be presented in a manner which will disclose upon a standard and comparative basis all data essential to test the justification of the amounts asked of or recommended by the committees to the respective houses,

[38] Macmahon, *op. cit.*, p. 401.

and which will permit adequate examination of the justification. And in order that fiscal trends may be brought to public notice, monthly reports should be promptly printed giving cumulative data on the several appropriations and on all proposed supplemental and deficiency appropriations.[39]

Open Hearings

Fifth, the veil of secrecy which shrouds the legislative phase of the budget process should be lifted. At the present time, subcommittee hearings on the departmental estimates are held in executive session from which are excluded not only the public and the press, but all other members of Congress, even the other 38 members of the Appropriations Committee who are not members of the subcommittee. No member of Congress, not even members of the Appropriations Committee (other than members of the particular subcommittee), to say nothing of the public or press, have any knowledge of what transpires within the subcommittee until its bill is reported. Opposition to the requested appropriation which, if informed through open hearings and publicity, might give much helpful information to the subcommittee, to the full committee, and to Congress, is at present stifled or, at best, placed at a decided disadvantage. Secret hearings have the advantage, however, of relieving subcommittees from the pressures of groups interested in larger grants for favorite projects. Nevertheless, the main stages of the budget process, including legislative consideration, should be made public, as Budget Director Smith asserted in his first principle quoted above, with the exception of executive sessions for voting or where national security requires secrecy.

As a further aid to informed public and congressional opinion, it is also recommended that the printed hearings and reports on appropriation bills be laid before each house a minimum of three legislative days before floor consideration of the bill will be in order. At present, these documents are not available to members of the House until the day the bill is reported to the House for consideration. The hearings are voluminous in size and complex in detail. Under these circumstances, plus the secrecy of committee hearings, the membership at large knows little about the financial aspects of departmental administration and debate on the bills is superficial and perfunctory.

---

[39] *Controlling Federal Expenditures*, Finance Department, Chamber of Commerce of the United States, June, 1944, pp. 16, 20. See also testimony of Prof. Fred A. Fairchild before the Joint Committee on the Organization of Congress on June 22, 1945.

One may wonder, in view of their forbidding form and volume and their technical character, whether the budget documents will ever have much appeal for the average citizen or legislator. Congressman Robert Luce thought it a "vain hope that a systematic presentation of the financial programme will secure the help of public scrutiny and criticism . . . No tabulation of dreary figures will have any charm for Mr. Average Citizen." As for himself, he candidly stated that "I have found not the slightest use in the huge volume delivered to me annually for this purpose. Nor have I ever heard any other member say he found it of use. It may help members of the Committee on Appropriations, though my suspicion is that they examine only the pages relating to the work of the subcommittees on which they serve . . . The great bulk of the other Senators and Representatives hoist the thing to a top shelf on the chance that they may want to refer to it some time, which in my case has never happened. This is not because of indifference or neglect. We simply have not the time to meet the expectations of the budgetary enthusiasts. Only by chance do we know the facts behind the figures. We feel ourselves lost in the deluge of dollars." [40]

Other Improvements

Several other improvements in appropriation procedures would also help to strengthen legislative control over the public purse.

1. It might well be made a standing rule that any motion on the floor to increase an appropriation item beyond the figure recommended in the committee report would be out of order. Only motions to reduce items would be considered. This is the practice in the English Parliament where no member may move to increase an item as proposed by the government. But if Congress is unwilling to abdicate its powers in this respect, the rule could require a two-thirds majority for any increase in the estimates beyond the request in the Budget.[41]

2. When a bill authorizing appropriations is reported by a legislative committee, it should be referred to the Appropriations Committee for report on the fiscal effects of the proposed measure. Under House rules no appropriation may be made unless it has been requested

[40] Luce, *op. cit.*, pp. 86–87. See pp. 69 et seq. for a thoughtful analysis of the limitations of budget reform.
[41] This was proposed by Representative McCormick of Illinois in 1918. 65th Congress, 2d Session, House Doc. No. 1006. Cited by Marx, *op. cit.*, p. 658.

by the executive and authorized by the proper legislative committee.[42] This proposal would permit the review of authorizations by a committee able to take an over-all view of their effects on the general financial program.

3. All appropriations for a fiscal year should be consolidated into two bills: one for civil expenditures and the other for defense outlays, so as to give a complete picture of total annual appropriations and achieve a more consistent congressional fiscal policy.

4. The practice of making permanent appropriations for indefinite periods should be abolished, except in the case of appropriations for trust funds and for servicing the public debt. All federal expenditures should be subject to annual congressional review.

5. The custom of reappropriating unexpended balances should be discontinued, except in the case of continuing appropriations for public works, and such balances should revert to the treasury. The new amounts appropriated each year should indicate the total money available to each agency for the next fiscal year.

6. The current practice of permitting transfer of funds between appropriation accounts and organization units should be discontinued.

7. Congress should move in the direction of reasonably broad appropriation bills and away from detailed itemization. Excessive breakdown of appropriation accounts impedes administrative flexibility and facilitates pork-barrel items. Separate items for this school and that post office may win votes for the subcommitteemen in his local district, but at the sacrifice of effective expenditure control.

8. More stringent rules should be adopted against the inclusion of legislative riders on appropriation acts. The practice of attaching legislation to appropriation bills is often destructive of orderly procedure. Riders obstruct and retard the consideration of supply bills. Sometimes they contradict action previously approved in carefully considered legislation. They also compel the President to accept measures which he might otherwise disapprove, for a veto of an appropriation bill might cripple essential departmental services. In most cases such riders are adopted under the parliamentary guise of "limiting provisos," avoiding points of order that would be made against them under ex-

---

[42] There have been exceptions to this rule, e.g., the Legislative Reference Service in the Library of Congress has no statutory authorization, but owes its continued existence to an item in the annual legislative appropriation act; while the postwar division in the Bureau of Labor Statistics was not requested by the President but was created upon the initiative of the House subcommittee on Labor Department appropriations.

isting rules by purporting to restrict the spending of government funds. This practice, which impinges upon the regular jurisdiction of the standing committees of Congress and complicates the codification of the statutes, should be prohibited by tightening of the rules.

9. And, finally, Congress should reexamine and, where feasible, repeal the numerous acts in which authority is granted administrative officials to spend money without regard to the general laws controlling and safeguarding the use of public funds. From time to time provisions of law have exempted certain federal agencies from general expenditure controls, thus affording them greater freedom in the use of public moneys than the general law contemplates or other agencies enjoy. In varying degrees the accountability of the agencies concerned and legislative control over the use of public funds has thus been reduced. The annual reports of the Comptroller General for 1941 to 1944 indicate that there has recently been a notable increase in the number of such provisions. With the end of the war the continuation of this practice seems highly dubious if Congress is to recover its control of the purse. "Now is the time," as Comptroller General Warren says, "to begin to draw in this authority." [43] There is also a fertile field for study, he suggests, in the removal of many small restrictions on the use of public funds which hamper administration without accomplishing the legislative intent." [44]

CONTROL AFTER EXPENDITURE

In order to complete our picture of legislative control of the spending power, it remains to consider the law and practice of retrospective oversight, the shortcomings of existing post-control measures, and proposed remedies.

Title III of the Budget and Accounting Act of 1921 created a General Accounting Office as an independent establishment directed by a Comptroller General appointed by the President with the advice and consent of the Senate. The Comptroller General may be removed at any time by joint resolution of Congress for specified causes; otherwise he holds office for 15 years and is not eligible for reappointment. The act authorized the G.A.O. to adjust the claims and settle the accounts of the government; to investigate all matters relating to the receipt, disbursement, and application of public funds; and to make recommen-

---

[43] Hearings before the Joint Committee on the Organization of Congress, p. 530.

[44] For an elaboration of several of the above recommendations, see especially the testimony of Carter W. Atkins and Fred A. Fairchild in the hearings of the Joint Committee.

dations to the President and Congress looking to greater economy or efficiency in public expenditures. The Comptroller General was directed to make special investigations when ordered by Congress or its fiscal committees; to report departmental expenditures or contracts made in violation of law; to advise Congress as to the adequacy of the departmental examination and inspection of accounts; and to furnish information relating to expenditure and accounting upon request to the Bureau of the Budget. The act also directed all departments and establishments to furnish the Comptroller General information upon his request regarding their powers, duties, activities, organization, financial transactions, and methods of business. From the legislative history and language of the law, it is clear that the Comptroller General was expected to be independent of the executive and responsible to Congress alone. The intention of the authors of the act was that he should be "more than a bookkeeper or accountant; that he should be a real critic," as Representative Good, who was in charge of the bill, expressed it during the debate.

Armed with these broad powers, the General Accounting Office has made thousands of investigations during the past 25 years and has reported hundreds of cases of erroneous or extravagant payments to the House Committee on Appropriations. From small beginnings the office has grown until now (1945) it employs 14,586 persons and spends over $31 million annually. Off and on through the years there has been a great deal of controversy between the Comptroller General and agency heads as a result of conflicting interpretations of the law and basic differences in their outlooks. Such friction was more conspicuous during the days of General McCarl, the first incumbent, than under the administration of his successor, Lindsay Warren, who had been a member of Congress for many years. With the growing tendency of Congress to exempt essential war and other programs from his review and of the office to focus its attention upon the minor "chicken-feed" aspects of public expenditure, conflict seems to have subsided. Busy with a million other tasks, succeeding generations of legislators have come and gone in the confident belief that the Comptroller General was the agent of Congress and the vigilant watchdog of the Treasury.

With the postwar resurgence of efforts to strengthen fiscal control, Congress is tending to place increased reliance upon the G.A.O. In the Government Corporation Control Act of 1945 it provided that the transactions of government corporations should be audited annually by the General Accounting Office which is to make reports to Congress on its audits. And the Independent Offices Appropriation Act for 1946 appropriated $67,980 to the G.A.O. for investigations for, and details of assistants to, the congressional fiscal committees. This appropriation may result in increased use of the facilities of the office by the designated committees.[45] Several ways in which retrospective control of expenditures could be implemented through the G.A.O. were suggested by Comptroller General Warren in his testimony before the Joint Committee on the Organization of Congress in May, 1945.

Lack of a Legislative Audit

Despite the high hopes of the framers of the Budget and Accounting Act and the long and arduous labors of the General Accounting Office, the attempt to improve fiscal accountability has fallen far short of its goal. Responsibility for this must be shared both by the office and Congress itself. On the one hand, the G.A.O. has turned out in practice to be primarily an accounting and not an auditing agency. Instead of furnishing Congress with the kind of independent review and audit of federal accounts that a certified public accountant would provide a private business concern, the office has devoted its time over the years to examining the details of individual expenditures, allowing this little item and disallowing that, approving this travel voucher and "docking" that per diem or contract according to their legality. Vested under the act with both audit and accounting functions, the Comptroller General and his employees have concentrated on the petty details of their accounting function. An army of workers produces tons of paper work of trivial significance, while there is a lamentable shortage of inspection of how the federal accounts are kept. As a result of this penny-wise and pound-foolish procedure, the board of directors (Congress) of the public corporation (the federal government) have never received a genuine post-audit showing how the management (the administration) has carried on the financial operations of the government. Moreover, few, if any, of certain types of special reports required by the Budget and Accounting Act have ever been made by the General Accounting Office, such as the reports of "every expenditure or contract made . . . in violation of law" or upon "the adequacy and effectiveness of the administrative examination of ac-

---

[45] In the absence of requests for assistance from these committees, none of this appropriation had been spent during the first half of the fiscal year 1946.

counts and claims . . . and . . . of departmental inspection of the offices and accounts of fiscal officers."

On the other hand, much of the blame for the breakdown rests on Congress. By assigning him both audit and control powers, the Budget and Accounting Act combines incompatible functions in the Comptroller General. By dividing authority to determine administrative policy and procedure between the Executive and the Comptroller General, the act creates a separation of powers at the administrative level. By allocating the task of making studies and recommendations looking toward greater economy and efficiency in the public service to both the Budget Bureau and the General Accounting Office, the act sets up potential rivals in administrative housekeeping. Fortunately, the Comptroller General has not exercised this part of his assignment, thus avoiding conflict with the Budget Bureau which is the principal management arm of the President. Moreover, Congress has failed to create any agency within itself to which the Comptroller General can report. The Committees on Expenditures in the Executive Departments are the appropriate ones to receive and act upon the Comptroller General's reports, but in practice Congress has disregarded these reports and the expenditure committees have failed to follow them up.[46] Such follow-up as there is has been on selected items by the clerks of the House appropriations subcommittees. "I have been forced to the conclusion," lamented General Warren, "that Congress has no idea whatever how appropriated funds are spent." [47] Incidentally, he stopped submitting annual reports to Congress back in 1933.

Appointed by the President but independent of the executive, putative agent of Congress, but ignored by it most of the time, the Comptroller General is effectively responsible to no one. "Rather he is a one-man commission, independent of all other branches of the Government, and to him the Executive is made administratively responsible." After an intensive study of the G.A.O. for the President's Committee on Administrative Management, Harvey Mansfield concluded that "the main feature of the act has broken down completely. Administrative

---

[46] Representative Alvan T. Fuller resigned from the House Committee on Expenditures in the Interior Department in 1918 because it was "wasting the taxpayers' money." "We continue to be," he said, "the most inefficient and expensive barnacle that ever attached itself to a ship of state." Eleven separate committees on expenditures in the several executive departments were combined into one committee of the lower House on December 5, 1927.

[47] Hearings before the Joint Committee on the Organization of Congress, p. 529.

action by the Comptroller General has been substituted for reports to Congress. In place of the constitutional division of authority over financial matters between Congress and the Executive, a third authority has been introduced which impairs the responsibility of the other two. The Executive has not the proper power, the Congress has not the information, adequate to the discharge of their respective tasks." [48]

Similar conclusions were reached by Lucius Wilmerding after studying the history of congressional efforts to control expenditures since 1789. "Congress has not now, and has never had, any practical means of ascertaining after the event whether its financial authority has been respected or infringed. The reports of appropriations, expenditures, and balances which, since 1791, have in one form or another been presented to Congress have never been efficient instruments of retrospective control . . . There is, and can be under the present system of procedure, no certainty that the expenditure reported is within the ambit of the appropriation, that the proper administrative sanctions have been obtained, and that the terms of every governing statute have been observed. The reports—which, it is to be noticed, are in no sense of the word appropriation *accounts*—are unaudited.

"The congressional committees on expenditures," continued Wilmerding, "have been inefficient for the purposes of their creation. Without appropriation accounts upon which to bottom their work, without an auditor general to assist and advise them, without any regular procedure of scrutiny, they have not been and cannot be organically in touch with the executive and departmental system.

"The efforts of Congress to take over, for its own purposes, the auditing machinery of the Treasury have likewise failed. By transferring to the Comptroller General those powers of the Treasury accounting officers which were inconsistent with a congressional audit, Congress succeeded in creating a new and very powerful officer—an officer perhaps unknown to the constitution—but it left itself unprovided with an auditor general. The Comptroller General decides what payments will be or will not be allowed as definitive charges against the appropriations, but he is hardly in a position to report on the propriety of his own decisions."

Wilmerding concluded that "the attempts of Congress to arm itself with the machinery of retrospective control have altogether miscarried.

---

[48] Harvey C. Mansfield, The General Accounting Office in the *Report of the President's Committee on Administrative Management* (1937), p. 191. See also his testimony before the Joint Committee, *op. cit.*, pp. 999–1006.

Congress has not yet succeeded in devising a system of procedure stringent enough to render efficacious its unquestioned right to control the public expenditure." [49]

Proposed Reforms in Retrospective Control

A correct system for controlling federal expenditures after the money is spent must be based upon recognition of the distinction between accounting and auditing. Accounting involves the recording of transactions and the making of financial reports. It is primarily an administrative function and should be performed by the executive. Auditing, on the other hand, is the systematic and scientific examination and verification of accounting records and vouchers, performed for the purpose of ascertaining the fidelity and legality of the accounts, presenting the financial condition of the government at a given date, and rendering an expert and impartial opinion on the economy and efficiency of the management. It should be performed by an agency completely independent of the executive, as the General Accounting Office is. The two functions should not be combined, however, as they now are in the G.A.O.

The changes that should be made in the system of retrospective control are indicated by the defects of the present system and are long overdue. In the first place, the power to settle accounts and claims should be transferred to the Treasury Department and the General Accounting Office should be transformed into a General Auditing Office, headed by an auditor general and confined to auditing the federal accounts and reporting to Congress on the general financial operations of the government. Under this change the function of determining the fidelity and legality of public expenditures would be handled by the Auditor General who would also investigate the wisdom or extravagance of the expenditures made. In other words, the General Auditing Office would make service as well as fidelity audits, advising Congress on the major administrative problems revealed by its investigations. Instead of an army of clerks searching for petty errors, however, the G.A.O. would be composed of a small staff of qualified investigators, organized in teams, who would go into the several agencies and make periodic audits on a sampling basis, spot-checking the accounts and stimulating the development of proper accounting

---

[49] Lucius Wilmerding, Jr., *The Spending Power: A History of the Efforts of Congress to Control Expenditures* (1943), pp. 307–308. See also his testimony before the Joint Committee on the Organization of Congress, pp. 973–991.

standards. Thus transformed and strengthened, the G.A.O. would become "an office of administrative intelligence" for the national legislature and a much more effective aid to Congress in exercising its power of the purse. Furthermore, Congress itself should choose the auditor general and make him fully responsible to it.[50]

In the second place, Congress should amend its standing rules so as to make it the definite duty of its Committees on Expenditures in the executive departments (or of a new Joint Committee on Public Accounts) to receive the reports of the Auditor General, to consider his recommendations for improvements in methods of financial administration, to hold hearings on such matters with his assistance, and to report general or special legislation to correct any condition of which it disapproves. The abolition of the eleven expenditure committees in the House in 1927 and their replacement by a single committee on expenditures was a step in the right direction, but lacking staff aids and a positive definition of its duties, it has failed to perform its supervisory function. Thus clarified and revitalized, with competent staff assistance and the privilege of reporting at any time to the appropriations, legislative, and policy committees of the two houses, chaired perhaps by a minority member to prevent the majority from pigeonholing criticisms of the administration, the Committees on Expenditures would then be equipped to enforce proper accountability to Congress for the execution of the budget.[51]

PARTNERSHIP IN FOREIGN AFFAIRS

In addition to its oversight of administration in regard to appointments, rule-making, and expenditures, Congress also shares in the control of America's foreign relations. Under Article II, section 2 of the constitution, the advice and consent of the Senate is a condition of treaty making and of the appointment of ambassadors, other public ministers, and consuls.[52] The concurrence of two-thirds of the Senators present is necessary before the United States may be bound by treaties with foreign nations. Under Article I, section 8, Congress has power

---

[50] Leonard D. White, "Congressional Control of the Public Service," *American Political Science Review*, February, 1945, p. 10.

[51] These reforms have been advocated by many political scientists in recent years. See Harvey C. Mansfield, *President's Committee on Administrative Management, Report with Special Studies* (1937), pp. 201–202; W. F. Willoughby, *Principles of Legislative Organization and Administration* (1934), pp. 162–172; Lucius Wilmerding, Jr., *The Spending Power* (1943), Part II; Leonard D. White, *loc. cit.*

[52] During the first session of the 79th Congress the President submitted to the Senate 30 nominations for ambassadors, ministers, and envoys and 660 foreign service officers.

to regulate commerce with foreign nations, to control immigration and naturalization, and declare war. It also has power to establish and maintain foreign missions and consulates. Both houses of Congress must approve acts regulating our commercial and financial intercourse with other countries, such as the Bretton Woods plan, the reciprocal trade agreements, and the Export-Import Bank program. Now that we are living in an interdependent planetary economy, many subjects of domestic legislation have international repercussions and implications. A trade agreement with Canada, a loan to Britain to help revive her economy, or an appropriation to UNRRA for the relief of starvation in Greece—all require congressional approval.

By giving the Senate a share in the treaty making and appointing powers, the founding fathers intended that the upper house should function as an executive council, advising the President in his handling of our foreign affairs. But after abortive attempts by President Washington and Secretary of the Treasury Alexander Hamilton to consult with the Senate in the early days of the young Republic, the advice phase of the "advice and consent" function fell into desuetude.

The role of Congress in the control of our foreign affairs has happily received increased recognition in recent times by the executive branch. The Department of State held many informal conferences on foreign policy with members of the foreign affairs committees of Congress after the outbreak of hostilities in 1939. The President and the Secretary of State reported in person to Congress upon their conduct of our foreign relations after their return from international conferences at Yalta and Moscow. The State Department named one of its assistant secretaries to supervise the department's liaison with Congress. Mr. Dean Acheson, who first functioned in this capacity, established an *entente cordial* with the Senate Committee on Foreign Relations and the House Committee on Foreign Affairs. And influential members of both houses of Congress participated by presidential invitation in the actual negotiation of great international agreements at Bretton Woods, San Francisco, and London—a practice which won widespread congressional approval and greatly improved the climate of legislative opinion, as well as congressional understanding, of international political and economic problems. On its part Congress sought, as Victory Day approached, to encourage and guide the administration by adopting the Fulbright and Connally resolutions as expressions of legislative attitude on foreign policy. These devices and procedures have gone far to eliminate some of the misunderstandings and suspicions that in the past have beclouded the conduct of our foreign relations. And they have reduced the temptation for Presidents to by-pass constitutional machinery by the negotiation of executive agreements in lieu of treaties and by the appointment of personal representatives abroad in lieu of ambassadors.

Treaties vs. Executive Agreements

The proper role of Congress and the President in the conduct of our foreign relations has been a subject of bitter controversy throughout our constitutional history. Some critics attack the constitutional two-thirds rule requiring Senate advice and consent to treaties as too cumbersome, slow, and undemocratic and advocate the substitution of executive agreements for treaties. They argue that this rule has often been used by the minority party to embarrass the administration and they blame it for the defeat of many important treaties, including the Treaty of Versailles after World War I. They insist that the reasons advanced more than 150 years ago for excluding the House of Representatives from the treaty-making power have now lost their validity, and they urge the adoption of a more democratic method of obtaining congressional approval of treaties.[53]

Others defend the two-thirds rule against these charges and advocate its retention as a direct brake on drastic changes in foreign policy, for its sobering effect on the Executive, and because of the binding and irrevocable character of treaties. The substitution of executive agreements for treaties, they believe, is open to many objections. They permit the inclusion of secret clauses such as were involved in the case of the Lansing-Ishii Agreement of 1917; they bind only the administration that makes them; they may be unilaterally terminated at any time; they cannot be relied upon since they can be disapproved by legislative bodies; they lack the constitutional force and dignity of a treaty; and unless expressly authorized or acquiesced in, they are open to the charge of constitutional evasion.[54]

In actual practice about three-eighths of all the international agreements signed by the United States have been arrived at by the treaty-making process, the other five-eighths having been entered into by

---

[53] Kenneth Colegrove, *The American Senate and World Peace* (1944).

[54] Hugh Gibson, *The Senate and Foreign Relations* (1944), pp. 174–187; Herbert Wright, "The Two-Thirds Vote of the Senate in Treaty-Making," *American Journal of International Law*, October, 1944, pp. 643–650; Edwin Borchard, "Shall the Executive Agreement Replace the Treaty?," *ibid.*, pp. 637–643.

executive agreements or similar means. Altogether, about 1,500 executive agreements have come into effect and over 900 treaties. In some cases this device has been used in order to avoid or to circumvent defeat of a treaty by the Senate, for example, the Louisiana purchase, the annexations of Texas and Hawaii, and control over the finances of the Dominican Republic. More recently, the Declaration of the United Nations, the Atlantic Charter, the establishment of the Combined Chiefs of Staffs, the Combined Food Board, and numerous other wartime organizations were created by executive agreements. In general, matters dealing with economic cooperation, postal service, regulation of radio and air navigation and similar matters have become the subject of such agreements, while more serious and vital matters such as the establishment of peace systems are embodied in formal treaties. According to Quincy Wright, treaties and executive agreements have been treated as having equal validity in both international and municipal law. The courts have made little distinction between them. "Not only is it legally permissible to by-pass the two-thirds rule, but it is politically practicable." [55] Nevertheless, nothing less than a treaty has as much constitutional and moral control over the conscience and conduct of the American people.

Obstacles to Cooperation

Despite the recent improvement in executive-legislative relations in the field of foreign affairs, the situation is still defective in certain respects. Although the discipline of two world wars in a single generation and the inexorable logic of events led to speedy and overwhelming Senate ratification of the United Nations Charter, with only two dissenting votes, the two-thirds rule still hangs like a sword of Damocles over the postwar peace treaties. Since 64 Senators (when all vote) are needed for treaty approval, 33 Senators from the so-called "acreage states" or elsewhere can reject any and all treaties, and thus negatively control our foreign policy. The 17 least populous states, with 34 Senators, contained in 1940 eight per cent of the national population. But since only one-third of the population votes, the voters of these 17 states were less than three per cent of our total population. And if the 34 Senators from these 17 states were elected by a bare majority of the voters, they would represent less than two per cent of all the people of the country. It is possible, in other words, for a minority of the

[55] Quincy Wright, "The United States and International Agreements," *American Journal of International Law*, July, 1944, pp. 341–355.

Senate, representing a small fraction of the American people, to defeat an international program that is advocated by the President and supported by an overwhelming majority of the population.

Moreover, recent innovations in the way of consulting Congress informally about foreign affairs are entirely optional with the President and may not always be followed. Even President Roosevelt, astute politician though he was, neglected to take Congress into his confidence about the Atlantic Charter meeting with Churchill, the exchange of destroyers for bases with Britain, and about the momentous decisions reached at Quebec, Cairo, and Teheran until some time after these events transpired. President Truman's secrecy about the projected conference at Rio de Janeiro, and his oversight of the "senatorial courtesy" custom in appointing ex-Senator Townsend as an alternate representative of the United States to the first session of the General Assembly of the United Nations in London, bred suspicion and resentment in Congress. Congressional participation with the Executive in foreign, as well as domestic, affairs needs to be regularized and provided for in some accepted and permanent machinery of executive-legislative partnership.

Furthermore, the internal organization and staffing of the congressional committees on foreign affairs are seriously inadequate to their heavy responsibilities and ever-increasing work load. The Senate Committee on Foreign Relations has not been divided into standing subcommittees, either by regions or subjects, as a means of giving specialized study to the various problems in its province. And although it nominally has a staff of ten clerks, none of these is of professional grade and most of them work in the office of the chairman on other than committee business. On the other hand, the House Committee on Foreign Affairs was divided in 1945 into five subcommittees, each with a subcommittee chairman and four other members, and each with a geographical region of the world in which it specializes. Chairman Bloom serves as *ex officio* member of each of the five subcommittees.[56] But the committee has only one clerk and no professional staff. The staff deficiencies of these two important committees were partially corrected during 1945 when the Legislative Reference Service made available to them the services of its newly appointed international affairs expert, Dr. Francis Wilcox, who rendered invaluable aid as an adviser to the American delegations at the San Francisco and London conferences.

The expanding role of the House of Representatives in the foreign

---

[56] The Far East; Eastern Europe, the Near East and the Balkans; Western Europe; Africa and the Mediterranean; Western Hemisphere.

relations field should not be overlooked. Although it was not explicitly provided in the original constitutional design, the House has come in latter years to play an increasingly important part in our foreign affairs. Hearings before the House Committee on Foreign Affairs help to influence the formation of public opinion on foreign policy. Passage by the House of resolutions like the Fulbright resolution reflect public sentiment in turn and influence the conduct of our foreign relations by the State Department. Moreover, there is an increasing tendency to use joint resolutions of both houses to obtain congressional consent to American membership in the new international organizations like the I.L.O. and the UNESCO. And the lower house also participates, of course, in the enactment of legislation designed to implement the execution of treaties and executive agreements. Thus the House as well as the Senate must be reckoned with in the foreign field.[57]

Finally, the day-to-day participation of American members of international organizations is seriously handicapped and embarrassed by the lack of adequate machinery for instructing them concerning United States policy on specific questions. Our ineffectiveness in the daily work of international negotiations was illustrated, as Howard Piquet has testified, in the work of the interim commission that drafted the constitution of the United Nations Food and Agriculture Organization. "This is not because Americans as individuals are not the equals, in negotiating ability, of the representatives of foreign countries . . . It is the fault of our system—or rather, lack of system . . . The American delegate has been ineffective solely because he had no definite instructions on specific questions . . . Policy does not implement itself. It is all very well to enunciate a broad objective in general terms, but unless adequate machinery is at hand for making prompt decisions, as questions arise, there is no way of insuring that the policy will be effectively carried out. In a real sense, policy is the sum total of day-to-day decisions. Someone with the authority of the sovereign body must be in a position to say whether a 'yea' or a 'nay' vote is called for on each question as it arises." [58]

Proposed Reforms

In order to perfect the partnership between Congress and the Executive in the field of foreign relations, which Cordell Hull did so much to improve, certain steps remain to be taken:

1. The constitution should be amended to provide for the ratification

---

[57] Cf. A. C. F. Westphal, *The House Committee on Foreign Affairs* (1942).

[58] Hearings before the Joint Committee on the Organization of Congress, pp. 1164–66.

of treaties by simple majority vote of both houses of Congress. Treaties would then require the same legislative majorities as statutes. It would facilitate matters were Congress to specify that the amendment be submitted to constitutional conventions rather than to state legislatures since the conventions, especially elected for the purpose, would be more clearly responsive to public sentiment. To avoid procrastination, Congress might indicate the day on which the constitutional conventions should meet in the several states. A resolution to this effect (H. J. Res. 60) passed the House of Representatives on May 9, 1945.

2. Some permanent machinery of partnership should be established through which the State Department could keep Congress informed of its international activities while policy is still in the making, and through which, in turn, Congress could participate at every stage in the negotiation of international agreements whose ratification will ultimately require the consent of the Senate or the provision of funds. By such participation the Senate will be able to implement the "advice" aspect of its foreign relations function and enhance the prospect of its "consent" to the final treaty. The majority and minority policy committees or the joint executive-legislative council, proposed in the previous chapter, would be appropriate mechanisms for this purpose.

3. The professional staff facilities of the Senate Committee on Foreign Relations and the House Committee on Foreign Affairs should be increased. The professional and clerical staffs of these committees should be segregated from the personal staffs of their respective chairmen, so as to avoid confusion in their work and assure the continuous service of the committee personnel regardless of changes in party control. Each committee should have as many qualified specialists, paid at least $7,500 per annum, as it has functional or regional subcommittees. It should be the duty of these specialists to do analytical and research work for the committee, prepare material for speeches and press releases, advise with committeemen, prepare reports, serve as functional or regional experts, and act as liaison persons with the corresponding subdivisions of the State Department and other government agencies operating in the international field.

4. Following the good example of the House committee, the Senate Committee on Foreign Relations should be divided into subcommittees, one for each of the principal geographical regions of the world, or one for each of the principal functional problems in the international field. In this way the committee will be better able to handle the increasing volume and complexity of world problems and become better informed

about economic, political, and social conditions in the various regions of the world.

5. Interdepartmental policy committees should be organized in the principal international problem areas, e.g., commercial policy, aviation, labor, immigration, currency stabilization, relief and rehabilitation, food and agriculture, foreign loans and investments, and the like. These committees should be composed of representatives of the administrative departments and agencies concerned with these problems and of the chairmen of the appropriate congressional committees having jurisdiction over legislation in these fields. It should be the responsibility of these committees (a) to provide definite instructions on specific questions to American delegates to international organizations for their guidance in day-to-day negotiations that involve the implementation of policy and require eventual congressional approval, and (b) to supervise international negotiations in their respective problem areas which will result in treaties or agreements involving Senate or congressional approval.

By taking these steps Congress can adequately equip itself to play its full and proper part as a partner with the President in the great international decisions of the future. Paul Appleby's proposal to permit the President to name the members of the foreign affairs committees is probably impractical. But his objective of united action could be realized by consultation among the party leaders via the policy committees and joint council proposed above and by measures to strengthen party responsibility. Appleby's suggestion of enlarging the powers of the foreign affairs committees and authorizing them to make commitments on behalf of Congress on specific matters is a possible alternative to my fifth proposal in the foregoing paragraph. The device of the legislative veto, which Congress has used as a check on domestic administration, might well be employed also in the conduct of our foreign relations.[59]

Conclusion

Supervising a powerful administration thus calls for a variety of changes in legislative organization and procedure. The combination of popular control with efficient administrative management is not easy to develop. It requires continuous readjustment to changing conditions. But the general principle seems clear: that Congress must concentrate on the control of broad policies and their execution and refrain from

[59] Paul H. Appleby, *Big Democracy* (1945), pp. 194–195.

intervening in the operating details of administration. To this end it should rely upon such devices as oversight by a reformed standing committee system, policy conferences via joint legislative-executive committees at the Cabinet and departmental levels, further extension of the provisional-order technique, better and more frequent departmental reporting to the corresponding legislative committees, strengthening the appropriation process, and transformation of the General Accounting Office. While general oversight of executive performance is a proper legislative function, congressional surveillance of the details of administration is impractical and disruptive. In lieu of detailed tutelage of the departments, Congress should endeavor to improve the administrative system and strengthen its internal controls. For the satisfactory performance of its oversight function Congress must rely in the last analysis upon its reorganized standing committees to inspect and review policy execution, and upon the over-all supervisory agencies—Budget Bureau, Civil Service Commission, and General Auditing Office—for surveillance of the details of administrative conduct.

9.

Representing and Informing the People

THE THIRD GREAT function of Congress is the two-way task of representing the people in Washington and of informing the people back home about governmental problems. Part of a Congressman's job is to represent the people, in all the diversity of their economic, social, and cultural interests, in the councils of the nation; and to represent the nation and the national interest in the councils of the world while serving as a delegate of the United States at international conferences. Senators represent the states in their equality, and Representatives the multifarious interests of the people in general. It is also part of their job to inform and guide public opinion on the great issues of the day, explaining the pros and cons and debating the merits of proposed courses of action. With the decline of Congress as an original source of legislation, this function of keeping the government in touch with public opinion and of keeping public opinion in touch with the conduct of the public business becomes increasingly important. Congress not only represents the states and districts in the national capital; it also informs the folks back home of national and international problems and how these problems affect them.

Origin of Representation

This two-way job of the modern American Congress had its origin 700 years ago in medieval England. G. M. Trevelyan, the eminent British historian, gives the following account in his history of England of the beginnings of representative government in the far year 1265:[1]

---
[1] G. M. Trevelyan, *History of England* 1937 (Longmans, Green & Company), pp. 176–178.

In the course of Henry III's reign it became an occasional but not an invariable practice to summon to this great assembly two or more knights elected in each shire court to represent the county. This was not to create a new assembly, or to originate Parliament; it was merely to call up some new people to the plenary session of the old *curia regis*. Neither was it a party move either of the King or of his opponents; both sides felt that it was best to know what the "bachelors" were thinking. It was a natural evolution, so natural as scarcely to attract notice. For two generations past, knights elected in the shire court had transacted local business with the King's judges and officers. It seemed but a small step to summon them collectively to meet the King among his judges and officers at some central point. Moreover, representatives from individual shires and boroughs had long been in the habit of attending the King's Curia to transact the business of their community. To us, with our knowledge of all that was to come, the step of summoning them collectively and officially may seem immense. But in the medieval world the representation of communities was a normal way of getting business done, and its application to the central assembly of the realm was too natural to cause remark. When the wind sows the acorn the forester takes little heed.

Then and for long afterward the summons to Parliament was often regarded as a burden, grudgingly borne for the public good, much as the companion duty of serving on a jury is still regarded today. Communities, particularly boroughs, often neglected to send their representatives; and even the elected knights of the shire sometimes absconded to avoid service. Doubtless it was galling, when you looked round the shire court to congratulate the new member ironically on his expensive and dangerous honor, to find that he had slipped quietly on his horse and ridden for sanctuary, leaving the court to choose you in his stead. "The elective franchise" was not yet a privilege or a "right of man." In Edward III's reign, the borough of distant Torrington in Devon obtained by petition the "franchise" of not being required to send members to Parliament; for the payment of members' expenses then fell on the communities that sent them up.

Nevertheless the presence of the knights of the shire strengthened the authority and aided the counsels of the Parliament of magnates. The government found it convenient and advantageous to enforce the presence of the "communities" or "commons" of the realm through their representatives. And so in the year of revolution after Lewes, Simon de Montfort summoned not only the knights of the shire, but for the first time two representatives from each of the chartered boroughs. He probably knew that the burghers would be of his faction, and he was the first of our rulers to perceive that the general position of a party government could be strengthened by calling representatives of all the communities together and talking to them. "It was a form of propaganda," over and above any financial or judicial use that was made of the Assembly. We learn from the writs that the burghers were summoned, but we do not know how many came, or what, if anything, they did. That particular Parliament was a revolutionary assembly to which only those barons were summoned who were of Simon's party, but it set a precedent for the summoning of burghers which was imitated in the more regular Parliaments of Edward the First.

The English Parliament had no one man for its maker, neither Simon nor even Edward. No man made it, for it grew. It was the natural outcome, through long centuries, of the common sense and the good nature of the English people, who have usually preferred committees to dictators, elections to street fighting, and "talking shops" to revolutionary tribunals.

Some Underlying Questions

Despite the hoary antiquity of this representative-informing function, parliamentarians have long differed as to how it should be interpreted and performed. How much independence should an elected representative have? How closely should he keep in touch with the people back home he is supposed to represent? Once a representative is elected, should he follow his own judgment while he is at the seat of government? Or should he always and unquestioningly act and vote just the way the people in his district want him to? Should he deliberately ignore the "popular will" if he thinks it is unintelligent or wrong? Should Congress lead or follow public opinion? How many people take part in the processes of self-government? How big a part do they take? How clear are they about the effect of federal legislation upon themselves and their interests? How familiar are people with reasoned arguments why certain legislation should or should not be passed? In a country as large as the United States and containing so many different types of people, how much unity of public opinion can be expected?

In performing this dual function a member of Congress comes in contact with his constituents, with the press, and with the Washington agents of so-called pressure groups. Let us examine each of these relationships in turn.

RELATIONS WITH CONSTITUENTS

If a Congressman is to represent the best interests of his state or district and reflect the views of his constituents in his votes on legislation, he must keep in close touch with them. When Congress was in session only a few months a year, long recesses made it possible for a legislator to cover his district and learn at first hand of the interests, needs, and sentiments of the people. But now that Congress is in almost continuous session, chief reliance is placed upon correspondence and personal visits from the folks back home. The volume of mail and visits varies from office to office and time to time, but much of the time of the average member and most of the time of his office force is consumed in writing and interviewing constituents and performing various chores for them. Congressman Dirksen of Illinois, for example, normally receives from 50 to 100 letters a day. Senator Tydings once stated that his typical day included 60 interviews and 300 letters besides committee and Senate meetings. Senator La Follette's incoming mail after the war leaped to a thousand letters a day. "Letters are a Congressman's bread and butter," said former Vice President Garner. They range from applications for jobs to material for high school debates, from requests for veterans' service to complaints about the rising cost of living.[1a] The callers want personal introductions, gallery cards, hotel accommodations, tourist assistance, political influence with this bureau and that commission, or whatnot. To keep in touch with the temper of the people, many members subscribe to and read the local newspapers published in their districts. Others maintain home offices to serve their constituents or send them questionnaires to ascertain their views on pending legislation. During the 79th Congress, for example, Representative Harless of Arizona mailed several thousand post-card questionnaires to his constituents on the subject of compulsory military training together with a compilation of the arguments on both sides of this important question.

In order to keep constituents posted on their activities and developments in Congress, many Congressmen send periodic news letters home which are published in the district press. Others make regular radio talks or recordings for the folks back home which are locally broadcast. Few members of Congress fail to avail themselves of the free mailing privilege to send their constituents communications reciting facts relating to their public record and requesting the views of the people on legislative matters. Harold Burton and Meyer Jacobstein, for example, while they were in Congress, used to send semiannual and annual reports to registered voters back home concerning their committee activities, voting record, and the like, as a means of educating the constituency.

[1a] See Representative George E. Outland, "Write to Your Congressman—But Do It Right," *Liberty*, May 25, 1946.

Relief from Errand-Running

If the folks back home confined themselves to telling their Congressmen how to vote on this strike bill or that foreign loan, relations with constituents would be comparatively simple. But the people have come to regard a Congressman not as their representative in Congress, but as their errand-boy in Washington. Most of his correspondence and callers are concerned, not with legislative questions, but with their personal problems or local benefits. They ask him to leave his duties at the Capitol and accompany them to this or that department and use his influence there to obtain the relaxation of some regulation, price ceiling, meat quota or whatnot. Out of 48 people who came to see Representative Priest of Tennessee one day, 46 came on personal matters not related to legislation. Veterans' claims, for example, are tremendously time-consuming and have nothing to do with lawmaking.

Many constituents regard Congress as sort of an appellate court and expect free legal service from its members. But a Senator or Congressman cannot serve as a lawyer for his constituents and at the same time function as a legislator. The public mind is confused, observed Senator White of Maine, over our legislative responsibilites and our administrative obligations. "They expect you to know all about this business, that business, and the other business . . . We are constantly giving of our time and energies to what are really administrative questions which we ought not, in a large sense, to be concerned about." "There come to my desk, and I know to every Congressman's desk," said Senator Bridges, "dozens of cases that lawyers in the community involved should have handled . . . I think Congress is really being a sucker on a lot of matters we are asked to handle." "All of us like to do things for our constituents," remarked Representative Ramspeck. "But we cannot do those things and do an intelligent job of legislating under present conditions." "We are the complaint desk for our districts," concluded Congressman Monroney.

Ex-Senator Ashurst once summed up the problem of errand-running in the following lament to his constituents:

You send me down to Washington to represent you in the Senate. But you do not send me there because you are interested in grave questions of national or international policy. When I come back to Arizona, you never ask me about such policies; instead you ask me: "What about my pension?" or "What about that job for my son?" I am not in Washington as a statesman. I am there as a very well-paid messenger boy doing your errands.

Defense of the Practice

Although many Congressmen privately deplore their "bellboy" activities, others frankly regard themselves merely as "the people's hired men" and seem reconciled to serving primarily as glorified lobbyists or chamber of commerce agents for their home communities. They defend errand-running as the road to reelection and as a means of humanizing relations between the people and a huge impersonal bureaucratic machine. The people must have some clearing house for their problems in the nation's capital, it is argued, and no other governmental agency could perform this function as cheaply or with the patience, understanding, and personal interest of congressional offices. Such services afford one of the few remaining direct contacts between the citizen and his elected representative. Constituent complaints also serve to keep Congressmen alert to the operation of the laws and administrative programs. In short, it is neither possible nor desirable, in the opinion of many members, to eliminate this non-legislative business.

Proposed Remedies

Nevertheless, there is widespread agreement in congressional circles that errand-running could be reduced or delegated without impairing the representative function of Congress. One way of reducing the departmental business of members would be to improve the procedure for the review of administrative decisions along the lines provided in the administrative procedure act which was discussed in chapter eight. Moreover, Congress might well adopt a self-denying ordinance prohibiting its members from appearing as counsel in controversies before administrative boards and commissions. Let constituent complaints of administrative rulings be referred by congressional offices to the appropriate legislative committees which have oversight of the agencies concerned. Let Congress adopt a Charter of Congressional Freedom in which members would forswear personal appearances before fact-finding boards on the ground that they are not technically qualified witnesses concerning matters which the boards are required to establish. Such appearances are a waste of time, both of the Congressmen and of the board, and are open to the misconstruction that legislators are trying to bring pressure to warp the board's findings on the facts. Let the law also disqualify any applicant for civil service employment or promotion who seeks congressional influence in getting a government job or a raise. By such a concerted agreement to refrain from specific interferences with administration in individual cases, Congress could at once rid itself of a large part of its non-legislative burden without jeopardizing one whit its undoubted right to issue general policy directives to the executive branch.

A less heroic step, which should be taken in any event, would be to authorize each congressional office to employ a high caliber administrative assistant for the purpose of relieving Senators and Congressmen of a substantial part of the non-legislative work-load they now carry. Familiar with governmental procedures, employed on merit, and paid at least $7,500, such an assistant would permit the overworked member to pay more attention to his legislative duties. He could assist in receiving visitors from back home and appear on behalf of his member before federal boards and commissions if this practice is not outlawed.

A general liaison office might be established on Capitol Hill to assist members of Congress in handling departmental problems. Correspondence and callers on administrative matters could be routed to this office which would be staffed with representatives of the principal federal agencies. Several departments now maintain contact or liaison offices at the Capitol to serve the convenience of Congressmen.

Congress might also establish a General Information Service to assist members' offices in handling routine constituent inquiries. A large part of the postwar mail flooding congressional offices every day consists of requests for information or expressions of opinion on demobilization matters, surplus property disposal, price control, housing, strikes, FEPC, minimum wages, unemployment compensation, compulsory military training, liquor advertising, foreign policy, regulation of firearms, the Missouri Valley Authority, and the various points in President Truman's legislative program. Every office receives hundreds of letters on these and similar popular subjects every week. Few offices have enough clerks to keep abreast of the incoming tide or send personal replies to each communication. And so the practice has developed of classifying the letters by subject matter and acknowledging them by form letters which furnish the desired information or give the Congressman's general views. Routine inquiries of this sort might well be handled on behalf of the member and in his name by a service bureau, leaving his office force free to concentrate on the more important inquiries that require personal attention. Congressional offices now refer many requests for miscellaneous information to the Legislative Reference

Service and to the division of public inquiries in the Bureau of the Budget. More extensive use might well be made of these excellent services.

Considerable congressional time could be saved if all post offices were placed entirely under the merit system and if military and naval academy appointments were transferred to civil service. Vacancies in the postal service are filled after competitive examinations held by the Civil Service Commission which certifies the three highest candidates to the Postoffice Department. After informal consultation with the Congressman concerned, the department transmits one of the three highest names to the President who in turn submits the nomination to the Senate. 3,662 postmasters were nominated by the President during the first session of the 79th Congress, each of whom presumably was cleared through a congressional office.

The selection of candidates for appointment to West Point and Annapolis is entirely at the discretion of Senators and Representatives. Each state is entitled to eight cadets at large (four for each Senator) in the Military Academy and each congressional district is entitled to have four cadets at one time. Likewise each state in entitled to have 10 midshipmen at large (five for each Senator) in the Naval Academy and each congressional district may have five at one time. Thus the total maximum enrollment in both academies is 4,779. Vacancies occur only on graduation, resignation, or expulsion of the cadet or midshipman. One principal and three alternates are nominated to fill vacancies in each academy. Outright nominations may be made or the facilities of the Civil Service Commission may be utilized for a preliminary examination of such young men as the Senator or Representative may designate. Many more boys make inquiries about these coveted appointments each year than vacancies occur. This is a minor item, of course, in the time schedule of a member of Congress, but it all adds up and it has nothing to do with lawmaking.

Home rule for the District of Columbia and the judicial or administrative settlement of private claims and pensions are further measures of relief from routine chores that should be adopted.

Moreover, representative democracy cannot remain truly representative if legislators are required to be absent from their constituencies for long periods of time. In recent years the sessions of Congress have been nearly continuous and both Congressmen and the people they represent have been denied that first-hand interchange of ideas so necessary to our system of government. If Congress is properly to perform its representative-informing function, arrangements must be made for regular refreshment of contacts with the folks back home. Periodic return of the member to his district is designed not for "fence building" or "vacations," but to enable him to feel the popular pulse and gain firsthand knowledge of the needs and sentiments of the people. To this end Congress should provide by law for a regular annual recess period beginning preferably at the close of each fiscal year (June 30) when appropriations have been made and continuing until October. Such recess arrangements would, of course, be suspended in case of national emergency and the legislature could be reconvened at any time upon call of its leaders. With a regular recess date fixed, the legislative program could be better organized and its consideration greatly expedited. A further step toward improving relations with constituents would be to grant each member a modest allowance to maintain a home office in his district or state in charge of a competent assistant who could intercept and handle many of the personal and local problems that now clutter up legislative desks in Washington.

On the eve of his recent retirement from Congress Representative Ramspeck proposed an heroic remedy for the errand-running problem. Convinced after seventeen years' service in Congress that "we cannot do an intelligent job of legislating under present conditions," he suggested dividing the job in two parts: the legislative part to be handled by elected representatives in Congress, the administrative part by elected representatives before the executive branch. Under the Ramspeck plan, the House of Representatives would be reduced to half its present size and members of Congress would be prohibited from contacting the executive branch except in regard to legislation. The problem cannot be solved, he argued, by providing additional assistants. He had found it "utterly impossible to delegate much of the departmental work, because your constituents simply think that you and you alone can do the job for them." Dividing the job, he thought, would make for a much better and more efficient representation of the people and for much better legislation. Sensible though it is, the Ramspeck solution is probably too radical an innovation to be accepted by Congress and the people. It would require a constitutional amendment and the redistricting of the entire country. A possible alternative, suggested by Congressman Monroney, would be for the several states to establish Washington offices to handle the federal business of their citizens and communities and to prohibit by law the transaction of district business by members of Congress.[2]

Unless Congressmen have the courage to adopt an emancipation proclamation and decline any longer to be messenger boys, they will have to educate their constituents not to bother them with their personal problems. This is a slow and uncertain process, but some relief might be gained by printing polite appeals on congressional letterheads, by posting appropriate notices describing the duties of members in their reception rooms, and by setting up a public relations department on Capitol Hill to teach the people not to contact their Congressmen on non-legislative matters. Civic groups like the League of Women Voters could help in such an educational campaign. Perhaps this is a forlorn hope, but unless the problem of errand-running is solved, "all else is whistling in the wind," as Benjamin Wallace has said.

PROBLEM OF PAROCHIALISM

One question which the conscientious Congressman must often ask himself, especially when conflicts arise between local or regional attitudes and interests and the national welfare, is this: "As a member of Congress, am I merely a delegate from my district or state, restricted to act and vote as the majority which elected me desire, bound by the instructions of my constituents and subservient to their will? Or am I, once elected, a representative of the people of the United States, free to act as I think best for the country generally?"

In a country as large as the United States, with such diverse interests and such a heterogeneous population, the economic interests and social prejudices of particular states and regions often clash with those of other sections and with conceptions of the general interest of the whole nation. The perennial demand of the silver-mining and wool interests in certain western states for purchase and protection, the struggle over slavery, and the recent filibuster of Southern Senators against the attempt to outlaw racial discrimination in employment are familiar examples of recurring conflicts between local interests and prejudices and the common welfare. These political quarrels are rooted in the varying stages of cultural development attained by the different parts of the country. It is the peculiar task of the politician to compose these differences, to reconcile conflicting national and local attitudes, and to determine when public opinion is ripe for legislative action. Some conflicts will yield in time to political adjustment; others must wait for

[2] Hearings before the Joint Committee on the Organization of Congress, pp. 296–300.

their legal sanction upon the gradual evolution of the conscience of society. No act of Congress can abolish unemployment or barking dogs or racial prejudices.

That it is the difficult duty of the legislator to transcend private and local influences and prefer the general interests of the community has long been the testimony of prominent politicians who have pondered the problem. Sir William Yonge, one of the leading politicians of his time, speaking of members of the House of Commons, said in 1745:

Every one knows that, by our Constitution, after a gentleman is chosen, he is the representative, or, if you please, the attorney of the people of England, and as such is at full freedom to act as he thinks best for the people of England in general. He may receive, he may ask, he may even follow the advice of his particular constituents; but he is not obliged, nor ought he, to follow their advice, if he thinks it inconsistent with the general interest of his country.

The classic description of a member's obligations is contained in Burke's address to the electors of Bristol in 1774. Burke felt that the chief duty of a representative was to use his own best judgment in deciding questions in the people's interest.

Certainly, gentlemen, it ought to be the happiness and glory of a representative to live in the strictest union, the closest correspondence, and the most unreserved communication with his constituents. Their wishes ought to have great weight with him; their opinion high respect; their business unremitted attention. It is his duty to sacrifice his repose, his pleasures, his satisfactions, to theirs; and above all, ever, and in all cases, to prefer their interest to his own. But, his unbiased opinion, his mature judgment, his enlightened conscience, he ought not to sacrifice to you, to any man, or to any set of men living. These he does not derive from your pleasure; no, nor from the law and the Constitution. They are a trust from Providence, for the abuse of which he is deeply answerable. Your representative owes you, not his industry only, but his judgment; and he betrays, instead of serving you, if he sacrifices it to your opinion.

My worthy colleague says his will ought to be subservient to yours. If that is all the thing is innocent: if government were a matter of will upon my side, yours, without question, ought to be superior. But government and legislation are matters of reason and judgment, and not of inclination; and what sort of reason is that, in which the determination precedes the discussion; in which one set of men deliberate, and another decide; and where those who form the conclusion are perhaps three hundred miles distant from those who hear the arguments?

To deliver an opinion, is the right of all men; that of constituents is a weighty and respectable opinion, which a representative ought always to rejoice to hear; and which he ought always most seriously to consider. But authoritative instructions; mandates issued, which the member is bound blindly and implicitly to obey, to vote and to argue for, though contrary to the clearest conviction of his judgment and conscience—these are things utterly unknown to the laws of the land, and which arise from a fundamental mistake of the whole order and tenor of our Constitution.

Parliament is not a congress of ambassadors from different and hostile interests; which interests each must maintain, as an agent, and advocate, against the agents and advocates; but Parliament is a deliberative assembly of one nation, with one interest, that of the whole; where, not local purposes, not local prejudices, ought to guide, but the general good, resulting from the general reason of the whole. You choose a member indeed; but when you have chosen him, he is not a member of Bristol, but he is a Member of Parliament. If the local constituent should have an interest, or should form a hasty opinion, evidently opposite to the real good of the rest of the community, the member for that place ought to be as far as any other from any endeavour to give it effect.

The authorities quoted above were speaking, of course, of England— a small, compact, homogeneous country where questions affecting private, personal, or local interests receive comparatively little attention from the member of Parliament. "He is primarily the representative of a national party elected to support or oppose the cabinet, rather than the delegate of a district sent to watch over the interests of his constituents, and push the claims of influential electors." [3]

Methods of Reducing Local Pressures

Under the American system where members of Congress represent and reside in states and local districts and depend upon their favor for reelection, the influence of localism is very difficult to escape. Members may aspire to be national statesmen rather than state and local politicians, but few Norrises or Maloneys emerge from the fray or long survive the physical and political hazards of legislative life. Certain steps might be taken, however, which would encourage the development of national leaders and attitudes.

Longer terms of office for members of the lower House might tend to increase their independence and improve the quality of their service. Under the laws of many states, in order to retain their seats, Congress-

---

[3] A. Lawrence Lowell, *The Government of England*, Vol. 1, p. 171.

men must be active candidates, including the primary and general election, for various periods ranging in length from three to ten months. Coming up for reelection every two years, members are so embroiled in politics that it detracts from their ability to function as effective legislators. To correct this condition, Representative Clarence Lea of California has introduced a proposed amendment to the constitution providing for four-year terms for members of the House and for staggering the congressional elections so that half of the membership would be elected every two years.[4]

The parochialism of American politics could really be remedied if we abandoned the usage which prohibits anyone from seeking to represent in Congress a district in which he does not himself reside. The constitution requires that a Representative must, when elected, be an inhabitant of the state in which he is chosen, but beyond that it imposes no geographical limitation. Providence has not blessed us with a geographical distribution of brains, as Charles Beard once said. But it would be political suicide for any party to attempt to abandon this fatuous custom.

Any steps which are taken to strengthen party government in both houses, through the creation of policy committees or by reviving the party caucus, should tend to counteract the influence of localism. Political parties are more likely to take a national viewpoint than individual Congressmen.

The traditional method of selecting standing committee chairmen is closely connected with this problem of sectionalism. For the repeated reelection of members from particular districts, especially in the South, so that they can achieve and hold ranking places on important committees means, in effect, when the Democrats are in power, that committee chairmen are locally chosen and locally responsible. To make the chairmen nationally chosen in some way, and somehow nationally responsible, is close to the heart of the problem of sectionalism and to the need for a system calculated to develop more national political leaders.

One of the defects of our representative system, as Paul Appleby has pointed out, is that it makes no provision for the development of "a pool of national politicians. They are under no particular pressure to become really national politicians, nor are they given any special opportunity or encouragement to do so. Some become sectional politi-

---

[4] H. J. Res. 315, 78th Congress, 2d Session.

cians, but very few attain national stature."[5] One possible, and I think practical, solution of this problem would be to provide a nucleus of national representation in the two houses of Congress. Such representation would not be at variance with the principle of representative government; rather it would strengthen it by freeing a few Senators and Congressmen from local pressures and making them truly national legislators. It is suggested that Congress submit to the states a constitutional amendment providing for the election by the people of the whole country of, say, 10 Senators and 24 Representatives. They might be nominated by the national party conventions or by disinterested civic groups. Thus, if the amendment were adopted, there would be in the national legislature a small group who could be the open defenders of the national interest. They could afford to be outspoken and could frequently furnish a nucleus around which legislators, elected by local and group interests, could rally when they felt deep down in their hearts that group and sectional pressures exerted by some of their more vocal constituents were not to the real advantage either of the country as a whole or of their own less vocal electorate. Under this plan men and women like the late Wendell Willkie, Alfred E. Smith, and Eleanor Roosevelt could be drawn into the national legislative counsels.

PUBLIC ATTITUDE TOWARD CONGRESS

Criticizing Congress has always been one of the favorite pastimes of the American people. James Bryce noted decades ago that Americans "are fond of running down Congressmen." In recent years the methods and accomplishments of our national legislature have come in for notably sharp criticism, some of which is addressed to faults of congressional structure, function, and facilities; and some of which is an indictment of defects in our form of government. The case against Congress varies with changing times and circumstances, but there is always more interest in and a wider market for fault-finding than for praise. "Congress has been a favorite target for the disgruntled, the disappointed, the intellectual snobs, and the doubters of democracy alike," writes Senator La Follette. "But most of this criticism is not constructive. It springs from personal prejudice, political bias, and above all from an utter lack of knowledge of the workaday problems with which a great legislative body must deal."[6]

---

[5] Paul H. Appleby, *Big Democracy* (Alfred A. Knopf, 1945), p. 134.

[6] Robert M. La Follette, Jr., "A Senator Looks at Congress," *Atlantic Monthly*, July, 1943.

The causes of public attacks on Congress are multiple. In a searching analysis of criticism of lawmakers, Representative Robert Luce attributed it to dissatisfaction with the results of democracy, emphasis in the press and cinema on the abnormal, the spectacular, and the eccentric aspects of lawmaking, ignoring the sober, serious, and solid achievements of Congress, its slow and cautious response to transient demands for political nostrums, and to the distortion of public opinion by the propaganda of pressure groups. The lack of special competence among legislators to deal with the technical problems of modern government, the multiplication of congressional tasks with the shift of formerly local and state problems to the national government, and the resentment of the strong against social legislation designed to protect the weak are other proximate causes. But Luce found the ultimate cause of the growing disrepute of Congress in its "interminable delays" in dealing with great issues which are caused in turn by the "steady increase in the volume of administrative detail" and by antiquated legislative procedures. "So year by year the petty work of a Congressman will become more burdensome, and he will perforce be less and less of a statesman, more and more of a mechanician . . . The old methods of representative government are nowhere equal to the problems springing from the complexities of modern life." [7]

Congress is also criticized by gallery visitors for the absence of members from the floor during sessions, for the occasional antics of eccentric members, and for the hazing of witnesses before committees. A more fundamental criticism, from the standpoint of its representative function, is that Congress is more responsive in shaping national policy to the spokesmen of pressure groups and special interests than it is to the ideas of the common man. On the basis of six years of continuous surveys of American public opinion, George Gallup concluded that the American public is far ahead of its legislators on most legislative matters and that the public is more willing to make sacrifices than its leaders suppose.[8]

The low esteem in which the public is currently reported to hold the national legislature may be due in part to the failure of Congress to acknowledge and develop its own peculiar functions, and in part to the obscuring of the performance of its solid, essential activities behind archaic forms of traditional parliamentary behavior carried on in public view. Unlike the President and the Supreme Court, Congress puts its

---

[7] Robert Luce, *Congress: An Explanation*, Lecture V and pp. 151–152.

[8] George Gallup, "The People Are Ahead of Congress," *Reader's Digest*, June, 1942.

worst foot forward to the public eye. Yet despite press conferences, fireside chats, columnists, commentators, and Gallup polls, Congress still possesses essential deliberative and representative functions which no other group is equipped to perform so well.

Remedies for Public Criticism

Public understanding and appreciation of Congress could be improved in several ways. A major improvement might be that of bringing congressional form into line with the realities of its peculiar tasks. This would involve three procedural changes which would require merely the revision of legislative rules and practice, not statutory or constitutional changes.

First would be the recognition of committee work as the heart of congressional activity. Here, actually, Congressmen organized in segments review the operations of administration, consider legislative and spending proposals, and, at times, themselves initiate new law. Committee work includes hearings as well as discussion in closed meetings. It involves contact with experts and written material. It is the center of legislative activity where criticism of administration and decision upon proposed legislation is largely made. Consequently, at least three days weekly during a congressional session should be specifically devoted to committee meetings. Hearings, preferably joint hearings for the concentration of attention, should be recognized by constituents and sightseers as the way to see Congress at work. Rather than looking down at a forlorn performance before empty chairs, the public might well choose between attendance at one or more parts of a twelve-ring committee circus where questions and argument would be lively and real. Congressmen might well encourage their constituents to attend committee hearings.

Full meetings of the two legislative bodies are actually used for two main purposes: i.e., to record votes on specific measures reported from committees, and to carry on debate, not so much to affect the votes of the other members as to influence public opinion among the Congressman's constituents and to explain the legislator's negative or affirmative votes on specific measures. These functions could readily be performed during two or three evenings a week. Thus there might be an evening once a week or, near the end of a session, a full day session—say Friday —during which formal committee reports and votes succeed each other with something like the simple dignity of an opinion day in the

Supreme Court. When contended measures are to be voted upon, such weekly voting sessions might be well attended, with galleries filled and a radio box informing the country and interpreting to it the decisions made. The public would see and hear the Congress acting out in a businesslike way one of its essential roles—that of recording decisive judgments on legislation.[9]

Actually a small number of Congressmen only could participate in these preferred positions of public national debate. But the others, instead of engaging in frustrating harangues before empty benches, could regularly be given places on the agenda of committee hearings to present their views and arguments. For this purpose places on the agenda would be open rather freely to non-committee members.

Most Congressmen are not national figures. They are not entitled to, nor will they gain the ear, of a national audience. But in practically all cases they are prominent state and local figures. It is their essential function to interpret national policy, laws and administration to the localities and *vice versa* to assess, to focus, to interpret local opinion to the national government. No other branch of the federal government is constituted to perform this essential representative function. It is important that the function be publicly recognized and regularized in the congressional time-table. This might be done by regular recess periods during which there would be no voting, debate or committee sessions in Washington and during which Congressmen and Senators would be expected to return to their states and districts there to give an account through radio or public speeches to their constituents of their votes and proposals and to receive at first hand delegations of citizens interested in controversial issues.

These three procedural changes leave out archaic practices which would not be missed. In their place would be solid days in committee rooms in the vital atmosphere of conversational or, at least, courtroom give and take; periodic evenings in the simple rite of a succession of polls or votes, a weekly congressional radio evening no longer than, occasionally as exciting as, and almost always as important as, a baseball game; a periodic return to the home folks to persuade, to explain, and to listen to the constituency which creates and may destroy the mandate under which the Congressman acts. Such a reorganization of procedure would leave unsolved many problems. But it would be a step in the

---

[9] On August 15, 1944, Senator Pepper introduced a resolution (S. J. Res. 145), authorizing the broadcasting of the proceedings of the Senate and House.

direction of uniting appearance with reality in the legislative process and would give promise of adding to the respect and understanding in which the legislative branch is held by the country at large.

Improvement of the physical conditions under which Congress works would also enhance public understanding of the operation of representative government. The legislative halls of Congress, which should be a model of acoustic perfection, present very difficult conditions under which to transact public business. Neither the membership nor the public can properly hear the proceedings on the floor due to acoustic defects which could easily be corrected. Lighting is bad in both the Senate and House chambers and the facilities for seating the public are inadequate and so noisy as to disturb the conduct of business. The halls of both houses should be remodelled to provide improved acoustics, better lighting, and adequate gallery facilities.

Large-scale public hearings on matters of great national interest—like the Pearl Harbor hearings—require a meeting room which can physically handle all those who wish to attend. At present there are only two rooms in the Capitol buildings—the Senate and House caucus rooms—which are large enough to accommodate the public at such hearings. In their present state, however, neither of these rooms is well adapted or equipped for this use. Both caucus rooms should be completely remodelled with acoustic and seating facilities and installed with equipment for the presentation of motion picture or other visual displays of matters of interest to Congress. David Lynn, the veteran and efficient architect of the Capitol, plans to make these and other physical improvements as soon as Congress recesses long enough to permit them to be completed.

In addition to these procedural and physical changes, much could be done to inform and arouse public interest in the legislative process. Congress could create a public relations department in the legislative branch and direct it to carry on an educational campaign designed to dramatize the role of Congress under our form of government and to discourage voters from bringing petty personal and local problems to their Senators and Representatives. Some members now submit periodic reports to their constituents describing and explaining their committee activities, their votes on public bills, and congressional action. Such reports are an excellent device for educating the constituencies and keeping them informed on the crucial problems of the day. The practice might well be generalized. Interest in public affairs and understanding of legislative problems do not automatically follow the right to vote.[10] They can only be achieved by making issues mean something to people and by presenting them in such a clear dramatic way as to make citizens realize that their own interests and welfare are involved. This teaching function is an important part of the Congressman's job.

In the last analysis, however, the place of Congress in public esteem will depend upon the extent to which it modernizes its structure and improves its procedures so that it is organized and equipped to perform effectively its essential functions. When Congress overcomes its timidity and inertia, rids itself of routine chores and minor lawmaking, and reconstructs its machinery and methods to meet the requirements of modern times, then public criticism will subside and the prestige of our national legislature will be restored.

RELATIONS WITH THE PRESS

In performing its public opinion function Congress has an indispensable ally in the Washington newspapermen who cover Capitol Hill. Contacts with reporters assigned to the Capitol "beat" are close, constant, and as a rule mutually advantageous. Congressmen are eager for favorable publicity for themselves and their legislative programs and it is the function of the press to print all the news in which their editors and readers might be interested.

Responsibility for covering Congress is assigned mainly to reporters for the three national press associations: the Associated Press, the United Press, and the International News Service which dispatch 100,000 words a day to newspapers throughout the world. Each of these agencies has several "leg-men" on the Capitol "beat" who cover the committee hearings and floor proceedings week in and week out and report congressional news of general interest.

Many newspapers maintain their own special correspondents in Washington, part of whose task is to cover and interpret congressional developments from the angle of vision of their particular cities, states, and regions and their various interests. Compared with the rather colorless stories of the press association reporters, the dispatches of the special correspondents deal with local aspects of national events and contain more comment and interpretation. Close and cordial relations usually exist between members of Congress and the Washington cor-

---

[10] In the 1942 congressional elections only 40 per cent of the adult citizens of the country voted, and only two-thirds of them went to the polls in the presidential election of 1944.

respondents of newspapers in their districts. The special correspondent is sometimes a vital link between local interests and district representatives in Congress. They compare notes, exchange tips, and otherwise collaborate in legislative matters of special concern to their communities. Sometimes Washington correspondents become secretaries to Congressmen from their districts. Congress is also covered by a group of "free-lance correspondents" who report the Washington news to several small-town newspapers in their states or regions, none of which could afford to have its own special correspondent in the capital.

Radio and Press Galleries

In addition to the press associations and special newspaper correspondents, legislative events have been reported over the radio in recent years by the several networks, stations, and services represented in the radio galleries of Congress. The radio correspondents' association now numbers more than 100 active members in Washington and some 400 associate members. Four national networks, seven radio press services, and 13 stations are presently represented in the radio galleries. Beginning in 1940 with a little space in the gallery corridors, the radio correspondents now have in the Senate wing of the Capitol their own sumptuous room walled with acoustically treated tile and equipped with five sound-proof, air-conditioned booths for the networks and independents, as well as a writing room for working news reporters. Comparable facilities are being installed in the House gallery. Television facilities and spot transmission of debates in Congress may come eventually. Senator Pepper and Congressman Coffee are sponsoring a move to put the proceedings of both houses of Congress on the air via short-wave government stations.

A recent innovation in the press coverage of the Capitol was the establishment in 1941 of Senate and House galleries for the periodical press. *Time, Life, Newsweek,* and 51 other magazines are represented in these galleries by 103 persons. Correspondents for periodicals have recently acquired their own neatly appointed room in the House wing of the Capitol, and have designs on Senator Vandenberg's room in the Senate wing. *Newsweek, Broadcasting, Pathfinder,* and McGraw-Hill Publications have the largest representation among the periodicals that cover the "Hill." Several magazines have regular congressional departments and others occasionally feature various legislative problems and aspects. In its issue of June 18, 1945, for example, *Life* devoted 14 pages to a tourist's view of Congress followed by a blueprint of its workings and shortcomings.

For the convenience of press and radio both houses have reserved special sections of their galleries directly over the presiding officers' desks where reporters have an opera-box view of the chambers in session. Immediately behind these galleries are the press and radio rooms fully equipped with typewriters and telephone booths where newspapermen write their stories, keep in touch with their offices, and relax when off duty. The press and radio galleries are governed by rules which confine admission to bona fide correspondents and news gatherers who represent daily newspapers or newspaper associations requiring telegraphic service or radio stations or systems. Standing committees of correspondents control the galleries, subject to the approval and supervision of the Speaker of the House and the Senate Committee on Rules. Symbolic of the close relationship between Congressmen and correspondents is a sign over one of the elevators in the House wing of the Capitol which reads: "Reserved for Members and the Press."

Thus Congress is well covered by the public-opinion industry. The men and women of the press and radio galleries are able, experienced, and hard-working. Covering committee hearings and floor sessions, interviewing Congressmen and filing dispatches day after day is a tedious and nerve-wracking task. Capitol correspondents like Richard Strout of the Christian Science Monitor and Robert Albright of the Washington Post—to mention only two—have covered Congress for many years and know the legislative ropes intimately. Serving thousands of papers representing every shade of political and economic opinion, the press association reporters who gather the raw material on the legislative assembly line must confine their dispatches to the cold facts. But the special correspondents are free to make their own selections out of the endless flow of congressional news and tend to slant their interpretation of events consciously or unconsciously according to the editorial policy of their papers or their own predilections. So voluminous is the daily output of the legislative mills that only the highlights and the most noteworthy developments are reported. House and Senate debates are not as well covered by the American press as are the proceedings of the British Parliament by their English colleagues— a circumstance attributed by one correspondent who has covered both legislatures to the comparative diffuseness and dullness of debates in Congress.

Publicity and News

On their part Congressmen utilize the press and radio to publicize themselves with their constituents and to air their views on public questions. A growing number of members send weekly news letters to the papers in their districts in which they inform the voters of developments on Capitol Hill and explain their own votes and activities. Others record their reports periodically in the radio rooms and send the recordings to the radio stations in their districts where they are broadcast to the folks back home. During their campaigns members advertise in the district press and display their features and platforms on bill boards along local highways. Some Congressmen issue hand-outs to the press, as Representatives Holifield, Douglas, and Voorhis of California did after the Pauley nomination, and hold occasional press conferences when they have important statements to make. Speaker Rayburn and Senate Majority Leader Barkley hold daily conferences with the press on the business pending before their respective chambers. Senator Borah made regular use of this sounding-board technique.

Newspapermen on the Capitol "beat" have free access to the legislators, conferring with them in their offices by appointment or calling them off the floor by sending in their cards. "It is not unknown," writes Rosten in his authoritative work on the subject, "for Washington correspondents to put ideas into the heads of their political favorites and, sometimes, to put felicitous words into their mouths. A Washington correspondent may type out a statement and ask a statesman if he 'would not like to say that for publication.' " [11] Reporters assigned to cover a congressional investigation of a presidential appointee or a departmental program sometimes become part of the entourage of the inquiry, handing up questions to committeemen and otherwise coaching them along. Congressmen reciprocate from time to time by supplying the press and commentators with confidential tips on what transpired during an executive session or what recommendations a forthcoming report will make. Pressmen are adroit in springing leaks and ferreting out supposedly confidential information; few secrets are long kept on Capitol Hill or anywhere in Washington for that matter. Rosten reports that "after a secret committee meeting in which seventeen Senators participated, two correspondents attempted, on a bet, to

---

[11] Leo C. Rosten, *The Washington Correspondents* (Harcourt, Brace and Company, 1937), p. 81.

discover how many men they could coax into telling what had gone on in the conference. With no particular effort they succeeded in getting the salient facts from thirteen Senators within one afternoon." [12]

Congress is thus a prolific source of news and comment to the press, and the press is an essential adjunct of the legislature. An extraordinary camaraderie exists between legislators and newspapermen. Ten Senators and 24 Representatives are now, or formerly were, newspaper editors and publishers or journalists and several of them are members of the National Press Club. They understand each other's problems and practices and exploit and cooperate with each other in pursuit of their respective purposes.

One aspect of the psychology of the Capitol press corps seems to me of dubious social value. I refer to their habitual quest for controversy. Conflict is news and often the first question a reporter will ask in an interview is: "Who opposes your proposal?" Or "what resistance have you encountered to that plan?" It is not unknown for Washington correspondents to create controversy where none exists in their restless search for copy. There is no news value in the prevalence of harmony and brotherly love. This constant emphasis on individual, group, and ideological conflict tends to give the reading public an exaggerated impression of friction in the nation's capital and hardly helps to mitigate the social tensions of the time.

RELATIONS WITH PRESSURE GROUPS

In performing its representative function Congress is bedeviled by a swarm of Washington lobbies claiming to speak for business groups, labor unions, taxpayers' associations, banking and insurance, utilities and railroads, shipping and air transport, agriculture and distribution, and all the other pressure groups. In 1929, when Pendleton Herring made his pioneer study of group representation before Congress, he found that there were well over 500 Washington lobbies. In 1941 Donald Blaisdell compiled an incomplete list of 383 national organizations having permanent representatives in Washington.[13] From the Air Line Pilots Association to the Western Pine Association they represented all the diverse economic, social, civic, and cultural interests produced by the division of labor and specialization of function in a com-

---

[12] *Ibid.*, p. 82.
[13] Temporary National Economic Committee, Monograph No. 26, *Economic Power and Political Pressures* (1941), pp. 197–201.

plex industrial society. Only one—the People's Lobby—purported to stand for the underlying population. Postwar Washington has become a bustling mecca for all manner of national and international lobbyists whose number is estimated to range between 1,500 and 2,000—three or four for every member of Congress.

Taken together, these large, powerful, and well-financed national organizations constitute kind of a fourth branch of the government. Tending to identify their special interests with the general welfare, they are constantly bringing pressure to bear upon legislators and administrators and threatening political punishment to all who oppose their demands. As the lawmaking, money-raising, and appropriating agency in the federal government, Congress has long been the object of much attention from these organized groups. They usually maintain skilled lobbyists in Washington who strive to influence Congressmen for or against legislation that will benefit or injure the particular groups they represent. When the St. Lawrence waterway project was under consideration by the Senate Foreign Relations Committee, for example, a swarm of opponents and proponents descended upon the committee from the affected states.

How Lobbies Operate

These "pressure boys" seek to transform the aims and programs of their groups into public policy by having them enacted into law. They use their influence to change the tax laws to suit their own purposes, to reduce or eliminate the appropriations for agencies they dislike, and to increase those of agencies they favor. They bring pressure to bear upon the Senate to ratify or reject treaties and to confirm or reject presidential nominations which their groups favor or oppose. In the old corrupt and contented days the old-fashioned lobbyist used to "buttonhole" legislators covertly and contact their political bosses. But modern public relations counsel appear openly as witnesses at committee hearings, lay down a barrage of letters and telegrams on congressional offices, and use all the techniques of high-pressure publicity—press, radio, movies, advertising, pamphlets, books, magazines, exhibits—in an attempt to arouse legislative and public support for their programs. "The old-time lobbyist has gone," as Congressman Robert Luce observed, "but the new brand, though more respectable, has perhaps a more damaging effect by working on the timidity of lawmakers rather than on their cupidity." [14] In these and similar ways organized interest

---

[14] Robert Luce, *Congress: An Explanation*, p. 130.

groups participate in the legislative process and constitute a real part of the legislative machinery of the nation.

As I write, a real estate lobby is attacking the government's housing program for veterans. Formulated by housing expediter Wilson Wyatt to meet an immense war-deferred demand, the Wyatt program was emasculated by a servile House of Representatives under heavy pressure from organized realtors, operative builders, and manufacturers of building materials. Majority Leader McCormack called it "the most powerful lobby in my time"—which included 19 years in Congress. Numerically insignificant in comparison with the millions of families in need of homes, the special interests opposing the Wyatt plan induced the House to reject essential features of the housing program. They did this by flooding Congress with "spontaneous" letters and telegrams from their local chapters, by marshalling clouds of witnesses, by open or veiled threats and promises, and by confusing public opinion on the issue. Nor was this preference for special interests over the general welfare an isolated phenomenon in the Administration's campaign to halt inflation and smooth the transition from war to peace.

The repeated crippling of public welfare programs by predatory pressure groups motivated only by their own selfish interests not only militates against the general well-being of the nation. It also raises a serious question as to the unrestricted right of individuals to form permanent irresponsible groups that can intimidate government officials and endanger the common good. In some continental states freedom of association has been severely restricted and the totalitarian powers of recent decades abolished all group organizations—labor unions, cooperatives, fraternal societies—that might in any way jeopardize the state or its custody of the general welfare. Thirty-five of the United States have enacted laws regulating lobbying in some way—usually by providing for publicity in the form of registration of legislative agents and counsel employed for compensation and for the filing of financial statements of all expenses paid, incurred, or promised in connection with the promotion of legislation.[15] In democratic countries freedom of association is a cherished right the exercise of which undoubtedly has beneficial social results. But now that organized groups have become so efficient and powerful and so disintegrating in their impact upon society, measures need to be adopted to bring them under control and discipline their conduct to democratic ends.

---

[15] Belle Zeller, "Public Relations and the State Lobbying Laws," *Public Relations Directory and Year Book* (1945), pp. 143–149.

Spokesmen for Minority Viewpoints

Moreover, the pressure boys speak for only a minority of the total population of the country. All Americans have an interest in congressional legislation that affects them as consumers, but there is no organized consumers' lobby in Washington. Home owners and parents are deeply concerned about legislation affecting their homes and the welfare of their children, but neither is organized as a pressure group. The great majority of the American people are not members of special interest groups and hence are much less articulate on particular issues than are the interested minority whose affiliation with some active organization gives them a greater political leverage. The result is that the strongest pressures from outside are essentially minority pressures representing particular local interests or specific occupational or political groups. Every minority group, to be sure, is entitled to its day in court in a democratic society and it would be political suicide for a Congressman to ignore strong pressures from his own district.

But the stand taken on matters of public policy by the leaders of organized pressure groups may not represent the majority opinion of their own groups or reflect the views of the American people. Some organized groups in American life have become so huge that their leaders cannot keep in close touch with the membership. Consequently, the leaders may sometimes, in the name of the pressure group, press for legislation that serves their own personal interests or predilections. Public opinion polls in recent years have sometimes shown a marked divergence between the attitudes of the official spokesmen of organized groups and the opinion of the rank and file.

Experience has taught many Congressmen that often their mail is neither reliable nor representative of general sentiments. This is because only people who feel deeply about a matter generally take the trouble to write letters to their legislators. Or a flood of mail on a particular topic may be artfully stimulated by some group with a special advantage to gain by the passage or defeat of a measure. Hadley Cantril cites the case of the congressional mail on the selective service bill as an example of its unrepresentative character. An analysis of more than 30,000 letters received by 14 Senators during the summer of 1940 concerning the Burke-Wadsworth selective service bill indicated 10 per cent of the writers were for it and 90 per cent were opposed. During the time the bill was under debate and letters to the Congressmen were pouring in, one of the public opinion polls asked a representative sample of the American people to record their attitude toward the provisions of the bill. The result showed that 68 per cent favored it, 27 per cent were against it, and 5 per cent expressed no opinion. Thus the mail these Senators received was a false guide to the state of public opinion on the question. It measured the intensity of feeling on the subject rather than the majority sentiment.

Types of Pressures on Congress

One can sympathize with the plight of the conscientious Congressman who is the focal point of all these competing pressures. The district or state he represents may need and want certain roads, post offices, courthouses, or schools. Irrigation dams or projects may be needed for the development of the area's resources. If the representative is to prove himself successful in the eyes of the people back home, he must be able to show, at least occasionally, some visible and concrete results of his congressional activity. Or else he must be able to give good reasons why he has not been able to carry out his pledges. The local residence rule for Congressmen multiplies the pressures that impinge upon him. Faithful party workers who have helped elect him will expect the Congressman to pay his political debts by getting them jobs in the federal service. Constituents affected by proposed legislation may send him an avalanche of letters, telegrams, and petitions which must be acknowledged and followed up. The region from which he comes will expect him to protect and advance its interests in Washington. All the various organized groups will press their claims upon him and threaten him if he does not jump when they crack the whip. Party leaders may urge a Congressman to support or oppose the Administration program or to "trade" votes for the sake of party harmony or various sectional interests. He is also under pressure from his own conscience as to what he should do both to help the people who have elected him and to advance the best interests of the nation. Besieged by all these competing pressures, a Congressman is often faced with the choice of compromising between various pressures, of trading votes, of resisting special interests of one sort or another, of staying off the floor when a vote is taken on some measure he prefers not to take a stand on, of getting support here and at the same time running the risk of losing support there. Dealing with pressure blocs is a problem in political psychology which involves a careful calculation of the power of the blocs, the reaction of the voters on election day, and the long-haul interests of the district, state, and nation.

Congress is not without its own devices for evading pressure when open resistance might be politically hazardous and yielding might be bad for the country. One house may pass the lobbyist's bill and rely on the other house or the conferees to amend it so as to nullify its effects. Or the party leaders may make a secret arrangement with the President to veto the measure and fail to pass it over his veto. Or the bill may be bottled up in the Rules Committee of the House to avoid embarrassment to the membership, or the advocates and opponents of the bill may be played off against each other. There are various parliamentary tricks by which the steam behind a legislative drive can be released and agitation allayed.

Federal Regulation of Lobbies [16]

Congress to date has passed no general lobbying law. On a number of occasions, notably in 1913 and 1935, Congress has investigated lobbying activities. Since 1907 bills regulating lobbyists have been introduced from time to time. In the 70th and 74th Congresses, there were extensive discussions of the bills introduced. In 1928, the bill sponsored by Senator Thaddeus H. Caraway of Arkansas passed the Senate.[17] Nationwide attention was attracted to the excesses of utility lobbies in 1935, when the Public Utility Holding Company Act was under discussion. On this matter, the House Rules Committee reported on February 27, 1936: ". . . the campaign to influence utility holding company legislation was probably as comprehensive, as well managed, as persistent and as well financed, as any in the history of the country." [18]

As a result, bills to regulate lobbies poured into the 74th Congress. Senate bill 2512, sponsored by Hugo L. Black of Alabama and H.R. 11663 introduced by Howard W. Smith of Virginia, passed their respective houses, but the wide divergence in these bills, while bridged by the conferees, did not meet with the approval of Congress.[19] Although additional bills were introduced in subsequent Congresses, no such serious consideration has since been given to the general regulation of the lobby.

---

[16] I am indebted to Dr. Belle Zeller, Professor of Political Science at Brooklyn College and a leading authority on the subject, for the information in this section which she originally submitted upon request to the Joint Committee on the Organization of Congress.

[17] S. 1095, 70th Congress, 1st Session, S. Report No. 342, February 21, 1928.

[18] H. R. Report No. 2081, p. 3, 74th Congress, 2nd session.

[19] H. R. Report No. 2925, June 2, 1936. This conference report was rejected by the House on June 17, 1936.

However, despite the fact that the Senate in 1935 had already passed the Black lobbying bill, the Congress was determined that the utilities would not escape regulation—no matter what the final outcome of the general lobbying bills introduced into that Congress. It was therefore written into the Public Utility Holding Company Act of 1935 not only that utilities could not contribute to party campaign funds, but that it is "unlawful for any person employed or retained by any registered holding company, or any subsidiary company thereof, to present, advocate, or oppose any matter affecting any registered holding company or any subsidiary company thereof, before the Congress or any member or committee thereof, or before the Commission (Securities and Exchange) or Federal Power Commission, or any member, officer or employee of either such Commission, unless such person shall file with the Commission in such form and detail and at such time as the Commission shall by rules and regulations or order prescribe as necessary or appropriate in the public interest or for the protection of investors or consumers, a statement of the subject matter in respect of which such person is retained or employed, the nature and character of such retainer or employment, and the amount of compensation received or to be received by such person, directly or indirectly, in connection therewith." The law goes on to state that financial statements must be filed with the Commission "within ten days after the close of each calendar month during such retainer or employment." [20]

Congress, having learned how the lobby of the shipbuilders and ship operators functioned, passed a statute the following year (1936) similarly regulating these pressure interests through registration with the United States Maritime Commission.[21]

With war clouds hanging heavily over Europe, and activity of foreign agents on the propaganda front intensified, the Congress took a protective step in 1938, by passing the first Foreign Agents Registration Act, amended in 1942, which required that every person who is an agent of a foreign principal must file with the Secretary of State a statement describing in detail the nature of his activities. Political propaganda disseminated by such agents must be so labelled and copies of such matter must be filed with the Librarian of Congress and the Attorney General. Under an Executive Order, effective June 1, 1942, President

---

[20] U. S. Code, 1940, Title 15, Ch. 2C, Section 79 (h) and 79 (i). See also Forms U-12 (1)—A & B of the Securities and Exchange Commission.

[21] See U. S. Code, Title 46, Section 1225; U. S. Maritime Commission General Order No. 9, July 13, 1937; and Forms 807-1 and 807-2, together with accompanying instructions for such Forms.

Roosevelt had transferred the administration of registering foreign agents to the Department of Justice. Registration statements, open to public inspection, must now be filed with the Attorney General every six months and a copy of each registration statement must be furnished the Secretary of State. It should be particularly noted that the Attorney General is also required to make reports from "time to time" to Congress concerning the administration of this Act.[22]

In reporting the special areas of lobbying activity upon which Congress has already acted, it is perhaps well to include the amendment to the Criminal Code in 1940. This provided against anyone endeavoring "corruptly or by threats or force, or by any threatening letter of communication, . . . to influence, intimidate or impede any witness . . . in connection with any inquiry or investigation being had by either House, or any committee of either House, or any joint committee of the Congress of the United States" or by such methods attempting to interfere with the proper administration of law or proceedings of inquiries. The above language appears to be sufficiently broad in scope to cover the "influence" exerted by lobbyists upon Congress.[23]

These federal regulatory measures reach only a very limited number of the interests which continuously exert influence upon Congress. In studying the problem of lobby regulation at the federal level, much can be learned from the experience of the states.[24] Thirty-five states regulate lobbying in some way. Of these, twenty-five states now provide that legislative agents and legislative counsel who are employed in such capacity for compensation register, in most states with the Secretary of State. The required information usually includes the name and address of such agents, by whom employed, date of employment, duration of employment if it can be determined and the special subject of legislation to which the employment relates. Seventeen of these twenty-five states also require the filing of statements of all expenses paid, incurred, or promised in connection with the promotion of legislation. Twelve states require that these expense statements be filed within thirty days after the adjournment of the legislature, three states within two months after adjournment. In 1945 both Nebraska and Wisconsin amended

[22] U. S. Code, Title 22, Sections 611–621; Executive Order No. 9176, Fed. Register Vol. 7, p. 4127, June 1942.
[23] U. S. Code, Title 18, Section 241a, approved January 13, 1940.
[24] See especially E. B. Logan, "Lobbying," *Supplement to the Annals of the American Academy of Political and Social Science,* July 1929; Belle Zeller, "State Regulation of Legislative Lobbying" in *The Book of the States,* 1943–1944, pp. 161–166; Belle Zeller, *Pressure Politics in New York,* 1937, pp. 251–262 for detailed examination of the administration of the New York State lobbying law.

their statutes to provide for the filing of expense statements *during* the legislative session.

These state lobbying provisions have at least established the principle that the public has a right to know who are the paid lobbyists and the source of their funds. It must be said, however, that the record of lobby control in these states has not been as effective as it should be because faulty definition has not included all lobbies operating as such and because of inadequate enforcement.[25]

Registration of Legislative Agents

On the basis of congressional experience in the regulation of public utilities, shipping interests, and foreign agents and benefiting from the experience of the states in the control of lobbies, it is recommended that Congress pass a general lobbying law requiring agents who for pay engage in influencing legislation to register with the Clerk of the House and the Secretary of the Senate. There is no stigma attached to registering. Congress should require reports, not only from those who devote their full time for compensation to this purpose, but also from others such as attorneys who, incident to other tasks, appear before the Congress to promote legislation for their clients. Such reports should show by whom the agent is employed, the period of such employment, and his special subject of legislation.

The regulatory legislation to be effective should cover in those organizations throughout the country whose principal business it is to influence legislation and who collect and expend money for this purpose. This legislation should require the identification of large contributors, the amount contributed and how expended. This provision of the law should be carefully drafted so as not to strike at "mass" groups such as labor unions or farm organizations by requiring the identification of persons who make small contributions. It should not entail reporting of memberships, dues paid, the total receipts and expenditures of these organizations. It should require registration of their paid lobbyists and the filing of the expenditures of these agents while engaged in influencing legislation. These provisions should convince such groups as labor and farm organizations which in the past opposed such federal regulation that they have nothing to fear. After all, they do register under many state laws.

It might be well if the first general lobbying law passed by Congress did not include registration by those who practice before administra-

---

[25] *Ibid.*

tive agencies. Additional difficulties in enforcing such provisions might impede congressional approval.[26] If in particular administrative areas the need for regulation is felt, the practice already begun in the case of the utility and shipping interests and the foreign agents could be extended. It would be well to maintain a close scrutiny of the results of lobby control in these areas.

Filing of expense statements should be required. Detailed reports should be on forms prepared by the government to assure full information and a uniform method of reporting. It is equally essential that these financial reports be submitted at stated intervals *during* the sessions of Congress. For example, at the federal level precedent has already been established in the Public Utility Holding Company Act of 1935. Among the states, Nebraska and Wisconsin may well have started, by the recent (1945) revision of their lobbying laws, a trend which will spread to other states. Nebraska now requires that financial statements be filed "each month during a session of the Legislature and upon the adjournment of such session." In Wisconsin, legislative counsel and agents are required to file detailed financial statements *weekly*. Filing of expense statements at monthly and three-month intervals has appeared in federal bills before the Congress.

The bill must make provision for adequate enforcement. The experience of many of the states which have failed in this respect must not be repeated. It is not sufficient to charge the Clerk of the House and the Secretary of the Senate with the responsibility of providing dockets in which appearance and expense statements are filed. These officers of the Congress should be required to make periodic and full reports to Congress and such reports should be incorporated in the Congressional Record.[27] It is hoped that members of Congress will from time to time consider the subject matter contained in these reports worthy of public debate and public information.

Publicity as a weapon in the enforcement of laws is powerful. Enforcement through unfavorable publicity of those who have something to fear has no substitute. However, it is customary for lobbying laws to carry penalties for violations. In some states, in addition to the customary payment of a fine, a light prison term is imposed, usually as an al-

---

[26] Perhaps the Conference Committee in the 74th Cong. 2nd Session (H.R. Report No. 2925), attempted too much when it recommended regulation of those who engage in lobbying before administrative agencies as well as Congress.

[27] U. S. Code Title 22, Sec. 621 requires the Attorney General to make reports "from time to time" to Congress concerning the administration of the Foreign Agents Registration Act. The lobbying law should provide for reports at definite periodic intervals.

ternative penalty. The provisions of the Black lobbying bill (S. 2512) which passed the Senate in 1935 seem reasonable. Violators were guilty of a misdemeanor and subject to a fine of $5,000 and/or imprisonment not to exceed twelve months—if guilty of perjury in making a false affidavit, imprisonment of not more than two years. Special consideration might be given to including disbarment as lobbyist in the list of penalties.[28]

Equally important to the regulation of lobbyists is the need for modernization of legislative machinery. Enough emphasis cannot be placed upon the value of adequate research assistance and more effective utilization of such aids and services now at the disposal of committees and individual members of Congress. Such official assistance would enable the Congress better to evaluate the data supplied by pressure groups which is so essential in the formulation of legislation. It must be recognized that pressure groups have a legitimate part to play in our democratic society and, to a considerable extent, these groups represent the public functioning in organized segments. The present is perhaps a more propitious time to recommend such regulation. In 1935–1936, when the Congress last gave serious attention to this problem, the excesses—the illegitimate practices—of lobbies had been called to public attention. Many lobbyists resented being associated with the practices and they had little difficulty in persuading a majority of Congressmen at that time to oppose general control.[29]

Regulation of the lobby does not interfere with the constitutional right of petition. It denies to no one the high right of appeal to the Congress or to the public for the purpose of influencing legislation. Regulation is imperative if only to bring home to pressure groups that their activities are clothed with a public interest. It should go a long way toward winning the battle against the bad pressure boys.

Counteracting Group Pressures

In addition to requiring legislative agents to register and file financial statements, other remedies are recommended for regularizing and

---

[28] Seven states provide for disbarment. See revised list of penalties in the state lobbying laws in Belle Zeller "Public Relations and the State Lobbying Laws," *Public Relations Directory and Yearbook,* 1945, pp. 143–149.

[29] Perhaps some Congressmen were reluctant to bring pressure groups under regulation because they did not wish to place obstacles in their own paths of future employment as ex-Congressmen. See H. J. Res. 227 (70th Congress, 1st Session) prohibiting ex-members of Congress from engaging in the practice of lobbying, and the statement on this subject in S. Report No. 342, p. 3 (70th Congress, 1st Session).

counteracting group pressures. Legislative counsel for private organizations should be required to submit statements of their testimony in advance of their appearance before congressional committees and should certify that they are advocating only measures that have been specifically approved by a majority of the membership of the organizations which they claim to represent. Moreover, lobbying by vested interests and pressures upon individual Congressmen would be reduced if the introduction of legislation were restricted to Administration measures and committee-sponsored bills. The disappearance of private member bills in the House of Commons has removed a source of corruption and improved the purity of British politics.

Anything which would strengthen the national political parties would also tend to offset the power of organized groups. The majority and minority policy committees, recommended by the La Follette-Monroney Committee, are conceived as trustees of the national interest and as an antidote to sectional and local group pressures. The grip of local loyalties would be relaxed and larger interests encouraged if a candidate could run for Congress from any district in his state instead of being limited by the local residence rule to the district in which he lives. Moreover, as Thomas K. Finletter has suggested, if the President had the right to dissolve the legislature in the event of a deadlock, the national parties would be stronger throughout the country and the power of pressure groups would be weakened.[30]

The great weakness of Congress, as Walton Hamilton has warned, is its susceptibility to pressure. "The public interest is noble but often hard to define; its support is usually too diffuse to register. Checks are required against special interest as an insurance of independence to Senators and Representatives. If the member of Congress is to transmit the will of the people to the agencies of administration, he must not be taken captive by the interested groups which move upon the agency set up for their control." Hamilton proposes that an Office of Public Counsel be established to assert the public interest and to create counter-pressures to those of private groups. The real balance of power in the government at Washington is between the electorate and organized interests which have converted some federal agencies into their own branch offices and staffed them with their own spokesmen.[31]

---

[30] Thomas K. Finletter, *Can Representative Government Do the Job?*, pp. 114–121.
[31] Hearings before the Joint Committee on the Organization of Congress, pp. 715–716.

Functional Group Representation

Since organized groups are an inescapable feature of modern industrial society and since the right of individuals having common interests to form permanent associations can hardly be denied in a democracy, the questions arise: what relationship might be established between these interest groups and the state that would at once tend to reduce their internal conflicts and convert them into more socially useful aids to government? Could representatives of the more important occupational and cultural groups be brought together in some council or federation which would provide a forum for the reconciliation of inter-group controversies and advise Congress on their areas of agreement? Can we turn lobbyists into advisers and make them a useful adjunct of the legislative machinery?

These and similar questions have intrigued political scientists in recent years. Several European countries experimented with national economic councils between the wars with mixed success. A congressional committee held extensive hearings in 1931 on Senator La Follette's proposal for a national advisory council. President Hoover's Committee on Recent Social Trends made a similar suggestion in 1933. More recently the idea of an official body representing business, labor, and agriculture for joint discussion of national policy has been advanced by farm and labor groups. The War Mobilization and Reconversion Act of 1944 provided for an Advisory Board nine of whose 12 members shall have had experience in functional groups. Congressman Voorhis of California has proposed a National Advisory Commission representative of industry, agriculture, labor, the churches, education, veterans' groups, cooperatives, consumer groups, et al. to advise Congress. An example of what can be accomplished in this direction is seen in the National Planning Association whose directorate represents a coalition of the three great interest groups: industry, labor, and agriculture. Operating through this private organization, spokesmen for these major segments of the American economy have declared their interdependence and have collaborated in a series of significant statements on various important issues of national policy.

Sentiment varies regarding the desirability of establishing an official relationship between Congress and the organized interest groups. Advocates of a national economic council composed of representatives of functional interests argue that it would canalize and divert their pressures from Congress, provide a forum for group thinking and a means of reconciling group conflicts, and bring the pressure groups and their Washington agents out into the open. As a purely advisory body, such a council, it is believed, would not become a rival of Congress. The advice of a body representing all employers, workers, consumers, and investors, as well as the press and the professions, it is argued, would carry great weight with Congress and the administration. It might contribute to that continuity of economic and social policy without which planning will give way to opportunism and improvisation.

On the other hand, opponents of the scheme fear that a national advisory council might become a super-lobby and that it would tend to sharpen rather than dull conflicts between occupational groups. Such a body, it is said, might in practice become a fascist institution that would fail to hold the balance among the interests. It might come in time to exert a coercive influence on Congress and become a menace to democracy. Moreover, European experience with similar councils between the wars demonstrates the dangers and limitations of such developments. If lobbyists had official standing, say as formal advisers to congressional committees, they might become buffers between the people and the legislature and give a special-group bias to public policy.

There is a place perhaps for functional group representation in the executive branch of the government, but to give the pressure boys official status in the machinery of Congress would be to magnify their weight and exaggerate their importance. The task of Congress is frankly to recognize these groups as component elements of our complex society, to provide an opportunity for all important interests to be heard, and to publicize their legislative activities by requiring them to register. Moreover, in view of the undemocratic internal structure and methods of some of these groups, which tax, regulate, and punish their members in various ways, Congress should set up standards governing the organization, powers, and procedures of these private associations in the public interest. Otherwise, government by pressure will replace government by law in these United States.

CONGRESS AND PUBLIC OPINION

As an organ of public opinion it is the function of Congress both to voice and instruct the popular will. Coming in daily contact through correspondence and visitors with people and conditions throughout the country and returning to their constituencies from time to time, Congressmen serve as channels of opinion and information between the people and their government. They bring to the halls of Congress a familiarity with local needs and problems and a knowledge of local attitudes and opinions. Through discussion and debate they learn something of conditions and sentiments in other parts of the country. And in their messages and trips back home they are able to interpret public policies and measures to their neighbors in national and international terms. In this way Congressmen serve in a liaison capacity between Washington and Main Street, farm and city, seaboard and hinterland. Committee hearings and departmental associations widen their mental horizons, while the amenities of congressional intercourse tend to ease sectional and social tensions. Congress functions as a forum through which public opinion is brought to bear upon all branches of the federal government, and as a medium for gathering and disseminating information for the instruction and enlightenment of the people.

In performing this two-way teaching task, it is not always easy for the legislator to discover what preponderant public opinion may be on any particular question. Few voters have the time or opportunity to become familiar with or develop an informed judgment on such technical questions as the British loan or the control of atomic energy. It is only on the broad objectives of social policy that public opinion can crystallize and be ascertained. The legislator learns what the people want from personally conducted referenda among his constituents, such as the questionnaires several members sent out on compulsory military training. Petitions and memorials bearing hundreds of signatures are a less reliable guide to public opinion and make little impression upon Congress. Likewise, little reliance is placed upon the resolutions of state legislatures which seldom reflect the views of a majority of the voters. Few legislators pay much attention to the printed and mimeographed propaganda which floods their offices from every source. Most of it is intercepted by their secretaries and consigned to the wastebasket. More useful as a guide to the public attitude are newspaper editorials which both reflect and mold public opinion, and to a lesser degree the editorial and gossip columns of commentators like Arthur Krock, Mark Sullivan, David Lawrence, Walter Lippmann, Anne O'Hare McCormick, Dorothy Thompson, Merlo Pusey, Marquis Childs, Drew Pearson, and Walter Winchell. These editorial columns enjoy a wide vogue, but Congressmen often resent the more gossipy kind.[32] *Reader's Digest* and *Time* are perhaps the two most effective media in the magazine field for stimulating congressional interest and inquiry.

Public Opinion Polls[33]

One of the most helpful methods of ascertaining what the people desire is the public opinion poll—an innovation of recent years. Legislators differ about the merits of this new device. Some hail it as the answer to one of democracy's great needs—that of determining quickly and accurately what people are thinking. Others condemn it as an instrument that undermines our theory of representative government, tending to make representatives into rubber stamps for the wishes of the people as discovered through the polls. The widespread use that has been made of this new device, its indirect power, and its adoption by various government agencies as a fact-finding method, all seem to indicate that, despite objections raised against it, this tool or some improved form of it is bound to be used and to exert a large influence on policy makers. The accuracy of the modern "scientific" polls has been repeatedly demonstrated on the basis of election returns. One polling organization has made over 120 election predictions. In the last nine years its average error in predicting these elections has been less than three per cent. It is of course to the self-interest of those who earn their living by making these polls that they should be accurate, honest, and unbiased.

Although the public opinion poll is used most frequently on a national scale, it seems likely that it will spread into state or more localized usage as time goes on. There are now in existence two state polls financed by newspaper interests to keep readers informed of what the people in the state are thinking. Some municipalities have their own polling organizations. And political parties employ polling facilities on local, state, or national bases before elections.

It would be very helpful to Congressmen to have public opinion polls conducted in their districts or states when they have to decide crucial questions in which their constituents are interested. But such polls are expensive to conduct. No way has yet been devised whereby an individual legislator, without considerable personal financial backing, can have a poll made for his own special use. But three nationwide organ-

---

[32] Cf. Luce, *Congress: An Explanation*, pp. 48–51.

[33] I am indebted to Hadley Cantril, director of the Institute of Public Opinion, for the material in this and the following section.

izations now exist that constantly poll the American people on questions of public interest and publish the results for anyone to read.

The value of public opinion polls as a corrective check on the letters, telegrams, and telephone calls a Congressman receives was well illustrated by two extensive polls conducted early in 1946 by Representative Corbett of Pennsylvania. Mr. Corbett sent two questionnaires containing ten questions each on as many outstanding issues of the day to an equal number of registered Republicans and Democrats in each voting precinct of the 30th Pennsylvania congressional district. This district includes four wards of the city of Pittsburgh and all of the boroughs and townships of northern Allegheny County. This is as representative a district as one could find, for its voters are almost evenly divided between the two major parties and economically it varies all the way from areas of extreme wealth to areas of extreme poverty. More than 2,500 signed replies were received to the first poll and more than 8,000 to the second. In presenting the results to the House, Mr. Corbett observed that "obviously many of the pictures of public opinion on given issues which I had believed to be true were found to be very false. I had been judging opinion on the basis of unsolicited letters and telephone calls from constituents. Like many others I tended to believe on a majority of questions that those who wrote, wired, or telephoned reflected typical opinion. They simply did not do so in most cases. Rather, they generally represented vocal minorities. Organized pressure groups and individuals have long since learned all the tricks on how to give members of Congress a false picture of public sentiment. There is one easy corrective—solicit opinion on a scale large enough to eliminate the possibility of error." [34]

What Polls Can Do

Many useful kinds of information can be obtained through this method of representative sampling. The following can be found out:

Some of the areas of public ignorance.
Some of the basic wants and desires of people in terms of their standard of living.
What people are worrying about.
What opinions people have on the various issues of the day and how these opinions compare with congressional sentiment.
What the vote of the people for a particular candidate on election day actually means.

---

[34] *Congressional Record,* March 15, 1946, pages A1473–1474, daily edition.

What popular resistances may be anticipated to legislative programs which a majority of Congress may consider to be in the public interest.

How the opinion of the total population compares with the opinion of special interest groups.

Differences of opinion between people of various political affiliations.

What contrasts of opinion there are in different regions of the country, among different occupations, or among different groups.

The results of public opinion polls should not be followed blindly and thoughtlessly by Congressmen. But representatives should have a maximum knowledge of public opinion as one of the factors upon which their decisions are based. For representatives of the people to act without getting the most reliable information they can on the state of the public mind would be like an army acting without having the most efficient military intelligence possible.

Public opinion polls in recent years have shown that the American public is far ahead of its legislators on many matters of social policy. The public is more willing to make sacrifices than Congressmen suppose. The farm bloc in Congress frequently does not speak for the farmers, nor labor leaders for the rank and file of labor. Gallup polls have shown that the people were ahead of Congress on hours, wages, price control, farm crops and prices, rearmament, conscription, and aid to Britain. A natural explanation of this legislative lag is that Congress may defer action until it knows how substantial popular support for a given policy is. The moral drawn from this is that, in shaping national policy, Congress should pay less attention to the spokesmen of pressure groups and special interests and more to the man on the street.[35]

It is difficult to generalize about the relationship between legislative proposals and public opinion, but the most common sequence appears to be somewhat as follows: (a) legislation is introduced by a Congressman or a certain policy is promoted by some pressure group; (b) the activity of pressure groups, the course of events, or planned discussion and publicity bring the issue to the attention of the people; (c) the people make up their minds as to what course to follow; and (d) several months later Congress takes action, generally following majority opinion. This description, of course, fits only those types of legislation that by their nature stir national interest.

In February, 1946, the National Opinion Research Center polled the leaders of six key groups (agriculture, labor, management, negro, press-radio, and veterans) and a sample of average Americans on what

[35] George Gallup, "The People Are Ahead of Congress," *Reader's Digest*, June, 1942.

they thought a Congressman should and does rely on most when he votes on a national problem: the opinions of the people who elect him, the opinions of the country as a whole, or his own judgment. Although there were some sharp differences between public and leadership opinion, both polls indicated that the opinions of the country as a whole play little part in determining individual congressional positions. Both also agreed that the welfare of the country should be much more seriously considered by legislators.[36]

Just as polls of the opinions of the average voter are helpful to individual legislators, so would surveys of expert opinion be useful to the committees of Congress in considering legislative proposals of a technical or specialized nature. With the advance of science and technology and the growing impact of modern inventions upon public affairs, many of the matters on committee calendars require expert knowledge and information which the average Congressman does not pretend to possess. Out in the nation, however, in universities, offices, research laboratories, and foundations, there are experts in the various fields who possess facts and information that could be of incalculable value to Congress and its committees. If, in advance of committee hearings, scientific surveys could be made of the views and opinions of the nation's leading experts on such problems as the control of atomic energy or the maintenance of full employment, the hearing process would be greatly expedited and the quality of the legislative product greatly improved. In order to tap the scientific and social intelligence of the nation and ascertain how much consensus there is among the experts on questions of public policy and procedure, as well as to stimulate creative thinking on national problems, Professor Norman C. Meier of the University of Iowa has proposed that a division be set up in the Legislative Reference Service to conduct expert opinion surveys upon the request of congressional committees.[37] Such surveys would supplement the formal committee hearings and might well prove to be an invaluable aid to the legislative process.

Methods of Informing Public Opinion

In his Farewell Address Washington wrote: "In proportion as the structure of a government gives force to public opinion, it is essential that the public opinion be enlightened." Jefferson urged that educa-

---

[36] Report of the American Leadership Panel for March, 1946, Vol. III, No. 3.

[37] In a memorandum submitted to the Joint Committee on the Organization of Congress.

tional opportunities be provided for the masses of the people, for he realized that "no other sure foundation can be devised for the preservation of freedom and happiness" than "the diffusion of knowledge among the people."

The conscientious Congressman conceives it to be his duty not only to voice the opinions of his constituents in the councils of the nation, but also to instruct them on the nature of national problems and to explain his own actions in committee and on the floor. This teaching function of the legislator, as we have seen, is one of his most important responsibilities, for he is in a better position than the people back home to understand the play of competing social forces and to explain the inevitable compromises that must be made in the determination of national policies.

Several devices are available to Congressmen in performing their instructive function. One of the best of these are investigations of current problems by congressional committees. The great inquiries conducted in recent years by the Truman-Mead committee on national defense, by the La Follette civil liberties committee, by the Tolan committee on interstate migration, the Murray committee on small business problems, the Pepper committee on wartime health and education, the La Follette-Monroney committee on congressional organization, and the O'Mahoney committee on the concentration of economic power made significant contributions to public understanding of important national problems. Robert Heller has recommended that Congress make more frequent formal and organized inquiries into basic national affairs.[38]

Public debates on the floor of Congress are usually aired in the press and help to enlighten public opinion. With its traditional right of unlimited debate the Senate is a better forum for this purpose than the House of Representatives where the special orders of the Rules Committee narrowly restrict debating time. Henry Hazlitt reminds us that the Rules Committee allowed the House only three hours of general debate on the famous Wagner labor relations act of 1935, "which might excusably have required several weeks of public discussion." [39] As the committees are the workshops of Congress, so the halls are its talking shops where public issues are ventilated and votes explained to the folks back home. Remarks made on the floor can be extended in the appendix of the *Congressional Record,* printed at the member's expense,

---

[38] Robert Heller, *Strengthening the Congress,* p. 29.
[39] Henry Hazlitt, *A New Constitution Now* (1942), p. 243.

and distributed wholesale under the franking privilege. After a careful study of the Senate debate on the Selective Training and Service Bill of 1940, Giraud Chester concludes that debate in the upper chamber serves effectively to clarify national issues, reconcile conflicting groups, educate public opinion, and hold the executive accountable. "To expect that debate within the chamber shall each day be on a superior level is an unfair and unwarranted expectation. An understanding of the duties and responsibilities of a Senator and of the demands made on his time by his constituents excuses occasional mediocrity in daily debate on passing matters. But it appears, from this study, that when an issue is important, when a major decision is to be made, Senate debate is of a higher and more skilled nature than we would imagine if we based our judgment solely upon the usual cursory or partisan observation of our upper house in action." [40]

Periodic news letters published in the local press, radio broadcasts, and personal speeches in their states and districts are familiar devices which Congressmen use to inform the people.

Broadcasting the Proceedings of Congress

Senator Pepper and Representative Coffee have proposed authorizing commercial radio stations to broadcast all or part of the proceedings on the floor or before the committees of Congress, and providing for complete transcriptions of the debates. Copies of the recordings would be sold at cost and the proceedings would be broadcast as a public-service "sustaining program."

In support of their proposal it is argued that putting Congress on the air would make for a much more intelligent interchange of opinion between the people and their Congressmen and hence a more democratic legislature. The people have a right to hear floor debates and would exercise that right. Uncensored broadcasts would serve as a check on those newspapers which sometimes delete or distort the news to make it fit their own bias. It would discipline demagogues and rabble rousers to more temperate speech. It would educate, enlighten, and inform the people, resulting in a more responsive and responsible electorate. It would improve the composition of Congress by exposing the stupid and unfit as well as the intelligent and hardworking members. It would improve the quality of debates. Greater citizen participation in government resulting from such broadcasts would strengthen

[40] Giraud Chester, "Contemporary Senate Debate: A Case Study," *Quarterly Journal of Speech*, December, 1945, p. 411.

democracy and keep government close to the people. And it would give millions of Americans front-line seats in the making of public policy. Experience with broadcasting the proceedings of the New Zealand Parliament and the New York City Council is cited as proof of the popularity and success of legislative broadcasts.

Opponents of broadcasting Congress raise the following objections: complete broadcasts would only bore and disillusion the people, making them less responsive to their obligations as citizens. The privilege might be misused by allowing members to "extend their remarks" on the air via radio transcriptions. The extension of congressional immunity from libel and slander suits to the air waves would encourage demagogues to step up their campaigns of personal slander and abuse. Members would not have a chance to amend "for the permanent Record" any inaccurate and extemporaneous remarks. Debate would have to be staged and Congress would be putting on a show instead of attending to its own business. Congress would lose its dignity by being exposed to public inspection. Oratory would be encouraged in preference to simple business-like debate. The Senate would have to surrender its right of unlimited debate on these occasions lest some demagogue get the floor and hold it during the entire time of the broadcast. And scrambling for the privilege of getting on the air would discredit Congress instead of boosting its stock in the eyes of the people.

The proposal to put Congress on the air raises several questions: how would the bills to be discussed over the air be selected? Who would be permitted to speak while Senate or House proceedings were being broadcast? Since the two houses often meet at the same time, which should be broadcast? Wouldn't the daytime listeners be mostly women? Should all the proceedings of both houses be put on the air or only certain selective parts? Would selective broadcasting provide a fair sample of Congress in action? Why broadcast floor proceedings when the real work of Congress is done in committee? Will Congressmen still enjoy "congressional immunity" on the air? What effect would broadcasting have on absenteeism? On traditional legislative procedures? How expensive would it be to broadcast Congress directly? Would the private networks be willing to give up much time to legislative programs? Would short-wave broadcasting of the proceedings of Congress be technically feasible? What would it cost?

Radio engineers say that short-wave broadcasting of the proceedings of Congress would be technically feasible. Since one station could not cover the United States, two plants would be required; one on the east coast and one on the west coast. Twelve frequencies would be necessary. The federal government now is operating 36 transmitters for short-wave broadcasting to foreign countries. Of these, 24 belong to the government and 12 are leased from private companies. All of them are currently being used by the Cultural Relations Office in the Department of State for foreign broadcasts. It is estimated that 25 per cent of domestic radio sets are now equipped to receive short-wave programs, and that the annual cost of operating two congressional stations would total approximately $800,000.

Congressmen are deeply divided on the desirability of broadcasting their proceedings. Some favor it on a selective basis. Others believe that only complete coverage would work. And others vigorously oppose any form of congressional broadcasting for the reasons mentioned above. My own view is that the proposal is well worth a trial. Congress could experiment at regular intervals with night sessions of one or the other house when proceedings of national importance could be broadcast to the nation. Arrangements could be made for equal division of the time between the parties. The coming of radio affords Congress a grand opportunity to perform its educational function by informing the public on both sides of great national issues. The provincial parliament in Saskatchewan, Canada, has recently put its proceedings on the air. It seems only a question of time before the American Congress will use radio and television as channels of direct communication with the electorate.

Should Congress Lead or Follow Public Opinion?

It is axiomatic to say that in a democracy public opinion is the source of law. Unless legislation is sanctioned by the sense of right of the people, it becomes a dead letter on the statute books, like prohibition and the Hatch Act. But public opinion is a mercurial force; now quiescent, now vociferous, it has various moods and qualities. It reacts to events and is often vague and hard to weigh.

Nor is public opinion infallible. Most people are naturally preoccupied with their personal problems and daily affairs; national problems and legislative decisions seem complex and remote to them, despite press and radio and occasional Capitol tours. Comparatively few adults understand the technicalities of foreign loans or reciprocal trade treaties, although congressional action on these aspects of our foreign economic policy may have far-reaching effects upon our standard of living. Moreover, "men in the mass are at times prejudiced, angry, impulsive, unjust. So at times the legislator must stand up against prejudice and passion, impulse and injustice. If resistance to opinion when it is wrong proves unavailing, the legislator should yield his office rather than his judgment. Nothing short of that will bring him peace of mind." [41] Perhaps this is why, along with his long-standing hostility to centralized government, Hatton W. Sumners retired from Congress after 34 years of able service in the House of Representatives.

In practice, a Congressman both leads and follows public opinion. The desires of his constituents, of his party, and of this or that pressure group all enter into his decisions on matters of major importance. The influence of these factors varies from member to member and measure to measure. Some Congressmen consider it their duty to follow closely what they think is the majority opinion of their constituents, especially just before an election. Others feel that they should make their decisions without regard to their constituents' wishes in the first place, and then try to educate and convert them afterwards. Some members are strong party men and follow more or less blindly the program of the party leaders. Except when they are very powerful in the home district, the pressure groups are more of a nuisance than a deciding influence on the average member. When a legislator is caught between the conflicting pressures of his constituents and his colleagues, he perforce compromises between them and follows his own judgment.

The average legislator discovers early in his career that certain interests or prejudices of his constituents are dangerous to trifle with. Some of these prejudices may not be of fundamental importance to the welfare of the nation, in which case he is justified in humoring them, even though he may disapprove. The difficult case occurs where the prejudice concerns some fundamental policy affecting the national welfare. A sound sense of values, the ability to discriminate between that which is of fundamental importance and that which is only superficial, is an indispensable qualification of a good legislator.

Senator Fulbright gives an interesting example of this distinction in his stand on the poll-tax issue and isolationism. "Regardless of how persuasive my colleagues or the national press may be about the evils of the poll tax, I do not see its fundamental importance, and I shall follow the views of the people of my state. Although it may be symbolic of conditions which many deplore, it is exceedingly doubtful that its

---

[41] Luce, *op. cit.*, p. 53.

abolition will cure any of our major problems. On the other hand, regardless of how strongly opposed my constituents may prove to be to the creation of, and participation in, an ever stronger United Nations Organization, I could not follow such a policy in that field unless it becomes clearly hopeless." [42]

A Two-Way Job

As believers in democracy, probably most Americans would agree that it is the duty of Congressmen to follow public opinion insofar as it expresses the desires, wants, needs, aspirations, and ideals of the people. Most Americans probably would also consider it essential for their representatives to make as careful an appraisal of these needs and desires as they can, and to consider, in connection with such an appraisal, the ways and means of accomplishing them. Legislators have at hand more information about legal structures, economic problems, productive capacities, manpower possibilities, and the like, than the average citizen they represent. They can draw upon that information to inform and lead the people—by showing the extent to which their desires can be realized.

In other words, a true representative of the people would follow the people's desires and at the same time lead the people in formulating ways of accomplishing those desires. He would lead the people in the sense of calling to their attention the difficulties of achieving those aims and the ways to overcome the difficulties. This means also that, where necessary, he would show special interest groups or even majorities how, according to his own interpretation and his own conscience, their desires need to be tempered in the common interest or for the future good of the nation.

Thus the job of a Congressman is a two-way one. He represents his local area and interests in the national capital, and he also informs the people back home of problems arising at the seat of government and how these problems affect them. It is in the nature of the Congressman's job that he should determine, as far as he can, public opinion in his own constituency and in the whole nation, analyze it, measure it in terms of the practicability of turning it into public policy, and consider it in the light of his own knowledge, conscience, and convictions. Occasionally he may be obliged to go against public opinion, with the consequent task of educating or re-educating the people along lines

---

[42] In an address on "The Legislator" delivered at the University of Chicago on February 19, 1946. *Vital Speeches*, May 15, 1946, pp. 468–472.

that seem to him more sound. And finally, since he is a human being eager to succeed at his important job of statesmanship and politics, he is realistic enough to keep his eyes on the voters in terms of the next election. But he understands that a mere weather-vane following of majority public opinion is not always the path to reelection.

The essence of true representative government was well epitomized twenty years ago by Representative Robert Luce. "The lawmaker is not to be purely an agent," he said, "vainly trying to decide what the majority of his principals desire. He is not to be purely a trustee, making wholly independent decisions, self-conceived and self-sustained. He is to be both agent and trustee as far as may be. He is to feel it as much his duty to try to modify in others opinions with which he disagrees, as to try to let his own opinions be modified by the advice of others. He is to deal fairly both by his constituents and by himself. Such a man deems it necessary to break with constituency or with party only on those very rare occasions when Judgment must step aside and let Conscience rule. The great mass of legislation is matter of expediency. Not once in a thousand times is it matter of what is usually thought of as right and wrong. Only when right and wrong are at stake may the legislator refuse to concede, to compromise, or to yield." [43]

_____
[43] Luce, *op. cit.*, pp. 52–53.

10.

Reorganizing Congressional Services

THE RECONSTRUCTION OF Congress will not be complete nor will it achieve maximum effectiveness until it modernizes its internal services and facilities along rational lines. The existing administrative and technical services available to members of Congress have grown up like Topsy over the years. And so scattered are they in the attics, galleries, basements, and byways of Capitol Hill that even some of the older members are unaware of their location or existence. Each house in times past has set up its own supply shops, folding rooms, document rooms, disbursing offices, mailing rooms, post offices, restaurants, barber shops, and other facilities. Each service is under separate management and there is little, if any, coordination between them.

The top administrative posts on the congressional staff are held by men of unquestioned competence and integrity who have served the legislature long and faithfully. But the lesser housekeeping services are largely manned by temporary and patronage employees with no particular training for their tasks and among whom there is a heavy turnover. Legislative positions are not classified in any systematic way and tenure in congressional and committee offices is exposed to all the hazards of political change. So tangled and twisted indeed are these varied services throughout the legislative structure that it would be difficult clearly to depict them on an organization chart.

Office of Congressional Services

In order to coordinate the scattered technical and administrative services that are now available in the Legislative Establishment and to improve their adequacy and efficiency, Congress should establish an

323

Office of Administrative and Technical Services on Capitol Hill. This office would operate under the general supervision of the Senate and House Committees on Administration, acting jointly, the chairmen of which would appoint the director of the office. It would be the function of this office to execute and coordinate the administrative policies and programs prescribed by the Joint Committee on Administration, to supervise the internal organization of the services necessary to carry out such policies and programs, and to handle liaison activities on administrative and technical matters between Congress and the other branches of the federal government. The Joint Committee on Administration would issue rules for the consolidation of duplicating offices and overlapping services, placing them under the jurisdiction of the office, centralizing the control of all appropriations for congressional services in the office, defining its authority and responsibility, and establishing the qualifications and tenure of all positions in the office. It goes without saying that only persons qualified in the field of administrative management should be chosen to staff the office and that they should continue to serve regardless of changes in party control.

The next step in providing Congress with good internal administration of its essential services will be to set up two divisions within the Office of Administrative and Technical Services: a Division of Technical Services and a Division of Administrative Services, each under a chief reporting to the director of the office. The Technical Services Division would furnish special technical assistance, advice, and professional services to members and committees of both houses, absorbing the work presently performed by the Legislative Counsel and the Legislative Reference Service and adding special investigative and information services. It would have legal, economics, investigation, and information departments whose heads would report to the chief of the division.

The Administrative Services Division would coordinate and centralize the various internal administrative services of Congress now split here, there, and everywhere. The scattered transportation and communication services would be regrouped into one department. The various purchasing activities would be brought together in a procurement department. The three payroll disbursing offices, the expenditure of the contingent funds, and the auditing and settling of House and Senate accounts would be centralized in a fiscal department which would also analyze the reports of the Comptroller General.

A personnel department would be established here to install a modern personnel system for all the service employees of Congress, covering their recruitment on merit, training for permanent work in the legislative branch, simplification of job standards, classification of work, salary grades, promotion, leave, retirement, insurance, and employee welfare programs. Personnel administration within Congress today is in a chaotic state. There are 531 appointing authorities. Employees are hired on patronage without any uniform standards of employment and with little regard to rights of tenure. (Tables X and XI, in the Appendix, show an analysis of legislative positions and payrolls.) Promotions and pay increases can be obtained only by changing jobs or by the cumbersome method of enacting special legislation. Such a lack of system leads only to duplication of services, underpaid personnel, overstaffing in some places and understaffing in others, and inequities in rates of pay. In brief, the entire situation relating to congressional employment is so confused and inefficient that only by setting up a central personnel department can it be corrected.

A management department should also be established within the Administrative Services Division to analyze administrative procedures for the office, coordinate technical and administrative work, conduct management surveys, make management consultants available for the use of committees in connection with oversight of executive branch operations, maintain liaison with the Bureau of the Budget, and recommend improvements in operating procedures. A budget department would assist both houses and the standing committees of Congress in preparing annual operating budgets for their activities, and would advise and assist the committees on appropriations to the executive branch. Finally, there would be a general services department which would provide a variety of miscellaneous services for Congress, including a stenographic and clerical pool, duplicating and photostat services, the services now furnished by the folding rooms, supervision of messengers and pages, janitor and custodial services, allocation of space in Capitol buildings, and free guide service.

Chart III in the Appendix illustrates this proposed reorganization and expansion of congressional services. Prepared by W. Darlington Denit and other experts in administrative management, this plan of organization is based upon the fruits of long experience in government and industry and profits by the lessons of the late war. It was presented in May, 1945, to the Joint Committee on the Organization of Congress by former Congressman Maury Maverick as a public service.[1] Its adoption, he pointed out, would give members of Congress services similar to those long enjoyed by persons in the executive branch. By rationalizing its internal administrative and housekeeping arrangements, it would enable Congress to function much more effectively. The plan contemplates no wholesale sacrifice of the prestige and experience of the present congressional staff. "Virtually all of the existing mechanisms," said Mr. Maverick, "and the personnel of which they are comprised, can be fitted into this proposal. The O.A.T.S. will sow the seeds of good administration within the Congress . . . and will handle the departmental business of constituents as the agent of Congress" without any increase in legislative costs. "No Congressman should have to look beyond the director of that office," added Mr. Denit, "to get any of the administrative and technical services which are outlined in the plan." Moreover, he agreed, these scattered services should be brought together at one point and housed in a new Administration Building on Capitol Hill which might also include rooms for the use of standing and joint committees. Part of the job of the personnel department of the office would be to certify qualified persons for appointment to the professional staffs of congressional committees. Based on the principle of central administration, this plan may err in minor details, but there can be no doubt that it would go far to improve the functioning of Congress by providing it with more efficient methods of internal administrative management.

Compensation of Personnel

In the early days of the Republic, members of Congress received six dollars for each day of attendance. This amount was increased to eight dollars in 1817 and remained at that level until 1855 when their rate of compensation was changed to $3,000 a year. From 1865 to 1907 congressional salaries amounted to $5,000, and from 1907 to 1925 they received $7,500 a year. From 1925 to 1947 the annual compensation of Congressmen was $10,000, except for temporary depression cuts during the 1930's.[2]

In addition to their salaries Congressmen currently receive the following allowances and perquisites:

---

[1] Hearings before the Joint Committee on the Organization of Congress, pp. 563–595.
[2] F. M. Brewer, *Compensation in Congress,* Editorial Research Reports, February 24, 1945, pp. 145–147.

	Senators	Representatives
Clerk hire	$13,920	$9,500
Expenses	2,500	2,500
Stationery	$400 a year	$700 a year
Phone calls between points outside Washington	$300 a year	———
Toll calls	26 per month	———
Air-mail & special delivery stamps	$105.66 a year	$75 a year
Mileage	One round trip per session—20 cents a mile each way	
Grant to widows of members who die in office	$10,000	$10,000
Franking privilege	government mail	government mail

It is interesting to compare congressional salaries and allowances with those of a member of Parliament and of officers of the executive branch. The salary of members of Parliament was raised in 1937 from 400 to 600 pounds a year (plus free travel between their constituencies and Westminster). Of this sum 100 pounds is allowed free of income tax for secretarial assistance, postage, and other expenses; and if these can be shown to exceed 100 pounds, a further allowance may be made. Ross points out that under modern conditions, with probably two homes to maintain, enormous correspondence, and many calls on his purse both at Westminster and in his constituency, the most economical member nowadays has difficulty in paying his way on less than 1,000 pounds a year, leaving a balance of 400 pounds to be found from other sources. It is not always easy for him to find part-time work in another occupation, and hence the direct or indirect subsidies from trade unions and industrial concerns which find it useful to be represented in Parliament.[3]

While the salary and allowances of Congressmen thus compare very favorably with those of members of Parliament, congressional allowances and perquisites are negligible compared with those of executive officials. They can travel at government expense on official business by plane or pullman. They receive six dollars a day expense money while in the field. They can make unlimited use of the communication services. They ride in automobiles which are purchased, operated, and maintained at public expense and driven by government chauffeurs. Uncle Sam furnishes their offices with all kinds of equipment, newspapers, stationery, supplies and materials. They are provided with large

---

[3] J. F. S. Ross, *Parliamentary Representation*, pp. 136–137.

research and clerical staffs, stenographic pools, and duplicating services. All the facilities of modern administrative organization are at their command. And they can retire at 62 on pensions to which the government makes a liberal contribution. These executive allowances and perquisites are paid for out of the contingent expenses of the departments which are granted by the Congress and which amounted, in the case of the Department of the Interior, for example, to $578,400 for the fiscal year 1946.

Congressmen have found it increasingly difficult in recent years to make ends meet on their present salaries. Under the 1946 rates of the federal income tax, a Senator and his wife must pay a tax of $2,117.25. If they have two dependents, their tax amounts to $1,798.75. The cost of living has greatly increased since their present salaries were fixed in 1925. Moreover, most members must maintain two residences: one at home and the other in Washington where rents are high. When a businessman comes to Washington on a business trip, his expenses are deductible for income tax purposes, but Congressmen cannot deduct the extra expense of their living quarters in the nation's capital. There are also the extraordinary costs of the biennial campaigns for members of the lower house. Current estimates of the average annual living expenses of a member of Congress range from $12,000 to $16,000. One careful calculation by a former member (based on personal interviews and the Heller budget) was itemized as follows:[4]

$1,798.00 federal income tax
90.00 other taxes
2,312.00 food
769.00 clothing
2,679.00 housing
1,260.00 house operation
82.00 furnishings
5,782.00 miscellaneous
_____
$14,772.00 total expenses

These cold figures measure the growing gap between a Congressman's income and outgo. They also explain the recent resignations of members like Robert Ramspeck and Clifton Woodrum—able men whom Congress can ill afford to lose—to take more lucrative positions in private business. "I couldn't afford to be a Congressman," Mr. Ram-

_____
[4] From statement by Maury Maverick before a subcommittee of the House Judiciary Committee, February 16, 1945, at hearings on H. R. 176.

speck remarked regretfully.[5] Now that legislative service has become a full-time job, members have no time to make money, as they did in the past through law practice or business operation, when their presence was not required in Washington.

Considering these circumstances and the increasingly heavy responsibilities that the top legislative positions in the nation entail, congressional salaries should certainly be raised. Persons in comparable positions in business and the professions are usually much better paid than Congressmen. Low salaries deprive the country of the services of many of its ablest citizens who cannot afford to give up their business or professional careers for a career in Congress. They tend to limit membership to those who are either rich or of mediocre ability or who patriotically are willing to accept economic sacrifices for themselves and their families. Recommendations for change range from $15,000 to $25,000. In determining the proper figure, the principle to follow was well stated several years ago by Ogden Mills who suggested that the salary of a member of Congress ought not to be so large that men would seek public office because of the attractiveness of the financial reward nor, on the other hand, should it be so small that only men of wealth or independent means could afford to come to the national legislature. A more adequate salary would not only tend to improve the quality of the membership. It would also make a direct contribution to independence of thought and to courageous action.

Provision for Retirement

Congress has authorized the extension of a wide range of social security benefits to many millions of citizens. It has provided retirement insurance plans for business and industrial workers. And it has extended retirement privileges to three million employees of the executive branch, to the officers and enlisted men of the Army, Navy, Marine Corps, and Coast Guard, to the foreign service personnel of the State Department, to the federal judiciary, and to the employees of Congress. But it has been reluctant to include its own membership in any form of retirement plan.

Bills to extend the existing contributory system of retirement benefits to elective officers (and heads of executive departments) were introduced in the 76th–79th Congresses, inclusive, and favorably reported by the Civil Service committees. One of these bills became law on January 24, 1942, but was repealed six weeks later after a "Bundles for

[5] See his article in Collier's for March 9, 1946.

Congress" campaign had ridiculed this alleged "pension grab." Only seven Representatives and five Senators had the courage to vote against repeal. The proposal was misrepresented by the press and misunderstood by the people. More sober reflection since then has evidently convinced the press and the public that their opposition was mistaken, for public opinion has now come to appreciate the justice of the case for congressional retirement allowances.

If it is proper to provide for the retirement of persons employed in business and industry and in other branches of government, it is likewise necessary in legislative service. The sense of security which comes from the assurance of a protected old age increases efficiency and enhances the value of the service rendered. Retirement allowances for Congressmen would strengthen their courageous inclinations and lead them to vote as conscience dictates. It would also tend to compensate them for the financial sacrifices they have made in giving up business or professional careers.

Employment in the federal service is long, continuous, and relatively secure. But service in Congress is comparatively short, intermittent, and subject to the hazards of recurring elections. Therefore, membership in the federal retirement system should be open to Congressmen on at least as favorable terms as to civil servants.

Such membership, moreover, would induce men who have reached advanced age or who face other infirmities to retire voluntarily, making way for younger men and women with fresh energies and new viewpoints on public problems. Congress is greatly handicapptd today by the inertia and hardened mental arteries of old age. Many of its key policy positions are held under the seniority rule by tired old men who have fought the good fight but have lost touch with modern ideas and social needs. An adequate retirement system would enable these veterans to withdraw gracefully from the legislative scene and make way for more vigorous, younger men with more objective views on governmental problems. It would also take the fear of poverty out of their souls. Fear makes Congressmen vote for bills they would otherwise oppose. The infusion of fresh blood in high places on Capitol Hill would be a great step toward the reconstruction of Congress.

Three retirement plans have been before Congress for its consideration. One is the plan favorably reported by the House Civil Service Committee[6] which would make Congressmen (and department heads) eligible to participate in retirement annuities on a contributory basis

[6] House Report No. 1343, 79th Congress, 1st Session, on H. R. 4199.

under the civil service retirement act, provided they have made contributions for all of their congressional service or have contributed at least $2,500—the equivalent of five years' contributions on a $10,000 salary at the regular five per cent rate. Another is the proposal of the La Follette-Monroney Committee[7] which would also permit members of Congress to join the federal retirement system on a contributory basis, but would require contributions at the rate of six per cent of base pay and provide more adequate annuities. Under this plan the annuity of members of Congress would consist of $2\frac{1}{2}$ per cent of the average salary received, multiplied by the number of years of congressional service, but no annuity would exceed three-fourths of the congressional salary. The third is the Heller plan under which members of Congress, with certain exceptions, would receive at age 55 annual service retirement pay of $1,000 for each full year of congressional service, up to a maximum of $10,000 annually.[8]

According to estimates of the Civil Service Commission, the cost to the government of matching retirement contributions by members of Congress under the first plan mentioned above would never be more than $500,000 a year, due to the small number who would retire and be able to meet the requirements of the law. Assuming that one-third of the membership would not elect to come under the La Follette-Monroney plan, or would not qualify, it would cost the government $198,000 a year and the total cost to the government of matching back contributions would be $2,896,000. The Heller noncontributory plan would be the most expensive to the government of the three schemes. But the cost to the treasury of any of the proposed retirement plans for Congressmen would be negligible in comparison with expenditures by the government for the retirement of other classes of public servants, as is shown by Table XII in the Appendix.

Congressmen will continue to be "the forgotten men of social security" until they bring themselves into the federal retirement system.

Improvement of Records and Reports

One final aspect of congressional housekeeping which deserves mention is the matter of the preparation and care of various records and reports. Extensive files of various records are systematically maintained by the Secretary of the Senate and the Clerk of the House. But the records of some committee proceedings are incomplete or nonexistent.

[7] Senate Report No. 1011, 79th Congress, 2d Session, p. 29.
[8] Robert Heller, *Strengthening the Congress*, pp. 34–35.

Each committee should be required to keep a complete record of all its proceedings, except executive sessions. Such records would include the attendance of members at committee sessions and the votes of all committeemen on bills and amendments on which a record vote is demanded. Such record votes should be printed in the *Congressional Record*. Concise summaries of the testimony heard and subject indices should be published with all committee hearings as an aid to their readers.

Much of the legislation now considered by Congress is so complex as to render difficult a complete understanding of its subject matter. Not only Congressmen, but the press, the radio, and the interested public are entitled to clear and concise explanations of bills being considered by the national legislature. To this end, simple digests of proposed legislation might well be incorporated in the committee report accompanying a bill. The report should also include supporting arguments for the passage of the bill and a statement of the national interest involved.

There is also room for improvement in the *Congressional Record*. Its usefulness to members and citizens would be greatly increased if each issue carried a daily calendar showing the scheduled meetings of the houses and their committees, their location, and the subjects on their agenda. A brief résumé of the previous day's congressional activities could also be incorporated in the Record, together with an index of its contents.

Since 1937 it has been the practice of the Secretary of the Senate to transfer the noncurrent records of the Senate to the National Archives, where they are stored under conditions that insure their permanent preservation and arranged in such a way as to make them readily accessible and quickly available for use. He retains in his custody the records of the Senate for the two Congresses immediately preceding the current Congress. This practice has eliminated the necessity of storing inactive records in numerous out-of-the-way places where they formerly suffered damage and deterioration. It has also enabled the Secretary of the Senate to provide adequate storage facilities for current records and to make them readily accessible.

No provision has been made, however, for the preservation of the noncurrent records of Senate committees, except those referred to the committees by the Senate which are required to be returned to the Secretary of the Senate at the close of each session. As a result, many of these records, which often have historic value and current utility, have been lost or destroyed. It is not unknown for committee records to disappear with their retiring chairmen. Senator Beveridge took the files of his Committee on Territories and Insular Affairs with him when he left the Senate in 1911. Mrs. Borah transferred the papers of the Senate Committee on Foreign Relations to the Library of Congress after her husband's death. And the records of the Dies committee are reported to have disappeared. The standing rules of the Senate should be amended to provide for the transfer to the Secretary of the Senate at the close of each session of Congress of all the records of the standing and special committees of the Senate from whatever source received, including bills, resolutions, hearings, committee prints, reports, and other pertinent papers.

The House of Representatives has taken no action with respect to the transfer of its noncurrent records to the National Archives, despite recommendations to this effect by the House Library Committee. As a result, the noncurrent records of the House are stored in eight different locations in the Capitol, in one depository in the Old House Office Building, and in three locations in the Library of Congress. According to the House Library Committee, many of the House records are disarranged and inaccessible and are stored in unsuitable places that contribute to their damage and deterioration. It does not appear logical for the noncurrent records of the Senate to be preserved in one place and the noncurrent records of the House to be stored in a number of other places. The best interests of the government and the people of the United States would be served by the preservation of the noncurrent records of the Senate and House in the National Archives.[9]

---

[9] The Legislative Reorganization Act of 1946 now requires this to be done.

11.

Congress Faces the Future

THE CASE FOR the reconstruction of Congress is clear. In three independent surveys political scientists, efficiency engineers, and a joint congressional committee have examined our national legislature and reached substantially the same conclusions concerning its defects and the appropriate remedies. They are agreed that Congress today is neither organized nor equipped effectively to perform its main functions of determining policy, reviewing executive performance, controlling expenditure, and representing the people.

According to their unanimous reports, Congress lacks adequate information and inspection facilities. Its internal structure is dispersive and duplicating. It is a body without a head. Leadership is scattered among the chairmen of 81 little legislatures who compete with each other for jurisdiction and power. Its supervision of executive performance is superficial. Much of its time is consumed by petty local and private matters which divert its attention from national policy-making. Elected by the people to protect the public interest, it yields too often to the importunities of lobbyists for special-interest groups. It lacks machinery for developing coherent legislative programs and for promoting party responsibility and accountability. Its posts of power are held on the basis of political age, regardless of ability or agreement with party policies. And its members are overworked and underpaid—the forgotten men of social security.

In order to overcome these handicaps and obstacles, it is almost universally agreed that Congress should have its own intelligence service to furnish it unbiased information essential to the performance of its legislative and supervisory functions. Congressional committees should have their own independent, qualified experts in whom they can have confidence. And the legislative reference and bill-drafting services—which are the research and legal arms of Congress—should be greatly strengthened.

Congress must also integrate and rationalize its committee system by dropping the inactive committees, which are merely ornamental barnacles on the ship of state; and by consolidating those with overlapping jurisdictions—so that the committee systems of both houses will correspond with each other and be correlated with the major functional divisions of the executive branch.

Furthermore, there must be reasonable continuity and coherence of legislative policies if domestic programs and foreign relations are not to be jeopardized. Otherwise, social planning will give way to opportunism and improvisation as in the past. Under a form of government which divides power between Congress and the President and permits opposing political parties to control them, with general elections every two years, continuous political direction cannot be assured. Continuity of public policy and unity of command would be facilitated, however, if Congress were to coordinate its scattered parts into a smoothly operating and responsible mechanism by setting up a legislative cabinet or policy committee. Such a congressional cabinet should be composed of the majority party leaders in both chambers, and it should be assigned the tasks of formulating consistent over-all legislative policies, expediting the passage of pledged party programs, and promoting more effective cooperation with the Executive via a joint legislative-executive council.

Moreover, Congress must develop techniques to implement its surveillance of administrative performance. This can be done by safeguarding delegated powers, improving appropriation procedures, transforming the General Accounting Office, adequately staffing the supervisory committees, and experimenting with the question period. It should also require the agents of pressure groups seeking to influence federal legislation to register and make full disclosure of their membership, receipts, and expenditures.

Committee chairmen should be chosen on the basis of ability and their approval of majority party pledges and programs rather than seniority alone, and all chairmen should automatically retire as such at age 65. Furthermore, the annual salaries of all members of Congress should be increased to at least $15,000, and they should be permitted to join the federal retirement system on a contributory basis. And an

Office of Congressional Services should be established to abolish the patronage system on Capitol Hill and install a modern merit system for the congressional staff.

Finally, Congress must divest itself of all delegable and less essential duties which divert its attention from national policy-making and with which it ought not to be burdened. This means granting home rule to the District of Columbia, delegating the settlement of private claims to the federal courts, and transferring other local and private matters to appropriate administrative agencies.

Such, in synopsis, is the congressional reform program. All impartial observers are agreed upon its essential features. It is long overdue. Its adoption will go far to restore the effectiveness of Congress as a coordinate branch of our national government, to simplify its operations and improve its relations with the Executive, and to prevent political frustration of well-laid plans for postwar economic and social reconstruction at home and abroad.

Obstacles to Reform

What are the prospects? We can count, I think, upon the support of the younger and newer members in both the House and Senate who have not yet been indoctrinated in the ancient ways and among whom reform sentiment is strong. But we have no illusions about the reaction and opposition from those who have vested interests in the status quo. There is a deep-set attachment to time-worn ritual and a massive inertia that must be overcome. The proposals for higher salaries, retirement allowances, and bigger and better staffs will be more popular than the more fundamental reforms in committee structure and operation. Under the guise of "practical politics" Congress will be tempted to take the sweet and leave the bitter.

The chief obstacle to the reform program is its proposal to consolidate the present standing committees and reduce their number from 81 to 34. This would deprive 47 Congressmen of their chairmanships and as many ranking minority members of the chance to become chairmen when the Republicans come to power. Here is an influential bloc of members who may be expected to resist by every stratagem the attempt to clip their privileges and prerogatives.

The proposed reforms will also be criticized by those who consider them good as far as they go, but who honestly believe that they do not go far enough. Friendly critics of the La Follette-Monroney Committee point to certain significant omissions from its report: its failure to recommend some substitute for the seniority method of selecting committee chairmen, and its silence on the powers of the House Rules Committee, the Kefauver question-time proposal, and Senate filibusters. They doubt that the proposed policy committees will achieve their avowed objectives if they are composed of committee chairmen chosen by seniority who are not truly representative of current public opinion as reflected in the most recent election.[1] "Only the best will do," writes Philip Broughton in urging more sweeping reforms.[2] Others, misconceiving a sincere effort to strengthen the machinery and facilities of Congress for an attack upon its parliamentary procedures, will cavalierly reject the entire reform program.[3]

On the one hand, the campaign to modernize Congress is in line with efforts to restore the balance of power between the legislative and executive branches upset by the great expansion of executive power since 1933. With the return of peace, Congress has been desirous of playing a larger part in policy-making, but has been handicapped by its antiquated machinery and archaic tools. On the other hand, the campaign has been hindered by congressional preoccupation with reconversion problems and by the intra-party conflicts between conservative and liberal factions.

Although little attention has been paid to the dynamics of congressional reform, there has also been some concern behind the scenes over the uses to which a renovated legislature might be put. Will a streamlined Congress be used by liberal legislators to facilitate the adoption of progressive policies and to cooperate with a liberal administration? Or will it be used by the reactionaries to strengthen Congress vis-a-vis the Executive and to hamstring programs of social welfare and international cooperation? Some who watched a coalition of southern Democrats and northern Republicans emasculate President Truman's domestic program in the House of Representatives during 1945–1946 thought that Congress was already much too strong for the good of the country.

The reconstruction of Congress will depend in the last analysis upon sustained public support. Only Congress can reform itself from within. But an aroused and informed public opinion can help in obtaining

---

[1] See letter by Caryl E. Cohen in *The New York Times,* March 31, 1946.

[2] Philip S. Broughton, *For a Stronger Congress,* Public Affairs Pamphlet No. 116, April, 1946, p. 31.

[3] See speech of Hon. Clarence Cannon in the House of Representatives, March 13, 1946, *Congressional Record,* March 25, 1946, pp. A1716–1725.

favorable action. Influential civic and professional groups like the League of Women Voters and the National Planning Association, as well as associations of taxpayers and chambers of commerce, which have endorsed the recommendations of the Joint Committee, can help further by informing the public of the facts and issues that are involved. Let them follow up the fine contributions they have already made toward the reorganization of our national legislature until the fight is finally and fully won.

Three Choices

In general, it seems to me that Congress now has three choices before it. First, it may endeavor to carry on unchanged. This course would mean that Congress would suffer from more and more pressure of work, mitigated slightly from time to time by haphazard delegation of powers; that its tasks would be on such a scale that it would be humanly impossible to do them well; and that consequently it would continue to decline in public esteem, leaving effective leadership to the President or running the risk of recurring deadlocks.

Second, Congress may adopt some minor changes designed to improve its research and staff facilities, make more efficient use of its time, and provide itself better pay and retirement benefits; but avoid the basic reforms in its committee structure and operation, in coordination of legislative policy, in strengthening party responsibility, in promoting better teamwork with the Executive, and in improving fiscal control. This course would be helpful to the individual members, but it would leave the fundamental institutional problems unsolved.

Third, Congress may raise its sights, overcome its inertia, and adopt the comprehensive and courageous program of reforms drawn up by its own bipartisan joint committee. This course would at once revitalize representative government in the United States, expedite the solution of our postwar problems, and renew popular faith in American democracy.

If "practical politics" and vested interests prevail, a few individuals will retain their transient powers and privileges, but Congress as an institution will continue to decline. Representative government will gradually fall into further disuse and disrepute. The conduct of public affairs will continue to shift to the executive branch and Congress will become, as Senator O'Mahoney has warned, "merely a timid and formal appendix to bureaucracy"—an anachronism in a totalitarian era—a monument to a noble past where tourists will come to watch and wonder at the ancient rites and parliamentary ceremony, and listen in Statuary Hall to the nostalgic echoes of bygone days.

Considering the pace of the legislative process, the complete reconstruction of Congress will be a matter, not of days or weeks, but of months and years. Meanwhile, conditions will change and new problems and relationships will arise that will require follow-up of the gains already achieved. The machinery of government at all levels needs continuous study and frequent readjustment to fit the changing requirements of the modern world. This applies, as William Y. Elliott of Harvard has pointed out,[4] not only to the organization of Congress, but also to the executive branch, to relationships between the federal government and the states and municipalities of the nation, and to the emerging relations betwen the United States and the new international organizations such as the UNO, UNRRA, UNESCO, et al. The reconstruction of Congress must be geared into the reorganization of the federal administrative structure; and the multifarious relations of the federal government to the states, on the one hand, and to the various aspects of world organization, on the other, must also form a part of any complete consideration of our total machinery of government.

Congress is the logical and responsible place where such continuing study of our entire governmental machinery should be carried on. For one of its principal responsibilities is to authorize adequate organizations for the execution of policies it has approved. In order to follow up, therefore, the work of congressional committees in this field, to evaluate the measures that are adopted to modernize the machinery of the national government, and to scrutinize those intergovernmental relationships at home and abroad—subsidies, federal aid, international aviation, telecommunications, etc.—that require the support and approval of Congress, provision should be made for this activity. This important task might be assigned to one of the standing committees in each house, or, as Dr. Elliott has suggested, to a new joint committee on the whole machinery of government with subcommittees on the organization of Congress, the federal administrative structure, federal-state-local relations, and on international machinery. In this way Congress could keep our governmental plant and equipment abreast of the needs of the atomic age.

---

[4] In a memorandum to Senator La Follette dated February 21, 1946.

Postscript

AFTER THIS BOOK was written and while it was in press, the 79th Congress passed the Legislative Reorganization Act of 1946. Upsetting the pessimistic predictions of Capitol Hill observers, the Senate approved the reform bill on June 10 and the House of Representatives followed suit on July 25. This legislative miracle was achieved by thumping majorities in both chambers: the vote being 49 to 16 in the Senate and 229 to 61 in the House. On July 26 the Senate concurred in the House amendments to the bill, instead of sending it to conference which would have been the normal procedure. The danger of the disappearance of a quorum in the lower house, caused by the exodus of members from Washington as final adjournment approached, precluded resort to this procedure. And on August 2 President Truman signed this epoch-making bill in an impressive ceremony at the White House in the presence of the members of the Joint Committee on the Organization of Congress.

Reforms Achieved

As a result of this forward step toward congressional self-improvement, several of the reforms recommended in this book will become effective at the beginning of the 80th Congress in January, 1947. The committee structure of both houses will be streamlined, reducing the number of Senate standing committees from 33 to 15 and those in the House from 48 to 19. Inactive minor committees will be abolished, those with overlapping jurisdictions merged, and roughly parallel systems set up in both chambers. The jurisdictions of the reorganized committees will be clearly defined in the rules. Hereafter no senator will serve on more than two standing committees, and (with minor exceptions) no representative will serve on more than one committee. Every committee will be a major active committee and every member will have one or two important, manageable committee assignments.

Each of the new committees, moreover, will be authorized to employ a staff of independent, qualified specialists in its field, appointed on merit, to aid it in lawmaking and in keeping watch over the execution of the laws in its province. The act also provides for a considerable expansion of the legislative reference and bill drafting services which are the research and legal arms of the Congress.

As steps toward reduction of the work-load and toward concentration on national problems, the reform act divests Congress of the mass of petty work connected with the settlement of private claims and pensions, the building of bridges over navigable waters, and other private and local legislation by banning the introduction of private bills.

The act also regularizes committee procedure as regards hearings, meetings, and record-keeping and expedites the reporting of bills. Committee powers are defined, and permission to sit while the Senate is in session is restricted. Conference committees will be confined to the consideration of matters in disagreement between the two houses, and legislative riders on appropriation bills are outlawed.

A long-sought reform is achieved in the provision requiring the registration of organized groups and their agents whose principal activity is seeking to influence legislation. They will also be required to file detailed quarterly accounts of their receipts and expenditures. This will not impair the right of petition or the freedom of citizens to make proper representations to their Congressmen. But it will help legislators to evaluate the pleas of pressure groups and weigh their worth. Beset by swarms of lobbyists seeking to protect this or that small segment of the economy or to advance this or that narrow interest, Congress has hitherto found it difficult to discover the real majority will and to legislate in the public interest. The true attitude of public opinion is often distorted and obscured by the pressures of special-interest groups.

Another major achievement of the reorganization act is the provision for a Legislative Budget fixing a ceiling on total appropriations. This budget is to be formulated by February 15 each year for the ensuing fiscal year by the taxing and spending committees of both houses, acting jointly. They shall recommend a reduction or increase of the public debt according as they estimate that federal receipts will exceed or fall below expenditures. While this provision is little more than a pious gesture in its present form, since no method is provided for its enforcement, nevertheless it constitutes a promising first step toward strengthening congressional control of federal expenditures. The reform act also makes several improvements in the legislative phase of the budget process by lifting the veil of secrecy from hearings on appropriation bills, allowing members time to study appropriation hearings and reports before their floor consideration, permitting the committees on appropriations to expand their professional staffs, forbidding the reappropriation of unobligated balances, and limiting permanent appropriations. Expenditure analyses of each executive agency by the Comptroller General will furnish a double check upon the economy and efficiency of administrative management.

It is expected that better organization, improved procedures, and a lighter work-load will enable the Congress, which has been in almost continuous session since 1940, to adjourn *sine die* at the end of July each year. This will allow Congressmen to keep in closer touch with their constituents and to recharge their physical batteries.

While the quality of the present personnel of our national legislature is as high as it ever was in the good old days of Webster, Clay, and Calhoun, the composition of Congress can still be improved. To this end, as well as to help members meet the rising cost of living and campaigning, the act raises congressional salaries 25 per cent to $12,500. It also grants each member a tax-free allowance of $2,500 a year to assist in defraying expenses incurred in the discharge of his official duties. This increase compares with equivalent advances in the compensation of federal employees since 1925 when the salaries of Congressmen were last raised.

Finally, the act makes members of Congress eligible to join the federal retirement system on a contributory basis—a step which will encourage super-annuated members to retire and conduce to the sense of security and greater independence of thought and action on the part of the younger members.

Significant Omissions

Thus, the Legislative Reorganization Act of 1946 was an impressive achievement. In one quick leap Congress jumped the hurdles of timidity, inertia, and vested interest and modernized much of its machinery and methods. All told, it added up to the most sweeping reorganization in congressional history. But at best it was only a beginning, although a good one. For the bill was considerably diluted before it finally passed, and several important reforms never went beyond the discussion stage.

On at least two significant matters the report of the Joint Committee was silent: the selection of committee chairmen by some better method than seniority, and the powers of the Committee on Rules of the House of Representatives. Although it is widely believed that the seniority custom has serious drawbacks and that the House Rules Committee has usurped powers it ought not to exercise, the Joint Committee was unable to agree upon workable changes in these existing practices. And so the new law does not change these customs.

Nor does it deal with the problem of filibusters in the Senate, upon which the Joint Committee was not at liberty to make any recommendations under its terms of reference. Nor does it make any provision for implementing party responsibility via the proposed majority and minority policy committees, or for promoting better teamwork between Congress and the President via the suggested joint legislative-executive council, or for assisting Congressmen with their departmental business through the appointment of executive assistants, or for making the legislative budget ceilings effective. The last four major provisions were struck from the bill as it passed the Senate by the House leadership as a price of its admission to the floor of the House.[1]

Several minor provisions in the Senate-approved bill met the same fate: (1) the ban on the creation of special investigating committees; (2) the "docket day" provision whereby Congressmen could appear before committees to urge public hearings on their bills; (3) permissive joint hearings of parallel Senate and House committees on the same bills; (4) nontechnical bill digests in committee reports; and (5) a requirement that committees keep records of the attendance of committeemen at their meetings. Thus it will be seen that several major reforms, as well as a number of minor procedural changes, remain to be achieved. The fight for these improvements will doubtless be resumed by members of the 80th Congress.

Chief credit for passage of the Legislative Reorganization Act rightfully belongs to Senator La Follette, chairman, and Representative Monroney, vice chairman of the joint committee which produced the reform bill. A pioneer advocate of congressional reform and an ac-

---

[1] Administrative assistants to senators and Senate policy committees were later provided for in a supplemental appropriation act for the fiscal year 1947.

knowledged master of parliamentary strategy, La Follette piloted the bill through four days of Senate debate to final approval on June 10. Almost single-handed he bore the brunt of the fight for the bill on the floor before galleries packed with attentive visitors. Despite the importance of the measure and the great public interest in it, floor attendance dropped at times to as few as seventeen senators. Opposition to the bill was confined to a few southern members who unexpectedly confined their attack to the relatively minor provision for the creation of a director of congressional personnel. This new officer would have been assigned the twofold task of coordinating the scattered internal housekeeping services of the Congress and recommending a modern system of personnel administration for its employees. This horrendous provision was denounced as setting up a "superlord over the Senate" by half a dozen senators who have a vested interest in the patronage system on Capitol Hill. One senator devoted two and one-half hours to a defense of his right to appoint page boys from his home state, although he admitted that he had never made any such appointments. Finally, to save his bill, Senator La Follette sacrificed this minor section, the opposition evaporated, and approval quickly followed.

After the bill passed the Senate almost intact, save for the decapitation of the personnel "director-generalissimo," as Senator McKellar described him, it was messaged to the House of Representatives where for six weeks it rested quietly on the speaker's table while Representatives Monroney and Dirksen dickered with the House leadership over the conditions of its admission to the House floor. The upshot of these protracted negotiations was the deletion from the Senate-approved bill of a group of provisions designed to bring about a better meshing of our governmental gears. Closer liaison between House and Senate via joint hearings of their twin committees on matters of mutual interest; coordination between the standing committees of each chamber and overall planning of the legislative program by means of policy committees; and better teamwork between Congress and the President via a joint legislative-executive council were the major items in the price that had to be paid before the bill received a "green light" to the House floor. Those who are familiar with the need for these improvements in our governmental machinery will appreciate how heavy a price it was. After eight hours of debate, brilliantly led by Representatives Monroney and Dirksen and ably supported by other members, the reorganization bill passed the House on July 25 substantially in the form in which it had been reported to that body.

Power of the Speaker

To students of government the role of the speaker of the House in the dilution of the legislative reorganization bill was illuminating. As presiding officer of the House and high priest of its rules, he was naturally deeply interested in the proposed changes. As the central figure in policy making in the lower chamber, he faced a probable diminution of his power through the functions to be assigned to the proposed seven-man majority policy committee. As one of the "Big Four" who meet every Monday with the President while Congress is in session to consider the legislative program, perhaps he saw no need of superseding these smoothly working informal conferences by a formal joint legislative-executive council. And so these important sections of the bill had to be deleted before it could leave the speaker's table and receive the blessing of the Rules Committee.

Responsibility for the pruning of the Senate-approved bill before it reached the floor of the House was shared by the speaker with Majority Leader John W. McCormack and Minority Leader Joseph W. Martin, Jr. with whom he conferred. He also acted to a considerable extent upon the advice of the parliamentarian of the House, Lewis Deschler, who sits at the speaker's table and is a real power behind the speaker's throne. The parliamentarian is an appointive officer and the present incumbent has served the House ably for twenty years. Mr. Deschler is unexcelled in his knowledge of procedure in the House of Representatives and has made himself indispensable to successive speakers. His political experience has been largely confined to the hall of the House and he claims no special acquaintance with committee or appropriation procedure or with the external relationships of the Congress. It would not be surprising, therefore, if he were more concerned with preserving the power of the speaker than with strengthening Congress as an institution in the entire scheme of government.

To the layman not learned in legislative ways it may seem an astonishing piece of political piracy that a few leaders can intercept a bill in its transit from the Senate to the House and prune it to fit their personal views. Press commentators at the time characterized it as a travesty on the democratic process that one man should be able to substitute his judgment for that of a joint committee which had studied the subject intensively for more than a year, for that of forty-nine senators who approved the measure in its unexpurgated form, and for that of those representatives who would have voted for the stricken provisions if given a chance. To others it also seemed a travesty on the Constitution which provides that "each House may determine the rules of its proceedings," not one or a few members thereof. But to those initiated in the inherited scheme of use and wont, whose minds were duly disciplined by the established order of legislative affairs, it all seemed quite fitting, proper, and inevitable.

Appendix

TABLE I

REGIONAL DISTRIBUTION OF SEATS IN THE HOUSE OF REPRESENTATIVES*

Region	1789–1791 1st Congress	1845–1847 29th Congress	1895–1897 54th Congress	1945–1947 79th Congress
New England..........	17	31	27	28
Middle Atlantic.......	18	63	72	92
North Central........	0	50	128	131
South Atlantic........	30	47	50	56
South Central........	0	39	62	79
Mountain............	0	0	7	16
Pacific..............	0	2	11	33
Total...........	65	232	357	435

* Based on the regional classification of states of the U. S. Bureau of the Census.

TABLE II

POPULATION AND POLITICAL POWER IN 1940

Region	Per Cent of Total Population	Per Cent of Senate Seats
New England..................	6.4	12.5
Middle Atlantic...............	20.9	6.2
East North Central............	20.2	10.4
West North Central............	10.2	14.6
South Atlantic.................	13.5	16.6
East South Central............	8.2	8.3
West South Central............	10.0	8.3
Mountain.....................	3.1	16.6
Pacific.......................	7.4	6.2

TABLE III

QUALIFICATIONS OF MEMBERSHIP OF 1ST, 29TH, 54TH, AND 79TH CONGRESSES

Qualification	1st Congress	29th Congress	54th Congress	79th Congress
Median Age of Representatives......	44	41	48	52
Education:				
College.........................	45	126	254	72*
High School....................	15	61	75	12*
Grammar School†...............	10	44	88	7*
Total........................	70	231	417	91*
Legal training:				
Senators.......................	15	53	65	62
Representatives.................	24	163	240	241
Total........................	39	216	305	303
Previous Legislative Experience:‡				
Senators.......................	25	52	72	49
Representatives.................	58	157	82	158
Total........................	83	209	154	207
Number of Senators...............	26	56	90	96
Number of Representatives.........	65	232	357	435
Total Membership...........	91	288	447	531

* Senators only.
† Attendance at "public schools" is classified under this head.
‡ Does not include previous consecutive terms in the same house in which the member was serving, but does include service in city councils, state legislatures, the House of Representatives in the case of Senators, and a previous non-consecutive term in the same house.

TABLE IV

OCCUPATIONAL DISTRIBUTION OF THE MEMBERSHIP OF THE 79TH CONGRESS, 1ST SESSION*

Occupation or Profession	Senate	House of Representatives	Total
Accountant	0	3	3
Agriculture	3	15	18
Author	0	2	2
Banking	2	10	12
Business and/or Manufacturing	10	47	57
Dentistry	1	3	4
Editing, Publishing or Journalism	10	24	34
Education	2	24	26
Investments	0	3	3
Law	62	241	303
Legislator	2	4	6
Medicine and Surgery	0	7	7
Municipal Officer	0	6	6
Pharmacy	0	2	2
Real Estate and/or Insurance	0	24	24
Secretary—Congressional	2	4	6
Social Welfare	0	2	2
Union Official	0	2	2
Miscellaneous	2	11	13
Vacancies	0	1	1
Total	96	435	531

* Sources: *Congressional Directory, Who's Who in America,* and *Martindale-Hubbell Law Directory.*

TABLE V

APPORTIONMENT OF 435 REPRESENTATIVES AMONG INDUSTRY
GROUPS BY THE METHOD OF EQUAL PROPORTIONS*

Group	No. of Employed 14 Years Old and Over	Representatives
Total Employed	45,166,083	
Industry not reported	688,836	
Basis for Apportionment	44,477,247	435
Agriculture, forestry and fishing	8,475,432	83
Mining	913,000	9
Construction	2,056,274	20
Manufacturing	10,572,842	104
Transportation, communications and other public utilities	3,113,353	30
Wholesale and retail trade	7,538,768	74
Finance, insurance and real estate	1,467,597	14
Business and repair services	864,254	8
Personal services	4,009,317	39
Amusement, recreation and related services	395,342	4
Professional and related services	3,317,581	33
Government	1,753,487	17

* Source of number of employed workers: Sixteenth Census of the United States, Population Volume II, Part 1, p. 99.

TABLE VI*

COMMITTEE ACTIVITY IN THE 78TH CONGRESS, AS MEASURED BY BILLS REFERRED, BILLS REPORTED, AND HEARINGS HELD

Senate

Committees	Bills Referred		Bills Reported		Hearings	
	Number	Per Cent of Total	Number	Per Cent of Total	Number	Per Cent of Total
Total number...........	[1]2,670	100.0	[1]909	100.0	[1]1,543	100.0
Agriculture and Forestry......	130	4.9	32	3.5	180	11.7
Appropriations...............	62	2.3	45	4.9	240	15.6
Audit and Control the Contingent Expenses of the Senate..	157	5.9	115	12.6	...	...
Banking and Currency.........	105	3.9	25	2.7	118	7.7
Civil Service.................	66	2.5	9	1.0	20	1.3
Claims.......................	909	...	579	...	41	...
Commerce....................	146	5.5	67	7.4	110	7.1
District of Columbia..........	93	3.5	52	5.7	76	4.9
Education and Labor..........	64	2.4	19	2.1	59	3.8
Enrolled Bills................	...	...	...	...	...	...
Expenditures in the Executive Departments................	17	.6	3	.3	2	.1
Finance......................	270	10.1	26	2.9	83	5.4
Foreign Relations.............	53	2.0	16	1.8	71	4.6
Immigration..................	79	3.0	22	2.4	5	.3
Indian Affairs................	105	3.9	37	4.1	5	.3
Interoceanic Canals...........	8	.3	2	.2	...	...
Interstate Commerce..........	88	3.3	18	2.0	97	6.3
Irrigation and Reclamation....	27	1.0	13	1.4	4	.3
Judiciary....................	240	9.0	56	6.2	144	9.3
Library......................	22	.8	3	.3	...	...
Manufactures.................	...	...	...	...	...	...
Military Affairs..............	301	11.3	88	9.7	191	12.4
Mines and Mining............	11	.4	5	.6	6	.4
Naval Affairs.................	203	7.6	117	12.9	34	2.2
Patents......................	6	.2	2	.2	2	.1
Pensions.....................	115	4.3	9	1.0	...	...
Post Offices and Post Roads....	98	3.7	27	3.0	22	1.4
Printing.....................	27	1.0	13	1.4	1	.1
Privileges and Elections.......	15	.6	4	.4	19	1.2
Public Buildings and Grounds..	14	.5	8	.9	6	.4
Public Lands and Surveys......	99	3.7	57	6.3	26	1.7
Rules........................	14	.5	1	.1	...	...
Territories and Insular Affairs..	26	1.0	16	1.8	22	1.4
Special committees	9	.3	2	.2	[2]204	...

[1] Excludes data for Claims Committee.
[2] Excluded from total.
* This and the following table compiled by H. B. Price and C. R. Gibbs, Federal Law Section, Legislative Reference Service, Library of Congress, Apr. 12, 1945.

TABLE VI*—*Continued*

House of Representatives

Committees	Bills Referred Number	Bills Referred Per Cent of Total	Bills Reported Number	Bills Reported Per Cent of Total	Hearings Number	Hearings Per Cent of Total
Total number..........	¹5,405	100.0	¹1,012	100.0	2,615	100.0
Accounts.....................	77	1.4	64	6.3	1	...
Agriculture..................	203	3.8	34	3.3	138	5.3
Appropriations..............	65	1.2	45	4.4	509	19.5
Banking and Currency.........	175	3.2	14	1.4	119	4.6
Census.......................	5	.1	...	...	2	.1
Civil Service.................	115	2.1	19	1.9	57	2.2
Claims.......................	1,612	...	737	...	...	...
Coinage, Weights, and Measures	16	.3	2	.2	6	.2
Disposition of Executive Papers	3	.1	...	...	...	...
District of Columbia..........	116	2.2	42	4.2	35	1.3
Education....................	26	.5	2	.2	21	.8
Election of President, Vice Pres-ident, and Representatives in Congress....................	36	.7	1	.1	12	.5
Elections No. 1................	...	...	1	.1	...	...
Elections No. 2................	...	...	1	.1	1	...
Elections No. 3................	1	...	3	.3	2	.1
Enrolled bills.................	...	...	...	...	...	...
Expenditures in the Executive Departments.'..............	65	1.2	8	.8	19	.7
Flood Control................	45	.8	5	.5	33	1.3
Foreign Affairs...............	116	2.2	12	1.2	93	3.6
Immigration and Naturalization	245	4.5	74	7.3	33	1.3
Indian Affairs................	107	2.0	30	3.0	25	1.0
Insular Affairs...............	23	.4	4	.4	39	1.5
Interstate and Foreign Com-merce......................	221	4.1	46	4.5	172	6.6
Invalid Pensions..............	406	7.5	6	.6	9	.3
Irrigation and Reclamation....	32	.6	14	1.4	31	1.2
Judiciary.....................	467	8.7	60	5.9	124	4.8
Labor.......................	43	.8	3	.3	55	2.1
Library......................	23	.4	5	.5	3	.1
Memorials...................	...	...	...	...	...	...
Merchant Marine and Fisheries	102	1.9	30	3.0	137	5.2
Military Affairs..............	765	14.2	68	6.7	181	6.9
Mines and Mining............	17	.3	6	.6	...	...
Naval Affairs.................	259	4.8	75	7.4	178	6.8
Patents......................	23	.4	4	.4	8	.3

, ¹ Excludes data for Claims Committee.

(*Continued*)

TABLE VI*—*Continued*

House of Representatives

Committees	Bills Referred		Bills Reported		Hearings	
	Number	Per Cent of Total	Number	Per Cent of Total	Number	Per Cent of Total
Pensions....................	96	1.8	1	.1	1	...
Post Office and Post Roads.....	117	2.2	27	2.7	61	2.3
Printing....................	66	1.2	40	3.9	...	...
Public Buildings and Grounds..	45	.8	11	1.1	68	2.6
Public Lands................	123	2.3	46	4.5	64	2.4
Revision of the Laws..........	6	.1	4	.4	1	...
Rivers and Harbors...........	88	1.6	2	.2	34	1.3
Roads......................	29	.5	4	.4	45	1.7
Rules......................	272	5.0	142	14.0	89	3.4
Territories.................	22	.4	9	.9	...	...
War Claims.................	59	1.1	1	.1	...	...
Ways and Means.............	430	7.9	31	3.1	173	6.6
World War Veterans' Legislation................	255	4.7	16	1.6	36	1.4
Special committees...........	...	...	...	...	[2]355	...

[2] Excluded from total.

TABLE VII

ANALYSIS OF CONGRESSIONAL STAFF AS OF JUNE, 1944

Department or Office	Number of Employees		
	Senate	House	Total
Office of the Secretary or Clerk...............	63	87	150
Office of Sergeant-at-Arms..................	190	50	240
Office of Doorkeeper.......................	39	187	226
Office of Postmaster.......................	27	45	72
Office of Speaker..........................	...	9	9
Office of Legislative Counsel................	5	7	12
Chaplain.................................	1	1	2
Clerks to Members........................	364	1,145	1,509
Standing Committee Employees.............	259	133	392
Joint Committee on Internal Revenue Taxation	...	...	16
Joint Committee on Printing.................	...	...	3
Joint Committee on Federal Expenditures.....	...	...	4
Special Inquiries and Investigations..........	62	83	145
Folding Documents........................	13	45	58
Joint Roll, Detailed Metropolitan Police......	...	...	20
Joint Roll, Capitol Police...................	...	...	60
Special and Minority Employees.............	2	19	21
Official Reporters*........................	...	28	28
Furniture & Repair Shop...................	6	14	20
	1,031	1,853	2,987†

* Reporting of Senate debates and hearings is handled by contracts with private firms.
† Including joint employees.

TABLE VIII

Cost of Congress in 1944

(rounded in thousands of dollars)

Items	House	Senate	Total
Salaries of Members........................	$ 4,339	$ 960	$ 5,299
Mileage of Members........................	170	47	217
Salaries—Officers and Employees.............	4,573	2,419	6,992
Salaries—Capitol and Detailed Police.........	86	96	182
Police Uniforms and Equipment..............	5	5	10
Automobile and maintenance, Speaker and Vice President................................	3	3	6
Legislative Counsel.........................	40	31	71
Reporting Debates and Hearings.............	33	75	108
Joint Committee on Internal Revenue Taxation	34	34	68
Joint Committee on Printing.................	7	7	14
Joint Committee on Federal Expenditures.....	9	9	18
Furniture, Repairs, etc......................	37	5	42
Special Investigations.......................	474	346	820
Folding Documents..........................	25	13	38
Kitchens and Restaurants....................	27	35	62
Fuel for Heating Apparatus..................	...	1	1
Mail Transportation........................	...	3	3
Postage....................................	23	5	28
Stationery.................................	282	41	323
Storage of Documents.......................	...	2	2
Miscellaneous Items........................	68	331	399
	$10,235	$4,468	$14,703

TABLE IX

STAFFING OF CONGRESS

79th Congress—1st Session‡

Committees	Senate			House		
	Clerks and Assts.	Janitors and Mesgrs.	Total Salary	Clerks and Assts.	Janitors and Mesgrs.	Total Salary
*Accounts				2	1	7,320
*Agriculture				2	1	7,320
*Agriculture & Forestry	6		15,780			
Appropriations	9	1	37,340	10	2	60,100
*Audit & Control the Contingent Expenses	5		13,200			
Banking & Currency	4†		17,400	2	1	5,760
*Census				1	1	4,020
Civil Service	5		13,500	1	1	4,020
Claims	6		17,400	3	1	8,820
*Coinage, Weights, & Measures				1	1	4,020
*Commerce	6		16,200			
*Disposition of Executive Papers				1	...	2,760
District of Columbia	6		21,480	2	1	7,020
*Education				1	1	4,020
*Education & Labor	6†		15,180			
*Election of President, Vice President & Representatives				1	...	2,760
*Elections No. 1				1	1	4,020
*Elections No. 2				1	1	4,020
*Elections No. 3				1	1	4,020
Enrolled Bills	5		12,120	1	1	4,020
Expenditures in Executive Depts	6		15,900	1	1	4,560
*Finance	9	1	29,720			
*Flood Control				1	1	4,020
*Foreign Affairs				2	1	7,020
*Foreign Relations	7	1	19,980			
*Immigration	6		14,700			
*Immigration & Naturalization				2	1	6,960
Indian Affairs	6		18,200	2	1	7,020
*Insular Affairs				1	1	4,020
*Interoceanic Canals	5		12,540			
*Interstate Commerce	6		17,760			
*Interstate & Foreign Commerce				3	1	10,200
Irrigation & Reclamation	5		12,300	1	1	4,020
*Invalid Pensions				4	1	13,020
Judiciary	5		14,160	3	1	9,900
*Labor				2	1	5,760
Library	5		12,720	1	1	4,020
*Manufactures	5		12,360			

(Continued)

TABLE IX—*Continued*

STAFFING OF CONGRESS

70th Congress—1st Session‡

Committees	Senate			House		
	Clerks and Assts.	Janitors and Mesgrs.	Total Salary	Clerks and Assts.	Janitors and Mesgrs.	Total Salary
*Memorials				...	...	...
*Merchant Marine & Fisheries				2	1	5,760
Military Affairs	7		19,460	2	1	6,960
Mines and Mining	7		15,720	1	1	4,020
Naval Affairs	5		13,620	2	1	6,960
Patents	5		12,720	2	1	6,110
Pensions	6		15,360	2	1	6,720
Post Offices & Post Roads	7		17,760	2	1	6,960
Printing	4		10,500	1	1	4,320
*Privileges & Elections	5		12,540			
Public Buildings & Grounds	6		14,120	2	1	6,300
*Public Lands				2	1	6,300
*Public Lands & Surveys	6		15,600			
*Revision of Laws				1	1	4,560
*Rivers & Harbors				2	1	7,020
*Roads				2	1	5,760
Rules	5		13,500	3	1	8,460
*Territories				1	1	4,020
*Territories & Insular Affairs	7		16,720			
*Un-American Activities				3	1	10,200
*War Claims				2	1	6,300
*Ways and Means				5	3	20,100
*World War Veterans				2	...	5,760

* Committee exists in one house only.
† $6000 of the total salary was given for additional personnel which was not enumerated.
‡ Based on the Legislative Appropriation Act for fiscal 1946. The table does not always fit the facts for the Senate committees because of the mixture of their staffs with the clerks of their chairmen.

TABLE X

ANALYSIS OF SENATE EMPLOYEE PAY ROLLS, BY TYPE OF POSITION AND
RANGE OF EARNINGS, FISCAL YEAR 1944*

Legislative Positions	Total Number of Employees	Range of Earnings											
		Under $1,000	$1,000 to $1,499	$1,500 to $1,999	$2,000 to $2,499	$2,500 to $2,999	$3,000 to $3,499	$3,500 to $3,999	$4,000 to $4,499	$4,500 to $4,999	$5,000 to $5,499	$5,500 to $6,000	Over $6,000
Secretary of the Senate	63	0	10	12	15	8	3	3	4	2	2	1	3
Sergeant at Arms†	344	4	72	208	18	24	10	2	0	2	0	1	3
Clerks to standing committees	32	0	0	1	0	0	1	9	3	16	1	0	1
Assistant clerks to standing committees	227	3	9	82	57	39	19	10	4	2	1	0	1
Chaplain	1	0	0	1	0	0	0	0	0	0	0	0	0
Clerks to Senators and Vice President	65	0	0	0	0	1	4	18	15	27	0	0	0
Assistant clerks to Senators and Vice President	299	4	10	116	105	37	16	9	1	1	0	0	0
Legislative counsel	5	0	0	0	0	1	0	0	2	0	0	0	2
Joint Committee on Internal Revenue Taxation	16	1	0	2	3	3	0	0	0	3	0	2	2
Joint Committee on Printing	3	0	0	0	0	2	0	0	0	1	0	0	0
Joint Committee on Federal Expenditures	4	0	0	1	1	0	1	0	0	1	0	0	0
Inquiries and investments	62	0	5	11	12	4	5	9	1	1	3	2	9
Folding documents	13	4	3	4	2	0	0	0	0	0	0	0	0
Total	1,134	16	109	438	213	119	59	60	30	56	7	6	21

* Source: Hearings before the Joint Committee on the Organization of Congress, pp. 1070–1071.
† Includes joint police roll and detailed police roll.

TABLE XI

ANALYSIS OF HOUSE OF REPRESENTATIVES EMPLOYEE PAY ROLLS, BY DEPARTMENTS OR OFFICES AND RANGE OF SALARIES, FISCAL YEAR 1944

Department or Office	Total Number of Employees	Under $500	$500 to $999	$1,000 to $1,449	$1,500 to $1,999	$2,000 to $2,499	$2,500 to $2,999	$3,000 to $3,499	$3,500 to $3,999	$4,000 to $4,499	$4,500 to $4,999	$5,000 to $5,499	$5,500 to $6,000	Over $6,000
Clerks to Members	1,145	12	58	106	221	196	189	110	204	27	22	0	0	0
Committee employees	133	1	3	27	25	17	24	21	4	3	5	1	0	2
Office of the Clerk	87	0	0	16	35	14	7	3	5	1	0	4	1	1
Office of Sergeant at Arms	50	0	0	1	39	1	2	3	1	1	0	0	1	1
Office of Doorkeeper	187	0	0	116	49	10	5	3	2	0	0	1	1	0
Office of Postmaster	45	0	0	1	40	2	1	0	0	0	0	1	0	0
Office of the Speaker and Parliamentarian	9	0	0	0	2	4	0	0	0	0	2	0	0	1
Chaplain	1	0	0	0	0	0	1	0	0	0	0	0	0	0
Special and minority employees, offices of majority and minority floor leaders	19	0	0	0	5	4	1	6	1	0	0	2	0	0
Official reporters of debates, official committee reporters and transcribers	28	0	0	0	0	13	0	1	0	1	0	0	2	11
Legislative counsel	7	0	0	0	0	2	0	1	0	0	1	0	0	3
Furniture and repair shop	14	0	0	3	2	1	8	0	0	0	0	0	0	0
Special and select investigating committees	83	0	2	1	10	22	6	5	11	5	4	2	7	8
Folding documents	45	13	14	14	3	1	0	0	0	0	0	0	0	0
Joint Committee on Internal Revenue Taxation	16	0	1	0	2	3	3	0	0	0	3	0	2	2
Joint Committee on Printing	3	0	0	0	0	0	2	0	0	0	1	0	0	0
Joint Committee on Federal Expenditures	4	0	0	0	1	1	0	1	0	0	1	0	0	0
Joint roll, detailed Metropolitan Police	20	0	0	0	0	16	1	3	0	0	0	0	0	0
Joint roll, Capitol Police*	60	0	0	0	59	0	1	0	0	0	0	0	0	0
Total	1,956	26	78	285	493	307	251	157	228	38	39	11	14	29

* Effective July 1, 1944, the "Joint roll, Capitol Police," was divided between the House of Representatives and the United States Senate under the jurisdiction of their respective Sergeants at Arms.

TABLE XII

ESTIMATE OF 1947 EXPENDITURES BY THE GOVERNMENT FOR RETIREMENT

Civil Service employees under Civil Service Retirement Act $220,000,000
State Department Foreign Service personnel 1,051,000
Judiciary: Supreme Court judges, Circuit judges, District judges, and mis-
cellaneous judges 527,000
Army:
 Officers 21,798,500
 Enlisted men 40,226,934
 Nurses... 6,481,650
 Warrant Officers 2,965,000
Navy:
 Officers 20,063,000
 Enlisted men.. 26,572,526
Marine Corps:
 Officers 2,900,000
 Enlisted men.. 1,650,000
Coast Guard:
 Officers and enlisted men 6,059,675
Members of Congress 3,871,000*

* If contributions are made only for the last five years of service.

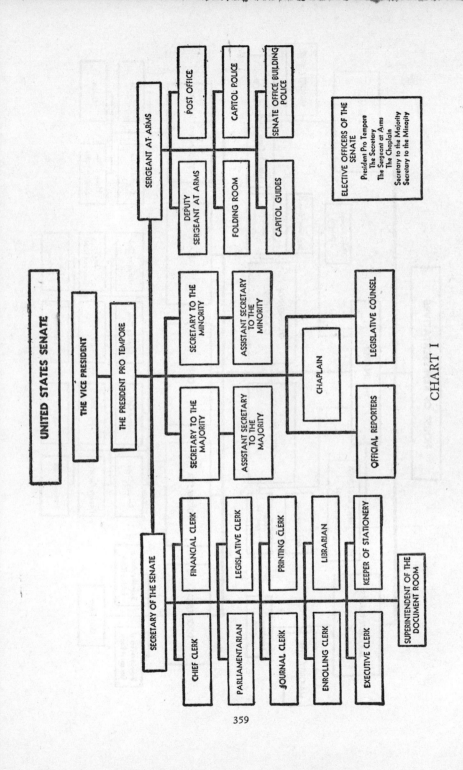

UNITED STATES SENATE

THE VICE PRESIDENT

THE PRESIDENT PRO TEMPORE

SERGEANT AT ARMS
- POST OFFICE
- CAPITOL POLICE
- SENATE OFFICE BUILDING POLICE
- DEPUTY SERGEANT AT ARMS
- FOLDING ROOM
- CAPITOL GUIDES

ELECTIVE OFFICERS OF THE SENATE
President Pro Tempore
The Secretary
The Sergeant at Arms
The Chaplain
Secretary to the Majority
Secretary to the Minority

SECRETARY TO THE MINORITY
ASSISTANT SECRETARY TO THE MINORITY

SECRETARY TO THE MAJORITY
ASSISTANT SECRETARY TO THE MAJORITY

CHAPLAIN

LEGISLATIVE COUNSEL

OFFICIAL REPORTERS

SECRETARY OF THE SENATE
- CHIEF CLERK
- FINANCIAL CLERK
- PARLIAMENTARIAN
- LEGISLATIVE CLERK
- JOURNAL CLERK
- PRINTING CLERK
- ENROLLING CLERK
- LIBRARIAN
- EXECUTIVE CLERK
- KEEPER OF STATIONERY
- SUPERINTENDENT OF THE DOCUMENT ROOM

CHART I

359

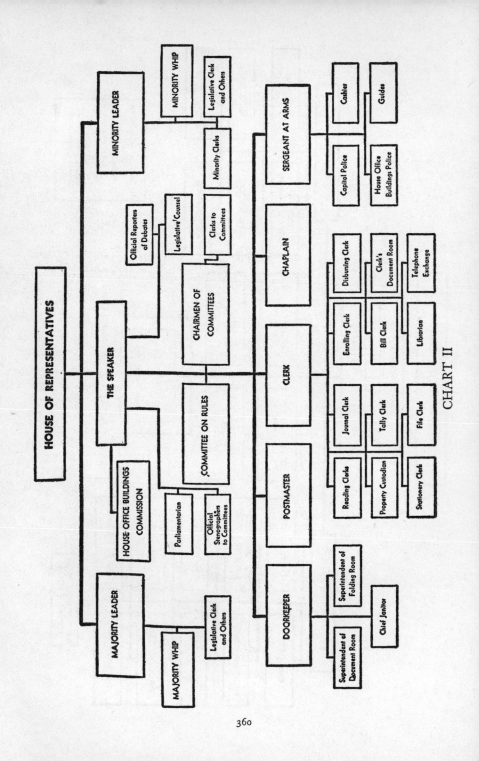

CHART II

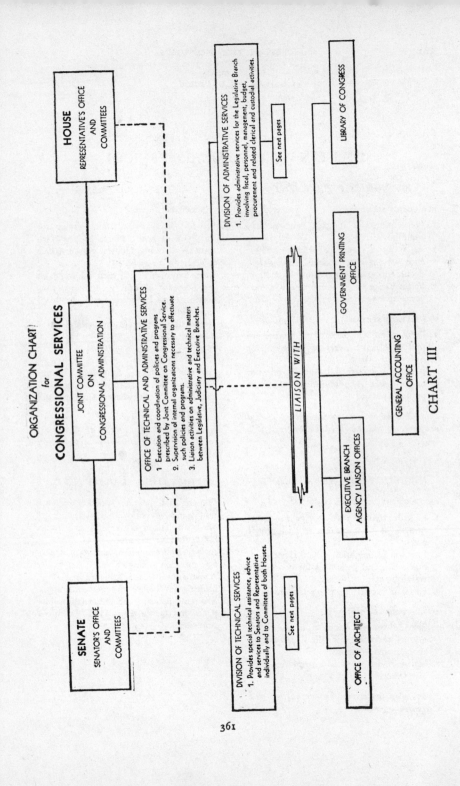

ORGANIZATION CHART
for
CONGRESSIONAL SERVICES

HOUSE
REPRESENTATIVE'S OFFICE
AND
COMMITTEES

SENATE
SENATOR'S OFFICE
AND
COMMITTEES

JOINT COMMITTEE
ON
CONGRESSIONAL ADMINISTRATION

OFFICE OF TECHNICAL AND ADMINISTRATIVE SERVICES
1. Execution and coordination of policies and programs prescribed by Joint Committee on Congressional Service.
2. Supervision of internal organizations necessary to effectuate such policies and programs.
3. Liaison activities on administrative and technical matters between Legislative, Judiciary and Executive Branches.

DIVISION OF ADMINISTRATIVE SERVICES
1. Provides administrative services for the Legislative Branch, involving fiscal, personnel, management, budget, procurement and related clerical and custodial activities.

See next pages

DIVISION OF TECHNICAL SERVICES
1. Provides special technical assistance, advice and services to Senators and Representatives individually and to Committees of both Houses.

See next pages

LIAISON WITH

LIBRARY OF CONGRESS

GOVERNMENT PRINTING OFFICE

GENERAL ACCOUNTING OFFICE

EXECUTIVE BRANCH AGENCY LIAISON OFFICES

OFFICE OF ARCHITECT

CHART III

361

Chart III—*Continued*

DIVISION OF TECHNICAL SERVICES

ECONOMICS DEPARTMENT

ECONOMICS SECTION

1. Preparation of indexes, digests and compilations.
2. Assembly of special collections of reference works, statutes, bills, reports and documents useful in framing legislation.
3. Performance of economic research, surveys, and reports.

TABULATING SECTION

1. Preparation of basic data studies of problems coming before Congress for committee work.
2. Assembly of statistical material relevant to proposed legislation, sampling of public opinion, etc.

Combines work now performed by special assignment and Library of Congress.

LEGAL DEPARTMENT

CONSULTATION SECTION

1. Provide legal consultation service for members of both Houses and to committees of both Houses on particular topics.
2. Keep committee chairmen informed on bills, executive orders, opinions, etc., pertinent to pending and proposed legislation.
3. Assist in drafting of proposed legislation and resolutions.

LIAISON SECTION

1. Assist in organizing committee hearings by liaison with Executive Branch.
2. Liaison with Legislative Counsel and Reference Service.

Combines work of Library of Congress; Loan Personnel; Committee Activity on Expert Legal Aid.

INVESTIGATION DEPARTMENT

GENERAL INVESTIGATION SECTION

1. Provide trained investigators for committees of Congress on an assignment basis.
2. Prepare confidential digest reports on businesses and personnel for committee activity.
3. Perform investigations on civil matters.

ACCOUNTING SECTION

1. Provide trained accountants for committees requiring specialized accounting analysis-investigations.
2. Maintain liaison with General Accounting Office.

Now being performed by committees and Executive agencies.

INFORMATION DEPARTMENT

1. Prepare materials for speeches on current topics of national interest.
2. Maintain liaison with press and radio for legislative releases.
3. Assist Congressmen in obtaining coverage on their speeches.
4. Assist committees in bringing important information before the general public.
5. Maintain liaison with information bureaus in the Judiciary and Executive Branches.

Chart III—*Continued*

DIVISION OF ADMINISTRATIVE SERVICES

TRANSPORTATION AND COM-MUNICATIONS DEPARTMENT

TRANSPORTATION SECTION

1. Secure itinerary routing and reservations for members of Congress, committee members, and employees of the Legislative Branch for foreign and domestic rail, air and steamship travel.
2. Perform liaison with State Department for purposes of obtaining passports for trips out of the country; and for subsequent visas from foreign embassies in the U. S.

COMMUNICATIONS SECTION

1. Provide direct contact service with telegraph, telephone and radio service; and on telephone service to perform such long distance and local service as required; maintaining constant switchboard and inter-communication service.

Combines railroad ticket offices; airlines ticket offices; telephone and telegraph space only for railroad and air offices.

PROCUREMENT DEPARTMENT

PURCHASE SECTION

1. Purchase all equipment, supplies and miscellaneous articles for the operation of the Legislative Branch exclusive of construction materials for major repairs to buildings and roads, and certain purchases for GPO, Library of Congress, and Office of Architect.

SUPPLY SECTION

1. Maintain stock room of supplies necessary for operation of Legislative Branch excluding Office of Architect, Library of Congress, Government Printing Office, Congressional Record and Agency Liaison Offices.

Combines committee activity; Architect's Office; Clerk's Office.

FISCAL DEPARTMENT

ACCOUNTS SECTION

1. Maintain accounts of all moneys allotted to Legislative Branch with exception of funds specifically appropriated to GPO, Office of Architect, Library of Congress for performance of their operations of a technical nature; maintain cost records as directed.

PAYROLL AND AUDIT SECTION

1. Prepare and disburse payrolls and paychecks; audit and pay vouchers for travel and other miscellaneous items; maintain cash fund for such banking services as check cashing and change and for other miscellaneous cash expenditures.

Centralizes appropriations now assigned to Clerks of Senate and House; committee clerks; Sgt. at Arms; Architect; Library offices.

PERSONNEL DEPARTMENT

1. Personnel orientation involving housing, recreation facilities, adjustment in new environment, liaison with state societies.
2. Recruitment of personnel
   a. When requested by members of Congress.
   b. Filling vacancies in organization.
   c. Promotion opportunities.
3. Liaison with Civil Service Commission and Executive Branch agencies on loan personnel for committee work.
4. Maintaining Employee Directory and Personnel Information Service for members of Congress.

Combines activity now in committee chairmen.

MANAGEMENT DEPARTMENT

1. Analyzation of administrative procedures.

Chart III—*Concluded*

2. Coordinate technical and administrative activities within Office of Technical and Administrative Services.
3. Perform management surveys within O.T.A.S.
4. Make available management consultants for committee activities in connection with Executive Branch operations.
5. Prepare digests for committee members' use on proposed organizations and changes in Executive Branch.
6. Maintain liaison with Bureau of Budget on management problems.

BUDGET DEPARTMENT

1. Preparation of tentative budgets for committee activities, showing suggested allocation of funds.
2. Preparation of operating budgets and comparative costs estimates for yearly appropriations of the Legislative Branch.

GENERAL SERVICES DEPARTMENT

1. Establish a Congressional Correspondence Unit for use of members in handling extraneous correspondence.
2. Provide automobile service or bus service for members of Congress for their official duties within the District of Columbia and environs.
3. Provide for use of Congressmen:
   a. Stenographic and clerical pool.
   b. Duplicating services.
   c. Assistance on local convention activities.
   d. Central point for obtaining housekeeping and special messenger service.

Custodial work now in Architect's Office and Sgt. at Arms; mail and messenger now in Architect's Office and committees.

Index

nesses, 184–185; work of individual Congressmen, 63–64; activity of, 350
committee system: development of, 87–96, 140–144; in House, 90; Legislative Counsel, 93–94; Legislative Reference Service, 94; personnel, borrowed, 95–96; staffing, 90–93; streamlining, 177
Commons, English House of, 13, 31
Comptroller General, 260–264
concurrent resolution, 102–103
conferences: committees, 98–100; news, 296
Congress, United States, vii, 13; admission to, 23–24; and public opinion, 310–322; as forum, 12; composition of, 22–48; conclusions concerning reorganization of, 334–339; functions of, 1–21, 234; housekeeping function of, 2; obstacles to reform of, 336–338; original design of, 1–4; oversight function of, 230; present pattern of, 4–21; public attitude toward, 288–293; relations with press, 293–297; size of, 24–25; theory of control, 231–232; three choices, 338–339; twentieth-century changes, 37–41
Congressional committees, 148–149
Congressional government, vii
Congressional Handbook, 154
Congressional Record, 153, 196, 219, 316; improvement of, 332
Congressional services: chart, 361; office of, 323–326; reorganizing, 323–339 (*see also* reconstruction of Congress)
Congressmen, 11–12; admission, conditions of, 23–24; age of, 28–29; committee work of, 63–64; expenses of, 42–43; floor attendance of, 64–65; health of, 65–67; historic, 32–34, 36; ideal, 45–48; improving quality of, 41–48; individual, work load on, 57–58; instructive function of, 316; new, training of, 43; qualifications of, 27–32; recalcitrant, 120; relations with constituents, 277–284; salaries of, 42–43, 326–329; tenure of, 26–28; today, 28–30; typical day, 58–60; Congresswomen, 29
Conkling, Roscoe, 35
Connally resolution, 267
Consent Calendar, 164
Constitution: amendments to, 3–4, 14–15; drafting of, 2
constituent chores, 3, 60–61
constituents, Congressmen's relations with, 277–284
Continental Congress, 13
control, conflicting theories of, 231–235; reconciliation of, 233–235
cooperation in foreign affairs: obstacles to, 269–271; proposed reforms, 271–273
Corbett, Robert J., 313
Cordozo, Benjamin N., 203
corporations, governmental, 250–251

correspondence of Congressmen, 82
Corrupt Practices Act, 42
cost of operating Congress, 87, 353
councils, departmental advisory, 224–225
Courts, James C., 247
Criminal Code, amendment to, 304
Crisp, Charles F., 37, 132
Crockett, John C., 86
Cultural Relations Office, 319
Curtis, Charles, 37, 38
Cutting, Senator, 92

David, Paul T., 237
Dawes, Charles G., 81
debate: decline of, 196; freedom of, 198; public, 290–291, 316; regulation of, 80–81
decentralization, regional, 79–80
delegated powers, safeguarding, 239–245
deliberation, decline of, 196
Democracy in Crisis, 45
Democratic Party, 106
Denit, W. Darlington, 325, 326
Department of Agriculture, 8
Deschler, Lewis, 13
Dies, Martin, 56
Dies Committee, 185; records of, 333
Dingley, Nelson, 37
Dirksen, Everett M., viii, 278; typical day of, 58–60
disbarment, 307
Discharge Calendar, 164
distribution, regional, Senate, 25; House, 347
District of Columbia, home rule for, 71–73, 282
Dodel, William E., Jr., 238
Dominican Republic, 269
doorkeepers, 84–86, 109
Douglas, Helen G., 296
Douglas, Stephen A., 33
Dowling, Noel T., 225
Downey, Sheridan, 57–58, 67, 81
Doxey, Wall, 41
Du Pont, Henry A., 38

Eberhart, John C., 90
Economics Department, 356
Economic Security, Committee on, 154
Edge, Walter E., 39
editorial columns, 311
education of Congressmen, 29, 44
Einstein, Albert, 205
electoral function of Congress, 4
Elliott, William Y., 220, 339
Emergency Price Control Act, 241
Emmerich, Herbert, 251
Engel, Albert, 250
England, Parliament of, 31–32, 210–211, 219–221, 286
English, George W., 16
English House of Commons, 13